THE NEW PATRIARCH DIGITAL CAPITALISM

This book offers an original critique of the billionaire founders of US West Coast tech companies, addressing their collective power, influence, and ideology, their group dynamics, and the role they play in the wider sociocultural and political formations of digital capitalism.

Interrogating not only the founders' political and economic ambitions, but also how their corporations are omnipresent in our everyday lives, the authors provide robust evidence that a specific kind of patriarchal power has emerged as digital capitalism's mode of command. The 'New Patriarchs' examined over the course of the book include: Sergey Brin and Larry Page of Google, Elon Musk of Tesla, Jeff Bezos of Amazon, Mark Zuckerberg of Facebook, and Peter Thiel. We also include Sheryl Sandberg. The book analyses how these (mostly) men legitimate their rapidly acquired power, tying a novel kind of socially awkward but 'visionary' masculinity to exotic forms of shareholding. Drawing on a ten million word digital concordance, the authors intervene in feminist debates on patriarchy, masculinity, and postfeminism, locating the power of the founders as emanating from a specifically racialised structure of oppression tied to imaginaries of the American frontier, the patriarchal household, and settler colonialism.

This is an important interdisciplinary contribution suitable for researchers and students across Digital Media, Media and Communication, and Gender and Cultural Studies.

Ben Little is a lecturer in Media and Cultural Politics and Associate Dean of Engagement and Innovation in the faculty of Arts and Humanities at the University of East Anglia. He works on celebrity, activism, generation, and digital culture. His last book (with Jane Arthurs) was *Russell Brand: Comedy, Celebrity, Politics* (2016). He is part of the editorial collective of *Soundings: A Journal of Politics and Culture*, series editor of generational politics series Radical Future, and a director of Lawrence and Wishart.

Alison Winch is a lecturer in Media Studies at the University of East Anglia. Her books include *Girlfriends and Postfeminist Sisterhood* (2013) and the poetry collection *Darling, It's Me* (2019). She is part of the editorial collective for *Soundings: A Journal of Politics and Culture*.

'This is a much-needed field guide to the apex predators of tech. Little and Winch reveal the ideological terrain, the cult of celebrity, and the dominant features of patriarchal capitalism that have shaped Silicon Valley and far beyond.'

Kate Crawford, *author of* Atlas of AI: Power, Politics, and the Planetary Costs of Artificial Intelligence

'Written at a cultural moment when people around the globe are necessarily engaging with technologies in everyday life, *The New Patriarchs of Digital Capitalism* is an incredibly timely and brilliant analysis of the deep interrelations between and within gender, technology, and capitalism. Resisting a simplistic analysis of the founders of tech companies, Winch and Little offer us an astute framing that positions these founders within the landscapes of patriarchy, celebrity, the household, and myths of the Western frontier. A true interdisciplinary project, the book engages with feminist theory, science and technology studies, political science, and cultural studies, and thus offers us complex conceptualizations of not only the role of technology in society, but also the ways in which patriarchies structure the way we use and understand technologies, and it clearly theorizes the ideologies, histories, and values of the people who run and organize the dominant media platforms in the world.'

Sarah Banet-Weiser, *Professor of Media and Communications, London School of Economics*

'For some time now, media scholars, political scientists and public commentators have been working to make sense of the manifold implications of data capitalism, surveillance culture and Big Tech ownership on democracy, the state and the future of society more generally. This book stands out as one of the most exciting and original interventions in this space. Organised as a series of case studies critiquing the world's richest and most powerful tech oligarchs, it provides a rich and meticulous account of digital capitalism's reliance on the construction of mythic celebrity personae in its pursuit of a new – and frankly terrifying – global social order. Little and Winch demonstrate how this new breed of founding fathers engage in stage-managed acts of philanthropy, environmentalism and progressive rhetoric to legitimate new forms of power and avoid scrutiny. Inspired by paradigms from celebrity studies, they deftly expose the self-mythologising of the capitalist super-elite as foundational to the complex political economy of data colonialism. Methodologically sharp and deeply compelling, this is a searing conjunctural analysis of the dynamics that shape the new networked monopoly of patriarchs that drives technocapitalism. A comprehensive, enlightening and deeply unsettling analysis of the tech industry's inordinate power over all aspects of human life.'

Debbie Ging, *Associate Professor of Media Studies, Dublin City University*

THE NEW PATRIARCHS OF DIGITAL CAPITALISM

Celebrity Tech Founders and Networks of Power

Ben Little and Alison Winch

LONDON AND NEW YORK

First published 2021
by Routledge
2 Park Square, Milton Park, Abingdon, Oxon OX14 4RN

and by Routledge
605 Third Avenue, New York, NY 10158

Routledge is an imprint of the Taylor & Francis Group, an informa business

© 2021 Ben Little and Alison Winch

The right of Ben Little and Alison Winch to be identified as authors of this work has been asserted by them in accordance with sections 77 and 78 of the Copyright, Designs and Patents Act 1988.

All rights reserved. No part of this book may be reprinted or reproduced or utilised in any form or by any electronic, mechanical, or other means, now known or hereafter invented, including photocopying and recording, or in any information storage or retrieval system, without permission in writing from the publishers.

Trademark notice: Product or corporate names may be trademarks or registered trademarks, and are used only for identification and explanation without intent to infringe.

British Library Cataloguing-in-Publication Data
A catalogue record for this book is available from the British Library

Library of Congress Cataloging-in-Publication Data
Names: Little, Ben, 1980-author. | Winch, Alison, author.
Title: The new patriarchs of digital capitalism: celebrity tech founders and networks of power/Ben Little and Alison Winch.
Description: Abingdon, Oxon; New York, NY: Routledge, 2021. | Includes bibliographical references and index. |
Identifiers: LCCN 2020056372 (print) |
LCCN 2020056373 (ebook) | ISBN 9780367260118 (hardback) | ISBN 9780367260156 (paperback) | ISBN 9780429291005 (ebook)
Subjects: LCSH: Internet industry–United States. | Businesspeople–United States. | Corporations–United States.
Classification: LCC HD9696.8.U62 L579 2021 (print) |
LCC HD9696.8.U62 (ebook) | DDC 384.3092/273–dc23
LC record available at https://lccn.loc.gov/2020056372
LC ebook record available at https://lccn.loc.gov/2020056373

ISBN: 978-0-367-26011-8 (hbk)
ISBN: 978-0-367-26015-6 (pbk)
ISBN: 978-0-429-29100-5 (ebk)

Typeset in Bembo
by Deanta Global Publishing Services, Chennai, India

This book is dedicated to Jonah: no more 'Chapter 1! Chapter 2! Chapter 3!...'

CONTENTS

List of illustrations viii
Acknowledgements ix

Introduction: The new patriarchs 1

1 Theorising the patriarchal network 27

2 Elon Musk: Geek masculinity and marketing the celebrity founder 56

3 Jeff Bezos: Beyond the American frontier 85

4 Mark Zuckerberg's corporate household 116

5 Peter Thiel's technological frontiers 144

6 Endorsed by Sandberg: Resilience not resistance 167

7 The limits of liberalism: Google's Larry Page and Sergey Brin 187

Conclusion 216

Appendix: A concordance of popular books on digital capitalism 223
Index 237

ILLUSTRATIONS

Figures

0.1	Trump Tech Summit 2016 (Tesla/SpaceX's Elon Musk is just out of shot to the right)	2
0.2	Network of case studies	9
2.1	Instagram promotion for a follow-up of Joe Rogan's Interview with Elon Musk in 2020 (Rogan 2020)	75
3.1	Jeff Bezos and the Ice Bucket Challenge	86
3.2	Jeff Bezos at the Axel Springer Award, 2018	99
4.1	'Live Grilling' Mark Zuckerberg (right), Sam Lessin (centre), and Joe Green (left), October 2016	121
4.2	Mark Zuckerberg at Iowa 80 Kitchen, 2017	131
5.1	The 'Paypal Mafia' from *Fortune.com* 2006	146
5.2	Peter Thiel giving a speech at the 2016 Republican Convention in Cleveland	150
6.1	Sheryl Sandberg and Oprah Winfrey *SuperSoul Conversations*, 2017	168
7.1	Larry Page with his grandfather's 'Alley Oop' Hammer, 2009	193

Tables

0.1	Famous tech executives full name mentions in the concordance	7
6.1	A gendered genre: pronouns and gender terms in the concordance	173
A.1	Authors: gender and coding	227
A.2	Distribution of authors by number of books	228
A.3	Complete list of texts with genre coding	228

ACKNOWLEDGEMENTS

Any book of this sort is a collaborative project. We are indebted to so many people, who have helped shape the direction of the book, refine its argument, and think through its case studies, methods, and conclusions.

We are lucky to have, and are enormously grateful for, some really excellent friends who read chapters and work in progress and gave sound advice and encouragement: Alan Finlayson, Jamie Hakim, Rachel O'Neill, Martin Scott, Karen Schaller, Eitan Tzelgov, and Alex Williams. For rich and sometimes pivotal discussions, thank you to Hannah Hamad, Georgia Walker Churchman (concordance!), Sarah Banet Weiser, Diane Negra, Yvonne Tasker, Debbie Ging, Michael Fraser, Yoav Segal.

As with any academic project, many of the most (constructively) critical people have been anonymous reviewers. Most notable are the ones from Routledge who offered hugely thoughtful and rigorous comments, but we have also had feedback on developmental articles from reviewers at *Open Cultural Studies*, *New Formations* and the *European Journal of Cultural Studies*. We would also like to thank all the editors of those journals for their support in bringing that earlier work into the light, especially Anna Malinowska and Toby Miller, Jeremy Gilbert, Zeena Feldman, Mike Goodman, Jo Littler, and Helen Wood. Thanks also to the *Soundings Journal* editorial collective who published an editorial on the Trump Tech Summit, that started moving the project in a more explicitly political direction.

We are also deeply grateful to all the conference organisers and attendees who have provided us with lively feedback on the work as it developed. These include: 'Digital Violence' at Anglia Ruskin (thanks to Tanya Horek), 'Toxic Digital Intimacies' at the University of Essex (thanks to Róisín Ryan-Flood), 'Media, Gender, Feminism' at LSE (thanks to Sarah Banet-Weiser and Shani Orgad), 'Digital Everyday' and 'Digital Foods' at Kings University

London (thanks to Zeena Feldman), Media and Politics Group of the Political Studies Association, 'Annual Celebrity Studies Conference' in Rome, 'Toxic Masculinities' at Birmingham City University (thanks to John Mercer), 'Debates in New Materialisms' at Middlesex University (thanks to Phoebe Moore), UEA politics seminar series, UEA Gender Studies Seminar Series (thanks to Tori Cann), and the 'mediated masculinities' symposium at UEA (thanks to Jamie Hakim).

We employed a superb student intern early on in the process, Abbie Mulcairn, who helped us work out our methodology and devised early lists of books to be included in our concordance. Thanks to Claire Cuminatto whose research internship scheme at UEA made that assistance possible. For invaluable assistance preparing the manuscript we are grateful to Sally Davison and assistance on the bibliography from Lynda Dyson.

We have been lucky to have had great institutional support from the UEA, who in various capacities over the years have made the book possible: Claire Jowett, Hussein Kassim, Lee Jarvis, Lee Marsden, Holly Dyer, Alex Russell-Davies, Katie Frost, Emma Pett, Sarah Garland. Ben is particularly grateful to the collegial media and cultural politics group: Helen Warner, John Street, Sally Broughton-Micova, Kate Mattocks, Delia Dumitrescu, Marina Prentoulis, Oli Brooks.

Many thanks to those who have helped with the childcare that has enabled us to do this project at all: Helena and Simon Hart, Cathy and Chris Winch, Caitlin Boylan, Fay Ikin and Hannah Powell-Smith, Sarah and Martin Falkingham. Honorary shout out to the board game crew Alex Murty (and for random Elon Musk knowledge), Brett Mills, Frederik Kohlert, and Sam Moon for listening to Ben witter on about the book for years over weekly sessions. For friendship and support thanks to Kat Christophy, Keri Finlayson, Deborah Grayson, Laura Hamilton, Sophie Herxheimer, Soonita Ramtohul, Daniel Sellers, Anna Webster.

INTRODUCTION
The new patriarchs

After Donald Trump won the 2016 US presidential election, one of the first things he did was to invite the founders and chief executive officers (CEOs) of tech companies to Trump Tower for a summit (see Figure 0.1). In the room were some of the most vocal opponents to his presidency and policy platform from within the ranks of the powerbrokers of American capitalism. Trump was deferential and flattering – 'There's no-one like you in the world' – and, in an attempt to echo the iconoclastic ideology of Silicon Valley, he insisted that there was no hierarchy in his administration. He told his visitors that his door was open: he was 'here to help [them] do well' (Streitfeld 2016).

Around the table were the CEOs, chief operating officers (COOs), and founders of technology firms: among them the five most valuable companies in the world: Apple, Amazon, Microsoft, Alphabet-Google, and Facebook (Cardenal 2016). Also present were executives from Palantir (whose co-founder Peter Thiel brokered the meeting), Oracle, Goldman Sachs, IBM, Cisco Systems, and Intel (Sonnad 2016). That this happened so fast and was inclusive of so many senior figures within the tech industry is quite remarkable. As a sector, technology companies, founders, and workers had thrown more money at Democrats during the 2016 election campaign – and progressive Democrats at that – than at Republicans. In the Democrat primaries it had been 'democratic socialist' Bernie Sanders who had been the largest beneficiary of tech workers' financial support; and in the election itself, donations to the Democrats' candidate, Hillary Clinton, from voters in California's Silicon Valley, the physical home to much of the tech industry, were 60 times the level of donations given to Trump (Levy 2016). The meeting was thus a performance of political pragmatism, by both the incoming president and the leading figures of an industry that has been hailed in the middle-brow and technology press as 'the #resistance' to Trump's administration (Smiley 2017; Vara 2017; Tarnoff 2017).

2 Introduction

FIGURE 0.1 Trump Tech Summit 2016 (Tesla/SpaceX's Elon Musk is just out of shot to the right)

The political tensions that were suppressed to allow for the production of the image in Figure 0.1 were soon to become visible through the actions of Elon Musk, CEO of Tesla and Space X, and a founder of PayPal (who was present at the meeting but not in the photo). Musk had originally threatened to move to China if Trump was elected, but in the end he joined one of Trump's advisory committees, persuaded by Peter Thiel, his fellow PayPal founder and a presidential supporter and advisor. But this presented a particular problem for Musk, whose celebrity persona is closely bound up with environmentalism. As is the case for many leaders of tech companies, Musk depends on celebrity as the primary driver of corporate publicity, in a trend that can be traced back to iconic Apple founder, the late Steve Jobs. Marketing for these companies has – in their beginnings at least – depended on the myth of the legendary founder: a young (white, male) genius capable of producing new products that change the world. And these founder identities have been closely bound up with the identities of the companies themselves. Musk's celebrity persona of a messianic environmentalist clashed with his more pragmatic concerns: his business's dependence on government contracts for rocket launches (Space X) and occasionally the need for state subsidy (as in the early stages of Tesla). Hence his need to cosy up to the president. In the end the circle was too hard to square. When Trump pulled America out of the Paris Climate Accord, Musk quit his advisory role in protest (Koren 2017). Maintaining a consistent public image, for Musk, trumped direct political influence as a means to promote his corporate agenda. There were, of course, many other tensions among the participants, but for most of them the opportunity to be at the top table was decisive.

While the meeting included some of the most powerful people in America, missing from the picture is Mark Zuckerberg. The Facebook founder and CEO has been declared by political theorist David Runciman to be an even bigger threat to democracy than Trump, partly because his company is seen to undermine the state itself (and also to indirectly contribute to the election of figures like Trump (Runciman 2018, 138–139)). Zuckerberg's responsibility for Trump's election is hard to quantify, but certainly Facebook was used ruthlessly by the Trump campaign, which had embedded Facebook staffers – something that was absent from the Democrat campaign (a strategic error it turns out: see Bartlett 2018). As the youngest of all these entrepreneurs by a small stretch, Zuckerberg most closely conforms to the general stereotype of the boy-genius-founder and thus bears the weight of being a significant cultural icon as well as a business leader. He is also, perhaps, the person who has most suffered the brunt of the so-called 'Tech-lash' – the reaction against tech companies in the years following this auspicious meeting that has spelled the end of their positive public image even as their wealth and influence has grown (Foroohar 2018). It was possibly a sign of Zuckerberg's potential political aspirations, rather than any broader consideration, that led to his absence from the meeting. Instead, he sent as his surrogate Sheryl Sandberg, one of only four women out of the 21 people present at the table – the others being the president-elect's daughter Ivanka Trump, Oracle CEO Safra Katz, and Ginni Romety, CEO of IBM.

Given Trump's usual implacable and relentless demonisation of opponents, this photo opportunity struck us as an exceptional moment. It indicated that this industry, in the unified form it presented at this meeting, was not an enemy that Trump could hope to overcome – or at least, not at a cost that made it worth it. For us, this picture put into sharp relief a series of emerging research questions on the people who run the tech companies that have risen to prominence since the financial crash of 2008. Who are these people that President Trump would so graciously and urgently court them? Why would he rehearse their language and invite them into his circles? Where does their power lie, how do they justify accumulating it, and for what ends do they wield it? More directly, why are they almost all white men? The answers to these questions are extensive and complex, bound up as they are with wider social, cultural, and economic processes. So in this book, we investigate these men by analysing their celebrity biographies: the best material for research we could find that addresses that complexity from multiple perspectives.

Thus, the image makes visible a group that represents a powerful industry that is ushering in a new era of 'data colonialism' (Couldry and Mejias 2019) and 'surveillance capitalism' (Zuboff 2019). These ideas describe, differently but with clear overlap, how digital technologies have introduced a new economic paradigm that is shaping social relations. That is how everyday life is surveilled or colonised by large technology companies for economic exploitation. And it is not yet clear what the social and political consequences of that will be. For Shoshana Zuboff it is the corporate penetration of the intimate sanctum of domestic life;

for Nick Couldry and Ulises Mejias it is a repetition in new form of capitalism's worst imperial impulses seizing the 'space of subjectivity' from us without asking permission (171). For all these writers, democratic accountability is worryingly absent from this socio-economic arrangement.

But this new economic order also brings into view a highly motivated and active network of men that dominates it – and that we should understand them as such is one of our key research findings. These are powerful individuals at the head of seemingly unassailable monopolistic corporations, and their network makes them an even more powerful collective social actor (Moore and Tambini 2018; Gilbert 2019). In short, these figures have benefited from, and contributed to – to an extraordinary degree – the full-spectrum social, cultural, economic, and political shift that is currently transforming the world. These new forms of power have led us to contextualise our research through a periodisation of 'digital capitalism': our way of understanding the present as marked by the 2008 financial crash, which can be seen as a tipping point in the transition to a new era. The crash opened the door to intensified collaboration between West Coast tech companies and the finance industry, with tech becoming the dominant partner in this new hegemonic bloc (Gilbert and Williams 2018). We see this period as being characterised by: the imbrication of data processes in all forms of economic activity (Zuboff 2019); the funnelling of capital from public welfare into a financialised platform society (van Dijck et al. 2018); and an increasingly casualised workforce legitimated through the branding of entrepreneurialism, choice, and control (Jarrett 2016). The scholars listed above (alongside others) have made considerable progress in understanding the nature of the socio-economic shift to this new set of social arrangements, and we draw on their work in this book. But our focus is on the network of founders itself: how they maintain their influence, how they justify it, and what cultural resources they use to explain and propagate their wealth and power.

Our aim is to identify and track connections between the tech oligarchs, and in particular to map their networks of ideas, people, and practices through how they are mediatised and narrativised. This makes our project different from traditional political science books like *Billionaires and Stealth Politics* (Page et al. 2019), where the authors are trying to fathom the ideological orientation of American billionaires and their concrete political activities. We make no such attempt: we approach our research with an understanding, informed by our background in media and cultural studies, that we will never access these men in such a way as to be able to assess their politics directly. We recognise that even a face-to-face interview with the subjects of our research would take place within the remit of corporate public relations activity (see also James 2018).

Our approach is nevertheless case-study based. Our aim in studying selected figures from the industry is to develop an understanding of their mythic narrative biographies and celebrity personae, which are an important element of their corporate strategies. Our chosen subjects are Jeff Bezos, Mark Zuckerberg, Sergey Brin and Larry Page, and Elon Musk, around each of whom we base a chapter of the book. We also have chapters on Peter Thiel, who is not as obviously wealthy as the others, and Sheryl Sandberg, who is not a tech-founder, but who are both significant to this discussion. Each of these core celebrity figures in the network illustrates a particular dimension or aspect of the wider phenomenon we are exploring; and in each case study we look at one of these founders (two in the case of Google's Page and Brin) and their celebrity strategy, focusing on a specific feature that most illuminates one aspect of such strategies. In most cases the insight offered by one of the subjects of our research also applies more broadly to others in the network. Thus, Elon Musk is best placed to illustrate the cross-overs between the celebrified founders and the Hollywood celebrity industry, but Jeff Bezos also has very strong ties to Tinsel Town – and, indeed, has a far larger financial stake in it. Similarly, nearly all the figures in question have tied their celebrity to mythic elements of American culture.

The omission of women in our selection is also significant. Why not include eBay's Meg Whitman or disgraced Theranos CEO Elizabeth Holmes? we have been asked. But Whitman did not found eBay and Holmes has been exposed as a fraudster who used the hype surrounding tech founders to generate great wealth, but without a product that actually worked (Carreyou 2018). Similarly, the other women around the table in the photograph are not founders, but appointed CEOs. They are not as wealthy, as successful, or as famous as the founders we analyse here. Indeed, there are no female founders operating at the scale of the men in the network we have identified. This is connected to a core quality of the network, which was immediately apparent from the beginning – the subaltern role of women within it. A central aim of this book is to understand more fully the gendered nature of the network.

Within this patriarchal world, women are permitted some roles, but not others. To explore the mechanics of this, at both a practical and ideological level, we have included Sheryl Sandberg as the subject of a case study, due to her obvious influence, and in recognition of the importance of looking at the interaction of the industry's most high-profile woman within the broader phenomena we are investigating. Sandberg's writing and career help us to make sense of how women are able to participate in and benefit from an elite patriarchal structure – through negotiating the cultural norms in terms of gender relations, and striking bargains to secure a place in its hierarchies.

Characteristics of the celebrity founders

In this section, we set out how the people attending the Trump summit constitute what we term a 'patriarchal network.' Much of the interest to readers in this book we expect to be in the detail found in the individual case studies. All of the figures whose celebrity personae we have analysed are of intrinsic interest, due to their wealth, influence, and media profile. These analyses are the product of extensive original research, but it is only in apprehending the case studies together that we start to see the real contours of their power and the modes by which they legitimate it.

Key to being able to articulate this argument has been through our methodological approach. We have mixed classical forms of textual analysis with more quantitative literary methods (corpus linguistic analysis) and general desk research. Central to these methods is empirical evidence drawn from a ten million word custom-built (by the authors) database comprised of digital scans of 95 popular books on the technology industry and surrounding culture. This database – or digital concordance – consists of four kinds of books – celebrity biographies, corporate 'how-to' books, ideological books, and polemical books. It exists as a database in the NVivo 12 software system for access to full text for the authors of this book and as a SketchEngine.eu corpus.[1] We note, in support of the validity of our selection of texts, and hence of the reliability of the database for making general inferences about the ideology of tech entrepreneurs, that in a recent documentary about Microsoft founder Bill Gates, there was significant overlap between the books listed (at length) by his assistant as being taken by Gates on his travels and the content of our concordance (*Inside Bill's Brain* 2019). Similarly, Facebook investor Robert McNamee, at the end of his insider critique of Facebook, *Zucked*, also lists many of the books we included for further reading (McNamee 2019, 313–320). For more detail about how we compiled this concordance, please see Appendix.

Our decisions about who to include in this network (and thus as our case studies) were rooted in three broad criteria, as well as judgement based on our desk research. The criteria were that our case studies should be *founders*; should have substantial *wealth*; and would be available for analysis through their *celebrity* profiles.

We focus on *founders* of companies as they have a particularly celebrated cultural location in the technology sector, and thus have been able to accrue excessive amounts of corporate power; many of the companies we discuss in this book are technically 'controlled companies': i.e. there is no standard mechanism to challenge executive power for the company's shareholders or investors. 'Founder' is an extraordinarily frequent word in our concordance, appearing 251 times per million words, 5 times the rate it occurs in the EnTenTen15 reference corpus. (The EnTenTen15 is a sample of 15 billion words of English scraped from the internet in the SketchEngine software. Throughout the book we use reference corpora – databases of examples of English usage created by other researchers – as baselines for comparison to indicate how word use in our concordance compares with general usage.) We also chose founders who were involved in day-to-day management at the start of our project.[3] Sandberg is perhaps the exception here. While she has founded organisations such as leanin.org and optionb.org – which mainly function as extensions of her personal brand – they are not her primary activities, nor the source of her wealth.

Wealth was also a criterion for inclusion. These are not just successful entrepreneurs; they are the wealthiest people in the world. All of our case studies

TABLE 0.1 Famous tech executives full name mentions in the concordance[2]

Name	Primary Company/Companies	Concordance References
Steve Jobs	Apple	1688
Bill Gates	Microsoft	882
Mark Zuckerberg	Facebook	504
Larry Page	Alphabet-Google	485
Peter Thiel	Paypal/Palantir	465
Jeff Bezos	Amazon	408
Eric Schmidt	Google	354
Elon Musk	Tesla/Space X/Paypal	323
Sergey Brin	Alphabet-Google	254
Marc Andreessen	Mosaic/Netscape/Investor	189
Sheryl Sandberg	Facebook/Google	171
Travis Kalanick	Uber	147
Meg Whitman	eBay	86
Larry Ellison	Oracle	81
Jack Dorsey	Twitter	67
Elizabeth Holmes	Theranos	65
Sam Altman	Y-Combinator	26
Michael Dell	Dell Computers	13
Evan Spiegel	Snap	4

are billionaires, though Sheryl Sandberg and Peter Thiel are not in the top 25 wealthiest people in the world.[4] While these men were incredibly rich before the coronavirus pandemic of 2020–21 that started as this book was going to publication, their collective wealth has since skyrocketed. Jeff Bezos and Elon Musk particularly have seen their wealth surge by a huge amount, making them the two wealthiest people in the world by some margin. As of 21 February 2021, Bezos is listed by Forbes (2021) as possessing an estate worth $190 billion (this is after Bezos signed over 25% of his Amazon stock to MacKenzie Scott in their 2019 divorce). Musk's wealth has increased from around $35 billion to a staggering $182 billion dollars – likely to be the greatest ever annual increase in wealth in history. At fifth in the world rich list sits Mark Zuckerberg with $95 billion and at eighth and nineth are Larry Page ($91 billion) and Sergey Brin ($88 billion). It is worth noting that no women appear in the top ten and two others (Larry Ellison and Bill Gates) also made their wealth from technology.

These figures demonstrate two things. Firstly, that to the founders go the rewards. Sandberg has been instrumental in monetising the services offered by both Google and Facebook; but her wealth is less than 2% that of her boss and work partner Zuckerberg. Here again, her inclusion is useful to indicate the significant differences between the founders and highly successful people who work in the same milieu but are not founders. Secondly, that technology now produces the world's biggest billionaires, reflecting both its centrality to the economy, and the possibility that an early, lucky, insight into the market opportunities offered by the digital economy can reap vast fortunes – on a scale not seen since the 1890s. The coronavirus pandemic, which has forced many of us to rely even more heavily on digital technology for social and economic life, has underscored these shifts by accelerating on ongoing transfer of wealth and power from the wider economy to digital monopoly platforms that are the source of most of our case studies' wealth.

The third criterion was *celebrity*. Our approach is focused on how tech founders are represented in popular media and other textual resources that legitimate and challenge their social power. We have, in general, limited our analyses to the narratives over which they exercise some control (often with possible deniability 'baked-in' as a precaution in texts such as semi-official biographies), rather than discussing unverifiable or paparazzi-style gossip journalism. This is because we recognise that the celebrity of the people in our selection, the stories they tell about themselves and their companies, and the social power they exercise, are deeply entwined.[5] From our desk research we understood that Thiel and Sandberg were extremely important to completing the network we had identified, and thus to understanding the ideological terrain that the others inhabit – and this was confirmed by our quantitative analysis of full names in the concordance, where the occurrence of references to these two was broadly within the range of frequency of the other figures (see Table 0.1).

Mapping the patriarchal network

> There are so few people this crazy I feel like I know them all by first name ... They travel as if they are pack dogs and stick to each other like glue.
>
> *Larry Page, commencement speech, Michigan 2009*
> *(Google 2009)*

In Figure 0.2 we map the connections between the people in our case studies. Most of the connections were found using broad-context collocations in the NVivo version of our concordance. This means that their names appear in the same paragraph in one of the books in our concordance. To indicate the complexity of the connections, we have identified four axes by which the different members of the group can be connected: business, friendship, rivalry, and political influence or lobbying connections. As clearly emerges from this mapping, this is a dense network where the links between the different members are intense and varied – some, like those between Musk and Page/Brin, are deep, and based on nearly two decades of friendship. Others, for example between Musk and Sandberg, seem limited from our sources. The results from the concordance are by no means comprehensive: an evidence base drawing on a wider range of media would have produced an even denser set of connections, but the aim here is to focus on confirmed connections between these figures (not including gossip press), and hence on legitimated public domain narratives

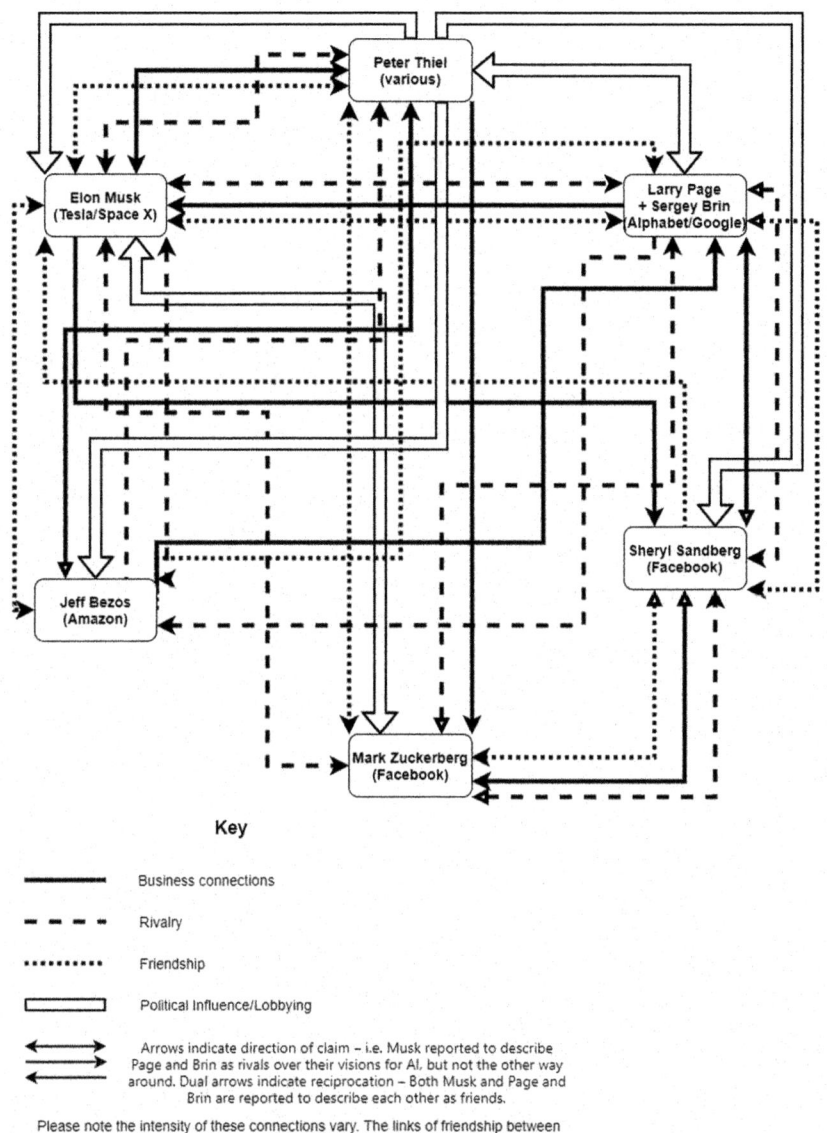

FIGURE 0.2 Network of case studies

about their relationships to one another and the manner in which their celebrity is constructed in relation to one another.[6]

At one end of the scale we can see close working relationships, as for example between Zuckerberg and Sandberg. The references to their connection in the data are numerous: Zuckerberg organised Sandberg's husband's funeral;

they meet several times a week; hug when appropriate; go on holiday together; agree on 'data-driven decision making'; Zuckerberg has endorsed Sandberg's books; and the two have shared financial interests through board membership of Facebook. They have disagreed over strategic decisions at Facebook, but not so much as to jeopardise their friendship. Both attended Harvard University, so they have a shared reference point that is distinct from the majority of the figures we discuss, who all attended Stanford University at some point except Bezos who went to Princeton.[7] At the other end of the scale, the least developed relationship is between Musk and Sandberg: all we learn from the concordance is that they have met and talked about the loss of loved ones and that at one point Musk wanted to hire Sandberg from Facebook.

Thematically, the types of connection tend to divide quite neatly. For instance, the friendship connections are clear even when there is also a demonstrable rivalry. In fact, it is rare to have one without the other – the only exception to this being the relationship between Zuckerberg and Musk, who have rivalries over AI and had a falling out over Zuckerberg's lobbying organisation strategy, but for whom there are no references citing their friendship. The connections under the terms of friendship and rivalry are often reciprocal in that the references indicate flow in both directions (Musk considers Page a friend and vice-versa). There are exceptions here too, however: for instance Musk is prepared to criticise the Google guys (who are largely inseparable so have been placed together), whereas they themselves are exclusively complimentary of him.[8] Peter Thiel has also, partly due to his different status, been cautious to name specific people in his rivalries (Musk from the PayPal years excluded, and Google more recently), but he will condemn Silicon Valley's liberal culture in general. But Thiel is also unlikely to be openly attacked by others in this network, despite clear lines of ostensible political disagreement.

The friendships among the network require rivalries – for strategic purposes. Rocket companies SpaceX and Blue Origin must not be seen to be colluding, in order to maintain a semblance of capitalist competition, so Bezos and Musk claim to be barely on speaking terms. They emphasise competition for staff (rocket scientists are thin on the ground) and present different visions for space explorations. Bezos wants man-made habitats in space, while Musk wants to 'Occupy Mars.' Both claim the other's plan is not viable. Meanwhile their companies focus their energies on different bits of the space market, while a steady stream of expertise moves from top universities to SpaceX to Blue Origin on a conveyor belt of talent.[9] Similarly, the big internet firms, Google, Facebook, and Amazon, operate a sort of '*Pax Britannica* type of non-competitive arrangement,' while still ostensibly competing in areas like search or social networking (Couldry and Mejias 2019, 50). The rivalries may or may not be real, but they are an important way in which the network as a whole legitimates its consolidation of power and tries to avoid the wrong kind of scrutiny.

These rivalries are dramatized in hyperbolic fashion by one former Facebook employee in our database:

> Zuck looked over at Bezos in Seattle, or Larry Page from Google in Mountain View, or (in the past) Steve Jobs from Apple in Cupertino, and he saw more than just a tech company and a chief executive. He saw a reflection of himself among those men, and that was terrifying. Other players in the tech or media worlds could be outwitted, out-engineered, or otherwise co-opted or bought off, but not these alpha companies. With Amazon or Google, the Facebook army had to close ranks and present a phalanx, and possibly battle an equal foe whose CEO was just as much of a kamikaze as Zuck was (Carthage must be destroyed!).
>
> *(Martinez 2016, 428)*

But once you look at another set of relationships from the concordance, it's hard to take these claims seriously, as the business interests are so interlinked. Thiel, Zuckerberg, and Sandberg all have substantial financial interests in Facebook, but Sandberg presumably has, or has had, significant shareholdings in Google as part of her remuneration while she worked there. Bezos was an early investor in Google, while Page and Brin have both invested in Musk's companies. Musk and Thiel made their first fortunes together at PayPal, and Thiel's venture funds invest in Musk's SpaceX. Both Musk and Thiel invest in companies like Stripe and organisations involved in AI research. Even Bezos and Thiel, who otherwise have few connections in the database, have both invested in the anti-ageing company Unity Biotechnology. So, as a collective, their material interests are shared not just at the general, sectoral level, but very literally through investment in each other's companies and outside interests.

Thus the network is held together through similarity, support, and common interest, but legitimated through disagreement and difference. It is a material intertwining of men, rivalries, and interests that seems to be self-sustaining politically, and mutually reinforcing. If one prospers against the stated interest of others, they all seem to thrive (as we saw with Thiel's ability to reconcile the patriarchs to Trump, despite the open opposition of many of them to his candidacy). Similarly, when one patriarch takes a publicity hit, as Mark Zuckerberg did over accusations of electoral interference, it allows the rest of the network to maintain business as normal, and thus, effectively, to also protect the one in the firing line, given that no structural challenge will take place. Instead any failure is seen as individual, and a fine or similar is administered, and then everything goes back to as before.[10] This, then, is a high functioning, if informal, network, operating with great efficacy.

Assemblage thinking

While this is an interdisciplinary project, taking insight from political science, internet studies, literary methodologies, and feminist theory (and more), our research is primarily framed by the conjunctural concerns of cultural studies – summarised by Jo Littler as seeking to identify 'the particular power dynamics and character of a particular moment.' Conjunctural analysis seeks out the key elements in power relations that contribute to the coming together of a historical period, and we have identified the technology sector, and certain paradigmatic characters within it, as one such element – our focus is on the most powerful people in the most powerful corporations. This is not least because, as Larry Grossberg notes, in the current moment 'many people who distrust established political institutions seem willing to place greater trust in the ability of corporations to address the needs of the public good' (Grossberg 2019, 39). Littler describes conjunctural analysis as a necessarily transdisciplinary space: one where scholars can draw from the 'psycho-social,' 'feminist activism,' 'literary analysis,' and 'philosophy,' as part of a 'multi-faceted investigation to consider the configurations of power which constitute contemporary life' (Littler 2016).

We have drawn on different disciplines in different ways in the writing of this book. Some we approach in a relatively utilitarian way to help us understand particular phenomena – for instance, we take the concept 'cultural strategy' from marketing scholars to help make sense of the corporate value the companies derive from their founders' celebrity (Holt and Cameron 2012). We have also drawn on political economist Shoshana Zuboff's work on surveillance capitalism (2019); the internet studies scholarship of Safiya Umoja Noble, who helps us make sense of the intersection of race and gender on the internet; and the sociological work of Bev Skeggs and Simon Yuill (2019), as well as that of Nick Couldry and Ulises Mejias, who help us see how these elements come together in the reinvigoration of colonial imaginaries in the current conjuncture (2018, 2019).

To get a better sense of the complexity of the network we are describing, we use the concept of *assemblage* as part of our analytic frame (Deleuze and Guattari 1988; Delanda 2006). This framework offers a way of understanding the social as a complex of human and non-human actors. It is a fruitful way of analysing the relationship between these companies, their founders, and the wider public, economy, and state. Conceptually 'assemblage' gives agency to people, things, and ideas as if all had a material impact on the other: understanding social phenomena as relational and interconnected. And it is also able to account for the multiple forms of resistance to the dominance of the tech founders. Whether that is within the industry itself (e.g. Google staff walkouts over sexual harassment), or from legislation in the European Union, or nation-states such as Australia and India, or through ideological challenge in academic and online fora. In addition, it allows for the, albeit limited and circumscribed, diversity, agency, and autonomy of, for example, the engineers and other relatively well-paid members of the key corporations' workforces (English-Lueck 2017). These external and internal points of contestation are understood as part of the normal function of the assemblage and central to its process of socio-economic and cultural legitimation. Moreover, we can also see the differences between the founders themselves as a productive part of these assemblages.

The companies we are discussing here have formed a particular kind of assemblage that has been ordered into a hierarchical relation — an 'apparatus' — which works in an *intentional* manner to intervene in the wider social terrain (Agamben 2009). While still subject in theory to the laws of the land they operate in, they have their own policies, technical affordances (Papacharissi 2010), physical infrastructure, workforces, publicity operatives, customer services, users (both individual and corporate), algorithms of various kinds, and so on. All work together to produce the things we know as Facebook, Google, Amazon, etc. And they interact with the cultural, political, social, and economic dimensions of the legal territories and lived locales in which they are present. Google's computational algorithms can tell us which route to take to get to work on time; Amazon organises its facilities based on tax efficiency and distance to key markets. In the control centres of these intention machines sit their founders, their power drawn from their ability to direct, in some fashion or another, the broad trajectories of the various components of their corporate apparatus.

We may not always directly refer to this body of theory in our analysis, but it consistently underpins our understanding of these men, their companies, and their network. We see the founders and their corporations as existing in this space of complexity, alongside points of resistance and agency outside of the active apparatus. That means that routine interventions into social life by corporations like Facebook, Google, or Amazon are usually messy in their outcome and have unpredictable or unintended effects, such as Facebook's contribution to Trump's election or Amazon's acceleration of the decline of high streets. This book, then, is an exercise in 'assemblage thinking' (Featherstone 2011) rather than an elaboration or development of assemblage theory; that is, in trying to think through the complexity of our subject matter we use assemblage theory as a tool for processing it. We are not looking to make bold claims about assemblages themselves (nor indeed conjunctural analysis).

The threat to the state and society posed by these men is a theme that has recurred throughout our research. Mark Zuckerberg has described Facebook as 'more like a government than a traditional company,' and as Facebook's ruler he gets to say how things work through making policy. In his own words: 'We have this large community of people, and more than other technology companies we're really setting policies' (quoted in Kirkpatrick 2011, 255). Some political commentators, including David Runciman, see Facebook in particular, but also, increasingly, other corporations such as Amazon and Google, as real challenges to democracy, social cohesion, and even capitalism itself (2018).[11] In legal and policy domains this kind of analysis is often a prelude to an argument to break up their monopolies — as happened in the early twentieth century with companies like Standard Oil, as a result of the activities of anti-trust movements — or at least to heavily regulate their activities (Wu 2018). We return to the similarities between these patriarchs and the Robber Barons in Chapter 1, but it is worth noting that these anti-trust movements may have had a net positive impact in terms of improving the normative performance of competitive capitalism in the early twentieth century, but the act of breaking up Standard Oil, for instance, increased the wealth of its founder John D. Rockefeller fivefold.

One way of understanding these corporate forms is to see these companies not as conventional businesses run with multiple stakeholders in mind, but as extended corporate households run to the whims of their masters: as conjoined apparatuses, these men and their companies are seen as agents of transformative social change, operating within a structure that is opposed to the conventional frameworks that constrain the role of the corporation as a vehicle for individualised power. As a group, these companies and their founders have created and now lead what Italian political theorist Antonio Gramsci in his writings on hegemony might have called a historic bloc – that is, in our terms, a wider assemblage that is involved in full-spectrum struggle for social and political leadership (Gramsci 1971). As Aeron Davis puts it of CEOs in general: 'they are the public face of the economy, the "primary definers" … of wealth creation in the media … they influence government policy making as they alternate between financial and political networks, providing vital connectivity between the two' (Davis 2019, 90). The subjects of our case studies reflect this, but with rocket boosters attached (and in the case of SpaceX and Blue Origin, these are very much actual rockets).

This tripartite structure, of founder, company, and the sector which they represent, puts the specific men that we look at in this book in a uniquely privileged social, cultural, and political position, as well as making them the dominant subset of the richest people in the world. They can be seen as constituting the vanguard of a new social formation. They build on the legacy of tech entrepreneurs such as Bill Gates of Microsoft and Steve Jobs of Apple, but form a generationally distinct group of the capitalist super-elite. They have thrived since the 2008 financial crash, which indeed, as we have noted, allowed their industry to seize a hegemonic position from finance in the economic imaginaries of the global North. White and under 60 (unusual for billionaires who haven't inherited their great wealth), these men own, are responsible for, and reap the benefits of, some of the fastest-growing companies of all time. We see them as constituting a mediated patriarchal network: a larger-scale assemblage bridging themselves and their companies and wielding significant power in the current conjuncture. Like the Robber Barons, it is likely their names will mark public space for decades to come: Zuckerberg, Musk, Bezos, Page, and Brin will join Guggenheim, Rockefeller, Carnegie, Vanderbildt, and Stanford as indelibly inscribed on the institutional landscape of the US, monuments to patriarchal capitalism. In analysing these men, we seek to understand how they collaborate – and compete – with one another, each claiming to hold the key to humanity's future.

The spirit of the founders

Political scientists David Broockman and Neil Malhotra, working with tech journalist Gregory Ferenstein, have suggested that tech entrepreneurs as a social group have particular and specific political beliefs: they are highly 'cosmopolitan'

– fiercely in favour of immigration for instance – and they are also staunchly against regulation, including trade barriers. Broockman et al. also suggest that the views of tech leaders may well be characteristic of the wider sector's politics, in that 'particular industries may attract individuals with distinctive predispositions, leading those in that industry to share a distinctive set of political views' (Broockman et al. 2019, 212–213). In their paper on the political preferences of economic elites, they explicitly use the tech industry as a case study, and do indeed find a distinct ideological affinity within the sector that stretches from the founders of companies through to the workforce, and even to undergraduates studying a relevant subject (in this case computer science). Thus, the tech founders are not just billionaires, but billionaires who are likely, broadly speaking, to have a shared ideology. They also wield that ideology in a manner that reflects the sector's 'growing political influence.' Broockman et al. identify four ways this power is exercised, and we elaborate on their categorisations below with reference to our own research.

Firstly, these entrepreneurs' extremely high levels of direct wealth can be used to buy influence through lobbying. As Benjamin Page and his co-authors (2019) point out, billionaires such as these have the capacity to spend on both sides of the political aisle to make sure they get their way. This is something that the people in the photograph at the beginning of this book (Figure 0.1) do quite regularly (particularly around immigration). For instance, Mark Zuckerberg's FWD.us lobbies on progressive immigration reform – usually associated with Democrats – while also supporting oil-pipelines to entice Republican policymakers to back their positions.[12] Such bipartisanship was also the case in the 2016 presidential election, as Jonathan Taplin reports:

> So while Eric Schmidt [Google] is advising Hillary Clinton's campaign, Larry Page [Google] flew with Sean Parker [Facebook] and Elon Musk [Tesla/Space X] in March of 2016 to a secret Republican meeting at a resort in Sea Island, Georgia, organized by the rightwing think tank the American Enterprise Institute. There they met with Republican leadership, including Mitch McConnell and Paul Ryan as well as Karl Rove, to plan Republican 2016 election strategy.
>
> *(Taplin 2017, 131)*

Secondly, tech entrepreneurs have 'enormous structural power over governments' (Broockman et al. 2019, 213), through how they can use their corporate investment strategy as leverage. This was seen very clearly in the highly publicised bidding process that Jeff Bezos's Amazon used to determine his company's second headquarters. After making a list of demands – including on tax breaks and infrastructure – directed at local governments bidding to host the site, Bezos decided on two new sites in New York and Arlington, Virginia. When New Yorkers expressed opposition, Amazon simply dumped their development plans for the city and focused their attention on Arlington, making the Pentagon their nearest significant neighbour. This was hardly a surprise given Amazon's multi-billion-dollar contracts with the Department of Defence. Moreover, this example is a reminder of the reciprocal and longstanding nature of the relationships that bind government and these firms. The internet has its origins in ARPANET, a distributed computer network designed by the military to ensure communications continued in the event of a nuclear attack. We can see Amazon's decision as contiguous with the longstanding historical links between the technology sector and military research and development. Similarly, Elon Musk's SpaceX is heavily integrated with and dependent on governmental agencies, for instance NASA and the US Airforce and Space Force, and his electric car company Tesla has relied on grants, subsidies, and loans from government at various points in its development (Sardar 1995; Turner 2006; Zuboff 2019; Cohen 2019).

Thirdly, tech companies build, run, or otherwise have frequent access to our smartphones – the emblems of the digital economy. This is significant in ways that Broockman et al. perhaps don't make fully clear, and which we expand upon here. The digital economy offers these corporations and their founders a form of power that not only elicits brand loyalty from consumers, but has also contributed to the development of a new economic paradigm, rooted in the expropriation of data – what we term 'digital capitalism.'[13] This power has been described in increasingly concerned terms by a number of contemporary political economists, social theorists, and legal scholars, and will be discussed further throughout this book. In this new milieu, the individual competition between the 'consumer-subjects' of neoliberalism is intensified through the competitive attention economy of social media, even as the espoused principles of a neoliberal free-market economy give way to the oligarchic monopoly characteristic of digital capitalism (Winters 2011; Gilens and Page 2014; Page et al. 2019; Moore and Tambini 2018).

Fourthly, as Broockman et al. put it: 'Millions of Americans work for companies technology entrepreneurs founded and run, and these numbers continue to swell' (p213). The influence wielded here is not straightforward. Although some US corporations compel staff, at least in workplace activities, to endorse certain political positions Page et al. (2019, 64–65) identify billionaire John Menard as incorporating conservative politics into staff training, in tech companies the relationship with staff is more complex than direct attempts at indoctrination. While some companies do explicitly select for ideological compatibility, ostensibly for effective teamwork (as with Peter Thiel's PayPal), this area is fraught with tensions. What we *can* say – complicating Broockman et al.'s claim that the industry is racially diverse – is that it is clearly the case that the tech industry has a deep cultural preference for young white, South Asian, and East Asian men, while at the same time publicly professing commitments to diversity (Broussard 2019). But perhaps the biggest consistent impact on employment by these men is their opposition to union organising (as Broockman et al. note). Most critically here – and as a central theme of this book – we would add a fifth dimension. The leading technology entrepreneurs are a tight-knit *network* who know each other, invest in each other, compete with each other, and self-identify in relation (and opposition) to each other. And as we will demonstrate through this book, the network is patriarchal, racialised, and subject to very particular American cultural logics.

Overview of the book

The case studies in this book demand specific methodological approaches. For example, following the practices of celebrity studies, we have distinguished between texts produced by the apparatuses around the men, which support the ideological and corporate work they do as founders, CEOs, and corporate representatives, and those that are part of the wider gossip press that claim to offer insight into the lives of the rich and famous. Our focus has been on the sites where a corporate apparatus is brought to bear on the development of celebrity for strategic reasons. In such a way we focus on a number of other specific celebrified locations: commencement speeches, prestige interviews, popular culture cameos, product launches, corporate communications, and social media content. We do not seek to offer a comprehensive analysis of each of these locations, nor do we draw on all of them in each case study: instead, we focus on paradigmatic examples. Each kind of location has a slightly different role in communicating the underpinning spirit which justifies the dominance of this patriarchal network.

Popular technology books and biographies are another primary resource here. On starting to explore the books that underpin this analysis, we noted that they constitute a genre in themselves. Contemporary writing about technology seems to work within a framework where certain values – innovation, brilliance, modernity, efficiency, youth – are taken for granted, and which then serve as a bedrock for a wider social description of a particular sort which these men, and tech culture itself, draw upon. Another feature that is of marked significance in these texts is how founder and firm, corporation and CEO, are folded together, often as if they were the same entity. This is most evident in biographical books (for instance Brad Stone on Bezos (2014), or Ashlee Vance on Musk (2015)), but it also emerges in more general books about technology and business, whether written by those praising the tech industry (such as *Abundance* by Peter Diamandis and Steven Kotler (2014)), or those critiquing its relationship to democracy (such as Jamie Bartlett 2018). Thinking through this evidence with concepts developed by a range of feminist theorists, we argue that these men collaborate and compete to secure their position in society.

Although usually presented as addressing universal themes, the celebrity narratives we identify in our case study chapters are fundamentally American stories. To understand how they are linked, Chapter 1 looks at the philosophical, ideological, and contextual forces that shape the network we have identified above. In this chapter we note Imani Perry's recommendation to think patriarchy through the 'architectures' of the concept to avoid reproducing the essentialised attitudes to race, class, and gender that it depends on. In doing so we look at how the conceptual frameworks of US tech culture are rooted in an imagined American frontier. These frontier myths go back centuries, from the seventeenth-century philosophy of John Locke, the 'father of liberalism,' to the myth of the nineteenth-century Wild West. Through recourse to these historical precursors, and looking at their deployment from the 1990s to our current case studies, we demonstrate how they are used to obfuscate a series of deep structural hierarchies that are embedded at the heart of American tech culture: from its commitment to dataism to the uneven ethnic, racial, and gendered configurations of its workforces.

In Chapter 2, noting that we see gender and patriarchy as complementary and co-constitutive terms, we move on to explore the gendered nature of the popular culture that is embraced by the celebrified persona of rocket engineer and electric car manufacturer Elon Musk. We start by looking at popular culture's role in disseminating the 'boy genius' narrative as a way of justifying a natural hierarchy that places men like Musk at the top. We explore a range of popular culture texts, from *The Big Bang Theory* to *Silicon Valley*, but with a main focus on the Iron Man movies, which are rumoured to have used Musk as a model for a playboy-entrepreneur-cum-inventor-cum-world saving superhero. We then look at how the geek masculinities embedded within these narratives are taken up by Musk and deployed as part of his celebrity profile for strategic corporate advancement, particularly in relation to marketing. We conclude the chapter with a look at a controversial interview where the publicity-seeking Musk smokes marijuana on Joe Rogan's YouTube podcast while wielding a samurai sword in front of a faded Stars and Stripes.

We then turn to a more detailed exploration of the significance of the American frontier. In Chapter 3 we focus on the narrative presented by Jeff Bezos's celebrity, starting with his participation in the viral internet Ice Bucket Challenge meme, which shows the celebrity founder network of West Coast tech culture in full flush. In Bezos's version of the video challenge, he invokes a range of world figures, from the Queen of England to Edward Snowden, before turning his attention to actors from the cult TV series *Star Trek*. From there we move on to his biography (which is in our concordance) and an interview in Berlin to mark his receipt of the Axel Springer Award 2018. We mark how the spirit of the frontier traverses these very different textual locations, and how it covers a wide variety of ground in the service of Bezos's ideological justification for his wealth and power. The frontier is simultaneously a business frontier that Amazon must conquer, the electronic or cybernetic frontier of the internet, the historic frontier of the American West, and the final or 'high' frontier of space. In each of these areas we can see how the basic legal and social unit of the historic frontier – the 'homestead' – is reproduced in corporate form to the benefit of the founder.

This key area of ideological content – the household as configured through the frontier homestead underpins our exploration of Mark Zuckerberg's celebrity. In Chapter 4 we examine his entanglement with Facebook as a corporate household. Zuckerberg usually spreads information via his own Facebook platform, which is then taken up as material for newspapers, blogs, and online journals (many of which will recirculate through Facebook itself). Using Zuckerberg's own Facebook Timeline we argue that he is represented through the signifiers of postfeminist fatherhood (Hamad 2014). This gives Zuckerberg legitimacy as founder and CEO of the largest global social network platform, as well as one of the key sites of 'surveillance capitalism' (Zuboff 2019). We then explore how he is portrayed as a celebrity statesman, including his explicit positioning of himself as a contrast to Trump, especially around immigration policies. Analysing his Year of Travel Facebook Timeline from 2017, where his aim was to visit every state in America, we investigate how he (and his corporate household) draw upon the tropes of home, food, and hospitality to be produced as a viable leader of civil society; in an economy built around data extraction from households.

We return to the themes of the frontier in our next chapter where we look at Peter Thiel, a key member (alongside Elon Musk) of the 'Paypal Mafia,' the group of men who made their first fortunes from the sale of PayPal to eBay and went on to found or invest in numerous successful tech companies. Thiel is a serial investor and founder as well as being on the Facebook board. He is also author of two books and a conservative blogger. We look in particular at his 1995 book *The Diversity Myth*, which was born out of Stanford University's provocative right-wing newspaper, *The Stanford Review*. This book is significant because the PayPal Mafia explicitly hired from *The Stanford Review*, and these recruits then went on to also become key venture capitalists, founders, and CEOs in Silicon Valley. Thiel is the broker between the apparently liberal founders of West Coast Tech and the Trump administration. Although he is not as wealthy or as globally significant as the other subjects of case studies in this book, his books and think pieces position him as a key disseminator of ideology: he carries out important work for the patriarchal network for wider audiences. In particular, his right-wing philosophy is an attempt to reconcile the celebrity assemblages of the patriarchal founder network with online conservative hubs who feel discriminated against by outwardly liberal organisations such as Google.

In order to understand how women can be reconciled to this misogynistic milieu, we look at the celebrification of Sheryl Sandberg in Chapter 6. Sandberg is not a founder, and she is not nearly as wealthy as the men that we look at (bar Thiel perhaps). She is also a woman. Like Thiel, however, she has written best-selling books and plays an important ideological role in the dissemination of Silicon Valley philosophy. In this chapter we look at her attempts to resolve the patriarchal structures of tech culture for an audience of women. She advises women, and models to them how to bargain with patriarchy; and she also displays the value of the gendered digital subject through her performance of the figure of the middle-class woman who shares her private and public data with Silicon Valley's corporate households. In response to Thiel (and his conservative networks) – who has remarked that the extension of suffrage to women made 'democratic capitalism an oxymoron' (Thiel 2009) – Sandberg advises women on how to participate in both the public and private spheres under digital capitalism: a pioneer woman on the founder's technological frontiers.

Our argument seemingly runs counter to the technology sector's own self-image as a progressive, liberal field. So in the final chapter we look at Google to explore how this sits alongside and in tension with the conservative, patriarchal ideological formations we identify in the book. We begin by examining Google's Initial Public Offering (IPO) letter, as well as Larry Page's commencement speech at the University of Michigan, where he tells the story of his grandfather's role in a trade union. We do this in order to show how the celebrification of Google's founders is built on the symbols of progressive liberalism. However, as Google's racialised patriarchal structures have become evident (as revealed by the work of Safiya Umoja Noble and Siva Vaidhyanathan, as well as prominent journalists), so the founders' progressive celebrity narratives have become untenable. We argue that this is because they cannot reconcile their progressive celebrity stories with the material reality of the Google corporate household. Google ended up becoming the very opposite of what Brin and Page once insisted a search engine should be. Perhaps this helps us to understand some of the contradictions that have emerged over time in Google's self-presentation – and why the two founders have now withdrawn from their roles as celebrity founders, and in effect from public life (as of December 2019 (Overly 2019)). We then look at Susan Wojcicki, CEO of YouTube, and former Google employee James Damore, who authored a memo that argued that women were biologically wired to be lesser engineers (for which he was fired). We do this in order to explore some of the problems inherent in the Google corporate household – in relation to the diversity of its workforce, its approach to content moderation, and its value-laden algorithms. Pinpointing dataism as a weapon of the patriarchal network, we conclude by arguing that the model of liberalism around which Brin and Page constructed their celebrity was itself grounded in the racialised, classed, and gendered hierarchies of the colonial household.

Some final notes on the underpinning research: the concordance and corpus linguistics

Emerging from our desk research we identified a very substantial 'fuzzy set' genre (Attebury 1991) of popular literary works that we believed provided a substantive way to address our case studies without simply chasing gossip or specific news agendas – this became our concordance: a substantial corpus that we have taken as the basis of our research. Using a body of work like this has parallels to the work of Luc Boltanski and Eve Chiappello on management texts, in their exploration of the ideological spirit of late capitalism in the 1990s. At the centre of our 'fuzzy set' ('the idea that there is a core likeness [among a group of texts] to which we can add ever more distant perimeters,' Mendlesohn 2008) are the celebrity biographies of the entrepreneurs, some of them semi-official, others verging on hostility. Similar to these are the memoirs of people in their near circles. Some in this vein are even written by the subjects themselves (Sandberg and Thiel are both published authors in their own right). Slightly further out are the corporate 'how-to' books that are often hagiographical in their praise of the founders. Similarly there were ideological books which present a world organised around technology as either inevitable or full of hope and promise; while at a similar distance, but with a far more critical tone, are the polemical books which denounce the industry and its leaders.

Concordancing is a method that was originally used for biblical study, to create lists of all the uses of key words in the Bible. The first known example was produced in the twelfth century (Higdon 2003, 52), a time when such work required great amounts of diligent labour – as they continued to do until the advent of the first computers. With contemporary digital technologies, however, the range of uses of this method, given that it now requires considerably less labour input, has been vastly increased. We can, for instance, see how many times a word appears and what its frequent collocates are in a few seconds, and can search within far larger bodies of text than the million words that was standard in the 1960s, the early period of digital corpus linguistics (Baker 2014, 75). The skill needed in this method is knowing how to work out which results are interesting and useful, as well as genuinely distinctive – given the speed at which these numbers can be generated. A key requirement is to generate comparative metrics, so we can work out how significant the frequency of a word is by looking at its uses in different contexts.

In this book there are three primary ways in which we analyse data generated through the concordance. In the first of these, a simple word-count frequency is compared to a baseline or 'reference corpus' (most often this is a sample of over 10 billion words scraped from the English language internet in 2015 or enTenTen15) (Baker 2014, 9). This data is expressed as ##/mw or the number of occurrences per million words. It is usually used to indicate the heightened relevance of a word in tech culture as compared to other subject areas or general usage. The second way is as a concordance sample. Here a random selection of 50 KWIC uses are chosen from the database and a selection is made by the authors to illustrate a point. This is usually employed to show the different uses of a particularly significant word or phrase: for instance how 'disrupt' is used in a positive way to indicate the destruction of competitor businesses. The third way consists of showing examples from a word sketch – i.e. showing the other words with which a key word is frequently associated. Frequent collocations (two words commonly appearing together) may also be indicated in these examples. There are other novel uses deployed throughout this book. In each case, we will explain how we are using the material and offer examples for comparison where appropriate.

We thus approach this concordance in a number of different ways, although we have largely been led by the corpus linguistics work of Paul Baker, whose *Using Corpora to Analyse Gender* has been a kind of guidebook for this research (Baker 2014). Baker's co-authored work with Gabrielatos and McEnery on race and representation, using the same software as we do (Sketch Engine), has also informed our underlying approach to the corpus (Baker et al. 2013). We also heed Baker's observation that we should be cautious in using this sort of quantitative language analysis. If we want to talk about the 'legitimation strategies' (2014, 124) that are observable through the use of these digital tools, these are best discussed alongside more discursive methods to avoid the dangers of misinterpretation of data. Thus, we recognise and are aware of the problems with these quantitative approaches: indeed we are acutely aware that positivist readings of gendered language have been subject to convincing feminist critiques (Mandell 2019). As a result, we deploy the quantitative approaches made available by the concordance mainly as a support for more traditional forms of textual analysis. We have generally tried to keep the methodological explanation of these research methods light, as we recognise that many readers will be less concerned with the technical details and more with the conclusions.

Notes

1 Unfortunately due to copyright restrictions we cannot make this corpus publicly available. Ironically, this has not been a problem for Google who have made 40 million books available online through their Google Books project.
2 Due to the common use of nicknames and the fact that 'Page' is a commonly used word this is solely a count of the number of times first name and surname appear together. It is not a representative figure of the total number of times they would be referred to, but more accurately the number of times they are introduced for discussion with their full name. If every instance was counted the top hits would run into the thousands (Over 4,000 for Zuckerberg for instance).
3 In the time between starting the research to publication of the book, Larry Page and Sergey Brin of Alphabet-Google have stepped back from active management of their companies and Jeff Bezos has moved from CEO to Executive Chairman of Amazon. In these cases, the men nevertheless retain significant influence and indelible association with these companies.
4 Thiel's wealth is difficult to quantify, however, given his interest in cryptocurrency – an asset class designed to be hard to identify with an owner.

5 Clearly it is also the case, as Page et al. note, that interviews with these figures are not really possible for academic researchers – 'even their gatekeepers have gatekeepers' (2019, 3–4). Furthermore, as Toby James argues, the use of interviews is 'a problematic approach when used with elite actors': individuals tend to portray themselves in the best possible light, and do not necessarily answer truthfully (James 2018).
6 Our method for finding the links in this network was threefold. First, we coded each of the entrepreneurs' names in our NVivo database as nodes, and then we searched for each of the others' names in 'broad context' around that node. We then recorded any relationships that emerged. Through this we found a set of links that varies in intensity between various pairings, but shows a dense network when considered collectively. This method did not immediately show some nodes that are obvious from desk research: these required additional, if minimal, piecing together by the authors – for instance around university networks or membership of lobbying groups or philanthropic organisations. Our primary method was thus lightly supplemented by desk research drawing on four years of notes.
7 It is, to be fair, not entirely clear if Musk actually ever attended Stanford, but he did, at least briefly, enrol in doctoral training there.
8 Generally, if only one of the Google founders is referred to it is Larry Page, although Brin does appear in reference to a secret fancy dress party (implied to be a sex party) that Musk also attended, in Emily Chang's book *Brotopia* (Chang 2018, 182).
9 Even in areas of seemingly direct competition there is clear differentiation. Both are contracted by NASA to develop Moon landing vehicles. Space X is proposing a vehicle which will be similar to the vehicle they aim to land on Mars, while Bezos is producing a specialist system for the lunar environment. These then are complementary, rather than competing technologies.
10 Facebook's record fine of $5billion in 2019 actually caused its stock to rise: the increased value of the company stock wiping out any cash losses. Whether the new wave of anti-trust suits currently being brought to court in the US will be similarly ineffective remains to be seen.
11 Runciman also uses the term 'assemblage' to describe these corporations, though his reference point is social-contract theorist Thomas Hobbes rather than materialist philosophers Gilles Deleuze and Felix Guattari.
12 Incidentally, this pro-oil lobbying led Elon Musk to resign from FWD.us on climate grounds, much as he resigned from Donald Trump's advisory board over withdrawal from the Paris Agreement on carbon emissions.
13 Elon Musk may seem to be an exception to this point about the smart phone economy, but Tesla is both a luxury car manufacturer and a data company. The latter is the more valuable part of the equation. Consider Ford's value of $28 billion versus Tesla's of $160 billion (as of March 2020). Ford sold 5.5 million cars in 2019; Tesla sold 367,000 in the same period. The price difference stems from the value of (1) being first to market with a popular electric car; and (2) the ability to gather data from over a million cars on the road for the purposes of improving self-driving algorithms. In other words, Tesla applies the logics of the smart phone to the automotive industry and this explains its valuation.

References

Agamben, Georgio (2009) *What Is An Apparatus?* trans. Davis Kishik and Stefan Pedatella. Stanford: Stanford University Press.
Attebury, Brian (1991) *Strategies of Fantasy*. New York: Zone Books.
Baker, Paul (2014) *Using Corpora to Analyse Gender*. London: Bloomsbury.
Baker, Paul, Costas Gabrielatos, and Tony McEnery (2013) *Discourse Analysis and Media Attitudes: The Representation of Islam in the British Press*. Cambridge: Cambridge University Press.

Bartlett, Jamie (2018) *The People vs Tech: How the Internet is Killing Democracy (and How We Can Save It)*. London: Ebury Press.
Boltanski, Luc and Eve Chiapello (2007) *The New Spirit of Capitalism*. London: Verso.
Broockman, D. E., G. Ferenstein, and N. Malhotra (2019) 'Predispositions and the Political Behavior of American Economic Elites: Evidence from Technology Entrepreneurs' *American Journal of Political Science*, 63: 212–233.
Broussard, Meredith (2019) *Artificial Unintelligence: How Computers Misunderstand the World*. Cambridge, MA: MIT Press.
Cardenal, Andrés (2016) 'The Most Valuable Companies in the World' *The Motley Fool*. www.fool.com/investing/2016/11/03/the-most-valuable-companies-in-the-world.aspx Last accessed 28/04/2020.
Carreyou, John (2018) *Bad Blood: Secrets and Lies in a Silicon Valley Startup*. London: Penguin Random House.
Chang, Emily (2018) *Brotopia: Breaking Up the Boys' Club of Silicon Valley*. New York: Penguin Random House.
Cohen, Noam (2019) *The Know It Alls: The Rise of Silicon Valley as a Political Powerhouse and Social Wrecking Ball*. London: Oneworld.
Couldry, Nick and Ulises Mejias (2018) 'Data Colonialism: Rethinking Big Data's Relation to the Contemporary Subject' *Television and New Media*, 20:4, 336–349.
Couldry, Nick and Ulises Mejias (2019) *The Costs of Connection: How Data Is Colonizing Human Life and Appropriating It for Capitalism*. Stanford: Stanford University Press.
Davis, Aeron (2019) 'Top CEOs, Financialization and the Creation of the Super-Rich Economy' *Cultural Politics*, 15:1, 88–104.
Delanda, Manuel (2006) *A New Philosophy of Society: Assemblage Theory and Social Complexity*. New York: Continuum.
Deleuze, Gilles and Felix Guattari (1988) *A Thousand Plateaus: Capitalism and Schizophrenia*. London: Athlone Press.
Diamandis, Peter H. and Steven Kotler (2014) *Abundance: The Future Is Better Than You Think*. New York: Free Press.
English-Lueck, J. A. (2017) *Cultures@SiliconValley*. Second Edition: Vol. Second edition. Stanford: Stanford University Press.
Featherstone, D. (2011) 'On Assemblage and Articulation' *Area*, 43, 139–142. doi:10.1111/j.1475-4762.2011.01007.x
Forbes.com (2021) 'The World's Real Time Billionaires' Forbes.com. www.forbes.com/real-time-billionaires/ Last accessed 21/02/2021.
Foroohar, Rana (2018) 'Year in a Word: Tech-Lash' *Financial Times*, December 16. www.ft.com/content/76578fba-fca1-11e8-ac00-57a2a826423e Last accessed 28/04/2020.
Gilbert, Jeremy (2019) 'Editorial' *New Formations*, Issue 96–97, 5–37.
Gilbert, Jeremy and Alex Williams (2018) 'Hegemony Now: Power in the Twenty-First Century' *Culture, Power and Politics podcast* available at https://culturepowerpolitics.org/2018/07/10/hegemony-now-power-in-the-twenty-first-century-part-1/ Last accessed 21/02/2021.
Gilens, M. and B. Page (2014) 'Testing Theories of American Politics: Elites, Interest Groups, and Average Citizens' *Perspectives on Politics*, 12(3), 564–581.
Gramsci, Antonio (1971) *Selctions from The Prison Notebooks*, trans. Quentin Hoare. London: Lawrence and Wishart.
Grossberg, Lawrence (2019) 'Cultural Studies in Search of a Method, or Looking for Conjunctural Analysis' *New Formations*, Issue 96–97, 38–68.

Hamad, Hannah (2014) '"Don't Let Him Take Britain Back to the 1980s": Ashes to Ashes as Postfeminist Recession Television' *Continuum*, 28:2, 201–212.
Higdon, David Leon (2003) 'The Concordance: Mere Index or Needful Census?' *Text*, 15, 51–68.
Holt, Douglas and Douglas Cameron (2012) *Cultural Strategy: Using Innovative Ideologies Build Breakthrough Brands*. Oxford: Oxford University Press.
Inside Bill's Brain. (2019) David Guggenheim (dir) Netflix.
James, Toby S. (2018) 'Political Leadership as Statecraft? Aligning Theory with Praxis in Conversation with British Party Leaders' *British Journal of Politics & International Relations*, 20:3, 555–572.
Jarrett, Kylie (2016) *Feminism, Labour and Digital Media: The Digital Housewife*. London and New York: Routledge.
Kirkpatrick, David (2011) *The Facebook Effect: The Real Inside Story of Mark Zuckerberg and the World's Fastest Growing Company*. London: Virgin Books.
Koren, Marina (2017) 'Elon Musk Quits Donald Trump' *Atlantic*, 1 June. www.theatlantic.com/science/archive/2017/06/trump-climate-change-elon-musk/528906/ Last accessed 28/04/2020.
Levy, Ari (2016) 'Silicon Valley Donated 60 Times More to Clinton Than to Trump' *CNBC News*, 7 November. www.nbcnews.com/storyline/2016-election-day/silicon-valley-donated-60-times-more-clinton-trump-n679156 Last accessed 28/04/2020.
Littler, Jo (2016) 'On Not Being at CCCS' in Kieran Connell and Matthew Hilton (eds.) *Cultural Studies 50 Years On*. London: Rowman & Littlefield.
Mandell, Laura (2019) 'Gender and Cultural Analytics: Finding or Making Stereotypes?' in Matthew K. Gold and Lauren F. Klein (eds.) *Debates in the Digital Humanities 2019*. Minneapolis: University of Minnesota. https://dhdebates.gc.cuny.edu/read/untitled-f2acf72c-a469-49d8-be35-67f9ac1e3a60/section/5d9c1b63-7b60-42dd-8cda-bde837f638f4#ch01 Last accessed 28/04/2020.
Martinez, Antonio Garcia (2016) *Chaos Monkeys: Mayhem and Mania Inside the Silicon Valley Money Machine*. London: EBury Press.
McNamee, Roger (2019) *Zucked: Waking Up to the Facebook Catastrophe*. London: HarperCollins.
Mendlesohn, Farah (2008) *Rhetorics of Fantasy*. Middletown CT: Wesleyan University Press.
Mies, Maria (1998) *Patriarchy and Accumulation on a World Scale: Women in the International Division of Labour*. London: Zed Books.
Moore, Martin and Damian Tambini (eds.) (2018) *Digital Dominance The Power of Google, Amazon, Facebook and Apple*. Oxford: Oxford University Press.
Noble, Safiya Umoja. (2018) *Algorithms of Oppression: How Search Engines Reinforce Racism*. New York: New York University Press.
Overly, Steven (2019) 'Google Co-Founders Hand Over Reains of Parent Company Alphabet' *Politico*, 3 December. www.politico.com/news/2019/12/03/google-co-founders-alphabet-brin-page-pichai-074974 Last accessed 28/04/2020.
Page, Benjamin, Jason Seawright, and Matthew Lacombe (2019) *Billionaires and Stealth Politics*. Chicago: University of Chicago Press.
Papacharissi, Zizi (2010) *A Networked Self: Identity, Community and Culture on Social Network Sites*. New York: Routledge.
Perry, Imani (2018) *Vexy Thing: On Gender and Liberation*. Durham: Duke University Press.
Rottenberg, Catherine (2018) *The Rise of Neoliberal Feminism*. Oxford: Oxford University Press.
Runciman, David (2018) *How Democracy Ends*. London: Profile Books.

Sardar, Ziauddin (1995) 'alt.civilizations.faq Cyberspace as the Darker Side of the West' *Futures*, 27:7, 717–794.
Skeggs, Beverly and Simon Yuill (2019) 'Subjects of Value and Digital Personas: Reshaping the Bourgeois Subject, Unhinging Property from Personhood' *Subjectivity*, 12, 82–99.
Smiley, Lauren (2017) 'The Tech Resistance Awakens' *Wired Magazine*, 2 September. www.wired.com/2017/02/the-tech-resistance-awakens/ Last accessed 28/04/2020.
Sonnad, Nikhil (2016) 'The Seating Chart at Trump's Table of Tech Giants' *Quartz*, 14 December. https://qz.com/863437/who-was-at-donald-trumps-tech-meeting/ Last accessed 28/04/2020.
Star Trek (1966–1969) Gene Roddenberry (creator). Desilu Productions/Paramount Television.
Stone, Brad (2014) *The Everything Store: Jeff Bezos and the Age of Amazon*. London: Corgi Books.
Streitfeld, David (2016) '"I'm Here to Help" Trump Tells Tech Executives at Meeting' *The New York Times*, 14 December. www.nytimes.com/2016/12/14/technology/trump-tech-summit.html?auth=login-google Last accessed 28/04/2020.
Taplin, Jonathan (2017) *Move Fast and Break Things: How Facebook, Google, and Amazon Cornered Culture and Undermined Democracy*. New York: Hachette USA.
Tarnoff, Ben (2017) 'Trump's Tech Opposition: An Interview with Kristen Sheets, and Matt Schaefer' *Jacobin Magazine*. www.jacobinmag.com/2017/05/tech-workers-silicon-valley-trump-resistance-startups-unions Last accessed 28/04/2020.
Thiel, Peter (2009) 'The Education of a Libertarian' *Cato Unbound*, 13 April. www.cato-unbound.org/2009/04/13/peter-thiel/education-libertarian Last accessed 28/04/2020.
Turner, F. (2006) *From Counterculture to Cyberculture: Stewart Brand, the Whole Earth Network, and the Rise of Digital Utopianism*. Chicago: University of Chicago Press.
Vance, Ashlee (2015) *Elon Musk: How the Billionaire CEO of SpaceX and Tesla is Shaping our Future*. London: Virgin Books.
van Dijck, Jose (2014) 'Datafication, Dataism and Dataveillance: Big Data between Scientific Paradigm and Ideology' *Surveillance and Society*, 12, 2. https://doi.org/10.24908/ss.v12i2.4776 Last accessed 28/04/2020.
Van Dijck, José, Thomas Poell, and Martijn de Waal, (2018) *The Platform Society Public Values in a Connective World*. Oxford: Oxford University Press.
Vara, Vauhini (2017) 'The Tech Resistance to the Trump Refugee Ban' *New Yorker*, 31 January. www.newyorker.com/business/currency/the-tech-resistance-to-the-trump-refugee-ban Last accessed 28/04/2020.
Winters, J. (2011) *Oligarchy*. Cambridge: Cambridge University Press.
Wu, Tim (2018) *The Curse of Bigness: Antitrust in the New Gilded Age*. New York: Columbia Global Reports.
Zuboff, Shoshona (2019) *The Age of Surveillance Capitalism: The Fight for a Human Future at the New Frontier of Power*. London: Profile Books.

1
THEORISING THE PATRIARCHAL NETWORK

Elon Musk makes cameo appearances in many popular films and TV programmes. In the comedy film *Why Him?* he plays himself at a party – his appearance authenticating the film's Silicon Valley setting. The film's plot is driven by the father v. fiancé conceit: two men from different generations engage in a struggle for authority over a woman and thus over generational supremacy. The father, Ned (Bryan Cranston), owns a print company in Michigan, and the fiancé boy genius Laird (James Franco) is a billionaire CEO of a video games company in California. The men compete and eventually bond over Stephanie (Zoey Deutch), whose intention to drop out of Stanford in order to run Laird's philanthropic foundation is a disappointment to her father. The film is a partial satire of Silicon Valley cultures playing on stereotypes of gender roles in tech: the boy genius founder, the female partner running the philanthropic foundation, female-voiced AI, as well as the pretentious food, the billionaires.

Significantly for our purposes, Laird's home is also a mocking portrait of the American frontier homestead, replete with farm animals which he tends in a haphazard fashion; he is even subject to unexpected ambushes – from his best friend, butler, and household manager Gustav (played by biracial actor Keegan-Michael Key), who is training him in martial arts. Although there are restaurant-style chefs in the household, the rest of the domestic staff are eclipsed by the husky-voiced AI (played by Kaley Cuoco, the 'sexy blonde' Penny in the geek sitcom *The Big Bang Theory* – a role referenced in the film). And Laird's home is also his business. His homestead is a corporate household, accommodating his workforce, the programmers and gamers producing and testing his products. The only components this head of the household lacks are the wife and children, and the film is driven by his need to overcome this lack.

The film's patriarchal plot, which is undergirded by the rivalry and collaborations between men, reveals the conservatism of the cultures it is mocking in a number of ways. One of the points of contestation between the two men is Stephanie's body. Stephanie is framed as belonging to her father; a tattoo of Laird's name on her hip – indicating a loss of possession – is a source of paternal rage. Another point of contestation is the shift from print to digital; Ned is on the verge of bankruptcy and Laird buys his business in an attempt to save it. Another is the depiction of the home. It is in Laird's home that Ned learns of the engagement, and of Stephanie's decision to work for Laird. The film ends with Stephanie's father, brother, and fiancé turning the printing company into a toilet factory, and Stephanie using this company – and staying true to the female caring (and American imperialist) role – to help improve sanitation in developing countries (this is a nod to Bill Gates' philanthropic work on sewage projects). Although she remains unmarried at the end of the film, Stephanie is economically tied to Laird, and he achieves what he has always wanted – a corporate household remade in the image of a white, middle-class, heterosexual family. And Stephanie's body has facilitated a form of homosocial bonding between Laird and Ned, bringing together their economic and generational differences – the movement from one form of patriarchy to another.

Although the film was badly reviewed (a 39% aggregate score on RottenTomatoes.com), it is worth dwelling on because of what it reveals about the patriarchal network that we are looking at. This film offers a useful introduction to some of the contexts within which the contemporary American tech industry is located. Although Silicon Valley likes to project itself as progressive, future-oriented, and innovative, we have been struck by how the ideologies of the founders are embedded in histories of white American settler colonialism. In particular, these ideologies are animated by the frontier spirit and its paradigm of the heteronormative white homestead. In this chapter we examine the myth of the frontier and 'patriarchal architectures' of the homestead or household (Perry 2018). That these myths are part of the stories that American West Coast Tech tells about itself is key in identifying and making sense of contemporary raced and gendered hierarchies. That contemporary tech has a colonial impulse has been identified by Zuboff (2019) as well as Couldry and Mejias (2019). Skeggs and Yuill (2019) note how Facebook is embedded in colonial paradigms of personhood and property. We develop these scholars' work to look at the specificity of the colonial and patriarchal histories that inform the corporations' 'data relations' (Couldry and Meijas 2019).

Why patriarchy?

Anthropologist Sherry B. Ortner gives a useful – if limited – description of a patriarchal system. She argues that it is organised around 'three dyads and their many kinds of interaction':

(1) The relationship between a patriarchal figure of some sort and other men;

(2) The many homosocial but heterosexual relationships among the men themselves; and
(3) The relationships between men and women (Ortner 2014, 532).

This definition is productive because it clarifies that patriarchal systems are not simply about the repression of women, but also relationships between men, and that these are constantly being negotiated. That is, men compete and collaborate with other men, and men hold power over other men. This seems to usefully describe the kind of network we are describing in this book. The focus on patriarchy as a set of relations rather than a static system is also key. However, it is important to note that patriarchy is always contextual; it is not a theoretical framework that can be applied without taking into account contemporary political structures, histories, specific colonial projects. Indeed, historically the term patriarchy has been highly contested on multiple fronts (e.g. Rowbotham 1981, Acker 1989), and it is still a concept that is not easily assimilated in many feminists' critical work (see McRobbie 2015). Our intention in using the term as a key part of our argument is to hold on to the clarity of the idea, while also being attentive to arguments criticising the often universalising, essentialist and unhistorical ways in which it has sometimes been deployed (Josephs 1981, Patil 2013, Miller 2017). We understand that patriarchy is fluid, moving, shapeshifting – in relation not only to what form it takes, but also to the identity of the recipient of its socioeconomic benefits. As Cynthia Enloe states, 'Patriarchy is not old-fashioned: it is as hip as football millionaires and Silicon Valley start-ups' (Enloe 2017, 15). As she goes on to argue, patriarchy is a 'system – a dynamic web – of particular ideas and relationships'; it is 'stunningly adaptable' and 'can be updated and modernized.' This is what makes it sustainable (Enloe 2017, 16). Our priority here is to show the specificity of one such system.

Ortner's definition above is limited for our purposes here because it does not directly take into account race, migration status, and class – structures of oppression that are crucial to understanding how patriarchy functions in US West Coast Tech. Because of this, we also focus on a conception of patriarchy that is articulated with histories of personhood in America. What is at stake in this is a concept of who counts, who gets to be a 'proper person' – in other words, who gets to *own* property rather than *be* property. Here we turn to Imani Perry's discussion of patriarchy and seventeenth-century theorisations of personhood as delineated by the logics of the American frontier household (Perry 2018). As Perry points out, John Locke gives us a very clear statement of how the ideal household is constructed. In his *Second Treatise of Government*, Locke has us consider 'a master of a family with all these subordinate relations of wife, children, servants, and slaves, united under the domestic rule of a family' (Locke 1689, 86). He compares 'the master of a family' to a monarch, arguing that the master 'has a very distinct and differently limited power.' Locke grants that the master does not have 'legislative power of life and death' over the members of the family

– with the exception of the slave. Nevertheless, the master is the patriarch of the household, and the other components are differentially striated beneath him. Our argument in this chapter (and this book) is that this racialised, gendered, classed shaping of personhood persists in the patriarchal network we have identified, as well as its workforces and exported products.

Rather than examining the categories of male and female as key to what she calls 'patriarchal architectures,' Perry examines the history of personhood, of what it means to be a full person. This is understood not in binary gendered or sexed terms but in hierarchical terms which also take into account race and class: what it means to be a full or proper person through legislation. Examining Lockean ideas of personhood, Perry notes that there is 'an embedded deception' and 'violence' in how categories of sex, race, and class are constructed, and then presented as natural. It is a form of coercion: 'They are philosophical fictions matching legal ones' which then 'instruct how the person would be treated' (Perry 2018, 55). Essentialising sex or gender, for example, reproduces categories as being grounded in truths rather than ideologies, policies, legislation. A focus on the metaphor of the household rather than the binaries of male and female is therefore productive inasmuch as it does not reify and repeat sex difference but at the same time is aware that particular patriarchal structures work to *replicate* sex and gender binaries. Indeed, our argument in this book is that gendered hierarchies are reinforced and legitimated by the patriarchal network.

Thinking in terms of the household also exposes the racialised structures of the celebrity assemblages we are looking at, as expressed in the claims to personhood made in relation to race, class, and social reproduction, among other factors. We follow the work of Patricia Hill Collins (1989), who argues for the centrality of the imaginary of the white middle-class family as reinforcing raced, gendered, and classed systems of oppression, as well as how the constitutive limits of personhood are prescribed therein. We also draw on the work of Lisa Nakamura by understanding race as 'a code that evokes a specific type of regulating response from the state that serves to make race "real"' (Nakamura 2008, 74); as well as Ruha Benjamin: 'if we consider race as itself a technology, as a means to sort, organize, and design a social structure as well as to understand the durability of race, its consistency and adaptability, we can understand more clearly the literal architecture of power.' (Benjamin 2019, 91). It is precisely this designation of a social structure that we see in Locke's philosophising above.

But why hold on to seventeenth-century philosophy and American history when discussing the apparently innovative and future-focused men of West Coast Tech? Understanding patriarchal architectures as articulated by Perry – as a hierarchical set of raced, classed, gendered relations with long and specific histories, but also the white heteronormative family as an idealised patriarchal unit – is productive for making sense of the ideological work and storytelling that we found, for example, in the concordance. We see the household structure re-appearing at many different scales, from the domination of tech by white men, to the location of the middle-class family as the site of data extraction and manipulation, to some of the founders' celebrity brands. If we turn to our concordance we can see that the 'household' is a highly gendered concept: the household use clearly maps onto questions of consumerism, decision-making, and demography as defined by work, class, location, and wealth. Occurring approximately 43 times per million words, we see from a random sample of 50 uses that women 'take care' of the household, its children, and even the 'household laundry'; they make medical decisions on behalf of the household; they staff their household (when they can afford to hire help). It is reported that households led by women are 12% poorer than male-led ones: Men are not generally associated with households directly, they are however implicitly assumed to lead them. But it should also be noted that gender isn't the only key divide: households of people over 65 have 47 times the wealth of people under 35 (it will be a larger multiple now Mark Zuckerberg is 36); we learn that in Nigeria the average household has four people to a room and that children brought up in two-parent families have better outcomes 'by most dimensions'; and that the 'top 5% of households are … responsible for nearly 40% of spending.' In short, the household does a lot of work across a wide range of relevant areas here, and the uses found in our concordance demonstrate that, as far as the literature on technology goes, when it is not a primarily demographic term, the idea of the 'household' resonates strongly with that of a normative 1950s America.

Looking more specifically at the tech companies and their founders that we have identified in this book, the idea of the household recurs in different ways. In Chapter 5, we will see that Thiel explicitly compares corporations to households. And the household is also part of the origin stories of Google and Amazon, as we discuss later in the book. Sean Parker, Facebook's first president, said of the social media company: 'I refer to Facebook as a family business. Mark and his heirs will control Facebook in perpetuity' (Kirkpatrick 2011, 148). Zuckerberg's celebrification is centred around his visible location in his household, as revealed in television interviews and photographs on his Facebook Timeline. His philanthropic organisation – the Chan-Zuckerberg Initiative – is run out of his home (Price and Peterson 2020). Sandberg's home also appears in her books, interviews, and commencement speeches as we discuss in Chapter 7 – and is a key site in her celebrity narrative. The household is a structuring force in different ways for the various patriarchs (for example the celebrification of Elon Musk in relation to his extended domestic household conforms less to the constraints of the nuclear family, and is more sprawling and aristocratic in tenor).

How the conservative household is imagined also structures the products made by these corporations. For many people, through family mobile phone contracts, domestic broadband, and the growing number of home consumer devices constituting the 'internet of things,' our domestic spaces are a key conduit for our interactions with tech companies. And their products reflect that. Couldry and Mejias note that the systems designed to capture data are 'constituted such that data is able to flow'; and they argue that 'the seeming naturalness of the relation [as configured by Facebook et al.] frames the resulting data as something that can be validly extracted from the flow of life' (2019, 27). In short, the household itself becomes a mechanism of data capture, and that mechanism means that data is captured in the form of the household. The household, then, is one of the key ways through which we 'enter into the ambit' of data extraction. This means that our social relations will be embedded in the relatively conservative form of the normative household, and that services will be provided that specifically and exclusively cater to it. As Couldry and Mejias also note: 'data is not natural but a resource whose extractive possibilities must themselves be socially constructed.'

Thus digital sociologist Murray Goulden examines the ways that AI captures, constructs, and remakes households through the design of Amazon Household and Google Families – the digital mechanisms that allow groups of people to share content or access devices without having to purchase multiple copies of a given book, film, single or video game (among other functions). Although Goulden doesn't specifically characterise households as interpellated by the AI of Amazon or Google as patriarchal, he argues that the technology reinvents the family according to 'a white suburban American middle-class ideal,' where roles are 'ascribed largely by gender, the husband in the instrumental role as wage earner, the wife in the affective role of family carer … This is at the expense of recognising variation, struggle and conflict, in the form of poverty, race, class, and gender, the latter being naturalised as deeply unequal' (Goulden, 4 2019). Although Amazon Household and Google Families – as Goulden notes – are not intrinsically gendered, they effectively take their gendered dimensions from normative assumptions. As he notes, 'Google's Family Manager derives ultimate authority from being the first adopter in the family,' and this means that the fact that the associated technologies are 'designed by and for men' will have 'deep implications for how agency is distributed within the platform family' (Goulden 2019, 12). In addition, the design assumes a specific kind of normative family, 'as being of a certain size, as co-located, as isolated, and as stable and enduring, in which authority over others is formally vested in one, or perhaps two, key roles.' In Goulden's words, digital households 'offer a technical, yet inevitably normative, account of what home is, and family does': 'As scripts, these categorisations carry material force – creating new possibilities for life's regularities, events and norms, whilst precluding others' (15).[1]

It is no surprise that the default voice on the home assistants of the companies under discussion here – Amazon's Alexa and Google Home – is both sultry and feminine, just like Kaley Cuoco's in *Why Him?* The assistants take on the role of both domestic help and sexy secretary, as Helen Hester puts it:

> They exploit our assumptions about feminised labour and our existing relationship to socially gendered caring and service behaviours, tapping into those elements of femininity that have historically enabled care-giving or service-providing subjects to better undertake specific obligations, activities, and tasks.
>
> *(Hester 2016)*

In these spaces, the virtual labour of the feminised home assistant effaces the traditional role of domestic help in affluent households. It has the effect of democratising access to servants where those on middle incomes can afford to extend their households by bringing in virtually the domestic labour that richer homes can afford to have physically: Amazon's Alexa, like a flesh-and-blood maid, can take shopping orders for instance. But these assistants also deracialise and declass that labour, particularly in the USA, where over half of domestic workers are African-American or Latina women (Wolf et al. 2020). Alexa's voice obscures the normative power-relation through the racial markers of whiteness as evident by Cuoco's character.

As we have noted, Imani Perry's theorisation of patriarchy and the household is productive because its complexity answers many of the critiques of the term patriarchy as universalist, essentialist, and reductive by instead focusing on histories and intersecting forms of oppression (see also Crenshaw 1989 on how patriarchy and intersectional inequality are mutually constitutive). And we have also found the focus on the household and on personhood extremely helpful for our discussion of the frontier. In the frontier imaginary, a figure goes into a disputed space as yet unexploited by capitalism, and claims it as America, through the mechanism of the household. It is through the domination and ownership of the household and the persons and non-persons therein that the colonising figure becomes a patriarch. It is important to remember that this is not primarily an ideological or philosophical construct, nor was it confined in practice to the seventeenth and eighteenth centuries when it was first theorised and justified. In legal terms, claiming land was made possible by the bureaucratic frameworks of the Homestead Acts of 1862 and 1866, in which nearly 10% of the land area of the US was given to applicants so long as they lived on the land. Homesteading continued in the US until 1976 and in Alaska until 1986 (National Parks Service 2019). In frontier mythology this legal framing of the household as territorial claim becomes where the wilderness is turned into civilisation. The household offers a man paternal power as head of a household and owner of a homestead. Without the hierarchies of gender and race structured by the heterosexual matrix (Butler 1991), a pioneer culture cannot form a household – i.e. without a woman to bear the children and without subaltern people to do the domestic and manual labour.

The frontier spirit

Why Him? ironically marshals the frontier spirit; for example, in its visual representation of the chickens running around the homestead. But significantly for our analysis, this American settler spirit animates Silicon Valley's attitude to technology; it is key to the stories that it tells about itself. The ranch, the range, and the cowboy figure heavily in many tech narratives. For example, let us turn to Adam Fisher's words from his 2018 book *Valley of Genius: The Uncensored History of Silicon Valley:*

> They come West seeking fame and fortune. They work their claims. Some even strike it rich. Swap the pickaxe for some coding chops and the six-shooter for a standing desk and suddenly Silicon Valley becomes a much more familiar place. It is what it has always been: a frontier – the boundary between what is and what could be. It's a place where the future is dreamed up prototyped, packaged, and ultimately sold. But what is the future of this place that makes the future? Where is Silicon Valley going? Where is its technology taking us? What are we to become? The best answers to those questions come from those who've already built the future: the one that we live in today.
>
> (Fisher 2018, 421)

The tech founders we look at are strongly linked to the frontier imaginary – and this in turn is deeply entwined with the myths of the pioneering homesteads of the American settlement of the West. The pervasiveness of the spirit of the frontier can be seen in the concordance. 'Frontier' is used 153 times; and it is particularly used in texts by Peter Thiel, and more generally in books we have coded as ideological in terms of the uses of technology. The manner of its use is also instructive, in its breadth of associated concepts. It is used in the following ways, which we have organised into themes:

- *Space* – as in 'earthly,' 'space,' 'high' (after Gerald O'Neill's book on space colonisation), 'final' (after *Star Trek*) frontiers;
- *Technologies* – 'computer-guided,' 'electronic,' 'digital,' 'technical,' and 'internet' frontiers;
- *Business opportunities* – 'promising,' 'payments,' and 'profitable' frontiers
- *Measures of time and space* – 'new,' 'last,' 'far,' 'open,' 'wide-open,' and 'next' frontiers
- *Physical boundaries* – 'microscopic,' 'physical,' 'broad,' 'actual' frontiers
- *Social practices and psychological limits* – 'ethical,' 'mind,' or 'bohemian' frontiers;
- *American history* – 'wild,' 'Western,' and 'American' frontiers.

Like the underlying mythic structure, the frontier is an expansive term. It offers a set of principles that can be applied in a number of different settings. At a basic level it is about liminality – the boundary between two things. But in its specific usage it tends to act as a defining space of American culture: America itself is defined through its ability to transform new spaces for capitalism. The West has been conquered, but new spaces must be imagined, whether in business, science, technology, or beyond the atmosphere.

In this book we use the term 'the frontier spirit' to explain the ideologies of the frontier that we see as animating the patriarchal network of US West Coast Tech. Drawing loosely on Luc Boltanski and Eve Chiapello's *New Spirit of Capitalism*, we argue that the patriarchal network is constituted through a set of material, legal, and discursive practices that have their roots in the colonial household of the seventeenth century; and that elements from these discourses are still pervasive in the popular texts we draw upon as evidence. We use this approach to demonstrate what a feminist perspective can contribute to more traditional disciplines working on the role and means of the powerful, such as political science. We also make the case for the specifically American character of these companies and their founders, noting that the frontier homestead deployed metaphorically at times by these men has long been a space for turning migrants into Americans (some of the men we discuss in this book are themselves first-generation immigrants – Thiel and Brin for instance). And we also note that these patriarchal structures are striated with race: digital capitalism's frontier is a space of possibility primarily for white people (and to some extent Asian people, especially if they are male). For Black, Latinx and indigenous people it largely reproduces in rhetorical and material terms the locations of longstanding oppression. We discuss this further below. Moreover, this frontier spirit legitimates itself within the tech sector precisely through its points of internal contestation ('critique' is the term used by Boltanski and Chiapello for a similar argument in their work), and these, at least partially, also serve to obscure the more reactionary aspects of its underpinning mythic structures. For the fantasy of the frontier, as imagined through the histories of the Western US – where the companies are based – has strongly colonial roots, and these are often consonant with the practices of the tech patriarchs, if not always foregrounded in their myth-making. While other scholars have picked up on elements of coloniality in this 'spirit,' our research adds to these observations in a number of ways. Most particularly, we think through the specificities of the spirit that motivates the sector in terms of its location in distinctly American rather than European cultural forms.

If we turn to the early 1990s, we can see how the frontier was key to the way that access to the internet was being struggled over. As mentioned in the Introduction, the American internet has its origins in ARPANET, a distributed computer network designed by the military to ensure communications continued in the event of a nuclear attack. In 1993 Howard Rheingold published the popular *The Virtual Community: Homesteading on the Electronic Frontier* (2000 [1993]), explicitly using homesteading as a means to advocate for colonial land-grabbing, albeit virtually. Rheingold uses the mythic language of the Wild West. For example, by comparing one 'online activist' to a frontier cowboy.[2] In 1990, the Electronic Frontier Foundation was founded by John Gilmore, John Perry Barlow, and Mitch Kapor (Stewart Brand later joined the board of directors and we pay considerable attention to Brand in the following chapter on Bezos). Barlow, a countercultural libertarian figure –a Wyoming rancher and Grateful Dead lyricist – wrote 'A Declaration of the Independence of Cyberspace' in 1996. This manifesto explicitly marshals the language of the American frontier in order to compare attempts to regulate the internet to British rule over the American colonies:

> These increasingly hostile and colonial measures place us in the same position as those previous lovers of freedom and self-determination who had to reject the authorities of distant, uninformed powers. We must declare our virtual selves immune to your sovereignty, even as we continue to consent to your rule over our bodies. We will spread ourselves across the Planet so that no one can arrest our thoughts. We will create a civilization of the Mind in Cyberspace. May it be more humane and fair than the world your governments have made before.
>
> *(Barlow 1996)*

Like the 'lovers of freedom' of white settler colonialism, personhood in cyberspace is circumscribed; there are those people who own the servers and those people whose data are owned as a result. In the end, it turns out, that digital era division looks, in demographic terms, much like the ones of the late eighteenth-century revolutionary period. Barlow obfuscates these hierarchies by invoking a postracial (Mukherjee 2011) and postfeminist vision when he states that the internet 'is not where bodies live': 'We are creating a world that all may enter without privilege or prejudice accorded by race, economic power, military force, or station of birth.' In a deft move, structural inequalities and material differences are erased. As Whitney Phillips argues,

> Barlow's utopian and decidedly libertarian message thus functioned not just as a Declaration of Independence, but also as Manifest Destiny version 2.0. To these early adopters – the vast majority of whom were white males – the Internet was a land of endless opportunity, something to harness and explore, something to *claim*.
>
> *(Phillips, 129)*

Republican House leader in the 1990s Newt Gingrich – who had ties to Barlow – has also made connections between the rise of digital media and the frontier spirit. And Gingrich was a consistent supporter of the racialised, classed, and heterosexual household in conservative policies that included welfare reform, anticrime legislation, and a pro-marriage tax. In Fred Turner's discussion of Gingrich, Turner states that: 'To settle the "biolectronic frontier" [Gingrich] seemed to imply, was a divine mission, not unlike the settling of America some two hundred years earlier' (Turner 2008, 231). This is also the context the celebrity founders have stepped into. And because they have not attempted to mitigate and contextualise the oppressions already present in the social field as well as occluding how they invoke historical precedents, so these inequalities have been perpetuated in, for example, the ideology of dataism widespread in the tech industry (that we discuss below).

Ziauddin Sardar's searing critique of the electronic frontier imaginary (published in the same year as David Sacks and Peter Thiel's anti-diversity screed *The Diversity Myth*) is worth quoting at length:

> As an idea, the frontier is a tool of domination that arises from the certainty that one already has total control. As an instrument, the function of the frontier is to pass the routine practice of domination into the hands of the populace, to give them the illusion of freedom while they merely act out the actual effective control that is already predetermined, scrutinized, and seen to be good by those with power. The frontier is the agency through which power elites get everyone to do their work while thinking they are acting on their own volition.
>
> *(Sardar 1995, 780)*

Significantly, this pre-empts Adam Fisher's own words cited above when he excitedly celebrates Silicon Valley as the place where 'the future is dreamed up prototyped, packaged, and ultimately sold.' It is sold to us as freedom and autonomy but it has already been built and controlled (Fisher 2018, 421).

This homesteading impulse – 'the act of declaring that this plot of land is now my plot of land, regardless of whose land it might be currently' (Phillips 2015, 129) – persists in the tech industry's harnessing of the frontier myth, as well as the stories the founders tell to legitimate their wealth. Part of the reason why the American tech industry lacks regulation (with devastating consequences) is because of the persistent belief in the myth of the frontier spirit. This spirit, combined with the postracial and postfeminist framing of early gatekeepers of the internet – 'there are no bodies here,' legitimates the reluctance of celebrity founders to address the flouting of civil rights in terms of product design, workforces, and online interactions. This, therefore, facilitates forms of discrimination, inequality, and violence. Cyberspace is seen as a space where 'people' rather than governments will work out how it is to be governed; it is explicitly seen as a site free of juridical oversight. Howard Rheingold, for example, states: 'I believe that most citizens of democratic societies, given access to clearly presented information about the state of the Net, will make wise decisions about how the Net ought to be governed' (Rheingold, xxxii). Here we can see that an appeal to liberal humanism ('citizens of democratic societies') can be used in such a way as to obfuscate the structures of power at play. A regulatory perspective on the internet's history needs to take account of its changing context: it has moved from the secrecy of the military domain to the rational universalism of higher education, before being thrown open to commercial exploitation. In each of these phases, legal frameworks have been either hidden or rejected – initially for national security and later in favour of the 'free' exchange of knowledge. In all of these contexts, because juridical oversight is suspended or rendered opaque, other forms of power can freely operate. Cyberspace, as a frontier domain without clear laws, can be dominated and controlled by the most powerful. This is what we see happening in Amazon, Google, Facebook.

Like the fortune seekers of the mythic Wild West, the tech founders are keen to avoid the restraints of modern lawmakers. Here we draw on the work of legal scholars, such as Olivier Sylvain (2018), as well as the work of scholars researching content moderation, including Sarah R. Roberts (2016) and Kate Crawford (2018). As we have outlined, the subjects of our case studies are keen lobbyists, spending millions of dollars in an attempt to avoid regulation, including regulation that protects minorities and vulnerable groups (Zuboff 2019; Van Dijck et al. 2018; Sylvain 2018). Their platforms do not need to gain consent in the kinds of ways that are usually necessary for achieving hegemony. For Gramsci, hegemony is a kind of socio-political leadership where consent to govern is negotiated with different sections of society in a series of trade-offs and through cultural–ideological constructs which naturalise the rule of the dominant class and assign places in the social order to different subaltern groups. While the tech giants also engage in that sort of hegemonic struggle (for instance with their allies in the finance industry), for most people consent is given, instead, through the widespread use of their monopoly products and services: we accept their terms and conditions in order to access the service, though rarely reading them - the political struggle for hegemony is circumvented through an automatic process (Couldry and Mejias 2018; Carmi 2018).

Legal consent is thus secured for the invisible exercise of their power, allowing them to focus on the task of legitimating their wider social control, given that their authority is both extreme and unaccountable. As Safiya Umoja Noble has argued, it is no accident that it was after governmental policy changes addressing the demands of civil rights groups in the US that decision-making processes within the sector started to be made by the apparently neutral processing systems of computerised technology (2018).[3] This disavowal of inequality and the mechanisms that sustain it is discussed in Dorothy E. Roberts's compelling critique of racialised technologies. As she points out: 'at the very moment that science, government, and business are promoting race-based genomics, the idea that we are living in a "postracial" America is gaining traction' (Roberts 2011, 287). It is clear to us that the battle against regulation, though often couched in libertarian terms, is a way of consolidating the power of the network, and freeing the frontiersmen for their project of occupying new territory. To give a specific example here, Noble is one of a number of critics who has pointed to how the Google search engine reproduces the racism it claims to have no truck with. She examines how Google harnesses and deepens racist structures through its indexing of information and its algorithms, and she discusses the detrimental impacts on Black women and girls in the US that arise from assuming a 'colourblind' algorithm. Noble contextualises Google as a key participant in the American imperialist project that profits from the bodies of Black people across the world: from the mining of coltan in the Congo, to the dismantling of e-waste in Ghana, to its bypassing of labour unions in its manufacturing activities (Noble 2018, 164–165). Google's abandoning of their 'Don't' be evil' motto seems appropriate in this light.

Of course, this is also not the first 'Frontier Era' to have produced these tensions, contradictions, and oppressions. The Gilded Age – and its associations with the history of US monopolies, oligarchs and industrialists is one of the historical contexts through which we must understand these patriarchal networks. In our concordance, the 'Gilded Age' (a period of rapid growth and prosperity in the US in the latter part of the nineteenth century) is referenced 13 times, while the term 'Robber Barons' (the unscrupulous tycoons that were also a feature of the period) appears 27 times. Indeed, the parallels between the late nineteenth-century monopolists and our subjects seem obvious. In both cases, a small group of men have dominated emerging industries, while there has been little regulation or effective governmental intervention to stop them garnering almost unimaginable levels of individual (then family) wealth in the process. And, as with their nineteenth-century counterparts, opinions about the West Coast patriarchs are sharply divided: 'robber baron or philanthropist, greedy imperialist or benevolent humanitarian' we are invited to ask (Guthey et al. 2009, 8). Zuboff states:

> The Gilded Age millionaires, like today's surveillance capitalists, stood on the frontier of a vast discontinuity in the means of production with nothing but blank territory in which to invent a new industrial capitalism free from constraints on the use of labor, the nature of working conditions, the extent of environmental destruction, the sourcing of raw materials, or even the quality of their own products. And like their twenty-first-century counterparts, they did not hesitate to exploit the very law that they despised, flying the banner of 'private property' and 'freedom of contract,' much as surveillance capitalists march under the flag of freedom of speech as the justification for unobstructed technological 'progress.'
> *(Zuboff 2019, 106)*

Responses among the founders to these differing perceptions have also varied: through the mechanism of the 'Giving Pledge' set up by Bill and Melinda Gates, Warren Buffet, Zuckerberg, Musk, and Sandberg have each promised to give away most or all of their wealth, while Page, Brin, Bezos, and Thiel haven't. In an interesting twist on this theme (and in the spirit of the Zuboff quote above), Larry Page leaned into the collective celebrity of our network of entrepreneurs and half-joked that instead of giving to charity he would bequeath his wealth to Elon Musk, because Musk's businesses were themselves philanthropic. Like Google's parent company Alphabet, he was suggesting, Musk's companies exist for the benefit of humanity. Instead of accepting the premise that his rewards for corporate success could be considered excessive, he doubles down and insists we should be grateful for his benevolent brand of capitalism.

In another similarity to the Robber Barons of the Gilded Age, many of the tech founders own their monopolistic companies in an exotic fashion to maintain control of their companies even as they sell their stakes in them. The trusts of the nineteenth century have been replaced in the twenty-first century by corporations that issue class B (and class C) shares, with varying voting rights, thus enabling founders like Zuckerberg, Page, and Brin to ensure that the companies they have founded avoid share-holder accountability – a key measure of oversight under liberal capitalism.[4] Bezos has no reliance on such mechanisms, but his authority over Amazon is so unassailable that there is little need for them, while Musk's private ownership of SpaceX seems to function as a respite from his constant frustration at having to deal with Tesla shareholders and its stock performance.[5] If the companies started to fail there might be some challenge to the absolute dominance of their founders and CEOs (as we have seen recently with Uber under the toxic leadership of Travis Kalanick, and with Adam Neumann and WeWork, a company run in a manner almost parodic of the founder myth). But for our primary case studies there is little chance of any such usurpation.

Racial hierarchies: workforces

The frontier spirit was credited by its nineteenth-century advocates as playing an important role in the dismantling of slavery. The opportunity offered by the frontier was seen as levelling the difference between North and South, citizen and slave, in the aftermath of the civil war (Turner 1893, 5). Thus the postracial assertions of Barlow and his ilk have a long pedigree in American culture. But race clearly striates the work cultures of Silicon Valley as much as they did in the imaginaries of the old American West: Chinese railway workers blowing holes in the hillsides while Mexicans were an unruly enemy of America to be faced at the Alamo. Indeed, Richard White has notably stated that it is in fact these racialised histories that characterise the history of the West as different to the East: 'Without the special experiences of its minorities, the West might as well be New Jersey with mountains and deserts.' White's argument is that the American West is dependent on a '*wage* labor system… [that] depended on a *racial* stratification of labor' (White 1986, 397).

This history is clearly reflected in the West coast tech cultures to this day. A different way of formulating contemporary workforces can be seen through Richard Barbrook's and Andy Cameron's argument from the early 1990s. They suggest that the 'Californian Ideology' they identify maintained older racial hierarchies: that is the general exclusion of Black and Latinx people from the tech sector. Seeing a form of rationalist coffee house style belief in liberal democracy as at the core of the emergent values of Silicon Valley, Barbrook and Cameron (like Perry cited above), also understood it as reproducing the hierarchies of those eighteenth-century liberals rather than being specific to the Western frontier. Focusing on the particular influence of the slave-owning president Thomas Jefferson, they frame the problem of the Californian Ideology through 'Jeffersonian democracy [becoming] a hi-tech version of the plantation economy of the Old South' (Barbrook and Cameron 1995). As such, while conflicts around race are shifting and open to interpretation as to their historical source, the strict hierarchies within the tech industry are, and have been, relatively stable over the last 20 years.

Considering this, it is also important to note that Silicon Valley is a profoundly diverse place. English is spoken as a first language in less than half the homes in the region (Massaro 2020, 10). The workforce exists in a cultural landscape that reflects 'this high-tech international interdependence as well as the impact of previous generations of immigrants'; while '[t]he importation of people is a constant feature of regional culture' (English-Lueck 2017, 115). This mix is not reflected evenly in the corporate workforces of the businesses we look at in this book, although East and South Asian people are well represented in the industry. Sundar Pichai, CEO of Google and Alphabet, as well as Satya Nadella, CEO of Microsoft, are two examples of Asian men in very senior leadership positions (albeit Nadella is based in Seattle rather than Northern California). Strikingly, women in high-status technology jobs tend to have not been born in the USA. It is hard to draw concrete conclusions without doing ethnographic work but in terms of demography: 'Three-quarters of Silicon Valley's female tech workers ages 25 to 44 are foreign born. These women are disproportionately married with children, and primarily come from Asian countries' (Massaro 2020, 17). This is not to say that Asian or Asian-American women do not face particular forms of discrimination as we can see in Ellen Pau's critique of Silicon Valley in her memoir *Reset: My Fight for Inclusion and Lasting Change* (2017). Migration status and national citizenship are also precarious, vulnerable, and highly contested in Trump's America.

In *Digitizing Race*, Lisa Nakamura discusses the front cover of a 2004 *Wired* Magazine depicting a veiled South Asian woman. The cover story is titled 'The New Face of the Silicon Age: Tech Jobs Are Fleeing to India Faster than Ever.' In tiny letters next to the dateline, it states 'help wanted.' The woman is exoticised by the veil, her made-up eyes, and the way that her hand hides her mouth. She has *mendhi* on her hands, which spell out code. Nakamura states that 'The *Wired* cover images Asians as technological, which is inscribed by strings of code and the language of machines.' She goes on to argue that Asians are often represented as 'products rather than users, creators of value rather than consumers' and this 'valences the ongoing formation of Asians in America' (Nakamura 2008, 199). In Jessie Daniels' discussion of the internet and racism, she notes how around 2014, Zuckerberg and 'a cadre of White male technology elites' positioned themselves as proponents of immigration reform. Daniels states that:

> What such a platform allows the technology elites to do is to advocate for a kind of reform that would benefit their industry and an elite group of highly educated, middle-class immigrants, consistent with the mythology of the United States as a land of opportunity and thus eschewing charges of bias in hiring and promotion.
>
> *(Daniels 2015, 2380)*

In her discussion of the history of immigration to America and Asian Americans, Lisa Lowe notes that US policies 'have placed Asians' within the nation-state, including its workplaces and markets, but that they remain 'racially marked' as outside the national polity (Lowe 1996, 8). What we are seeing here are hierarchies based on the intersections of race, class, and immigration status.

Set against this, Black and Latinx workers are largely excluded from high-status positions, though they make up a large proportion of the service staff – catering, maintenance, and so on. (Benjamin 2019, 58). These roles are often outsourced, and recruitment policies have produced a racialised subclass who lack access to the high salaries, stock options, and the considerable benefits of those directly employed by technology firms. As English-Lueck puts it tactfully about one of her case studies, a Mexican immigrant engineer who struggles with prejudice against Latinx people: 'the hierarchy of technical diversity does not assume that Hispanics are top performers' (2017, 121). Moreover, 'the number of black students who have computer science degrees is not reflected in the numbers hired by the Silicon Valley companies' (Wong 2017). These hierarchies pit minorities against each other:

> Different minorities have different functions in the cultural landscape of digital technologies. They are good for different kinds of ideological work … seeing Asians as the solution and blacks as the problem [i.e. cybertyping] is and always has been a drastic and damaging formulation.
> (Nakamura 2013, 22–23)

There is, to those who benefit from the racialised hierarchies of the industry, a very real cosmopolitanism to tech culture. But it is not open to everyone, old oppressions based on race persist.

It is notable that while white, many of the founders are also Jewish, an ethnicity that remains vulnerable to white supremacist attack in America, especially in the Trump and post-Trump eras due to the widespread circulation of anti-semitic conspiracy such as QAnon, but it is also the case that the Jewish founders' whiteness and maleness operate as forms of privilege within American society. But we must understand that this access to whiteness for Jewish men has come at a cost for Jewish women on whom the burden of cultural difference falls. As Karen Brodkin argues, it is the stereotypes of the Jewish American Princess, spoiled and demanding, and the Jewish mother, interfering and food obsessed, who translate racial difference into acceptable misogyny (1999). As Brodkin puts it, the racialised experiences of Jewish Americans reveal whiteness as 'patriarchal and heterosexual' (Brodkin, 184). Thus, we similarly understand that South and East Asian men and some Asian women have been incorporated into the racialised structures of the industry while leaving its basic configurations and hierarchies intact. Access to racial privilege is circumscribed by gender, migration, perceived adjacency to whiteness, and citizenship in intersectional ways.

Dataism

Bringing together the racial hierarchies of West Coast Tech, along with the history of the internet and the animation of the frontier spirit including the structuring role of the household, brings us to consider the ideology of dataism which inform the corporations we are looking at. Here we follow José van Dijck's definition of dataism as the 'widespread belief in the objective quantification and potential tracking of all kinds of human behavior and sociality through online media technologies' (van Dijck 2014). Much as the frontier myth's rhetoric of freedom, progress, and opportunity obfuscates its racialised and gendered hierarchies, so too does the ideology of dataism serve to present as valid only that which is already preselected as significant and important. And like the frontier values, this is 'baked' into the products of the sector reproducing dominant forms of oppression and discrimination. We have focused on the frontier to this point but would argue that dataism is a 'new' ideological component that buttresses and supports the frontier spirit in the formation of tech culture hegemony.

Indeed, most scholars agree that the concepts of data and algorithms are at the heart of current social transformations (van Dijck et al. 2018; Cheney-Lippold 2017; Beer 2018; Zuboff 2019; Couldry and Mejias 2019). It is not surprising then, that, at 645/mw, 'data' is one of the most frequently used words in our concordance (according to NVivo it occurs 8,796 times and accounts for 0.14% of all words – excluding prepositions and other words with a primarily grammatical function). That's close to half as often as the word 'Google' 1,390/mw (at 17,493 or 0.29%) and just behind 'Facebook' at 701/mw (8,784 words). It is one of a few lexically specialist words (with 4 letters or greater) in the top 20 by frequency across the whole concordance; other specialist words include 'company,' 'business,' 'computer.'[6] 'Data' occurs in every single book in our concordance bar two (*Girl Boss* and *Hatching Twitter*); in the celebratory book *Dataism* it appears 1,068 times in 246 scanned pages, whereas in *We Were Yahoo* it appears only once. On average it appears 95 times per book, with books we coded as ideological/futurological having the most occurrences, with an average of 131 times, and books we coded as corporate/industry-how-to having the least, at 55 average.

There are significant findings when comparing this specialist corpus against baselines generated from the internet. Through these, we can see a rapid increase in the use of the word 'data' since 2013. In the 2008 EngTenTen, it appears 336/mw; in 2012, it is 298/mw; and in 2013 285/mw; but the 2015 version on Sketch Engine shows 545/mw. This is likely indicative of the widespread expansion of dataism as a popular ideology. As tech companies like Google have assumed positions of leadership in the economy following the financial crash, so too have their driving concepts become increasingly absorbed within our language. In the academic literature we have engaged with as part of our wider research (i.e. those not in the database, but that we position this book in discussion with), data as a concept is subject to wide critique, and is seen as the mechanism – material and ideological – through which a new era of capitalist exploitation has been launched. All these elements are mutually reinforcing in coming to understand the significance of this belief system.

Data in these monopoly companies are prediction-driven – albeit usually in terms of predicting what you are likely to want to buy. Datafication locks us into identities – we can't really escape how it captures past experience and activity – and then reproduces us to ourselves. Data – and the calcification of digital identity through data (to an algorithm we are the aggregate of our records of past online behaviour) – is thus a key way that gendered and sexed logics are re-entrenched (the Lockean sorting and categorising we referred to earlier). The uncritical acceptance of dominant definitions by platform designers, and their subsequent reproduction within the system's algorithms, means that dataism has the effect of entrenching oppressions of the social field, especially along the lines of gender, race, and class (Eubanks 2017). In theory we could be 'more than human' online, but, as Cathy O'Neil argues, data is about the past, not the future – or it's about predicting the future using data from the past (O'Neil 2016, Zuboff 2019). Although this book is not about design or algorithms, we draw on the arguments of these scholars' work because they reveal how intersecting oppressions can be deepened by the logic of dataism. We argue that dataism is one of the ways that patriarchy is re-entrenched – by presenting as neutral, universal, and horizontal that which is specific, contingent, and hierarchical.

And data-oriented approaches are often partial: 'big data relies on what is available and obscures that which is not' (Bolsover and Howard 2017, 275). Dataism is also often mobilised in service of the idea that 'subjective opinion' can somehow be eliminated (Bolsover and Howard 2017, 151). Implicit within it is the belief that, with enough information, context can be flattened out and all information can become comparable and all decisions made objectively. But data is not neutral – it is always an applied form of knowledge that has been gathered (i.e. removed from context) and organised in specific ways. So data is radically decontextualised knowledge; and it is also constantly being recontextualised in the service of finding solutions to problems. As a universalised imaginary, dataism helps bind together dominant and subaltern groups within the hegemonic bloc forming around Silicon Valley: it shapes the actions of the founders, engineers, investors, and users of tech products. And dataism works in specific ways as it is processed by the monopolies that we are looking at.

Problems are identified by the visionary, genius founders – a specific group of acquisitive entrepreneurs with an engineering mindset – and products are then designed to solve that problem using data. The success of a given product is determined by the willingness of the founder-CEO to greenlight it, or the venture-capitalist funders to invest in it. Thus, founders and venture capitalists represent the two dominant class fractions of this bloc, while the subaltern class of jobbing engineers aspires to have the right idea to become the former; or to join the right start-up, along with stock options, to become the latter. The rest of us consume their products and ideas. As we have discussed, this is a business culture that is endemically raced, classed, and gendered. Indeed, its 'technochauvinism' (Broussard 2019) or 'technological solutionism' has undergone sustained critique by Eugene Morozov (2013), as well as Adele Hasinoff and Marina Levina (2017). As many critics have pointed out, the formation of the problem, as well as the kinds of solutions that are designed, are themselves subjective (Hasinoff 2017). Thus dataism is both a set of concepts and values to which people subscribe, and a social, cultural, and economic practice. And this is where we can see the links to the historic paradigms of the frontier and the household. In both the frontier and dataist ideological and technical formations there is a mobilisation of different kinds of nostalgia: an extrapolation from a partial view of the past (that is romanticised and overinvested in) is used to present a natural idea of progress into the future. The two are, neatly, mutually reinforcing.

Further thoughts on colonialism

We are indebted to the work of Zuboff as well as Nick Couldry and Ulises Mejias. In this final section, we note where and how we depart. Specifically our intervention into the discussions on digital culture and power is how US West Coast Tech — and the data relations they forge — are patriarchal and specifically colonialist by harnessing the frontier spirit. We make these claims using the concordance and our analyses of the founders' celebrity assemblages.

Couldry and Mejias argue that 'data relations' reconstitute a generalised form of coloniality that has its roots in European colonial capitalism. They argue that this form of data colonialism, which they call 'cloud empire,' is not, however, unique to the global North: the processes of data-led economic expropriation and exploitation can be seen in China, India, and Russia as much as they can be found in American-owned companies (Couldry and Mejias 2019, 53–57). There is some truth in this at the general level of political economy, but at the ideological, legal, and cultural levels the differences are stark. The intensification of data relations in China and the powerful role exerted by the government draws on a millennia-long history of bureaucratic culture and population control. While the technologies may be similar the cultural orientation is quite different. The Chinese internet is characterised by its great Firewall and state surveillance, the closing of space for controlled dissent and an intensity of social connection (Howard 2015). The American internet companies may be doing almost exactly the same thing technologically, and – especially in the light of the Edward Snowden revelations – have a similar relation with state security apparatuses, but the culture surrounding the use of this technology is quite different. Its legitimating structure at the level of the 'spirit' is instead about freedom, individualism, and open space: the frontier.

The idea of the frontier is so deeply embedded in American culture that even the critics of data colonialism are sometimes entangled within it. The subtitle of Shoshana Zuboff's book is 'The Fight for a Human Future at the New *Frontier* of Power' (our emphasis); and the tension between the frontier and the home is a central rhetorical motif in her book. These frontiers are still American ones: in essayist style, she presents herself as the honest pioneer and homesteader, with introductory statements such as: 'This book is intended as an initial mapping of a terra incognita, a first foray that will pave the way for other explorers' (Zuboff 2019, 17). She also uses her home as a key metaphor, a sovereign space to be defended against the incursions of the tech companies – after her old house burned down, her family 'foraged for durable natural materials: old stone and scarred wooden beams that had weathered the storms of time'(2019, 477). Thus her critique of the tech founders is couched in the same rhetorical frameworks that many of them rely on themselves. In her work, they are the frontier bandits stealing cattle and she is the honest deputy protecting us from their predations of our data herds. This trope of the good settler is something we will look at in the chapter that focuses on Jeff Bezos, in relation to his deployment of the *Star Trek* captain as part of his frontier-based celebrification. It is important to recognise here that even Zuboff's potent critiques of digital capitalism normalise and naturalise this very American conception of morality that binds the home and the colonial adventure in tight unity.

On the other hand, Zuboff also uses the language and metaphors of colonialism in instructive ways that are genuinely helpful for understanding how capitalism is changing. But they tend to be examples drawn from Spanish colonial history in the Americas. This is significant, as White et al. argue: 'The notion that the West was something we settled, rather than conquered, pervades American storytelling and iconography; the contrast with the Spanish conquistadores has never been subtle either in popular culture or in elementary and secondary education texts' (White et al. 1994, 13). This distinction allows Zuboff to frame her struggle over the frontier as the battle to restore American values. As she puts it: 'If there is a fight, let it be a fight over capitalism' (Zuboff 2019, 194). And in her discussion likening the contemporary moment to that of the nineteenth-century Robber Barons – as discussed earlier, she again returns to the imaginary of the Western Frontier – the empty space free for the taking that pushes the limits of capitalism. In the conclusion to Zuboff's book, she sees the struggle to free ourselves from the yoke of big tech companies as equivalent to the revolutionary impulse in the eighteenth century to free the colonial settlers from their dependence on 'Baubles of Britain,' citing Samuel Adams (Breen 2005, 20 cited in Zuboff 2019, 503). Without doubt, her critique of the tech companies is the most comprehensive on offer from a socio-technical perspective, but it continues to rest ideologically, in part at least, on her idea that their practices are inimical to American values of freedom and self-reliance, to the sanctity of the homestead, and to the self-reliant individualism of the frontier.

This valorisation of the frontier spirit, even from critics of the technology companies, reinforces, obscures, and naturalises a huge ideological edifice on which tech culture depends. For example, by presenting earlier European forms of colonialism – the explorers, trading companies, and imperial territorial claims – as the real problem, the American frontier variant can be seen as not only morally superior, but also desirable. This ideology, then, can act to reinforce the racial hierarchies that pervade West Coast tech culture. Shifting the blame to the European settlers that predate the foundation of the US offers no challenge to the traditions of the precursors of the technologists – the cyberneticists and communards of the Back to the Land movement – who, when they bought up estates in Texas and New Mexico for their communes in the 1960s and 1970s, displaced the Hispanic communities that had been there for generations (Turner 2008). These twentieth-century settlers reified and fetishized Native Americans, in a form of colonial celebration, but at the same time fed the myth of a 'blank territory' (terra incognita) that Zuboff references. While Zuboff uses these metaphors differently, and with a different target for critique, we can see the same tropes of American revolutionary and frontier sentiment deployed that Barlow did in his manifesto.

And how does all this play out in the real world? Native Americans, Mexicans, Latinx and Hispanic communities remain hugely underrepresented in technology firms. Their symbolic erasure was highlighted in outrage online when millions of VC dollars were invested in a vending machine company called Bodega, started by two Google employees. This company claimed it could use data analytics and customer tracking to ensure that vending machines stocked the most useful products for any given location. The idea of the company is to put its namesake – the small convenience stores called bodegas – out of business: that is, to replace human judgement (and human operators) with a data-driven process (Aran 2017, Lazzarro 2017). Because the human relationship between the bodega owner and their regular customers cannot be reliably quantified, it is discounted. Because the cost of (often Spanish-speaking and/or migrant) employment can be reduced and displaced by computational processes to deliver greater profits, this is framed as efficiency, not redundancy. The problem the Bodega company seeks to solve is the inconvenience and inefficiency of human contact, and it does that through the processes of datafication that Zuboff analyses. Yet by presenting her critique of dataism within the traditions of American frontier colonialism, her perspective could only ever tell half the story here. But if we understand Bodega as a dataist enterprise through a critique of the frontier imaginary, and its raced and gendered hierarchies, then it appears entirely congruent with the continuing history of the American West.

Notes

1 Facebook can also offer a contemporary example of the ways these gendered binaries are reproduced despite marketing themselves as progressive. As the work of Rena Bivens reveals: since 2014 Facebook has offered users a 'custom' option in addition to 'male' and 'female' (previous to this these were the only options available). But these non-binary possibilities of identification only exist at the front-end (i.e. user interface) level of the software. Deeper into the database, non-binary users are re-classified in order to meet the needs of advertisers and marketers to match users to gendered products (Bivens 2017). In this book we look at the multiple ways that gender and patriarchy are co-constitutive thus reproducing and reinforcing binary and hierarchical gender and sex categories.
2 In Rheingold's words, this 'old infantryman' 'rides into town' where he 'meets the locals, who are frustrated by the old ways of doing things.' The story continues as our hero:

> takes out his laptop, plugs it into the nearest telephone, reveals the scope and power of the Net, and enlightens the crowd. He tempts them in outputting their

hands on the keyboard, and they're hooked. When Hughes rides out of town, the town is on the net.

(Rheingold 2000 [1993], 255)

3 Noble describes this shift as 'a coordinated effort to delegitimise decisions made in policy': https://youtu.be/Q7yFysTBpAo Digital Diaspora; see also Simone Browne (2015).
4 Presumably, although they have recently stepped down from day-to-day involvement in Alphabet-Google, this also means that Page and Brin could step back in to take over at any time.
5 In early 2021 we note that Bezos has changed role at Amazon from CEO to Executive Chairman. While he may no longer manage the day-to-day running of the company, we see no need to modify the argument here as a result. Amazon will remain a company that he is forever associated with and over which he will continue to dominate at the level of strategic decision making whether formally as Chairman or informally as founder and largest shareholder.
6 The remainder of the most frequently occurring words are common words, such as 'even,' 'time,' 'work,' and 'just' (they might be very particular ones, but they are not lexically specialist to our topic).

References

Acker, Joan (1989) 'The Problem with Patriarchy' *Sociology*, 23:2, 235–240.
Agamben, Giorgio (2009) *What Is an Apparatus?* trans. Davis Kishik and Stefan Pedatella. Stanford: Stanford University Press.
Ahmed, Sara (2017) *Living a Feminist Life*. Durham: Duke University Press.
Alderson, David (2016) *Sex, Needs, and Queer Culture*. Chicago: University of Chicago Press.
Anderson, Aran Isha (2017) 'Call the Silicon Valley 'Bodega' Plan What It Is: Racist and Gross' *Splinternews.com*, 13 September. https://splinternews.com/call-the-silicon-val ley-bodega-plan-what-it-is-racist-1806012781 Last accessed 28/04/2020.
Aschoff, Nicole (2015) *The New Prophets of Capital*. London: Verso.
Banet-Weiser, Sarah (2018) *Empowered: Popular Feminism and Popular Misogyny*. Durham: Duke University Press.
Banet-Weiser, Sarah and Kate M. Miltner (2016) '#MasculinitySoFragile: Culture, Structure, and Networked Misogyny' *Feminist Media Studies*, 16:1, 171–174.
Barbrook, Richard and Andrew Cameron (1995) 'The Californian Ideology' *Mute*, 1:3. www.metamute.org/editorial/articles/californian-ideology Last accessed 03/05/2020.
Barlow, John Perry (1996) *A Declaration of the Independence of Cyberspace*. www.eff.org/cyberspace-independence Last accessed 29/04/2020.
Beer, David (2018) *The Data Gaze: Capitalism, Power and Perception*. Basingstoke: Palgrave.
Benjamin, Ruha (2019) *Race After Technology: Abolitionist Tools for the New Jim Code*. Cambridge: Polity.
Bhattacharyya, Gargi (2018) *Rethinking Racial Capitalism: Questions of Reproduction and Survival*. New York: Rowman and Littlefield.
Bivens, Rena (2017) 'The Gender Binary Will Not Be Deprogrammed: Ten Years of Coding Gender on Facebook' *New Media and Society*, 19:6, 880–898.
Bolsover, Gillian and Philip Howard (2017) 'Computational Propaganda and Political Big Data: Moving Toward a More Critical Research Agenda' *Big Data*, 5:4, 274–276.
Boltanski, Luc and Eve Chiapello (2007) *The New Spirit of Capitalism*. London: Verso.

Brah, Avtar and Ann Pheonix (2004) 'Ain't I A Woman? Revisiting Intersectionality' *Journal of International Women's Studies*, 5:3, 75–86.

Breen, T. H. (2005) *The Marketplace of Revolution: How Consumer Politics Shaped American Independence*. Oxford: Oxford University Press.

Brodkin, Karen (1999) *How Jews Became White Folks and What That Says about Race in America*. New Jersey: Rutgers University Press.

Broockman, David E., Gregory Ferenstein, and Neil Malhotra (2019) 'Predispositions and the Political Behavior of American Economic Elites: Evidence from Technology Entrepreneurs' *American Journal of Political Science*, 63:1, 212–213.

Broussard, Meredith (2019) *Artificial Unintelligence: How Computers Misunderstand the World*. Cambridge, MA: MIT Press.

Browne, Simone (2015) *Dark Matters: On the Surveillance of Blackness*. Durham: Duke University Press.

Butler, Judith (1991) *Gender Trouble*. New York: Routledge.

Carby, Hazel (1988) *Reconstructing Womanhood: The Emergence of the Afro-American Woman Novelist*. Oxford: Oxford University Press.

Carmi, Eleanor (2018) 'Do You Agree?: What #MeToo Can Teach us about Digital Consent' *Open Democracy*. www.opendemocracy.net/en/digitalliberties/what-metoo-can-teach-us-about-digital-consent/ Last accessed 29/04/2020.

Carreyou, John (2018) *Bad Blood: Secrets and Lies in a Silicon Valley Startup*. London: Penguin Random House.

Carroll, Hamilton (2011) *Affirmative Reaction: New Formations of White Masculinity*. Durham: Duke University Press.

Chang, Emily (2018) *Brotopia: Breaking up the Boys' Club of Silicon Valley*. New York: Penguin Random House.

Cheney-Lippold, John (2017) *We Are Data: Algorithms and the Making of Our Digital Slaves*. New York: New York University Press.

Cohen, Noam (2019) *The Know It Alls: The Rise of Silicon Valley as a Political Powerhouse and Social Wrecking Ball*. London: Oneworld.

Collins, Patricia Hill (1989) 'The Social Construction of Black Feminist Thought' *Signs*, 14:4, 745–773.

Collins, Patricia Hill (2000) *Black Feminist Thought*. London: Routledge.

Collins, Patricia Hill and Sirma Bilge (2016) *Intersectionality* Cambridge: Polity.

Connell, Raewyn W. and J. Messerschmidt (2005) 'Hegemonic Masculinity: Rethinking the Concept' *Gender and Society*, 19:6, 829–859.

Cooper, Brittney (2018) *Eloquent Rage: A Black Feminist Discovers Her Superpower*. New York: St Martins Press.

Couldry, Nick and Ulises Mejias (2018) 'Data Colonialism: Rethinking Big Data's Relation to the Contemporary Subject' *Television and New Media*, 20:4, 336–349. ISSN 1527-4764. Article first published online: September 2, 2018; Issue published: May 1, 2019.

Couldry, Nick and Ulises A. Mejias (2019) *The Costs of Connection: How Data is Colonizing Human Life and Appropriating it for Capitalism*. Stanford: Stanford University Press.

Crawford, Kate (2018) 'You and AI – Machine Learning, Bias and Implications for Inequality' https://royalsociety.org/science-events-and-lectures/2018/07/you-and-ai-equality/

Crawford, Kate and Tarleton Gillespie (2016) 'What is a Flag for? Social Media Reporting Tools and the Vocabulary of Complaint' *New Media & Society*, 18:3, 410–428.

Crenshaw, Kimberle (1989) 'Demarginalizing the Intersection of Race and Sex: A Black Feminist Critique of Antidiscrimination Doctrine, Feminist Theory and Antiracist

Politics' *University of Chicago Legal Forum*, 1989, Article 8. https://chicagounbound.uchicago.edu/uclf/vol1989/iss1/8

Criado Perez, Caroline (2019) *Invisible Women: Exposing Bias in a World Designed for Men*. London: Chatto and Windus.

Daniels, Jessie (2015) '"My Brain Database Doesn't See Skin Color": Color-Blind Racism in the Technology Industry and in Theorizing the Web' *American Behavioral Scientist*, 59:1, 1377–1393.

Davis, Aeron (2019) 'Top CEOs, Financialization and the Creation of the Super-Rich Economy' *Cultural Politics*, 15:1, 88–104.

Delanda, Manuel (2006) *A New Philosophy of Society: Assemblage Theory and Social Complexity*. London: Continuum.

Deleuze, G. and F. Guattari (1988) *A Thousand Plateaus: Capitalism and Schizophrenia*. London: Athlone Press

Driessens, O. (2013) 'The Celebritization of Society and Culture: Understanding the Structural Dynamics of Celebrity Culture' *International Journal of Cultural Studies*, 16:6, 641–657. doi:10.1177/1367877912459140

Duggan, Lisa (2003) *The Twilight of Equality: Neoliberalism, Cultural Politics, and the Attack on Democracy*. Boston, MA: Beacon Press.

English-Lueck, J. A. (2017) *Cultures@SiliconValley*. Second Edition: Vol. Second edition. Stanford: Stanford University Press.

Enloe, Cynthia (2017) *The Big Push: Exposing and Challenging the Persistence of Patriarchy*. Oxford: Myriad Editions.

Eubanks, Virginia (2017) *Automating Inequality: How High-Tech Tools Profile, Police, and Punish the Poor*. New York: St Martins Press.

Federici, Silvia (2017) *Caliban And The Witch: Women, the Body and Primitive Accumulation*. Brooklyn, NY: Autonomedia.

Fenton, Natalie (2016) *Digital, Political, Radical*. Cambridge: Polity.

Fisher, Adam (2018) *Valley of Genius: The Uncensored History of Silicon Valley, as Told by the Hackers, Founders, and Freaks Who Made It Boom*. New York: Twelve.

Forbes. www.forbes.com/billionaires/ Last accessed March 2020.

Gilbert, Jeremy and Alex Williams (2019) *Twenty-First Century Socialism*. Cambridge: Polity.

Gilens, Martin and Benjamin Page (2014) 'Testing Theories of American Politics: Elites, Interest Groups, and Average Citizens' *Perspectives on Politics*, 12:3, 564–581.

Gill, Rosalind. (2007) 'Postfeminist Media Culture: Elements of a Sensibility' *European Journal of Cultural Studies*, 10:2, 147–166.

Ging, Debbie (2017) 'Alphas, Betas, and Incels' *Men and Masculinities*. doi:10.1177/1097184X17706401.

Ging, Debbie (2019) 'Bros v. Hos: Postfeminism, Anti-feminism and the Toxic Turn in Digital Gender Politics' in Debbie Ging and Eugenia Siapera (eds.) *Gender Hate Online: Understanding the New Anti-Feminism*. Basingstoke: Palgrave Macmillan, pp. 45–68.

Google (2009) 'Larry Page's University of Michigan Commencement Address' *YouTube.com*. www.youtube.com/watch?v=qFb2rvmrahc Last accessed 02/05/2020.

Goulden, Murray (2019) 'Delete the Family': Platform Families and the Colonisation of the Smart Home' *Information, Communication & Society*, doi:10.1080/1369118X.2019.1668454

Gramsci, Antonio (2005) *Selections from the Prison Notebooks of Antonio Gramsci*, eds. Quintin Hoare and Geoffrey Nowell-Smith. London: Lawrence and Wishart

Gregg, Melissa (2011) *Work's Intimacy*. Cambridge: Polity.
Guthey, Eric, Timothy Clark, and Brad Jackson (2009) *Demystifying Business Celebrity*. London: Routledge.
Haggerty, K. D. and R. V. Ericson (2000) 'The Surveillant Assemblage' *British Journal of Sociology*, 51, 605–622. doi:10.1080/00071310020015280
Hakim, Jamie. (2016) '"The Spornosexual": The Affective Contradictions of Male Body-Work in Neoliberal Digital Culture' *Journal of Gender Studies*. doi:10.1080/09589236.2016.1217771.
Hakim, Jamie (2019) *Work That Body: Male Bodies in Digital Culture*. London: Rowman & Littlefield International.
Hamad, Hannah (2014) *Postfeminism and Paternity in Contemporary U.S. Film: Framing Fatherhood*. London: Routledge.
Hartmann, Heidi I. (1981) 'The Family as the Locus of Gender, Class, and Political Struggle: The Example of Housework' *Signs*, 6:3, 366–394. www.jstor.org/stable/3173752 Last accessed 12/4/2020.
Hasinoff, Adele Amy and Marina Levina (2017) 'The Silicon Valley Ethos: Tech Industry Products, Discourses, and Practices' *TV and New Media*, 18(6). doi: 10.1177/1527476416680454
Hasinoff, Adele Amy (2017) 'Where are you?: Location Tracking and the Promise of Childhood Safety' *TV and New Media*, 18:6, 1–17.
Hester, Helen (2016) https://salvage.zone/in-print/technically-female-women-machines-and-hyperemployment/
Hicks, Marie (2017) *Programmed Inequality: How Britain Discarded Women Technologists and Lost Its Edge in Computing*. Cambridge, MA: MIT Press.
Hoffman, Reid and Chris Yeh (2018) *Blitzscaling: The Lightning-Fast Path To Building Massively Valuable Companies*. London: Penguin, Random House.
hooks, bell (2010) 'Understanding Patriarchy' *No Borders: Louisville's Radical Lending Library*. http://imaginenoborders.org/pdf/zines/UnderstandingPatriarchy.pdf
hooks, bell (2016) www.bellhooksinstitute.com/blog/2016/5/9/moving-beyond-pain
Howard, Philip (2015) *Pax Technica: How the Internet of Things May Set Us Free or Lock Us Up*. New Haven, CT: Yale University Press.
James, Toby (2018) 'Political Leadership as Statecraft? Aligning Theory with Praxis in Conversation with British Party Leaders' *British Journal of Politics & International Relations*, 20:3, 555–572.
Jarrett, Kylie (2016) *Feminism, Labour and Digital Media: The Digital Housewife*. London: Routledge.
Josephs, Gloria (1981) 'The Incompatible Menage à Trois: Marxism, Feminism and Racism' in L. Sargent (ed.) *Women and Revolution: The Unhappy Marriage of Marxism and Feminism*. London: Pluto Press, pp. 91–107.
Kirkpatrick, David (2011) *The Facebook Effect: The Real Inside Story of Mark Zuckerberg and the World's Fastest Growing Company*. New York: Virgin Books.
Kreiss, Daniel and Shannon C. Mcgregor (2018) 'Technology Firms Shape Political Communication: The Work of Microsoft, Facebook, Twitter, and Google With Campaigns During the 2016 U.S. Presidential Cycle' *Political Communication*, 35:2, 155–177, doi:10.1080/10584609.2017.1364814
Lazzaro, Sage (2017) 'Start-up Company Called Bodega Is Slammed for 'Cultural Appropriation' and 'Racism' after it Reveals Plan for Vending Machines That Could Replace Corner Stores' *dailymail.com*, 14 September. www.dailymail.co.uk/sciencetech/article-4881578/Bodega-startup-cat-logo-infuriates-internet.html

Littler, Jo (2018) *Against Meritocracy: Culture, Power and the Myths of Mobility*. London: Routledge.
Locke, John (1689/2017) *Two Treatises of Government*, ed. Jonathan Bennett. www.earlymoderntexts.com/assets/pdfs/locke1689a_2.pdf
Lowe, Lisa (1996) *Immigrant Acts: On Asian American Cultural Politics Duke*. Durham, NC: University Press.
Manne, Kate (2018) *Down Girl: The Logic of Misogyny*. Oxford: Oxford University Press.
Martinez, Antonio Garcia (2016) *Chaos Monkeys: Obscene Fortune and Random Failure in Silicon Valley*. New York: Harper Collins.
Massaro, Rachel (2020) *Silicon Valley Index 2020*. San Jose: Joint Venture Silicon Valley. https://jointventure.org/images/stories/pdf/index2020.pdf Last accessed 02/05/2020.
McRobbie, Angela (2009) *The Aftermath of Feminism: Gender, Culture and Social Change*. London: SAGE.
McRobbie, Angela (2015) 'Notes on the Perfect: Competitive Femininity in Neoliberal Times' *Australian Feminist Studies*. doi:10.1080/08164649.2015.1011485.
Mies, Maria. (1986/1998) *Patriarchy and Accumulation on a World Scale: Women in the International Division of Labour*. London: Zed Books Ltd.
Miller, Pavla (2017) *Patriarchy*. London: Routledge.
Mills, Charles (1997) *The Racial Contract*. New York: Cornell University Press.
Moore, Martin and Damian Tambini (eds) (2018) *Digital Dominance The Power of Google, Amazon, Facebook, and Apple*. Oxford: Oxford University Press.
Morozov, Evgeny (2013) *To Save Everything, Click Here: Technology, Solutionism, and the Urge to Fix Problems That Don't Exist*. London: Allen Lane.
Mukherjee, Roopali (2011) 'Bling Fling: Commodity Consumption and the Politics of the "Post-Racial"' in Michael G. Lacy and Kent A. Ono (eds.) *Critical Rhetorics of Race*. New York: New York University Press, pp. 178–193.
Nakamura, Lisa (2008) *Digitizing Race: Visual Cultures of the Internet*. Minneapolis: University of Minnesota Press.
Nakamura, Lisa (2013) *Cybertypes: Race, Ethnicity, and Identity on the Internet*. New York and London: Routledge.
National Parks Service (2019) 'Homesteading by the Numbers' www.nps.gov/home/learn/historyculture/bynumbers.htm Last accessed 29/04/2020.
Netflix (2020) 'Culture' *Netflix: Jobs*. https://jobs.netflix.com/culture Last accessed 02/05/2020.
Noble, Safiya Umoja (2018) *Algorithms of Oppression: How Search Engines Reinforce Racism*. New York: New York University Press.
O'Neil, Cathy (2016) *Weapons of Math Destruction: How Big Data Increases Inequality and Threatens Democracy*. London: Penguin Random House.
O'Neill, Rachel (2018) *Seduction: Men, Masculinity and Mediated Intimacy*. Cambridge: Polity.
Ortner, B. Sherry (2014) 'Too Soon for Post-Feminism: The Ongoing Life of Patriarchy in Neoliberal America' *History and Anthropology*, 25:4, 530–549.
Osirim, Mary Johnson. (2003) 'Carrying the Burdens of Adjustment and Globalization: Women and Microenterprise Development in Urban Zimbabwe' *International Sociology*, 18:3, 535–558. doi:10.1177/02685809030183005.
Oyewumi, Oyeronke (1997) *The Invention of Women Making an African Sense of Western Gender Discourses*. Minneapolis: University of Minnesota Press.

Page, Benjamin I. and Martin Gilens (2018) *Democracy in America? What Has Gone Wrong and What We Can Do About It*. Chicago: University of Chicago Press.

Page, Benjamin, Jason Seawright, and Matthew Lacombe (2019) *Billionaires and Stealth Politics*. Chicago: University of Chicago Press.

Pao, Ellen (2017) *Reset: My Fight for Inclusion and Lasting Change*. New York: Random House.

Papacharissi, Zizi (2011) 'Conclusion: A Networked Self' in Zizi Papacharassi (ed.) *A Networked Self Identity, Community, and Culture on Social Network Sites* New York: Routledge, pp. 304–318.

Pateman, Carol (1988) *The Sexual Contract*. Stanford: Stanford University Press.

Patil, Vrushali (2013) 'From Patriarchy to Intersectionality: A Transnational Feminist Assessment of How Far We've Really Come' *Signs*, 38:4, 847–867.

Perry, Imani (2018) *Vexy Thing: On Gender and Liberation*. Durham: Duke University Press.

Phillips, Whitney (2015) *This is Why We Can't Have Nice Things: Mapping the Relationship Between Online Trolling and Mainstream Culture*. Cambridge, MA: MIT Press.

Price, Rob and Becky Peterson (2020) *Business Insider*. www.businessinsider.com/mark-zuckerberg-family-office-weststreet-misconduct-allegations-2020-2?op=1&r=US&IR=T

Qiu, Jack Linchuan (2016) *Goodbye iSlave: A Manifesto for Digital Abolition*. Urbana: University of Illinois Press.

Rheingold, Howard (2000 [1993]) *The Virtual Community: Homesteading on the Electronic Frontier*. Cambridge, MA: MIT Press.

Roberts, Dorothy E. (1993) 'Racism and Patriarchy in the Meaning of Motherhood' *Faculty Scholarship*, Paper 595.

Roberts, Dorothy E. (2011) *Fatal Invention: How Science, Politics, and Big Business Re-Create Race in the Twenty-First Century*. New York: Free Press.

Roberts, Sarah T. (2016) 'Chapter Eight: Commercial Content Moderation: Digital Laborer's Dirty Work' in Safiya Umoja Noble and Brendesha M. Tynes (eds.) *The Intersectional Internet: Race, Sex, Class, and Culture Online*. New York: Peter Lang, pp. 147–160.

Rottenberg, Catherine (2018) *The Rise of Neoliberal Feminism*. Oxford: Oxford University Press.

Rowbotham, S. (1981) 'The Trouble with "Patriarchy"' in Feminist Anthology Collective (eds.) *No Turning Back: Writings from the Women's Liberation Movement 1975–1980*. London: Women's Press.

Runciman, David (2018) *How Democracy Ends*. Profile.

Sacks, David O. and Peter A. Thiel (1995) *The Diversity Myth: Multiculturalism and Political Intolerance on Campus*. Oakland, CA: Independent Institute.

Salter, Anastasia and Bridget Blodgett (2018) *Toxic Geek Masculinity in Media: Sexism, Trolling, and Identity Policing*. Basingstoke: Palgrave.

Sandberg, Sheryl and Nell Scovell (2013/2015) *Lean In: Women, Work, and the Will to Lead*. London: Penguin Random House.

Sardar, Ziauddin (1995) 'alt.civilizations.faq Cyberspace as the Darker Side of the West' *Futures*, 27:7, 717–794.

Siapera, Eugenia (2019) 'Online Misogyny as Witch Hunt: Primitive Accumulation in the Age of Techno-capitalism' in Debbie Ging and Eugenia Siapera (eds.) *Gender Hate Online: Understanding the New Anti-Feminism*. Basingstoke: Palgrave Macmillan, pp. 21–44.

Skeggs, Beverly (2011) 'Imagining Personhood Differently: Person Value and Autonomist Working-Class Value Practices' *The Sociological Review*, 59, 3.

Skeggs, Beverly (2013) 'Values Beyond Value? Is Anything Beyond the Logic of Capital?' *British Journal of Sociology Annual Public Lecture*, Thursday 17 October.

Skeggs, Beverly and Simon Yuill (2019) 'Subjects of Value and Digital Personas: Reshaping the Bourgeois Subject, Unhinging Property from Personhood' *Subjectivity*, 12, 82–99. doi:10.1057/s41286-018-00063-4

Stone, Brad (2014) *The Everything Store: Jeff Bezos and the Age of Amazon*. Corgi.

Sylvain, Olivier (2018) 'Discriminatory Designs on User Data' The Knight First Amendment Institute's Emerging Threats series. Discriminatory Designs on User Data: Exploring how Section 230's immunity protections may enable or elicit discriminatory behaviors online.

Taplin, Jonathan (2017) *Move Fast and Break Things: How Facebook, Google, and Amazon Cornered Culture and Undermined Democracy*. New York: Hachette.

Teen Vogue (2019) 'horoscopes' www.teenvogue.com/gallery/weekly-horoscopes-october-6-12

The Big Bang Theory (CBS) (2007–2019).

'The Combahee River Collective Statement' (1978) Zillah Eisenstein. https://americanstudies.yale.edu/sites/default/files/files/Keyword%20Coalition_Readings.pdf

Thiel, Peter. (2009) 'The Education of a Libertarian' *Cato Unbound*, 13 April. www.cato-unbound.org/2009/04/13/peter-thiel/education-libertarian

Thiel, Peter and Blake Masters (2014) *Zero to One: Notes on Startups, or How to Build the Future*. London: Penguin Random House.

Turner, Fred (2008) *From Counterculture to Cyberculture: Stewart Brand, the Whole Earth Network, and the Rise of Digital Utopianism*. Chicago: University of Chicago Press.

Turner, Frederick Jackson (1893) 'The Significance of the Frontier in American History' *National Humanities Centre*. http://nationalhumanitiescenter.org/pds/gilded/empire/text1/turner.pdf Last accessed 23/02/2021.

Tyler, Imogen (2013) *Revolting Subjects: Social Abjection and Resistance in Neoliberal Britain*. London: Zed Books.

Vaidhyanathan, Siva (2012) *The Googlization of Everything*. Berkeley: University of California Press.

Vaidhyanathan, Siva. (2018) *Anti-Social Media: How Facebook Disconnects Us and Undermines Democracy*. Oxford: Oxford University Press.

van Dijck et al. (2014) '(ref p14) Datafication, Dataism and Dataveillance: Big Data between Scientific Paradigm and Ideology Surveillance and Society 2014' doi:10.24908/ss.v12i2.4776

Van Dijck, José, Thomas Poell, and Martijn de Waal (2018) *The Platform Society Public Values in a Connective World*. Oxford: Oxford University Press.

Wachter-Boettcher, Sara (2017) *Technically Wrong: Sexist Apps, Biased Algorithms, and Other Threats of Toxic Tech*. New York: W.W.Norton & Company.

Walby, Sylvia (1989) 'Theorising Patriarchy' *Sociology*, 23:2, 213–234.

White, R. (1986) 'Race Relations in the American West' *American Quarterly*, 38:3, 396–416. doi:10.2307/2712674

White, R., J. R. Grossman, P. N. Limerick, and Newberry Library. (1994) *The Frontier in American Culture*. Chicago: University of California Press. https://search.ebscohost.com/login.aspx?direct=true&db=nlebk&AN=21404&site=eds-live&scope=site

Why Him? (2016) John Hamburg.

'Why Him?' (n.d.) *RottenTomatoes.com.* www.rottentomatoes.com/m/why_him Last accessed 04/05/2020.

Wilson, Julie (2018) *Neoliberalism.* London: Routledge.

Winters, J. A (2011) *Oligarchy.* Leiden: Cambridge University Press. www.cambridge.org/core/books/oligarchy/5CC556B4483F7F3FDE1CADF928C04671 Last accessed 6/4/2020.

Wolf, Julia, Joli Kandra, Lora Engdahl and Heidi Shierholz (2020) 'Domestic Workers Chartbook' *Economic Policy Institute* www.epi.org/publication/domestic-workers-chartbook-a-comprehensive-look-at-the-demographics-wages-benefits-and-poverty-rates-of-the-professionals-who-care-for-our-family-members-and-clean-our-homes Last accessed 23/02/2021.

Wong, Julia Carrie (2017) 'Segregated Valley: The Ugly Truth about Google and Diversity in Tech' *The Guardian*, 7 August 2017.

Wu, Timothy (2018) 'Will Artificial Intelligence Eat the Law? The Rise of Hybridge Social-Ordering Systems' *Columbia Law Review*, 119, 7.

Zuboff, Shoshona (2019) *The Age of Surveillance Capitalism: The Fight for a Human Future at the New Frontier of Power.* London: Profile Books.

2
ELON MUSK

Geek masculinity and marketing the celebrity founder

From boy geniuses to world saviours

Paige: Don't tell me that he needs help. He's challenged. Have some empathy.
Walter: Challenged huh? Look at Sylvester and him. Do you know what they're doing? The matches are the king, the jelly is the queen, the sugar packets are the knights. He's playing chess with a grandmaster who's about to lose.
Sylvester: Walter, you see this? Check mate in 8 moves. This kid is amazing!
Walter: And he doesn't like to paint your nails. He does it because he wants to hold your hand, but he can't process physical contact. So help him. Or he will never connect with you. I'm sorry to be the bearer of bad news, but your son is a genius.

Scorpion Pilot Episode (2014)

All the men we focus on in this book have something in their public biography – an integral part of their repertoire of self-promotion – that lets them stake a claim to early signs of genius. It is a key factor that is used to set them apart: Mark Zuckerberg and Elon Musk wrote computer games when they were kids; Peter Thiel was a chess champion; Sergey Brin graduated college a year early; Larry Page made a printer out of Lego; Jeff Bezos programmed his high school timetable using a computer and so on (all from our concordance). The boy genius trope is a claim to intrinsic exceptionalism. That the emergence of abnormal capabilities for abstract and/or applied thought happens early is important because it signifies that these capabilities are biological rather than about social environment or upbringing.[1] In most cases, the boy genius narrative is intrinsically conservative: it is an assertion of natural hierarchy.

In this cultural script, the unusual and sometimes surprising and uncanny abilities demonstrated by such boys often lead to social exclusion and childhood bullying. This in turn produces two possible life trajectories for men such as these in popular narratives: either one based on a strong sense of social and natural justice (the genius superhero), or one shaped by a deep and abiding bitterness at their inability to assimilate their 'difference' to social norms, and thus a turn to misanthropy (the super villain). It is perhaps the ambivalence within this trope that, in part, leads to wildly divergent views among the general public about people like Mark Zuckerberg or Elon Musk.[2] But it is certainly the case that such stories give us clues about the kinds of cultural readings of masculinity within which celebrity tech founders are located.

The dialogue that opens this chapter is from the TV show *Scorpion*, which ran on American network CBS from 2014 to 2018. This is a digital era version of the *A-Team*, where instead of four different variants of heroic military masculinity, we have four variants of the super-intelligent geek hero – a computer hacker (Walter, the leader), statistician (Sylvester), psychologist (Toby), and engineer (Happy). All these geniuses are white men, except for Happy who is an Asian-American woman. The team is rounded out by a white woman Paige (not a genius) and her son (Riley – age nine, the biggest genius of all). All the genius characters have flaws emphasised in the narrative: Walter struggles with the emotional part of social interactions, Sylvester has obsessive–compulsive disorder, Toby is a self-sabotaging addict, and Happy has post-traumatic stress disorder (PTSD) from a childhood spent in care. While Riley is the current boy genius in the crew, the series opens with a young Walter being hauled off by the Department of Homeland Security (who are mysteriously operating with impunity in rural Ireland) for hacking into NASA to get space-shuttle blueprints for his bedroom wall. We are told in the opening credits that precede the scene that the show is inspired by a true story – that this fiction at one level reflects a lived reality.

A key role for Riley in *Scorpion* is to show the early innocence of these genius figures and to demonstrate their generational reproduction as a caste of men. Riley and Walter are characters in continuity with one another – Riley is the young Walter a generation apart, although the relationship is complicated by Walter and Paige's sexual tension and later blossoming romance. Walter and Riley are a dyad, the same person at different life stages, but at the same time Walter is a father figure to Riley, and his mother's partner. Paige embodies the very extensive role that women must play in support of such men. She is a mother, a lover, social support, and coach as well as a corporate administrator. Paige is the only character in the series able to process human emotions and participate in conventional social interactions. Her narrative has a dual function: on the one hand she interprets the social world for the rest of the team; on the other hand she is there to render empathetic responses to them for the audience. This is a trope in these forms of popular culture (other examples of related texts are listed below): smart men are complemented socially by beautiful women; men do the hard thinking and inventing, women do the socialising, time management, and perform professionalism. In these contexts, men are forgiven their awkwardness for brilliance, and women are forgiven their average intellect for translating the priorities of feminised care work into a professional context. Men might be flawed or sensitive, but they lack empathy and rely on women to interpret their and other people's feelings. Gone are the alpha males of previous eras, for whom showing emotion was a weakness; instead the 'most honoured' form of contemporary masculinity often can't interpret emotion at all (Connell and Messerchmidt 2005, 832).

This representation of geek masculinity includes a number of characteristics that are distinctly recognisable as having an affinity with the 'visionary founders' of Silicon Valley, or at least as mirroring their celebrity mediatisation (Massanari 2017, Banet-Weiser 2018). Indeed the 'true story' behind *Scorpion* is the biography of Irish hacker-turned-entrepreneur Walter O'Brien, who also produced the show (although some commentators contend the 'true story' is also largely fictional (Karlin 2014)). This popular culture configuration also reflects the actual gendered organisation of labour in the tech industry where, as we will see in Chapter 6, women must 'lean-in' to the brilliant entrepreneurs to share in the proceeds of their genius (Sandberg and Scovell 2013). This shift to geek masculinity as hegemonic is manifest across a growing and relatively diverse (in terms of genre at least) range of fictional texts, as documented by Salter and Blodgett (2018). With them, we understand this shift as a symbolic challenge to what has conventionally been understood as hegemonic masculinity (Connell and Messerschmidt 2005).

In these influential representational worlds, the emotionally repressed meatheads of the 1970s through 1990s (think Arnold Schwarzenegger, Sylvester Stallone, or Jean-Claude Van Damme), with their flashing biceps and chiselled pecs, are far less visible, and when they are present they are far less straightforwardly heroic. The classic male hero, troubled and angry at times but rising to assured leadership and moral certitude based on rational control over emotion, is no longer the predominant cultural archetype; although it does, of course, persist in other texts (see Jamie Hakim 2019). Instead, a new generation of entrepreneurial geek masculinity is emerging as the paradigm of a heroic man: at its most stereotypical extreme these characters appear as cerebral, wounded by early trauma (bullying schoolmates or angry/absent fathers), emotionally incapable rather than repressed, and they are armed with computer and engineering expertise rather than mechanical or martial skills. Instead of performing (often violent) 'morally correct' actions to defeat adversaries (Tasker 1993, 111), these heroes outthink their opponents, manipulate the system or find loopholes to enable them to win.

Like previous variants of 'hegemonic masculinity,' these forms of geek or 'hacker' heroism inaugurate a social order where they dominate (Connell and Messerschmidt 2005). They organically allocate subordinate roles to other men with different attributes and organise women into their orbit around generally heterosexual principles (mother or lover figures – often with some overlap). Class and race also play important and intersecting roles in this pattern of social organisation. Happy might be a female genius in the core *Scorpion* team, but as an Asian-American woman different cultural logics apply to her in this milieu; and her representation must negotiate entrenched Orientalist stereotypes such as the Lotus Blossom (Tajima 1989), including being 'available for white men' (Pyke and Johnson 2003, 36). In the context that we are exploring in this book, it is also more acceptable for her to display technical intelligence as Asians '*are* the business' of technology (Nakamura 2008, 199). At one point Happy performs a Portuguese pop song while dressed in pink, and with a large flamingo on her chest that recalls the East Asian pop cultures of Manga/Anime and K-Pop that are highly fetishised in the West, and particularly within geek subcultures. Moreover, as the programme develops she is seen as conceding to maternal desires, asking to have a child with her future husband Toby. Thus her 'difficult genius' behaviour is eventually subsumed within more traditional forms of femininity.

These configurations are also present in non-fictional representations of contemporary masculinity that we explore below: they represent on screen existing sociological dynamics. That is, this masculinity is not simply a feature of the representational texts discussed here: it is part of a set of wider social and cultural transformations around gender, transformations that ultimately reassert conservative gender roles within a high-tech, high-status social milieu. These popular media texts provide a good way into understanding what's at stake in the arrival of the geek as a new dominant form of masculinity: a masculinity which is co-constitutive with the forms of patriarchy that we are mapping. And these popular media texts also provide cultural materials for the genre of celebrity performed by the men that are the primary subjects of this book. But though our main focus here is on gender, it is important to note that this is only one element in understanding the social and representational phenomena we are discussing. Furthermore, we need to locate this gendering within the wider racialised patriarchal power structures of the technology industry. The main way we do that in this chapter is with reference to billionaire inventor Elon Musk – who was present but just out of picture in the screenshot of Trump and the tech leaders that opened the introduction. Musk's performance as a celebrity founder is strongly connected to these evolving new forms of masculinity within popular culture.

'The real-life Iron Man': Elon Musk and Tony Stark

The paradigmatic example of this shift in popular culture to embrace entrepreneurial celebrity can be seen in the cinematic superhero genre. Here Iron Man, a billionaire genius businessman, has replaced Superman as the favoured archetype of the modern superhero (by box office takings as much as any other measure (Nash Information Services 2020)). Indeed, this tech-entrepreneur-cum-witty-playboy-cum-world-saver is mentioned 23 times in our concordance: mostly when comparing the fictional Tony Stark to Elon Musk. This is a comparison Musk's PR apparatus eagerly endorse: in 2008 they placed an Iron Man statue near the elevators at his Space X headquarters (Vance 2015, 226), and they arranged well-documented exchange visits between Musk and Iron Man actor Robert Downey Jr as part of the publicity for the first film in the *Iron Man* series. Musk also had a cameo in the 2010 sequel, *Iron Man 2*. The Tesla co-founder isn't the only subject of this book to be compared to the superhero, however: in a PR blitz around the failed Google Glass project, Google founder Sergey Brin was also named as a 'real life' Iron Man in *Vanity Fair*, and Mark Zuckerberg and Jeff Bezos have also been described in this way, albeit to a lesser extent (Grigoriadis 2014, Sharman 2016, Yurieff 2017). In this section we look at how the superhero narrative crosses over with the figure of the celebrity entrepreneur – embracing both stories of new heroes and their romances and the world of technology product launches.

In the Iron Man story – mirroring similar patterns in the Walter and Paige story in *Scorpion* – Tony Stark's dependence on (and eventual marriage to) his live-in personal assistant, the dependable Pepper Potts, sets up the kinds of gender dynamics we have identified as playing a central role in our broader analysis. Stark is the protagonist, a brilliant but difficult man who depends on Potts to be the responsible one. She helps him to see the limits of his brilliance and direct his inspiration. She is a mothering caregiver, and organises the social and emotional elements of Stark's life, and eventually the two of them become lovers. Back in the real world, the role of nurturing social secretary is explicitly how Talulah Riley, Musk's second wife is portrayed in Ashlee Vance's biography *Elon Musk: How the Billionaire CEO of SpaceX and Tesla Is Shaping Our Future (2015)*. In the introduction, describing the elaborate parties Musk throws for his friends, Vance highlights Riley's central role in the care of the circle's social activities, while referencing the early trauma trope typical of these narratives:

> Riley turned planning these types of parties for Musk into an art … 'I try to think of fun things he has not done before where he can relax,' Riley said. 'We're trying to make up for his miserable childhood now.'
>
> (2015, 20)

As with many of these fictional characters, Musk's celebrity is partly explained through reference to his difficult early life, with his father being painted as a monstrous figure: 'a terrible human being,' Musk himself calls him. And it is also stated in descriptions of Musk's early life that he was bullied and beaten at school (Strauss 2017). We are invited to understand this early history as a generic side effect of his celebrity genius, and also as the source of his performed desire to save humanity. Indeed, these early experiences of injustice at the hands of bullies and his father are explicitly claimed as his motivation for developing transformative technologies by *Rolling Stone*'s Neil Strauss in a 2017 biographical profile (discussed further later in this chapter). And in Vance's biography, Riley's care of Musk is represented as resolving, holding, and taking care of that early trauma typical of the boy genius – while also justifying his need to participate in elaborately decadent social activities. Yet if his genius is a source of trauma, it is also seen as making him sexually attractive: describing their return from a date to Musk's hotel room, Vance writes: 'Musk told Riley, a virgin, that he wanted to show her his rockets' (195); an innuendo which also reveals the gendered position of the biographer.

In the 2010 film *Iron Man 2*, Tony Stark and Pepper Potts kiss for the first time in a manner that reinforces the "real-life" parallels with Musk and Riley as portrayed by Vance. Stark saves Potts (Gwyneth Paltrow) with his flying robot suit, but as he lands Potts announces she can't take the lifestyle anymore and resigns as his personal assistant. Stark then says: 'You've taken such good care of me,' and as they begin to talk about role transitions to a new post-holder, in mid-sentence, they start kissing. Thus, the boundaries between domestic support and romance are broken down: the figure of the professional woman attached to the entrepreneur's household is unable to maintain the sexual boundaries of professionalism.

While romantically attached women perform the role of mother–lover, other women must be visibly hypersexual. In the same film we learn that Stark, like Musk, is a fan of flamboyant product launches. After the opening credits, he lands on a platform in his flying suit to a cheering stadium crowd with a line of can-canning models in Iron Man–themed bikinis behind him. The star-spangled banner is displayed on a giant screen at the back of the stage, while a pyrotechnic display goes on announcing his presence. Technology, virility, and patriotism are bound together in a formulation that ties this new masculine order very clearly to common cultural tropes of American exceptionalism. Tony Stark claims that ideological formation with false modesty: 'I'm not saying that the world has enjoyed its longest period of uninterrupted peace in years because of me …' And he adds in a more serious tone: 'It's not about me … It's about legacy.' As with Musk's real-world space exploration or electric cars project, Stark's work is framed as something of intrinsic historic value, but also as having a specific national context. And Stark's triumphs in the film reflect classic American heroism: he will defeat an evil Russian scientist, as well as the corrupt military-industrial complex, while also wooing the dependable Potts.

The theatrical product launch that ties founder, product, and company in a tight formation was a promotional technique developed by Steve Jobs. Jobs became indelibly marked on the products that he sold through such events. The 2015 biopic *Steve Jobs*, directed by Danny Boyle, focused on these events as a way of showing the tension between celebrity and human being, through a narrative that wove off-stage and on-stage Jobs into a retelling of his tumultuous career. But Jobs's launch events were not predicated on the sexualisation of his products or his persona. As Sharma and Grant put it: 'Jobs' wit and originality is as much an expression of Apple's identity as it is his own: a centred, good-humoured, and achievement-oriented organisation that celebrates learning and growth' (2011). Musk's product launches are closer to Tony Stark's than those of Steve Jobs. There may be fewer models, but the cheering crowds, light show, and faux-modest script are strikingly similar. And in the Tesla car launches, the names of the range of cars spell S3XY, just in case anyone was missing the can-can girls. At the Model 3 launch, the visuals behind Musk's presentation show pictures of the Earth from space – thereby emphasising both the world-saving mission and the availability of service centres (as well as referencing his other company SpaceX). Musk's key message is that Tesla's mission is to 'accelerate the world's transition to sustainable energy' (Tesla 2016). At the Cybertruck launch he emphasised masculine values with feats of strength enacted by Gothic costumed circus performers, while spinning lines like: 'You want a truck that's tough, not fake tough.' The colour motif to these launches tends to be red, blue, and bright white lights – again not quite the star-spangled banner of Tony Stark, but clearly indicative of the national identity of the initial primary market (Digital Trends 2019). And Musk, a Canadian-South African migrant, is also presented as quintessentially American. It is worth noting here how references to American patriotism are evoked through the representational similarities between the performance of the Iron Man hero and Musk's persona as the electric car and rocket ship inventor. Inventing, in this matrix, becomes specifically articulated to American exceptionalism. Here is Scott Galloway, a popular business commentator and academic:

> Culturally, we have elevated the entrepreneur to iconic status along with sports heroes and entertainment stars … Entrepreneurs are seen as individual, self-made visionaries with vast wealth. They are perhaps the purest expression of the American hero. Superhero, even. Superman can reverse the rotation of the Earth, but Iron Man Tony Stark would be better on an earnings call and is a very human superhero – Elon Musk.
>
> *(2017, 260)*

Musk also performs a Tony-Stark-level superstar virility. Since his divorce from Justine Musk in 2010 he has had a love life comparable to that of an A-list Hollywood celebrity. As well as his relationship with his now twice-divorced ex-wife Talulah Riley, who is a successful actress in her own right, he has been associated with movie star Amber Heard and Canadian popstar Grimes. These romantic connections have also (intentionally or not) reinforced Musk's own celebrity links with science fiction, superhero and dystopian futures. Amber Heard has an, albeit small, part in the DC comics universe cinematic franchise, as part of the cast of the eco-aware *Aquaman* (2018), while Riley had a significant role as an AI hostess in the dystopian *West World* (2016). Here she is reprising one of Musk's favourite themes – the existential threat to humanity posed by general artificial intelligence. Similarly, Grimes's electronic music reflects and reinterprets many of Musk's interests: 'We Appreciate Power' (2019) is a cautionary song about the dangers of AI, with the refrain 'What will it take to make you capitulate? We appreciate power.' Power here puns on the capacity to act and the electricity needed to make AI run. It is also, perhaps, a comment on appreciating the power that her boyfriend has accumulated through wealth and technology: the implication being that Musk's power is also erotic.

Musk and Stark both strive to save the world. For Stark, the villains tend to be characters – the rogue Russian scientist, the corrupt corporate boss, the Malthusian Alien overlord. For Musk it is the dangers posed by a technological society, physics or both: artificial intelligence, asteroid impact, climate change. For both characters – the fictional superhero and Musk's celebrity persona – their great wealth is a means to an end. Stark uses his resources to produce the technology to support his superheroic activities, whereas Musk's businesses in rocketry and electric cars aim to directly solve the problems their founder has identified. Tesla helps to combat global warming by electrifying transport and moving it away from fossil fuels. SpaceX is developing commercial space flight to help build a colony on Mars. The ostensible aim of this project is to provide 'planetary backup' for 'humanity' – or at least a wealthy subsection of it – in the event of something wiping out life on Earth (an asteroid, AI, global warming etc.). Heroism, sexuality, and genius come together in a formation that presents an almost messianic figure for his fans: someone in whom humanity can place their hopes for the future.

The rise of geek masculinity

Iron Man is just one, highly visible, part of a spectrum of geek masculinities (see Ging 2017, Banet-Weiser 2018). At times dysfunctional, he is nevertheless the more suave fantasy realisation of the tech-visionary 'hacker' hero. Another paradigmatic text that embodies the shifting status of geek masculinity, as identified by Salter and Blodgett in their media studies book *Toxic Geek Masculinity* (2018, 1–3), is *The Big Bang Theory* (2007–2019). This *Friends*-style sitcom relocates its generationally recognisable cast of buddies from New York to Pasadena, and turns 90s slackers into 00s scholars. Gender divides are enforced more rigidly for the scientists than in generation X's paradigmatic sitcom; and romantic relationships are higher on the agenda sooner than they were in *Friends*. Indeed, one of the main quartet of men, the 'lovable' Rajesh Koothrappali, cannot talk to women at all unless he has consumed alcohol – in the early seasons at least. This is a show that Musk has staked a claim to – appearing in a 2015 Thanksgiving episode as a soup kitchen volunteer.

Similar geeky casts pepper other genres too. Young adult spy hero 'Chuck' of the eponymous TV show *Chuck* is a hacker and Stanford drop-out who becomes the Californian version of a tech-Bond with his 'hot blond' handler-soon-to-become-girlfriend Sarah; science fiction disaster series/political thriller *Salvation* sees a thinly disguised Elon Musk saving the world from an incoming asteroid while navigating a love triangle with a political press officer/single mom and the secretary of defence, mentoring his boy genius sidekick and eventually becoming president.

Ostensibly closer to reality, perhaps, are the parody figures of the HBO *Silicon Valley* TV show (2014–present), in which a team of misanthropic coders attempt to take over the world (or at least the internet) and get rich, while bringing down a thinly disguised Google/Oracle-esque CEO in the character of Gavin Belson. In this world, men are coders and women tend to be attractive and work in marketing or client relations for venture capital. This is a parody, and the tech industry's gender relations are part of what is being parodied, but after four seasons the lead character Richard Hendricks, a tech entrepreneur modelled after Mark Zuckerberg, is, despite the satire, quite clearly a hero that the programme is rooting for. While some female figures do eventually appear as programmers and powerful venture capitalists, the female leads are normally relegated to the periphery. The show has received some criticism for its poor gender portrayals (Berger 2014), but after reading insider accounts of life in the Valley for women (see Losse 2012, Chang 2018, and Pao 2017 – all in the concordance), it could be seen as positively progressive in comparison. The more strait-laced, less successful *Betas*, which had a short run in 2013 on the Jeff Bezos-run Amazon prime before being canned, was effectively the same show, but with less successful satire, and it reproduced exactly the same problems. On the other hand, the historical drama *Halt and Catch Fire* attempted to rewrite the recent past of the computing industry through a far more mixed-gender cast – after season 1 at least (2014–2017). But by its final season the nature of its gender representations indicated that the show had quite clearly recognised that it was a fantastic alternative history rather than an accurate representation of reality (we pick this up in Chapter 5 on Peter Thiel).

These forms of 'nerdy' or 'geek' masculinity, which were once thoroughly subordinate or oppositional – the savant hacker, the geek sidekick, the evil genius – have shifted their location in cultural hierarchies. Why has this 'geek cultural revolution' come about? For Salter and Blodgett the answer lies partly with the tech companies, their founders and their followers, who have helped launch the new era:

> Social media has particularly enabled this trend, as viewers of the same show gather using hashtags on Twitter, share memes and insider knowledge on Tumblr, and complain bitterly about bad season finales or cliffhangers on Facebook. These are platforms built and powered by geeks that have relied upon geeks as a base of support for building their cultural capital.
>
> (Salter and Blodgett 2018, 4)

Salter and Blodgett are right that there is a relationship between the platform founders (the celebrity subjects in this book) and these sorts of characters on TV, but this observation needs fleshing out. One way to do this is to recognise the role of culture as a site of contestation for rival forms of hegemonic leadership. (Gramsci 1971, Gilbert and Williams 2019). As we outlined in the Introduction, Gramsci argues that leadership involves struggle across a range of sites, both for the winning of hegemony and for sustaining it. This holds true both for leadership in the wider society and, more specifically, for the maintenance of hegemonic masculinity. Indeed, we would argue that understanding the nature of contemporary male social, political, and economic dominance is essential for grasping the wider pattern of social change wrought by digital technologies.

Connell and Messerschmidt find resources of hope in the idea that 'there could be a struggle for hegemony, and older forms of masculinity might be displaced by new ones' (Connell and Messerschmidt 2005, 883). However, the possibility of transformation quickly turns sour in the writing of Salter and Blodgett, who see the emerging dominance of geek masculinity as 'an inevitable evolution of hegemonic masculinity in a culture where dominance and technical mastery are increasingly interwoven' (Salter and Blodgett 2018, 47). In the view of these authors, rather than replacing conventional ideals of aggressive or athletic masculinity, geek masculinity is absorbing some of those values as it transcends them. To an extent we agree with this argument: such a change is apparent, for example, in Mark Zuckerberg's attempts to negotiate the boundaries between geekery and more athletic, hunter-gatherer forms of masculinity, as we explore in Chapter 4. Successful geek leaders continue the performance of existing forms of hegemonic masculinity 'even while apparently expanding its boundaries,' as Salter and Blodgett put it (2018, 68). Jeff Bezos, too, has built on his geeky obsession with *Star Trek* by turning himself into the owner of a rocket company, Blue Origin, while references to *Star Trek* narratives have also become part of his heroic CEO myth, as we will see in Chapter 3.

But it is Elon Musk – more than any other of the founders discussed in this book – who is keenest to harness these new forms of hegemonic masculinity, in both their mundane (*Big Bang Theory*) and superheroic (*Iron Man*) forms; they form the cornerstone not just of his celebrity persona, but also of his marketing strategy for Tesla; and it is these new forms of geek masculinity that provide legitimation for the activities of his rocket business SpaceX. He has embraced – and been embraced by – geek popular culture more extensively than any other of the men in this book. As well as his *Iron Man* and *Big Bang Theory* cameos, he has also appeared in films such as *Thank You For Smoking* (2005), *Machete Kills* (2013), *Transcendence* (2014), *Why Him?* (2016), and *Men In Black: International* (2019). His appearances in TV shows are almost more interesting, as they have been in some of the irreverent niches that are popular among mainstream geek audiences, such as *The Big Bang Theory*, spin-off *Young Sheldon* (2017), or cult favourite *Rick and Morty* (2019). In a 2015 *Simpsons* episode, his celebrity is gently mocked through praise: 'He's the guy who perfected electric cars and then gave away the patents: He's changed the way Hollywood drives!' says Lisa Simpson. Although many tech figures in this book have appeared in long-running satirical animation *South Park*, only Musk has done his own voice-acting, and as a result he gets perhaps a better representation there – as a benign inventor – rather than receiving the traditional roasting the show offers celebrities. As is the case with all the patriarchal founders we explore, Musk's celebrity is the mechanism for legitimating his actions; but each of them uses their public profile differently, with varying degrees of success and strategic ends. For Musk, the relationship with popular culture and the cultivation of subcultural fandom are central to his overall corporate strategy.

The myths of Musk's celebrity

At the start of an extended interview in 2017 for rock-and-roll-into-politics-and-counterculture magazine *Rolling Stone*, the terms of Elon Musk's celebrity are made clear. Written by reformed pick-up artist Neil Strauss (see O'Neill 2018) and titled 'Elon Musk: The Architect of Tomorrow,' the article states in its second paragraph:

> Musk will likely be remembered as one of the most seminal figures of this millennium. Kids on all the terraformed planets of the universe will look forward to Musk Day, when they get the day off to commemorate the birth of the Earthling who single-handedly ushered in the era of space colonization.

The next paragraph opens with: 'And that's just one of Musk's ambitions.' Later in the article Strauss is similarly hyperbolic:

> Musk is a titan, a visionary, a human-size lever pushing forward massive historical inevitabilities – the kind of person who comes around only a few times in a century.

Strauss gives us the version of Musk that his fans echo throughout the internet: that Elon (as the fans refer to him) is 'The Most Important Person of Our Generation.' Significantly the interviewer is a very particular type of person to be given this interview and to be making these claims. Strauss is the author of *The Game* (2005), which Rachel O'Neill describes as being an urtext for the heterosexual men involved in the 'seduction community.'[3] Strauss has built his career on advising heterosexual men that they *should* exercise control over women (O'Neill 2018, 24). In the *Rolling Stone* interview, Musk is portrayed as in great emotional pain after his recent break-up with Amber Heard. In response Strauss dispenses relationship advice; his diagnosis centres on Musk's abusive father, which he sees as meaning that Musk seeks co-dependency in his relationships with women. At points in the interview Musk is portrayed as tearful and shaky – a vulnerable and wounded genius. Here, Strauss cannily weaves together the 'discourses of injury' typical to online misogyny (Banet-Weiser 2018) that might appeal to his personal fanbase (who can access the article through his website) and the representation of Musk as working consistently to 'a scientific method' (a scientific method which includes the working proposition that 'our personalities might be 80 percent nature and 20 percent nurture': a perspective that conveniently naturalises his exceptionalism in the manner of the boy genius trope (Strauss 2017)). There are multiple audiences for this interview, all of whom are consumers (primarily men with disposable income) to whom Musk might want to sell cars: the *Rolling Stone* readership, online Musk fans, followers of Strauss.

But Strauss is far from alone in his hyperbolic praise for Musk. Many of Musk's advocates frame his celebrity in terms of his pioneering work on the 'frontier,' a prominent theme in this book, as we have already noted. Thus celebrity physicist Neil deGrasse Tyson writes: 'We are on the frontier of the future of civilisation – thanks to Musk,' and goes on to describe the various sectors in which he is 'pioneering.' Similarly, in books from the concordance there are a number of references to Musk couched in the language of heroism and genius. Kevin Kelly compares him to late physicist Stephen Hawking while calling him a 'genius inventor'; Peter Diamandis and Steven Kotler say he 'will bring prosperity to billions'; while Peter Thiel calls him a 'sales grandmaster' – implying also that there might be a bit more self-interest in his activities (a good thing from Thiel's perspective).

Perhaps the role that Musk plays within the wider patriarchal network of tech founders is most telling. We can see it here in this passage by Jamie Bartlett in *The People vs. Tech* (which is critical of the founders, but this has no bearing on the point we take from it):

> And to whom do we look in order to solve our collective social problems? It's no longer the state, but the modern tech-geek superhero. Space travel and climate change has fallen to Elon Musk. We look to Google to solve health problems and sort out ageing. Facebook gets to decide what free speech is and battle against fake news, while Amazon's Jeff Bezos saves the Washington Post from bankruptcy.
>
> *(159)*

This is part of a polemical argument (and the book is labelled as such in our concordance), but Musk's role as outlined in this passage is key to the wider rhetoric. For Musk, space travel and electric vehicles (hence the climate change reference) are his primary businesses. But for the other patriarchs referred to here, the issues mentioned are peripheral to, or side effects of, their main activity. Indeed, Bezos disavows any editorial control at *The Washington Post*; Facebook's Zuckerberg has strongly resisted responsibility for free speech; and the anti-ageing company Calico (hence ageing reference) is a separate entity from Google within the umbrella company Alphabet. But Musk is referred to first, and the fact that he clearly is working in both space travel and climate-friendly transport then justifies the further claims made, which are perhaps less tenable. Musk's role here is to legitimate the references to the work of the others.

This role as legitimator of the wider tech-founder group, usually in a more favourable context, operates in other areas. And is also a two-way street: the wider network gives Musk's celebrity a cultural logic. He is not simply a 'genius inventor,' but one who can be located in a wider cultural discourse of masculine genius; and he is also empirically networked – socially, financially, ideologically – with these other men. As we demonstrated in the Introduction, they make up a mutually reinforcing patriarchal system.

Musk's celebrity is thus fed by his membership in this group, even though he may not like these other men or approve of their companies: in the Strauss interview, for example, it appears that one of the things Musk wants to save us from is the other companies whose founders are profiled in this book:

> 'Between Facebook, Google and Amazon – and arguably Apple, but they seem to care about privacy – they have more information about you than you can remember,' he elaborates to me. 'There's a lot of risk in concentration of power. So if AGI [artificial general intelligence] represents an extreme level of power, should that be controlled by a few people at Google with no oversight?'
>
> *(Strauss 2017)*

Musk's businesses are also different from those of the other tech patriarchs in other ways. Both SpaceX and Tesla are transportation companies, albeit of very different sorts, rather than internet companies. Space X is a rocket company that is reducing the cost of getting into orbit by developing reusable rockets. Tesla is an electric car company that is also developing self-driving capabilities.

But nevertheless, Musk remains part of the group. He made his first fortune on the internet, like the others, at first with maps and listings company Zip2 (bought by Compaq), and then, alongside Peter Thiel and others in the 'PayPal Mafia,' with the sale of online payments company PayPal to eBay. These activities left him with around $180 million dollars which he reinvested in the two companies he currently runs. So, although Musk talks with frustration about still being referred to as 'the internet guy' (ThirdRow 2020), after spending a decade in transportation, he does still carry the ideological perspective and management techniques of the world of Silicon Valley and the start-up culture that comes with it. At core, his companies are designed to 'disrupt' mature industries (in the same way that Instagram 'disrupts' the photography industry or Google 'disrupts' directory services and libraries), through the application of transformative technological innovations: i.e. through the projection of a new paradigm for the industry. In Musk's case this is to be achieved through electrification and autonomous driving for the car industry; and through reusability for rocket ship building.

It is worth dwelling on this term, which is an important part of the tech founders' vocabulary: 'disrupt' is found in the concordance 299 times through a lemma-based search which reveals its uses across all its forms (e.g. 'disrupt,' 'disrupting,' 'disrupted,' and so forth). This is approximately 30 times per million words – three times as often as our baseline sample of enTenTen15 English language web corpus on Sketch Engine. This means it is a hugely significant word in the language of technology. It is used particularly in relation to collocates (words appearing next to or near to it) like 'industry,' 'economy,' 'market,' and 'sector,' and also with more specific objects like 'education,' 'publishing,' 'banking,' 'employment,' 'manufacturing,' 'police,' 'journalism,' 'transport,' 'medicine,' and so on. Fundamental to the business practice of the tech industry, then, is the ideological deployment of disruption – normally seen as inconvenient and stressful – *as if it was a good thing*. Internet entrepreneurs put established corporations out of business or force them to dramatically change their practices. The classic comparison is Kodak and Instagram. Instagram, a digital photo-sharing platform with 13 staff, was bought by Facebook for a billion dollars in 2012, the same year that photography and film company Kodak filed for bankruptcy. Kodak now employs around 5,400 people, down from a peak of 145,000 (Leslie 2014, Brynjolfsson and McAfee 2014).

Musk's two main businesses are doing similar things in the automotive and rocket industries. Indeed, he is so hated in some spaceflight circles that one book in our concordance reports that his face was taped to the toilet at an industry party so that the executives could urinate on him when they relieved themselves (Davenport 2018, 204). Yet, despite clearly acting as a textbook case for the practice, Musk rejects the discourse of 'disruption,' saying in 2015 that he is 'not really a fan' of the term, preferring to think about his activities as 'fundamental change' (Pramuk 2015). This is an important part of his persona, and it is significant in that it places the technological innovation above the business opportunity: he presents his motivations as changing the world not simply getting rich. In contrast to this, 'disruption' is a discourse about business success. To maintain his fanbase Musk must disavow that his businesses are about succeeding as such – they are portrayed as vehicles for wider socio-technical transformation, and his personal wealth is simply a side effect of those processes.

His negotiation of a performance-based bonus of up to $50 billion for his work at Tesla seems to suggest, however, that his indifference to great wealth might be overstated (Rushe 2018). Musk learned his business skills in the world of Silicon Valley start-ups, as well as being immersed in the exceptionalist narrative of US tech companies driven by the venture capitalists of Sand Hill Road. He has learned about 'disruption' from within a culture that has generated unprecedented private fortunes through it. And Musk is currently one of the two richest men in the world as a result. Whatever he says, this is not something that has happened by accident.

Moreover, regardless of what the practice of 'disruption' is called, technical innovation is never the sole driver of success: the management techniques of the Valley are fundamental too. While reusable rockets of the type developed by SpaceX have dramatically reduced the cost to get to orbit, and Tesla has proved the concept that electric cars are a viable alternative to the internal combustion engine, the ability to pull off those two feats has rested not simply on engineering skills, but on brutally demanding work practices and implacable opposition to unionisation. That, rather than simple technological innovation, seems to be the decisive factor: there are other electric car companies and even other spaceflight companies, but the key for Musk's business success seems to be his labour practices. But he does not disavow this aspect of his practice. Instead, he portrays it as part of his heroism.

When asked on Twitter 'What's the correct number of hours to change the world?' he replies: 'Varies per person, but about 80 sustained, peaking about 100 at times. Pain level increases exponentially above 80' (Musk 2018b). If his staff work 100-hour weeks (which some reportedly do), whereas his unionised competitors work 40 hours, it is apparent that, with the same staff base, his companies can do in four or five months what the established firms can do in a year. The key here is to turn extreme employment practices into an individual virtue. Indeed, Musk's work ethic is firmly engrained in his superheroic persona.

For this long-hours culture to be sustainable a few other elements are required: a young labour force with few family responsibilities (or who have, or can pay, other people to take care of the domestic arrangements); aggressive, continuous recruitment to replace burned-out staff (often hired straight from university so they know no better about conditions in other employers); a time-limited target-based reward system (usually stock options that vest under specific conditions); and the heroic mythologisation of the company so that exploitative practices become the method for a collective mission. Musk's celebrity helps to achieve all those things: it attracts talent through its online fan base; it presents a higher purpose tied to mythologised heroic leadership; and it maintains the necessary conditions to keep the companies operating to these logics, through facilitating the leveraging of stock price and investment capital to ensure large paper-based financial rewards to staff. Musk aggressively defends these practices in a 2018 interview for *60 Minutes*:

> There's been relentless criticism, relentless and outrageous and unfair. Because what actually happened here was an incredible American success story. All these people work their ass off day and night to make it happen. And they believe in the dream. And that's the story that really should be told.
>
> *(2018)*

While Elon Musk's employment practices are framed firmly in line with wider Silicon Valley narratives of hard work, great reward, and social mission, he denies their ideological basis and the celebrification that gives us access to him. Instead he presents himself as a man of the scientific method: whatever he does as, broadly speaking, objective. Everything should be boiled back to 'first principles thinking' (Strauss 2017) and there is no subtext to anything. As he says to Strauss:

> I think being precise about the truth works. Truthful and precise. I try to tell people, 'You don't have to read between the lines with me. I'm saying the lines!'

We agree that he is saying lines: 'lines' performed from a script. They may indeed be accurate, but they are also constructing a form of celebrity. This celebrity takes shape through a set of narratives, key phrases, and framing that is profoundly ideological in the way it mediatises his life and his businesses. That doesn't make his statement untrue, but truth isn't really the point: rather, we must recognise his missionary zeal for his products as solutions to global problems, and his careful curation of a public persona, as part of his strategic business practices.[4]

Celebrity as business strategy

Media theorists have long understood that celebrity is a form of labour that has an entire industry to support it. And Musk is firmly a part of the well-established Hollywood celebrity industrial complex (Turner 2007), attracting regular interest from gossip websites and newspapers. As Gamson set out in 1994:

> Paid specialists surround the celebrities to increase and protect their market value, and linked subindustries make use of celebrities for their own commercial purposes, simultaneously building and using performers' attention-getting power ... the specialists form support industries around the development of celebrity products: personal publicists and public-relations firms handle the garnering of media coverage and help manage the packaging of the celebrity; agents, managers, and promoters handle representation, affecting the pricing and distribution of the celebrity; coaches and groomers of various sorts help with the presentation. Linked industries, in particular the communication-media and entertainment industries, distribute the celebrity image to consumers. Celebrities are sold to consumers in specified or mass markets through these intermediate distributors, who buy and resell the celebrity product – either in the form of celebrity information (programs, magazines, newspapers) or celebrity performance vehicles.
>
> *(Gamson 1994, 61–62)*

Celebrity is also something that can be measured: it is a key word in our concordance, appearing in 64 books, and around 400 times, or double the background rate in the 2015 English internet sample.

Many of these features remain firmly in place for digital technology celebrities, with some adjustment geared towards the specificities of the sector. The point of all this labour is to produce something that appears natural, so that when Musk speaks to his audiences he is 'precise about the truth,' and he appears genuine, natural, and 'authentic' (Banet-Weiser 2018, Marwick 2013). Despite competent claims to this affect of authenticity, however, Musk's celebrity does occasionally show its seams. Thus in an interview with Joe Rogan, reference is made to his manager being present (discussed further below), and in another, with a fan collective called Third Row, two 'helpers' sit in on the interview alongside Elon's mother Maye Musk and younger brother Kimbal. His celebrity is produced by his PR teams and used extensively in the promotion of his products.

Our analysis in this book is concerned with the celebrification of tech founders, not with their actual personalities, opinions, or lives. The phenomenon of founder celebrification has been a key driver in the transformation of this particular industrial sector: it has played a role in the shift away from its origins as a primarily economic sector, to become one with a significant political, social, and cultural influence. In part this shift is due to the changing nature of the products themselves (from hardware and operating systems to social software and apps for instance), but the industry has also become significant through the 'becoming celebrity' of its key leaders (such as Jobs and Gates) and the sorts of stories they self-generate (Driessens 2013). These celebrity figures are then able to migrate their influence from the field they started in (technology) to other areas (Chadwick 2013, Arthurs and Little 2016).

Celebrity logics are increasingly spreading from the entertainment industry to other domains, through a process of what Olivier Driessens calls celebritisation (as opposed to celebrification – the process of an individual becoming a celebrity); and, as they do so, those logics, and the apparatuses that support them (agents, PR workers, media outlets and networks, specialist journalists, etc.), are becoming increasingly entangled in public life (Driessens 2013). We have celebrity presidents, celebrity chefs, even celebrity academics. Celebrity studies is now a well-established academic field, with a specialised journal and regular international conferences. Normally located within media and cultural studies, it addresses all aspects of celebrity, from A-List scandal to celebrity presidents to micro-celebrity communities online. Within this, political celebrity has garnered (and rightly so) a significant amount of attention. The study of politics and celebrity emerged in the 1990s through the work of people like P. David Marshall (2014). In 2004, John Street wrote a seminal article on the difference between politicians who utilise celebrity logics, and celebrities who move into the political arena; and in 2013 Mark Wheeler drew on this work to present a thoroughgoing survey of the extent to which these two spheres collide (Wheeler 2013, Street 2004). Research in this area is ongoing, and regular contributions to cultural studies, media studies, and political science journals are exploring the links between politics, entertainment, and celebrity.

There is a less extensive but still longstanding body of writing on the rise of the celebrity CEO in the business domain, including work by Jo Littler, Eric Guthey, Timothy Clark, and Brad Jackson. Littler notes the importance of thinking about business leaders as celebrities in order to avoid reproducing the idea of the heroic CEO as a real figure as opposed to a mediated construct, as with other celebrity figures. Discussing Lowenthal's dismay at the emergence of the entertainment celebrity, which displaced an early twentieth-century focus on the heroic industrialist in popular magazines, she argues:

> Lowenthal's account ... normalises the category of business celebrity as somehow allowed and respectable. Business celebrities are not distracting figures of mass entertainment; they aren't somehow not 'real' celebrities, not the real false idols.
>
> *(Littler 2007, 232)*

Instead, she suggests that analysing the media and forms of cultural mediation through which we access business celebrities is just as important for understanding them (if not more so) as it is for other forms of celebrity. The difference between the average CEO and a business celebrity is that the latter's profiles 'extend beyond the financial or business sectors of the media' (2007, 233). The celebrity of CEOs is an intrinsic part of their business practice. For instance, in their book *Demystifying Business Celebrity*, Guthey et al. note that, for Richard Branson, '[he] and Virgin are inseparable, so that both the company and the media invariably spice up news about Virgin with tales of Branson's flamboyant personality' (Guthey 2009, 2). This is certainly the case with the companies and CEOs that we look at. Guthey et al. emphasise the labour that goes into producing this celebrity, and the number of people involved in such work, both inside the company and externally. There is a dispersed apparatus that produces and distributes the CEO's celebrity so it can be consumed by its audiences. This involves, among other things, journalists, editors, publicists, photographers, websites, image rights, publications, and consumer devices. A list directly comparable to Gamson's.

For Guthey and co-authors, business celebrities have an important sociological function:

> in large part ... they function both to highlight and smooth over some of the key cultural and ideological tensions generated by the dominance of business institutions in contemporary society, as well as some of the key challenges and struggles faced by the people who must work and manage inside these institutions.
>
> *(4)*

Indeed, the example of Branson is instructive: he is a role model and friend to many of the billionaires that are the subjects of our case studies here (so much so that we eventually decided to include his autobiography, *Losing My Virginity*, in our concordance). Larry Page got married on Branson's private Caribbean island and Branson was reported to have been the best man. Elon Musk also hangs out on his island, apparently networking with luminaries such as Tony Blair, even though Musk also competes with Branson in the area of space technologies (Vance 2015, 184, 366). Branson is one of the endorsers of Sheryl Sandberg's *Lean In*, and he is cited by Brad Stone as an inspiration for Jeff Bezos at Amazon (2013, 89). Indeed, the Branson/Virgin model of using CEO celebrity to drive business growth is now a key underpinning of the founder cults of Silicon Valley.

While there has been a trend of leveraging the personality of a CEO for the benefit of promoting a business since at least the 1980s (although this waned somewhat in the 1990s, see Littler 2007, 236), it is important to note that billionaire celebrity on the scale we are looking at here is rare. Despite having their own dedicated media sphere in terms of publications like *Forbes*, *Fortune*, *Bloomberg* and the newspaper business pages, Page et al. note that, in general, 'billionaires … are very busy … protect[ing] their privacy … [and] have no desire at all to reveal their private lives to strangers' (2019, 3). These tech billionaires, then, are a specific breed. After Guthey et al., we would argue that this visibility is directly connected to the depth of the 'cultural and ideological tensions' to which their activities contribute (2009, 4).

As a group, the tech CEOs are exceptionally public facing. And they are not simply celebrified business leaders: they also represent a form of visionary social philosophy, a collective engagement in a goal of societal transformation (recall the Jamie Bartlett quote above). Moreover, their great wealth and high social status stand in deep symbiosis with their business practices in the public eye. There is a reciprocal entanglement here: the business depends on their celebrity profile which depends on their claims that their business is socially transformational. The men and their companies should be seen as relatively stable assemblages. Facebook and Zuckerberg are as one, as are Bezos and Amazon: and each of them is presented as a man who revolutionises his respective sphere – sociality and consumption. For Elon Musk, Tesla and Space X are extensions of his heroic celebrity brand 'to save humanity'; and they, in turn, are reliant on him to drive their marketing and publicity. Moreover, the men and their companies have a pre-assumed historic significance: they are seen by critics as having ushered in a new socio-economic era in the movement from liberal capitalism to 'surveillance,' digital capitalism, or data colonialism (Zuboff 2019, Pace 2018, Couldry and Mejias 2019).

'Fuss and noise': a joint, a sword, a car

It would be missing the point to see this desire for celebrity as driven by some sort of narcissism or vanity as some have argued (Coren 2019). Those sorts of psychological attributions to distant figures confuse the mediated celebrity performance of an 'authentic self' with the actual internal drives of a personality, which will never be accessible through the processes of representational media. Instead we should look at the detail of how these celebrity personae do important strategic work for the companies with which they are associated. The generic assemblage of founder-celebrity and disruptive company is something that has worked extremely well for West Coast tech firms, and it has enabled some to become the most valuable companies in the world. This assemblage is the template that venture capitalist investors look for[5]; and it is the cultural form through which observers make sense of the social processes that emerge from these companies. The boy genius myth is integral to this assemblage: it makes the social cost of economic disruption palatable – 'those dinosaurs working for Kodak deserved to lose their jobs.'⁶ We should therefore understand the cultural mechanisms behind Tech CEO celebrity as the product of a serious sectoral expertise that has been developing since at least the 1980s and the celebrification of Steve Jobs.

Musk's celebrity performances are a brilliant place to see this 'cultural strategy' in action (Holt and Cameron 2012). His public appearances are often quite awkward affairs – he is not a traditionally charismatic public speaker, although his deportment can be quite variable and has changed over the years. At times he can come across as rather wooden, at others animated and engaging. In all his appearances, however, he presents an intellect bound into the service of urgent and/or serious issues that threaten humanity.

The final section of this discussion of Musk's celebritisation focuses on his controversial appearance on the wildly popular YouTube channel and podcast *The Joe Rogan Experience* in September 2018. From the point of view of traditional commentators on CEOs in the business pages of broadsheet newspapers, this interview would have been seen as an absolute disaster. During the podcast, Musk is seen to accept a joint from presenter Joe Rogan (who is a former Mixed Martial Artists and fight commentator turned comedian and podcast host who advocates for drug liberalisation). The interview came on the heels of a tweet in August 2018 suggesting that Musk would delist Tesla from the stock exchange at $420 a share, which had landed him in trouble with the Security and Exchange Commission on the grounds of share price manipulation. The SEC complaint against Musk resulted in a $40 million fine and he was forced to stand down as Tesla chairman, although he remained as CEO. In media coverage of all this,

FIGURE 2.1 Instagram promotion for a follow-up of Joe Rogan's Interview with Elon Musk in 2020 (Rogan 2020)

it did not escape attention that 4:20 is code in American drug subcultures for marijuana. So the joint could be seen as further playing into ongoing speculation within the mainstream press and among his online fanbase about Musk's experimentation with drugs (Keck 2018). Musk claimed in a tweet that the fine was 'worth it.' From our reading of the Rogan interview as effectively a Tesla advert – understanding the whole performance as part of his celebrity marketing strategy – he is probably right.

In the aftermath of the interview, in response to Musk taking a drag on the joint (though not inhaling), newspapers reported a huge drop in Tesla's market value of nearly 6%. This was nearly two billion dollars at the time, making it probably the most expensive toke in history. Two executives also resigned from Tesla and the company was forced to issue a public statement about the executive reshuffle which followed. The statement was addressed to staff, asking them to ignore the 'fuss and noise in the media,' and reminding them (and anyone who could navigate to the site) of more important concerns: 'What you are doing is vital to achieving an amazing and sustainable energy future for all of humanity and life on Earth.' It was signed 'Elon' (Musk 2018a).

For, of course, the 'fuss and noise' in the media is precisely the point. No-one forced Musk to do the show. Instead, as with all his celebrity interviews (including the one with Strauss), it was seen as an opportunity to promote Musk's profile and, importantly, his products. The company did not suffer from the fallout in the longer term: Tesla has since become the most valuable car company in the world. Musk has also been reported as having received scoldings from NASA and the US military, but any suggestion of a threat to have his security clearance revoked has been denied by the US Air Force (Reuters 2018). And while these possible sanctions are arguably threats at the level of a business analysis, they are assets when considered through the lens of celebrity publicity. There may be a tension between Musk's promotional strategy and a stable share price for his companies, but as a longer-term means to increase the value of his companies, the celebrity strategy seems to be working.

The trick to a Joe Rogan interview is to just keep talking. They last for hours: Musk's here lasts for two hours and thirty-seven minutes. The longest we have found among the 1,200+ podcasts is with far-right conspiracy theorist Alex Jones, which lasted four hours and forty minutes (Feb 2019). The viewing figures are astronomical. Musk's interview has been watched over 32 million times. Jones's, by comparison, has been viewed a little over 19 million times, though it was filmed six months later and so is still catching up. Conservative self-help guru Jordan Peterson, once a regular on the show – he appeared at least five times between 2016 and 2018 – has viewing figures ranging from 4.5 million to nearly 9 million, with each episode lasting somewhere between two and a half to three and a half hours. The interview with Bernie Sanders, whom Rogan supported for president before switching his endorsement to Trump when Sanders dropped out, had 12 million views, and lasted a little over an hour.

Rogan occupies a new location in cultural politics that hybridises libertarian and conservative views with populist elements from the political left. He conducts his interviews sitting in front of a dulled Stars and Stripes, thus positioning his interviews within a tradition of rebellious nationalism commonly found among the American right. Other symbols of countercultural rebellion adorn the table at which he sits, providing both a theatrical "set" for the interviews and objects of interest with which to direct the flow of conversation. These include bottles of whisky, Buddha statues, and a King Kong lamp.

Rogan is a key node in what the *New York Times* dubbed 'The Intellectual Dark Web' [IDW]: a network of self-publicising intellectuals that say on the internet the sort of contrarian anti-feminist and 'heretical' content that has circulated in places like *Sp!ked* Magazine in the UK for many years (Weiss 2018). Key to this network is Eric Weinstein, the managing director of Peter Thiel's investment vehicle Thiel Capital. (We discuss Thiel's role in bringing conservative values to Silicon Valley companies later in this book.) Links to the 'Alt-Right' have also been made through this network, in spaces – such as Rogan's podcast – that have offered far-right provocateurs like Milo Yiannopoulos and neo-fascist Proud Boys founder Gavin McInnes a platform to share with the IDW heretics. Rogan also interviewed former Google employee James Damore, a figure celebrated by the alt-right for criticising diversity initiatives at his employer, discussed more fully in Chapter 7 of this book. Although Rogan himself does not voice the sort of racist views for which some of the interviewees on his show have become famous, he has been accused of transphobia and racism on other platforms (Matthews 2020), and he uses controversy as a central part of his performances. In one stand-up routine, Rogan imitates a feminist critic, adopting a falsetto voice and complaining, 'Your point of view is terrible,' before responding, 'Yeah it's how I make a living' (*Strange Times* 2018) – a joke that works through its proximity to the accusations levelled at him.

Yet Rogan also provides a space for Democrat presidential hopefuls like Tulsi Gabbard and Bernie Sanders, although it's important to note that these are politicians whose views are contrary to the Democrat mainstream. As Bhaskar Sunkara, editor of successful socialist journal *Jacobin* puts it, this is good news for the Democrats, as Rogan's fans represent 'a group of people we can't afford to cede to Trump' (Sunkara 2020). Sunkara admits to being a long-term fan of the show, albeit one who is critical of much of the content and appalled by some of the guests:

> His appeal for me, and I imagine the same goes for much of his mostly male and mostly young viewership, is that he seems more immediately familiar to us than most custodians of culture in 21st century America.

This might go some way to explain Elon Musk's appearance on the show. It appeals to, and is targeted at, young, intellectually curious men. Its audience is based in, drawn from, and produces crossover demographics between mixed martial arts, comedy, and contrarian politics. This is a potent audience for Musk to market to. It is perhaps worth noting here that Tesla do not do paid advertising. All their marketing is done below the line, through the live events discussed earlier or through the celebrity performances of their founder.

Musk's interview with Rogan circles around a few points that allow him to rehearse promotional material for his new companies – Neuralink (brain-electronics interfacing) and The Boring Company (drilling tunnels and selling blow torches as flame-throwers) – while repeatedly cycling back to Tesla. Neuralink and The Boring Company both operate as interlinked marketing devices for the sale of cars. Just as SpaceX reinforces the visionary image of its founder and thus scaffolds his other companies, these two new companies allow Musk to expand his repertoire of potentially world-saving activities to include dealing with both the perils of AI (let's merge with it through Neuralink) and the notorious LA traffic (Tunnels!).

The chat moves from Musk's products to his general brilliance and back again to his products. The discussion also loops to the themes of natural hierarchy offered by the boy genius narratives, as Rogan tries to assert that Musk might have a genetic mutation or be an alien, as a way of explaining his superior intellect. Musk modestly demurs – 'not bad for a chimp,' he says – but the comparison stands. Musk also discusses being on the set of a Hollywood action movie while at the same time floating a pet theory about reality being a simulation, thus combining his science fiction dystopianism with his celebrity insider status – folding the two together.

The key moment in this interview – which we identify as getting to the heart of the concatenation of forms of masculinity on display, both on the *Joe Rogan Experience* and in Musk's wider celebrity performances – starts by following a discussion of AI with one about social justice campaigns and social movements, before making a bizarre segue to weapons, and then back to Tesla. We reproduce the transcript at length here so that the reader can see what is going on, although we would recommend watching the video itself for full clarity (Rogan #1169 2018, 53.10 and onwards):

Musk: We should take the set of actions which are most likely to make the future better.
Rogan: Yes. Right. [Musk: Yeah]. Right, right.
Musk: And then re-evaluate those actions to make sure that's true.
Rogan: Well I think there's a movement there, I mean in terms of a social movement, I think some of it's misguided, and some of it's exaggerated and there's a lot of people who are fighting for their side out there. But it seems like the general trend of like, uh, social awareness seems to be much more heightened now than there's ever been at any other time in history. Because of our ability to express ourselves instantaneously to each other through Facebook or Twitter or what have you. And that the trend is to

abandon pre-conceived notions, abandon prejudice, abandon discrimination and promote kindness and happiness as much as possible. Look at this knife, somebody gave it to me. Sorry.

Musk: Yeah what is this?

Rogan: [inaudible] What the fuck did you do? Ah my friend Donny he brought this with him and it just stayed here. I have a real samurai sword if you want to have a play with that. I know you're into weapons. That's from the 1500s.

Musk: Really?

Rogan: Samurai sword at the end of the table, yeah I'll grab it.

Musk: Well that's cool.

Rogan: Hold on.

[Musk examines combat knife, Rogan fetches sword.]

Rogan: [passes to Musk] That's a legit samurai sword from an actual samurai from the 1500s. If you pull out that blade, that blade was made the old way. [Musk: folded metal?] Where a master craftsman folded that metal and hammered it down over and over again. Over a long period of time and honed that blade into what it is now. What's crazy is that more than 500 years later that thing is still pristine. I mean, whoever took care of that and passed it down to the next person who took care of it until it got to the podcast room. It's pretty fucking crazy.

Musk: Yeah.

Rogan: One day someone's going to be looking at a Tesla like that. Oo these fucking back doors they pop up sideways like a Lamborghini.

Musk: You should see what a Tesla can do!

(*Joe Rogan Experience #1169 53–55mins 2018*)

There are a number of notable things happening in this segment. The jumping-off point is Musk's particularly geeky way of framing his moral mission. But Rogan's role becomes to reconcile that with the more traditional forms of masculinity that he demonstrates. He creates a space for the two forms of masculinity to merge. The discussion of social justice and kindness must immediately be transformed into a discussion of weapons to maintain the masculine status of the two men. It is Rogan who reaches for first the dagger and then the sword, but Musk is absorbed by both. Rogan sets up the comparison between the sword and a Tesla to preserve Musk some modesty, but Musk takes the cue and runs with it. See Figure 2.1.

Musk and Rogan, between them, smooth the tensions between the heroic-world-saving-work that Tesla does through the sale of electric cars, and the lack of a personified opponent to defeat in climate change, by shifting the register to weapons and weaponry, and making Tesla equivalent both to the ultimate prestige weapon – the samurai sword – and the ultimate car-as-status-symbol, a Lamborghini. And we can all be part of this superheroic narrative through becoming one of Musk's army of sidekicks; we can defeat the ultimate video-game boss-level challenge of our age, climate change, by buying a $35,000 car.

Particular forms of masculinity are invoked to go beyond the geeky language at the beginning of the quote. These include, to be sure, the invocation of the noble warrior of traditional hegemonic masculinity, but also the story of the sword's patrimonial standing, passed down from father to son: a patriarchal legacy for a warrior caste. The combination of this with the comparison to Tesla as a similar object – a prized possession to be handed down within families as a marker of particular social standing – brings the sword-car into the ambit of a patriarchal transmission of status and authority. Like the samurai to the daimyo, a Tesla-branded car marks the standing of a household as part of the Musk clan. It binds its owners in service to his household – not entirely symbolically, given the fervour of his online following. The sword also recalls the comments that Tony Stark makes in his product-launch style entrance at the start of *Iron Man 2*, here quoted in full: 'It's not about me, it's not about you, it's not even about us, it's about legacy. It's about what we choose to leave behind for future generations.' A sword, a car, a robotic flying suit bristling with weapons: in Muskland, broadly speaking, all these hold an equivalence – and what is at stake with all of them is the world.

We have no reason to doubt Musk's sincerity in believing that he wants to tackle climate change, or stop runaway artificial intelligence, or build a 'planetary back-up' on Mars. But equally, we recognise that his method for getting there involves laying claim to an emerging celebrified form of hegemonic masculinity, and, as a result, accruing great wealth, power, and influence.

Notes

1 This is moderated sometimes by claims of the benefits of Montessori schooling in the Google example.
2 See YouGov indexes on celebrity popularity where most of the entrepreneurs in this book have net popularity ratings (positive views less negative views) of close to 0 or lower: https://yougov.co.uk/topics/finance/explore/public_figure/Elon_Musk
3 O'Neill describes the seduction community as 'a very particular set of knowledge-practices organised around the belief that the ability to meet and attract women is a skill heterosexual men can cultivate through practical training and personal development.' (O'Neill 2018, 3).
4 Evgeny Morozov (among others) critiques this framework as 'solutionism' arguing that is 'dangerously reductionist' (2013, 14).
5 See for instance insiders making the case explicitly for this form of celebrity: 'founders should ultimately be product/engineering types and … there should be a tight coupling between the product visionary and the individual responsible for driving the company's strategy and resource allocation decisions' (Kupor 2019, 22).
6 The dinosaur narrative informs the plot of the 2013 film *The Internship* where two watch salesmen, played by Vince Vaughn and Owen Wilson, are told by boss John Goodman that they're 'dinosaurs' as he lets them go. They then reinvent themselves as Google employees and learn to adapt to this new world post internet-meteor strike.

References

60 Minutes (2018) 'Tesla CEO Elon Musk: The 60 Minute Interview' *CBS*. www.cbsnews.com/news/tesla-ceo-elon-musk-the-2018-60-minutes-interview/ Last accessed 02/05/2020
Aquaman (2018) James Wan (dir) Warner Brothers.
Arthurs, Jane and Ben Little (2016) *Russell Brand: Comedy, Celebrity, Politics*. London: Palgrave Macmillan.
Banet-Weiser, Sarah (2018) *Empowered: Popular Feminism and Popular Misogyny*. Durham, Duke University Press.
Bartlett, Jamie (2018) *The People vs Tech: How the Internet is Killing Democracy (and How We Can Save It)*. London: Ebury Press.
Berger, Esther (2014) 'The Boring Sexism of HBO's "Silicon Valley"' *New Republic*, 30 May. https://newrepublic.com/article/117963/hbos-silicon-valleys-boring-sexism Last accessed 02/05/2020.
Betas (2013–2014) *Amazon Prime Video*. www.amazon.co.uk/Pilot/dp/B00ET0MZDW/ Last accessed 02/05/2020.
Branson, Richard (2002) *Losing My Virginity: How I Survived, Had Fun, and Made a Fortune Doing Business My Way*. 2nd Edition. London: Virgin Books.
Brynjolfsson, Erik and Andrew Mcafee (2014) *The Second Machine Age: Work, Progress, and Prosperity in a Time of Brilliant Technologies*. New York: W. W. Norton.
Chadwick, A. (2013) *The Hybrid Media System: Politics and Power*. Oxford: Oxford University Press.
Chang, Emily (2018) *Brotopia: Breaking Up the Boys Club of Silicon Valley*. New York: Penguin.
Chuck (2007–2012) NBC.
Connell, R. W., and J. Messerschmidt (2005) 'Hegemonic Masculinity: Rethinking the Concept' *Gender and Society*, 19, 829–859.
Coren, Michael (2019) 'Elon Musk May Not Be the Narcissist Tesla Needs Right Now' *Quartz*, 3 March. https://qz.com/1561985/elon-musk-may-not-be-the-narcissist-tesla-needs-right-now/ Last accessed 02/05/2020.
Couldry, Nick and Ulises Mejias (2018) 'Data Colonialism: Rethinking Big Data's Relation to the Contemporary Subject' *Television and New Media*, 20:4, 336–349.
Couldry, Nick and Ulises A. Mejias (2019) *The Costs of Connection: How Data is Colonizing Human Life and Appropriating it for Capitalism*. Stanford: Stanford University Press.
Davenport, Christian (2018) *The Space Barons: Elon Musk, Jeff Bezos and the Quest to Colonize the Cosmos*. New York: Public Affairs (Hachette).
Digital Trends (2019) 'WATCH LIVE! Elon Musk Presents the New Tesla Cybertruck Launch' *YouTube*. www.youtube.com/watch?v=SwvDOdBHYBw Last accessed 02/05/2020.
Driessens, Olivier (2013) 'The Celebritization of Society and Culture: Understanding the Structural Dynamics of Celebrity Culture' *International Journal of Cultural Studies*, 16:6, 641–657. doi:10.1177/1367877912459140
Friends (1994–2004) NBC.
Galloway, Scott (2017) *The Four: The Hidden DNA of Amazon, Apple, Facebook and Google*. London: Transworld (Penguin).
Gamson, Joshua (1994) *Claims to Fame: Celebrity in Contemporary America*. Berkeley: University of California Press.
Gilbert, Jeremy and Alex Williams (2019) 'Hegemony Now: Power and Politics in the 21st Century Part 1' *Culture, Power, Politics Podcast*. https://culturepowerpolitics

.org/2018/07/10/hegemony-now-power-in-the-twenty-first-century-part-1/ Last accessed 02/05/20.

Ging, Debbie (2017) 'Alphas, Betas, and Incels: Theorizing the Masculinities of the Manosphere' *Men and Masculinites*, 22(4), 638–657.

Gramsci, Antonio (1971) *Selections from The Prison Notebooks*, trans. Quentin Hoare. London: Lawrence and Wishart.

Grigoriadis, Vanessa (2014) 'O.K., Glass: Make Google Eyes' *Vanity Fair*, 12 March. www.vanityfair.com/style/2014/04/sergey-brin-amanda-rosenberg-affair Last accessed 02/05/2020.

Grimes (2019) *We Appreciate Power*. London: 4AD.

Guthey, Eric, Timothy Clark, and Brad Jackson, (2009) *Demystifying Business Celebrity*. Abingdon: Routledge.

Hakim, Jamie (2019) *Work That Body: Male Bodies in Digital Culture*. London: Rowman & Littlefield.

Halt and Catch Fire (2014–2017) AMC.

Hamilton, Carroll (2011) *Affirmative Reaction: New Formations of White Masculinity*. Durham: Duke University Press.

Holt, Douglas and Douglas Cameron (2012) *Cultural Strategy: Using Innovative Ideologies Build Breakthrough Brands*. Oxford: Oxford University Press.

Iron Man 2 (2010) Jon Favreau (dir) Marvel Studios.

Joe Rogan: Strange Times (2018) Netflix. www.netflix.com/title/80215419 Last accessed 02/05/2020.

Karlin (2014) 'Hackers vs. Scorpion: Walter O'Brien Responds To Scrutiny of Real-Life Claims Fueling TV's "Scorpion"' *Fast Company*, 15 October. www.fastcompany.com/3036897/hackers-vs-scorpion-walter-obrien-responds-to-scrutiny-of-real-life-claims-fueling-tvs-scorp Last accessed 02/05/2020.

Keck, Catie (2018) 'Elon Musk Claims "420" Tweet with $20 Million SEC Fine Was "Worth It"' *Gizmodo*, 27 October. https://gizmodo.com/elon-musk-claims-420-tweet-with-20-million-sec-fine-wa-1830050362 Last accessed 02/05/2020.

Kupor, Scott (2019) *Secrets of Sand Hill Road: Venture Capital and How to Get It*. London: Virgin Books.

Leslie, Ian (2014) 'Kodak vs Instagram: This Is Why It's Only Going to Get Harder to Make a Good Living' *New Statesman*, 28 January. www.newstatesman.com/politics/2014/01/kodak-vs-instagram-why-its-only-going-get-harder-make-good-living Last accessed 02/05/2020.

Littler, Jo (2007) 'Celebrity CEOs and the Cultural Economy of Tabloid Intimacy' in S. Holmes and S. Redmond (eds.) *Stardom and Celebrity: A Reader*. Los Angeles, CA: SAGE, pp. 230–243.

Losse, Katherine (2012) *The Boy Kings: A Journey Into the Heart of the Social Network*. New York: Free Press.

Machete Kills (2013) Robert Rodriguez (dir) Quick Draw Productions.

Mark, Wheeler (2013) *Celebrity Politics*. Cambridge: Polity Press.

Marshall, P. David (2014) *Celebrity and Power: Fame in Contemporary Culture*. Minneapolis: University of Minnesota Press.

Marwick, Alice (2013) *Status Update: Status, Publicity and Branding in the Social Media Age*. New Haven: Yale University Press.

Massanari, Adrienne (2017) '#Gamergate and The Fappening: How Reddit's Algorithm, Governance, and Culture Support Toxic Technocultures' *New Media & Society*, 19:3, 329–346.

Matthews, Dylan (2020) 'The Joe Rogan Controversy Revealed Something Important about the American Left' *Vox*, 27 January. www.vox.com/future-perfect/2020/1/27/21081876/joe-rogan-bernie-sanders-henry-kissinger Last accessed 02/05/2020.
Men In Black: International (2019) F. Gary Gray (dir) Colombia Pictures.
Morozov, Evgeny (2013) *To Save Everything, Click Here: Technology, Solutionism, and the Urge to Fix Problems That Don't Exist*. London: Allen Lane.
Musk, Elon (2018a) 'Company Update' *Tesla.com*, 7 September. www.tesla.com/en_GB/blog/company-update Last accessed 02/05/2020.
Musk, Elon (2018b) 'Varies Per Person…' *Twitter*. https://twitter.com/elonmusk/status/1067175527180513280 Last accessed 04/05/2020.
Nakamura, Lisa (2008) *Digitizing Race: Visual Cultures of the Internet*. Minneapolis: University of Minnesota Press.
Nash Information Services (2020) 'All Time Worldwide Box Office for Super Hero Movies' *The Numbers*. www.the-numbers.com/box-office-records/worldwide/all-movies/creative-types/super-hero Last accessed 02/05/2020.
O'Neill, Rachel (2018) *Seduction: Men, Masculinity and Mediated Intimacy*. London: Polity.
Pace, Jonathan (2018) 'The Concept of Digital Capitalism' *Communication Theory (1050–3293)*, 28:3, 254–269.
Page, Benjamin, Jason Seawright, and Matthew Lacombe (2019) *Billionaires and Stealth Politics*. Chicago: University of Chicago Press.
Pao, Ellen (2017) *Reset: My Fight for Inclusion and Lasting Change*. New York: Spiegel & Grau.
Pramuk, Jacob (2015) 'Elon Musk: "I'm Not Really a Fan of Disruption"' *CNBC Disruptor 50*, 8 June. www.cnbc.com/2015/06/08/elon-musk-im-not-really-a-fan-of-disruption.html Last accessed 02/05/2020 Last accessed 02/05/2020.
Pyke, Karen D. and Denise L. Johnson (2003) 'Asian American Women and Racialized Femininities: "Doing" Gender Across Cultural Worlds' *Gender and Society*, 17:1, 33–53.
Rachel, Massaro (2020) *Silicon Valley Index 2020*. San Jose: Joint Venture Silicon Valley. https://jointventure.org/images/stories/pdf/index2020.pdf Last accessed 02/05/2020.
Reuters (2018) 'Reports That Musk Security Clearance under Review Are Inaccurate: US Air Force' *Technology News*. www.reuters.com/article/us-tesla-musk-air-force/reports-that-musk-security-clearance-under-review-are-inaccurate-u-s-air-force-idUSKCN1LN2OF Last accessed 02/05/2020.
Rick and Morty (2013-present) Adult Swim.
Rogan, Joe (2018) '#1169 – Elon Musk' *The Joe Rogan Experience YouTube*. www.youtube.com/watch?v=ycPr5-27vSI Last accessed 02/05/2020.
Rogan, Joe (2020) 'Round 2 with the super genius!' *Instagram* www.instagram.com/p/B_4E38blUaf/?hl=en Last accessed 21/02/2021.
Rushe, Dominic (2018) 'Elon Musk Wins Approval for "Staggering" Pay Deal with Potential $55bn Bonus' *The Guardian*, 21 March. www.theguardian.com/technology/2018/mar/21/elon-musk-tesla-bonus-pay Last accessed 02/05/2020.
Salter, Anastasia and Bridget Blodgett (2018) *Toxic Geek Masculinity in Media: Sexism, Trolling, and Identity Policing*. Basingstoke: Palgrave.
Sandberg, Sheryl and Nell Scovell (2013) *Lean in: Women, Work, and the Will to Lead*. New York: Alfred A. Knopf.
Scorpion (2014–2018) CBS.
Sharma, A. and D. Grant (2011) 'Narrative, Drama and Charismatic Leadership The Case of Apple's Steve Jobs' *Leadership*, 7, 3–26.

Sharman, Jon (2016) 'Facebook's Mark Zuckerberg Reveals Iron Man-Style AI System Installed In His House: Morgan Freeman-Voiced System Even Makes the Toast' *Indy/Life*, 21 December. www.independent.co.uk/life-style/gadgets-and-tech/mark-zuckerberg-facebook-edwin-jarvis-ai-home-made-artificial-intelligence-morgan-freeman-a7488301.html Last accessed 02/05/2020.
Silicon Valley TV Show (2014-present) HBO.
South Park (1997-present) Comedy Central.
Star Trek: The Original Series (1966–1969) NBC.
Steve Jobs (2015) Danny Boyle (dir) Legendary Pictures.
Stone, Brad (2013) *The Everything Store: Jeff Bezos and the Age of Amazon*. New York: Transworld.
Strauss, Neil (2005) *The Game*. New York: Regan Books.
Strauss, Neil (2017) 'Elon Musk: The Architect of Tomorrow' *Rolling Stone*, 15 November. www.rollingstone.com/culture/culture-features/elon-musk-the-architect-of-tomorrow-120850/ Last accessed 02/05/2020.
Street, John (2004) 'Celebrity Politicians: Popular Culture and Political Representation' *British Journal of Politics and International Relations*, 6:4, 435–452.
Sunkara, Bhaskar (2020) 'Why the Joe Rogan Endorsement Is a Good Thing for Bernie Sanders' *Guardian*, 25 January. www.theguardian.com/commentisfree/2020/jan/25/joe-rogan-bernie-sanders-endorsement-democrats Last accessed 02/05/2020.
Tajima, Renee E. (1989) 'Lotus Blossoms Don't Bleed: Images of Asian Women' in Asian Women United of California (ed.) *Making Waves*. Boston: Beacon.
Tasker, Yvonne (1993) *Spectacular Bodies : Gender, Genre, and the Action Cinema*. Abingdon: Routledge.
Tesla (2016) 'Tesla Unveils Model 3' *YouTube*. www.youtube.com/watch?v=Q4VGQPk2Dl8 Last accessed 02/05/2020
Thank You For Smoking (2005) Jason Reitman (dir) Room 9 entertainment.
The Big Bang Theory (2007–2019) CBS.
The Internship (2013) Shawn Levy (dir) Regency Productions.
The Simpsons (1989-present) Fox.
ThirdRow (2020) 'Episode 7 – Elon Musk's Story – Director's Cut' *YouTube*. www.youtube.com/watch?v=J9oEc0wCQDE&t=565s Last accessed 02/05/2020.
Transcendence (2014) Wally Pfister (dir) Alcon Entertainment.
Turner, Graeme (2007) 'The Economy of Celebrity' in S. Holmes and S. Redmond (eds.) *Stardom and Celebrity: A Reader*. Los Angeles, CA: SAGE Publications Ltd, pp. 193–205.
Vance, Ashlee (2015) *Elon Musk: How the Billionaire CEO of SpaceX and Tesla Is Shaping our Future*. London: Virgin Books.
Weiss, Bari (2018) 'Meet the Renegades of the Intellectual Dark Web' *New York Times*, 8 May. www.nytimes.com/2018/05/08/opinion/intellectual-dark-web.html Last accessed 02/05/2020.
Westworld (2016–present) HBO.
Why Him? (2016) John Hamburg (dir) 21 Laps Entertainment.
Young Sheldon (2017–present) CBS.
Yurieff, Kaya (2017) 'Jeff Bezos Tests Giant Robot Suit' *CNN Business*, 20 March. https://money.cnn.com/2017/03/20/technology/jeff-bezos-giant-robot/index.html Last accessed 02/05/2020.
Zuboff, Shoshona (2019) *The Age of Surveillance Capitalism: The Fight for a Human Future at the New Frontier of Power*. London: Profile Books.

3

JEFF BEZOS

Beyond the American frontier

> Explorers are cool.
> Conquerors are not cool
> …
>
> Missionaries are cool.
> Mercenaries are not cool.
>
> Jeff Bezos 'Love Amazon memo' (Stone 2014, 389)

In August 2014, Jeff Bezos, founder of Amazon, rocket ship company Blue Origin and investment umbrella Bezos Expeditions, took the Amyotrophic Lateral Sclerosis Association (ALSA) Ice Bucket Challenge.[1] This 'viral challenge meme,' which spread across the world that summer and has been repeated in various forms for various causes every year since, involves pouring a bucket of ice water over your head and filming it (Burgess, Miller and Moore 2018). Before doing the challenge you nominate three more people to do it after you, who can either accept or donate money to the ALSA, but preferably both.

Bezos's video is organised around his laugh – which is a defining part of his celebrity and an impressive strategic asset. When you hear it, distinctive and piercing, it's disarming. One might, of course, wonder how a famously demanding boss and manager, who runs a company that, according to one investigative report, turns its 'warehouses into injury mills' (Evans 2019), can have such a warm and interesting laugh. Bezos biographer Brad Stone says the billionaire uses his laugh 'like a weapon.' He gives a florid description of encountering it in a meeting where he was setting out the scope of his book to its primary subject:

> When he realized what I was up to, he laughed so hard that spit came flying out of his mouth. Much has been made over the years of Bezos's famous laugh. It's a startling, pulse-pounding bray that he leans into while craning

his neck back, closing his eyes, and letting loose with a guttural roar that sounds like a cross between a mating elephant seal and a power tool. Often it comes when nothing is obviously funny to anyone else. In a way, Bezos's laugh is a mystery that has never been solved; one doesn't expect someone so intense and focused to have a raucous laugh like that, and no one in his family seems to share it.

(Stone 2014, 22)

In the ALSA challenge video, after Bezos pours the bucket of ice over his head, a slow-motion replay is then shown with his laugh edited over the soundtrack (Figure 3.1). Water and ice crash down over his light blue shirt and black denim jeans before he waves goodbye to camera, promising to see us next time (Amazon 2014). While people close to Bezos assert it has long been part of his identity (we learn from Stone that 'his booming, uninhibited laugh occasionally' embarrassed his siblings (Stone 2014, 190)), we can also see clearly that Bezos's PR team use it as a deliberate part of his celebrity performance. And the viral videos for the ALSA were all about performing celebrity.

In this chapter we focus on Bezos's mythic celebrity narrative, taking his participation in the Ice Bucket Challenge as an example, and as a way of revealing the gendered networks of which he is a part. We understand Bezos's philanthropic performance in this video to be indicative of how he asserts his power on a global stage. We also consider Bezos's fandom for the geek popular text *Star Trek* – which he invokes in his nominations for the Ice Bucket Challenge. This, in turn, is closely linked to his connections to 1960s counterculture. These elements of the Bezos persona coalesce to create a tech-culture variation on the great American industrialist. And this also extends to his view of the state, which

FIGURE 3.1 Jeff Bezos and the Ice Bucket Challenge

should support his herculean efforts at transforming digital 'wilderness' into productive civilisation or stay out of his way. This heroic American figure depends on the frontier spirit that has played a major role in the creation of Silicon Valley: this is a mythology to which Bezos consistently returns.

Frontier mythology glosses over the violence of settler colonialism, and organises itself around the American identity of the gritty and resourceful pioneer, as well as a specific imaginary of the colonial household. The old pioneer myths obscure the intersecting forms of oppression – race, class, and gender – that were involved in establishing the frontier lands. Our argument is that the specific structures of power and control this produced persist today; in the twenty-first century, this ideology – and its imaginary of the colonial household – is marshalled as a digital era re-invocation of the American frontier spirit.

We also extend these ideas about the frontier and the household to think about the Amazon assemblage more generally. This is a company that was founded in the private Bezos household, by a man who seeks parsimony and 'leanness' in his organisation. We ask what effects the founder's impulse to explore, and his missionary zeal – as invoked in the quotation at the beginning of this chapter – have had on workers, consumers, products, and citizens.

Ice Bucket Challenge: philanthropy and celebrity

Tech leaders were prominent participants in the Ice Bucket Challenge phenomenon, and through this we can see the networks of influence and patronage that they command. Mark Zuckerberg was nominated by then Republican governor of New Jersey Chris Christie, and in turn nominated his COO Sheryl Sandberg, as well as Microsoft's Bill Gates and Netflix's Reed Hastings. Sandberg's nominees were three women, including Melinda Gates and tech journalist Kara Swisher (see Chapter 6), and she stood alongside baseball player Jimmy Rollins to do the challenge. The challenge became a form of celebrity daisy-chain, crossing spheres of celebrity from politics, to technology, to entertainment, to sports. Nominating someone became a cheeky marker of respect, inviting them to a form of public humiliation that, while ridiculous, would also provide them with an opportunity to demonstrate their philanthropic good humour. Gates accepted Zuckerberg's challenge and nominated Elon Musk. Gates and Musk both built contraptions to deliver the icy water, ensuring that even in this whimsical activity, their celebrity was bound up with their technological aptitude. The challenge 'set the parameters for expressions of individuality,' according to Burgess et al. (2018, 1040): it was an opportunity to refine a celebrity public image and project an idea of your peer networks in a way that was playful, virtuous, and indicative of a claim to equality of status with those you nominated.

Jeff Bezos was nominated, alongside Google's Larry Page, by present Microsoft CEO Satya Nadella. The challenge was presumptuous: it asserted an equality within Founder/CEO networks that isn't there for Nadella (as reflected in our concordance for instance). Page and Brin (the latter presumably nominated by someone else) responded, in their 'don't be evil' playful fashion, by emphasising the charity itself, while bravely wearing t-shirts from the satirical HBO series *Silicon Valley* (see Chapter 2), which presents tech CEOs such as themselves as deranged, vicious narcissists. In the video, Brin claims that the meme is an intra-executive 'taunt,' but he fails to mention anyone else he would challenge (Google 2014). Presumably, the 'Google Guys' are without peers.

These are key moments for the assertion of a particular kind of celebrity – Chris Rojek's idea of 'celanthropy': a bringing together of the logics of celebrity and philanthropy to solve problems previously reserved for the state, in this case researching treatment for a chronic disease (Rojek 2014). For the tech founders, this sort of cultural opportunity enables them to perform their social value, while simultaneously demonstrating how the social media technologies they develop could solve major societal problems in a 'fun' way – many of the videos were hosted on Google's YouTube challenge, while circulating on sites like Facebook and Twitter. Yet, the Ice Bucket Challenge is also typical of celebrity fundraising in that it fails to 'go beyond event consciousness' (Rojek 2014): it does not even seek to educate audiences about what ALS is, let alone feed any discussion of how medical research is funded and prioritised. Instead, it serves to show how wealthy celebrities and social media can come together to raise vast sums of money for an interchangeable worthy cause.

A brief, multi-author network analysis of the ice bucket phenomenon in the *British Medical Journal* suggested that the net worth of the challenger was a key indicator of whether a challenge was likely to be accepted (Ni et al. 2014). That Mark Zuckerberg triggered the longest chain of celebrity ice bucketeers in their analysis supports this idea. Bezos himself described the question of who to challenge as 'very important … and not one to be taken lightly' (Amazon 2014). Effectively, these videos perform networks of celebrity status, offering patronage, supplication, and competition within a neat format. As discussed in earlier chapters (and following Ortner 2014), these networks are formed through the tension between collaboration and competition that characterises the patriarchal tech founder milieu. They are also, here, heavily inscribed with gender. Aside from the special case of Sandberg (see Chapter 6), who was nominated by Mark Zuckerberg, in all the tech industry examples we watched at least, men nominated men and women nominated women.

For his challenge, Bezos appears on a large stage with an Amazon-branded podium to his right (Amazon 2014). There is an echo in the room (perhaps indicating size) and the audience is barely shown beyond a few clapping hands at the end. Given Bezos's ready supply of employees and the fact that Amazon regularly uses theatres and other public venues for large staff meetings, we are tempted to infer that it is staged before a real audience of Amazon employees, with minor editing undertaken by Amazon's PR team before posting online. Bezos graciously acknowledges his friend and fellow Seattle-based tech CEO 'Satya,' before going into a sort of stand-up routine where he associates himself with figures who both indicate his claims to social status and offer the opportunity for jokes. His first – 'Obviously [I'd challenge] Edward Snowden … but if [he took] the Ice Bucket Challenge it would just leak' – lands to some audience laughter, and he follows by saying he could ask the Queen and Pope, before explaining that they wouldn't do it due to wearing hats. He ends these joke suggestions by selecting Kim Jong Un as his potential third nominee, before noting that unfortunately Kim can't accept, because he isn't on American social media.

From our perspective, these jokes are revealing. Unsurprisingly, given that Amazon now controls nearly 50% of the cloud infrastructure market (Gartner 2019), Bezos's thoughts quickly turned to the matter of large-scale digital leaks, like the one for which former intelligence operative turned whistle-blower Edward Snowden was responsible, and to digital security for government in general. We don't know if Snowden leaked CIA files for which Amazon had the hosting responsibility. But it was in August 2014, the month that this video was posted to YouTube, that Amazon Webservices (AWS) announced they had received a large contract from the US Department of Defence. The current AWS website states that Bezos's company is a major provider of these services to the government:

> AWS provides commercial cloud capability across all classification levels: Unclassified, Sensitive, Secret, and Top Secret making it possible to execute missions with a common set of tools, a constant flow of the latest technology, and the flexibility to rapidly scale with the mission.
>
> *(Amazon 2019)*

The joke can thus be read as perhaps signalling that Bezos's bucket won't be leaky; and the US government's apparent agreement with this is confirmed by the signing of the deal: '"The security was really superb,"' said Gus Hunt former Chief Technical Officer at the CIA' (Whitaker 2014). Bezos's celebrity is clearly here entangled with his corporation's business activities: they are parts of the same assemblage.

The 'jokey' idea that the Queen, the Pope, and Kim Jong Un are 'obvious' choices for Bezos is also sending a message: as the then eighteenth richest person in the world at the time, he is suggesting that he is of equivalent status to these figures. The test of that equality, under the celebritised logics of the meme, would be if they accepted his challenge – which of course they wouldn't. But the suggestion of parity is made – and the joke about the Queen and Pope not being able to participate because they wear hats is also significant, given that their headwear is a key marker of their high status. The implication is that Bezos is their equal but lacks similar symbolic trappings of importance – so he can still participate in the challenge without shame or threat to his standing: he is a different kind of leader. The function of the joke is nevertheless the assertion of status equivalence: Bezos occupies the same level of global significance as the world's longest-reigning living monarch, a murderous totalitarian despot, and the spiritual leader of 1.2 billion people. 'Take that "Satya,"' Bezos could be inferred as saying.

Bezos and the state

In some ways these comparisons are not as farfetched and presumptuous as they seem. When Bezos's phone got hacked in 2020, allegedly by the Saudi Crown Prince, the FBI, DNI, and even the UN got involved (Kirchgaessner 2020) – a very different response to what happens when a normal person's data security is breached. Moreover, it could be – and has been – argued that Amazon has already taken on the role of the state in some sectors, as in the hosting of its digital security infrastructure mentioned above. Both the *Guardian's* Julia Carrie Wong and CNN (among others) have dubbed the contemporary USA the United States of Amazon. Wong has written: 'my theory of Amazon is that they are looking to replace the state and be the primary institution that people interact with on a day to day basis' (Rakusen and Wong 2019). She argues that, given that 50% of American households are Amazon Prime subscribers (the regular fee that gives access to improved video on demand, faster free delivery, and other services), this is effectively a tax paid to Bezos's company. Amazon could thus be seen to be offering services similar to those of a state – or at least with the same level of coverage: as Amazon increasingly moves into areas such as health care and insurance, the horizontal service omnipresence of Amazon risks turning 'citizens into customers' (Rakusen and Wong 2019). This comparison with statehood has been made with regard to a number of other companies featured in this book. For instance, legal scholar Anupam Chander (2012) has argued that Facebook meets at least two of the four conditions of statehood as listed under the Montevideo Convention on the Rights and Duties of States.

José van Dijck, Thomas Poell, and Martijn de Waal take a different tack. They argue that the relationship between the 'platform ecosystem' (in which Amazon plays a key part, alongside Apple, Alphabet-Google, Facebook, and Microsoft) and the state is complex, and marked by key points of ideological contestation:

> The platform ecosystem ... is moored in paradoxes: it looks egalitarian yet is hierarchical; It is almost entirely corporate, but it appears to serve public value; it seems neutral and agnostic, but its architecture carries a particular set of ideological values; its effects appear local, while its scope and impact are global; it appears to replace 'top down,' 'big government' with 'bottom up' 'customer empowerment,' yet it is doing so by means of a highly centralised structure which remains opaque to its users.
>
> *(van Dijck et al. 2018, 12)*

Concerns about the relationship between state, platform, and citizen-consumer are shared by scholars such as Lina Khan, who are worried about the way markets and competition are currently ordered and understood. She argues that one way to tame Amazon's corporate power is to understand it as a public utility like water or electricity, and to regulate it as such (Khan 2018, 121). As the products and services of tech companies become intrinsic to the contemporary state – running essential services for the military and intelligence establishment, becoming integrated into education and healthcare, being a primary source of news and used by citizens on an hourly basis and so on – this approach makes some sense. Yet it must also take into account the studied disdain that tech entrepreneurs like Bezos (and indeed most of the case study examples in the book) demonstrate for the state and public sector.

Bezos has gone to great lengths to avoid the key contribution that corporations are supposed to make to nations and states in the form of taxation. Amazon, like Facebook, Google, Apple, and many others, actively seeks to minimise its tax exposure. Indeed, Amazon-Bezos biographer Brad Stone argues that the competitive advantage brought about by avoiding sales tax in the company's early years was what allowed it to gain such a strong foothold in the online retail business. The measures taken to ensure that Amazon couldn't be accused of operating outside of its domiciled state (Washington), and so would not be liable to pay or charge sales tax in a customer's home state, were extreme:

> The [tax avoidance strategy tied to geographic location] guidelines approached the surreal. Amazon employees had to seek approval to attend trade shows and were told to avoid activities that involved promoting the sale of any products on the Amazon website while on the road. They couldn't blog or talk to the press without permission, had to avoid renting any property on trips, and couldn't place orders on Amazon from the company's computers. They could sign contracts with other companies, such as suppliers who were offering their goods for sale on the site, only in Seattle.
>
> *(Stone 2014, 356)*

It was only in the aftermath of the 2008 financial crash that Amazon started recognising that the public relations liabilities of that approach might outweigh the tax benefits (Stone 2014, 352). By that point, however, the work had been done: Amazon had become a household name and largest retailer on the web. Amazon does now, as far as we can tell, pay sales tax in almost all US states and in most other countries in which it operates, but it remains structurally committed to what is sometimes called 'tax efficiency' (Shaxson 2012) – legal tax avoidance through the use of subsidiaries and accounting measures to reduce the total tax it pays. In the UK for instance, Amazon's total tax contribution in 2018 was around £220 million on sales of £10.9 billion, and this figure includes payroll taxes like national insurance (Butler 2019).[2] This is typical behaviour for the tech monopolies we are looking at. In 2019, for instance, Google used a delightfully named corporate instrument – the 'double Irish, Dutch sandwich' – to move

£20 billion to Bermuda as part of its efforts to reduce its tax contributions. It is worth remembering (as many have noted) that, as tax revenues have fallen it has been not just poorer people in general but disproportionately women and people of colour who have suffered as a result of public-sector cuts and austerity regimes (Pashkoff 2014; Hall et al. 2017). As Zuboff points out, not only have these companies stepped into the deregulated space opened up by neoliberal capitalism: they have also deepened and entrenched inequalities through their ruthless approaches (2019). When we consider the patriarchal effects of these assemblages, the outcomes of these tax avoidance activities should be understood as part of the social intervention the companies make. Peter Thiel is explicit in this regard (see Chapter 5): he blames women and poorer people for their dependence on the state (despite Silicon Valley in general and his company Palantir specifically being part-funded by US government contracts and subsidies). Bezos and our other case studies, however, are usually invested in appearing to espouse 'progressive' values. For this reason, tax avoidance must be carefully managed, avoided, or spun as positive through the character of the CEO (e.g. through marshalling a unique laugh).

But for Bezos, the relationship with the state is also masked by the ambivalent invocation of the frontier spirit. One of the foundational theorists of the American Frontier, popular Victorian historian Frederik Turner Jackson, described the settler household's attitude to government in the following terms:

> It produces antipathy to control, and particularly to any direct control. The tax-gatherer is viewed as a representative of oppression.
>
> *(Jackson Turner [1893], 6)*

The contradictory attitudes of the frontier – where new property rights are enforced by the state, while individual pioneers see themselves as beholden to – and responsible to – no-one, can clearly be seen in the positions adopted by Bezos. In the following section we explore how his corporation and corporate personae dig deep into wells of the do-it-yourself attitude of this distinctly American mythology – and how this combines with the tech geekery that suffuses the networks we are looking at.

Seattle, the final frontier

The people Bezos finally nominates in the Ice Bucket Challenge are stars from the cult science fiction TV series *Star Trek*. This is a key cultural location for geek culture, and, as we will see, it plays a central part in Bezos's celebrity. His specific nominations are actors who played officers from the Star Ship Enterprise: William Shatner (Captain Kirk), Patrick Stewart (Captain Picard), and George Takei (Lieutenant Sulu). It is notable that, rather than opting for a female captain – for example Voyager's Kate Mulgrew (Captain Janeway) – Bezos instead nominates a lower-grade officer, the male Takei, who is a supporting character in the series (albeit one who was very popular with fans and has since developed a substantial celebrity profile in his own right, not least as a famous advocate for LGBTQ+ rights). The character of Takei was 'not once the focus of a main storyline' in the original Star Trek series (Bernardi 1997, 218). In some ways the choice of Takei ties to Bezos' longstanding support for LGBTQ+ rights, but equally reflects the strongly gendered spaces of both tech geek fandom and the frontier myth. All three actors accept the challenge – unsurprising given Bezos's rising influence in TV and film through Amazon Prime Video and Amazon Studios.

Star Trek registers a significant presence in our concordance, but there are some difficulties in measuring its frequency. It occurs often, but the Optical Character Recognition software struggles with the italicised *k* so at least some instances are missing from our searches. Nevertheless, Sketch Engine identifies its use 124 times across the books: so the phrase appears at least 12.4 times per million words in our concordance (roughly six times the background frequency on the Web enTenTen15, which does not suffer from OCR accuracy issues). *Star Trek* is frequently used as a reference point for the development of new technologies, and its leading characters are discussed as sources of inspiration: 'bold' explorers of new worlds who push humanity on to further frontiers. Google executives Eric Schmidt and Jonathan Rosenberg (2017, 256) even apologise for the number of *Star Trek* references in their book *How Google Works*.

Yet the merits of the franchise are contested among the founders. Bezos's fandom goes deep: he has even had a cameo role in a recent *Star Trek* film (Lin 2018). He invokes *Star Trek* to represent hope and the utopian future of humanity. His mother shared with Stone a copy of the high school valedictorian speech of the young Bezos:

> [it] includes the classic Star Trek opening, 'Space, the final frontier,' and discusses his dream of saving humanity by creating permanent human colonies in orbiting space stations while turning the planet into an enormous nature preserve.
>
> *(Stone 2014, 193)*

Peter Thiel, on the other hand, who like many of our celebrity subjects shares Bezos's enthusiasm for space travel, thinks *Star Trek* is a communist fantasy – as opposed to the more capitalist *Star Wars* (Thiel 2009).[3] *Star Trek* is perhaps less overtly 'capitalist,' but it is an enthusiastic embracer of the explorer mentality ('to boldly go'); later in its run, an early-phase settlement of new solar systems is explored – though it is based on a form of settlerism that 'reject[s] the farmer's implements in preference for the scientist's rockets and missiles' (Jones and Wills 2009, 43). Indeed, the original pitch for the series referred explicitly to the traditions of American settler colonialism: '*Wagon Train to the stars*,' as its creator Gene Roddenberry described it (Booker 2008, 196).

Star Trek is seen in academic literature as a key location of ideological struggle in popular culture in ways that are salient for our discussions of tech culture and the frontier. We do not want to rehearse the detail of those debates here, but we agree with Daniel Bernardi when he argues that: '*Star Trek*'s liberal-humanist project is exceedingly inconsistent and at times disturbingly contradictory, often participating in and facilitating racist practice' (Bernardi 1997, 211). As Bernardi continues, both the underpinning logics of space exploration and *Star Trek*'s liberalism are firmly located within a specific Judeo-Christian imaginary. *Star Trek*'s captains boldly go into the unknown and find it full of other life whose problems the humans can usually overcome through recourse to their superior moral values – of inclusivity and difference of course. As Booker argues, *Star Trek*'s assertion that it is 'an anticolonialist enterprise' is made problematic by 'its very connection to the taming of the American frontier, with its associated legacy of racism and genocide' (Booker 2008, 196). Moreover, the *USS Enterprise*, the starship at the centre of the series, is a name that links the colonial-era navy with contemporary military force projection through a long list of vessels bearing the name, including an aircraft carrier due to launch in 2028 (Booker 2008, 214; Newport News ND).

The military concerns that maintain a presence in *Star Trek* appear relatively few times in our database, at around half the levels in our benchmarks. (The term 'military' itself appears 67 times per million words in our concordance vs. 140/million words in the enTenTen15, and 120/million words in Google Ngram for 2008.) This might seem surprising, given the deep and historical links between the tech industry and the federally funded US defence industry. However, we would argue that hiding the military roots of the consumer-facing technology industry is a key part of its marketing strategy, and the location of American militarism in the ideological productions of West Coast tech is something that is consistently underplayed: the friendly face of the Amazon logo and Google's retired motto of 'don't be evil' mask the fact that the Silicon Valley culture – the cyberculture as counterculture narrative we discuss at length below – was rooted in Stanford University Administrator Frederik Terman's success in bringing US military research money for computing into Stanford University (Turner 2008; Cohen 2019). Both Silicon Valley and these geek fictions are a piece with the widespread downplaying of the history of violence in the US national story: the *Star Trek* that Bezos invokes so emphatically as a symbol of naïve dreaming and innocent ambition is a far more complex and contradictory cultural location than this would imply. It inhabits a world that naturalises the American settler colonialism of the Western frontier and blends it with US militarism and countercultural progressive values.

The starting point for the *Star Trek* imaginary is that 'all non-Western-style societies have, by the twenty-third century, been swept away (along with the working class) into the ashcan of history' (Booker 2008, 198). This is in line with some of the ideas of the pioneers of the 'electronic frontier' (Rheingold 1993) such as John Perry Barlow, who sees – in this case – race as an anachronistic social factor as technology and cyberspace promise a freedom from bodily constraints. Yet it is significant that, for *Star Trek*, in a post-capitalist world that has managed to dispense with race, class, and gender discrimination, the one thing they retain is American patriarchal militarism. Thus, Captain Kirk's romantic attachments with aliens (and others) in his Enterprise voyages call to mind Cynthia Enloe's observation that a primary concern for military operations outside of national borders is the conduct of soldiers and local or refugee girls and women in the vicinity. Enloe's work on the structuring links between gender and militarism is a provider of other useful insights about such parallels (Enloe 2017).

Moreover, the Star Ship Enterprise is a kind of frontier homestead in the stars, firmly under the virile authority of James T. Kirk, and with a clear hierarchy of underlings – raced, ranked, gendered and classed, and deriving their status and role in relation to the captain. This location makes visible some of what is at stake in the imaginary of the frontier household. In Chapter 1 we discussed the social unit that constitutes full personhood. As Imani Perry argues:

> The family, heralded by a man whose wife, children, and chattel attended, was the basic social unit. The patriarch represented and led the family. He was the one possessed of full personhood. People to whom he was legally related as family (rather than chattel) garnered ancillary benefits and partial benefits of personhood. The relationship between the patriarch and the other members of his household was analogous to a king or parliament's reign over the nation, and later, postmonarchy, the patriarch was analogous to the nation itself, which possessed a form of legal personality, as well.
>
> *(Perry 2018, 23)*

This understanding of the social unit of the family helps us to locate the patriarchal networks that are based on it as raced and classed, as well as gendered and bound up with heteronormative sexualities. It is hard not to see how the tech founders replicate the imaginary of this social unit in the running of their corporations.

In *Star Trek*, the patriarch – James Kirk – is attended by a hierarchy of subordinate persons, none of whom can embody his sovereignty. Most significant in this reading is the 'exotic and erotic' (Vettel-Bekker 2014) Lieutenant Uhura (played by African American Nichelle Nichols), who is, famously, the recipient of America's first televised interracial kiss. Uhura has been seen as a symbol of Black women breaking through the barriers of segregation, and *Star Trek* was reportedly praised by civil rights leader Martin Luther King Jr (Geraghty 2003), but it is telling that this first kiss is a symbolic rape: Uhura is kissed by Kirk under duress from super-powerful aliens who derive sexual pleasure from forcing lesser beings into compromising situations (*Star Trek* 1968). In the scene Kirk is also struggling to help Uhura, and is a source of inspiring authority for her: he is both her assailant and an equal victim in an unfolding mythological drama. While he is kissing her, he is looking at a white female alien who is getting aroused. The gaze is between the two white characters over the frightened Black woman. The attitudes being reproduced by this key popular culture text of the 1960s – and the sorts of structures surrounding race and gender that it draws on – still form the tech imaginary's relationship with American frontier culture. Kirk then represents the 'good settler': he uses his authority to protect and maintain his crew. He understands he has a responsibility to the aliens he encounters in his exploration and uses force for moral and defensive reasons. He embodies a traditional form of liberal masculinity that reflects the moral use of violence to resolve threats to the general good. As such he is a key figure to be mobilised in reconciling the differences between earlier forms of hegemonic masculinity and the ascendant geek cultures (as we discussed in the previous chapter).

Bezos's employment of *Star Trek* as a component in his celebrification is thus significant not only for its connections to the fan bases and geek masculinities that pervade tech culture (Ging 2017; Blodgett and Salter 2018), but also for what it reveals about both tech culture and his own relationships to the ideologies of settler colonialism and patriarchal power. There are illuminating links to be made between the idea of the frontier household and recent conceptualisations of digital capitalism as a form of colonialism (see Couldry and Mejias 2019). Indeed, we can read *Star Trek*'s conception of the bold explorer as a liberal hero as a way of helping to obscure the colonial practices that Couldry and Mejias revisit in relation to the concept of Terra Nullius (9) – the practice of treating inhabited places as legally empty, thereby justifying dispossession. In his history of the American West, Frederik Jackson Turner argued that it was the intermingling of people and values on the Western frontier that brought an end to slavery (1893, 6); in a similarly tenuous fashion, *Star Trek*, despite its ideological roots in American settler colonialism, attempts to deny its links to the racist practices of colonial history through its (in practice oft-circumvented) 'prime directive' of non-interference in alien cultures.

So Bezos has revealed a lot about himself, and the ideological space that he and Amazon occupy, simply by pouring water over his head and comparing himself to unelected world leaders and fantasy space captains. In our concordance, the possessive form 'Bezos's' is most frequently placed in relation to a 'vision' (eight times), followed by a 'dream' (five times), followed by 'laugh' (four times). In his commencement speech at Princeton, he was introduced as a 'dreamer and doer,' 'entrepreneur and engineer' (Princeton Academics 2010). Bezos presents himself not as a despot or king (that is expressly denied), but as a visionary and pioneer. His sovereignty is tied to the myth of the American frontier and reconstructed as liberal paternalism. Inspired by James T. Kirk, we are told, he dreams of exploring space and flying to new planets. However, it is precisely this conception and legitimation of his sovereignty that links him to the idea of violent colonial enterprise and its deeply entrenched hierarchies of proper personhood.

Life on the ranch

Bezos's love of *Star Trek* has been a consistent part of his public persona. But his 'trekkiness' is also part of a wider performance of celebrity that emphasises his (albeit geeky) frontier spirit. In virtually all popular media accounts of the Amazon and Bezos story, the two are completely integrated. Bezos is a striating element in the Amazon assemblage: it's very hard to look at one without seeing the mark of the other. Significantly, Stone's biography is of both Bezos and Amazon, equally, with little distinction made between the two. Everything in the book is orientated to Bezos in some way, crediting him with every success that Amazon achieves, even if in reality the company sprawls in both human and geographic terms: far beyond the mastery of a single man. Some may argue that this is a literary conceit, but this linkage is consistent across not just the biographical books in our corpus, but in all varieties of them. And it also features in the celebrified award events that the business world is currently using to mimic the star circuits of Hollywood (discussed below).

The elements of Bezos's life that appear in the biography are not, of course, his real life. Some version of them may have happened to him, but the events discussed are the carefully edited highlights, used to present him as a heroic business leader; to selectively explain the rise of Amazon; and to justify both the company's dominant market position and his own dominance of the business. In short, they are a strategic mediation. As Guthey et al. put it:

> Let's face it, no matter how much we insist upon their many fine achievements, or their authenticity, or their humility, heroic leaders and guru heroes are still elaborate media productions. Otherwise, we would never even hear about them. Except on the personal level of everyday interaction, it is not possible to have a business hero who is not also a media phenomenon. They are not *like* business celebrities, they *are* business celebrities.
>
> *(Guthey et al. 2009, 153)*

The celebrity biography of Bezos tends to cohere around a few specific themes and events – *Star Trek*, his laugh, and the location that frames his background: his childhood summers spent with his grandparents on their ranch in Cotulla, South Texas. In a recent interview with Mathias Döpfner, Bezos describes these summers in quite practical terms. He emphasises how it was always a working holiday: though the ostensible purpose was providing his parents with a break, his grandfather created the illusion, even when he was only four, that he was helping out on the ranch. As the story, goes by the age of 16 he was actually helping: he and his grandfather did everything themselves from fixing fences to veterinary work. His grandfather never asked for help from experts, he just figured out what to do himself. The lesson was 'be resourceful': 'If there's a problem, there is a solution' (Döpfner 2018).

Bezos here is tapping directly into the myth of the American West as foundational to American culture. Sloughing off the complex dependencies of European civilisation, the frontier ranch enables Americans to prove themselves as men once more:

> the advance of the frontier has meant a steady movement away from the influence of Europe, a steady growth of independence on American lines. And to study this advance, the men who grew up under these conditions, and the political, economic, and social results of it, is to study the really American part of our history.
>
> *(Turner 1893, 3)*

The 'do everything yourself' attitude presented in this celebrified childhood narrative is seen to fold over into Amazon's corporate practices.

In the Döpfner interview, Bezos is representing not just himself but also the sprawling assemblage that is Amazon and his other business ventures. He is telling a compelling story about both the Bezos family and the approach taken by his companies. One illustration of this approach in the biography is its description of what happened when Amazon needed to change its computer hardware infrastructure during a period of rapid growth: they created a solution that would not only meet their needs, but would also provide spare capacity to be rented out at periods of lower demand (Stone 2014, 263–267). That, in turn, became Amazon Web Services, now the commercial backbone of the internet with more than 50% of the cloud computing market, and which has also tended to be the most profitable of Amazon's divisions. Rather than approach another company to assist, the story goes, necessity became an opportunity for invention and entrance into a new market – and one that led to market leadership, if not monopoly. This is the DIY ranch ethic in the service of an expansionist corporate form.

The Döpfner interview was given to mark Bezos receiving the Axel Springer Award (Figure 3.2) – which, since its inauguration in 2016, has gone to Mark Zuckerberg (2016), Tim Berners-Lee who invented the World Wide Web (2017), Jeff Bezos (2018) and, remarkably, in 2019, to leading critic of digital capitalism Shoshana Zuboff (Axel Springer Award 2019). The primary platform that disseminates news of the awards is Business Insider, a company in which, having previously been an investor, Bezos had retained a small financial interest after it was bought by Axel Springer.[4] This promotional interview with Bezos is typical of the sort of celebrity business news that the Insider brand promotes.

The award was accompanied by video link-ups from Warren Buffet, Bill Gates, and Steven Spielberg, all praising their friend's achievement. Behind Bezos is a giant screen showing footage of a Blue Origin rocket in the Texan wilderness. In a pot in front of the screen, framing the spaceship, sit a pair of cacti. There are no people there, just the 'Wild West' and a rocket that looks remarkably like a phallus. Here the award ceremony has precisely represented on

FIGURE 3.2 Jeff Bezos at the Axel Springer Award, 2018

screen the specific character of Bezos's myth – its blending of space technologies, the American frontier, and geeky-but-dominant masculinity.

This image is contiguous with other managed representations of Bezos's celebrity. As we have seen, Stone's biography also feeds into these narratives. In its discussion of Bezos as a great explorer and space enthusiast, it reinforces the Bezos-Amazon corporate strategy for managing the link between entrepreneur, firm, and brand. For instance, this is Stone discussing his early years:

> His childhood was a launching pad, of sorts, that sent Bezos rocketing toward a life as an entrepreneur. It also instilled in him an abiding interest in the exploration and discovery of space, a fascination that perhaps one day may actually take him there.
>
> *(Stone 2014, 178)*

Stone also makes clear the link between these stories and how Amazon has taken shape: 'Bezos … reinforce[s] his values within the company' (Stone 2014, 220); and, as he also notes: 'Repeating all these anecdotes isn't rote monotony – it's calculated strategy' (Stone 2014, 410). Thus, we should all pay close attention.

Another recurring part of the Bezos celebrity story is that his family, as a household, are, like the ranch household, extremely self-reliant and efficient. On one level this is a – relatively common – simple but effective way to deflect moral questions of great wealth and power, but on another level it is part of a strategic obfuscation of Amazon's working practices. At Amazon, a moral interdiction against lavish spending enables a corporate plan that is all about undercutting market price-floors and gaining an informational advantage over competitors (Khan 2018). The way this plays out is embedded within a deep double talk.

Moral authority is rehearsed repeatedly, but the corporate enaction of this supposed wisdom becomes a form of ruthless market behaviour.

The myth of Amazon founding is in line with these parsimonious frontier logics, and through a ritualised road trip across America, Bezos symbolically moved his household out of New York (with its prohibitive sales taxes), via his spiritual home in Texas on to the Grand Canyon before reaching sparsely populated Washington State on the Pacific coast. There the company was initially run from the family's house: Bezos was CEO while his wife MacKenzie managed the accounts (in line with the gender roles we saw emerging popular culture in Chapter 2). This entrepreneurial origin myth aesthetically locates Amazon as a household enterprise within a physical landscape that reflects material aspects of its founder's life. It's not just that Bezos grew up in Texas (as well as Florida): by his acquisitions for Blue Origin, he has gone on to become one of the twenty-five biggest landowners in the entire US (he owns 420,000 acres in West Texas). Meanwhile, through his cousin, country music superstar George Strait Sr, he also has a family connection to one of the West's most prominent cultural icons. He thus has both a physical and cultural stake in the culture of the American West.

A frontier company?

One of the key symbols of the company is a table made out of a door. The 'door desk' emerged out of this early period of Amazon's founding, representing its modest DIY roots. The anecdote goes that Bezos worked out that it was cheaper to buy a door and attach legs than to pay for tables. This 'door desk' has become a symbol of American start-up culture in general – and the idea that hard work, a frugal can-do attitude, and the occasional stroke of genius can lead to globe-spanning success (cf Schlosser 2018; Fichau 2016).

The 'door desk' (Karlinsky and Steadman 2018) values of its founder are refracted throughout Amazon. One of the main ways that this is seen is in the idea of frugality and 'leanness.' Unlike other tech companies, which tend to offer numerous benefits to employees as well as share options, Amazon, in its formative years at least, mostly relied on share options on their own to keep staff loyal (so that they were literally invested in the company); other common perks like luxurious canteens or free parking were absent at Amazon, and the staff experienced few of the cornucopia of benefits sometimes associated with tech firms like Google.

Instead of an orientation towards creating a comfortable working environment for employees, Bezos continuously emphasises that his focus is exclusively on his customers. In his 1997 'day one' letter to shareholders, he states that a core part of Amazon's philosophy is to 'obsess over customers' and 'maintain a lean culture.' Permanent staff from executives to (some) packers have their compensation 'weight[ed] ... to stock options rather than cash,' because employees 'must think like, and therefore must actually be, an owner' (Bezos 2017). Rather than an employee–employer relationship, Bezos describes an environment where there is a shared investment in a communal project: evoking a frontier town or colonial settlement where everyone pulls together for the sake of survival rather than a commercial enterprise located at the heart of advanced capitalism.

This is a particular form of paternalistic orientation to employment, which forecloses complaint about conditions through the promise of extravagant future reward, and promotes a relationship between staff and company that mirrors that of its founder. However, while co-ownership of companies can be used to promote equality and democracy, for instance in the cooperative movement, Bezos used it here to legitimate extreme working practices and cement his authority. Indeed, one telling quotation in the Stone biography suggested that there was no easy way to be an early Amazon employee: 'Kim Rachmeler shared a favorite quote she heard from a colleague around that time. "If you're not good, Jeff will chew you up and spit you out. And if you're good, he will jump on your back and ride you into the ground"' (2013, 167). The frontier spirit not only justifies ruthless working conditions but celebrates it. Work becomes the proving ground that taming the landscape was under the nineteenth-century iteration of the frontier. This gives frontier capitalism a cruel momentum that harks back to the high-risk, high-reward promise of the mythic American West, but here the threat is not 'restless natives' or dangerous animals. Instead, as we saw with Elon Musk in the previous chapter, it is simply relentless demands for overwork.

As Amazon expanded, its physical footprint grew in a way that distinctly reflected the dual ideologies of digital colonialism and dataism. New fulfilment centre (i.e. warehouse) locations were selected algorithmically to maximise efficiency; the world was flattened out into a canvas for corporate conquest of new lands that were desirable because of their merits within the logistics chain. While some had access to stock options, warehouse staff were nevertheless paid poorly, had bad contracts, and were then heavily policed to minimise theft. Rather than simply pay them more so that there was less economic imperative to steal, the company, initially at least, treated their logistics workers as unruly and untrusted natives. A point system was devised that led to dismissal after a relatively small number of infractions: for instance, six days of illness was grounds for firing. Amazon made it clear that unionisation would not be tolerated. Similarly, temperature controls (heating and air conditioning) were shunned as far as possible on grounds of cost, and when a fulfilment centre reached uncomfortable or even dangerous temperatures the mitigation measures were woefully inadequate (Stone 2014, 238). Indeed, stories have circulated in the press of staff peeing in bottles and fainting from fatigue during shifts (Bloodworth 2018). But it was this early extreme 'leanness' (i.e. ruthless exploitation of staff) which gave Bezos a competitive edge while he was establishing Amazon's current position.

While these driving logics remain in place, some of the excesses seem to have now been addressed due to pressure from journalistic exposés and criticism from prominent political figures and campaigners, including Bernie Sanders. Facilities are now temperature-controlled, staff in warehouses are paid at the widely campaigned-for wage of $15, and all staff get given annual and parental leave and so on. Yet they are also highly time managed and mostly on agency contracts rather than employed directly – a strategy that simply exists to minimise rights in employment. Furthermore, workers use 'wearable terminals' to ensure that 'every minute' they are at work is monitored. This application of the logics of the 'quantified self' to the hard physical labour of warehouse work is a form of cybernetic Taylorism that exacts a heavy toll on its workers (Moore and Robinson 2016). Like for previous generations of American industrialists, the worker's body becomes a new frontier in the quest for time and motion efficiency.

Amazon's corporate frontier first expanded East across America, then to the UK, and then to everywhere it could seemingly all at once. Following Jackson Turner's mythic pattern, the trials of the initial conquest gave way to more established settlements and then full civilisation, as further waves of expansion consolidated the logistical infrastructure. Amazon re-enacted the popular histories of the American frontier.

Bezos still insists on the culture from his 'day one' letter, however, reproducing it annually in his report to shareholders. In a passage from the letter he says:

> It's not easy to work here (when I interview people I tell them, 'You can work long, hard, or smart, but at Amazon.com you can't choose two out of three'), but we are working to build something important, something that matters to our customers, something that we can all tell our grandchildren about. Such things aren't meant to be easy. We are incredibly fortunate to have this group of dedicated employees whose sacrifices and passion build Amazon.com.
>
> (SEC 2017)

Here Bezos is reflecting a wider tech-culture maxim that 'work defines worth' – a philosophy that breaks the boundaries between public and private, the intimate and professional; where one 'works' on relationships, spirituality, and parenting a pattern that (unevenly) crosses gender divides under neoliberal values (English-Lueck 2017, 28). But he is also engaging in a project that is equal in grandeur to the 'manifest destiny' of the American settlers.

As on the frontier, the kind of work you do and the conditions under which you do it are often defined by race and gender. It is telling that in the PR video that accompanied the announcement that Amazon's minimum wage in the USA would now be at campaign group Fight for $15's suggested hourly rate, we see the announcement being made by a white male manager, and women and people of colour weeping with gratitude (Amazon 2018). It is possible, of course, that these are genuine tears of thanks, but public and collective displays of crying of this sort are unusual in workplaces: perhaps they indicate relief, instead, and just how hard it was to live on the sort of salary that was on offer before.

However, as when any shift such as this occurs, no matter that it has usually happened as a result of campaigning or public relations considerations, the announcement was accompanied by fanfare and lobbying. Thus, in what should have been an uncomfortable moment for Amazon's PR – one employee is shown in the video explicitly stating that previously she wasn't earning enough to support her family – the story about not being able to provide for children on Amazon wages becomes integrated into a narrative about Amazon's virtue. Extreme exploitation of workers is repurposed to the positive as part of the brand's crisis management activities.

The idea of 'leanness' has become part of the wider culture of the tech sector as much as the dataism that we discuss in other chapters, and Bezos's celebrity persona bears some degree of responsibility for this widespread parsimonious work/pay ethic. In his Business Insider interview, Döpfner describes Bezos as an inspiration to younger entrepreneurs – suggesting that other business leaders should take on his values in their own companies. Certainly, approaches drawn from Amazon appear in lots of different contexts – not just desk construction: they appear in different forms throughout our concordance. For instance, we see a modified version of the Amazon strategy being advocated in influential industry 'how-to' books such as the *Lean Startup* found in our concordance (Ries 2011).

Lean, as an adjective, appears under six times per million words in our enTenTen15 control corpus, but in our concordance it appears nearly three times as often. It is used to describe men – in formulations such as 'lean and hungry look,' 'lean and wiry' – and business strategy – '[Musk]'d learned in Silicon Valley to run SpaceX lean and fast,' 'lean start-up style hypotheses,' and so on. It's perhaps worth noting that appearing 'lean' is also a physical attribute of most of the men we focus on in this book, so perhaps the philosophy is at least partially inscribed in the bodies of our subjects. This 'leanness' is of course another term which slots into the conception of the Wild West: nothing can be wasted by the explorer, the prospector, or the cowboy; it becomes a moral imperative of self-sufficiency.[5]

There are clearly parallels between this expression of the frontier spirit of settler colonialism and some of the lines of argument in the work both of Shoshana Zuboff and of Nick Couldry and Ulises Mejias as we discussed in Chapter 1. Moreover, this understanding of tech companies has popular and political purchase: on a recent trip to India, Bezos was greeted by protestors holding banners comparing Amazon to 'the East India Company' (Punit 2020). Thinking about Bezos's activities as a colonial enterprise is helpful, so long as we recognise the specifically American character of its activities.

Frederik Jackson Turner, a figure who strongly shaped American popular narratives of the settlement of the Western States, argued that American national culture was driven by its progressive capture of empty land – a frontier spirit that pushed the settlers' European roots further into the past as ingenuity demanded a new cultural form. This colonial vision was in stark contrast to the Spanish and even British variants, as White argues:

> This story of the peaceful settlement of 'free' land, framed as a sweeping explanation of the evolution of a uniquely democratic, individualistic, and progressive American character, attained its initial influence among Turner's academic colleagues. Partly because of its resonance with existing images and stories, Turner's version of American history and character spread easily – through the classroom, through journalism, and through popular histories.
>
> *(White et al. 1994, 13)*

The embrace of this particular form of American colonial ideology, tied to the idea of manifest destiny, marked the end of European colonialism as a vital force in the shaping of the Western hemisphere. It offered the means of turning (European) migrants into Americans, through the catalysing hardships of the frontier. Moreover, as F. J. Turner himself puts it:

> The result is that to the frontier the American intellect owes its striking characteristics. That coarseness and strength combined with acuteness and inquisitiveness; that practical, inventive turn of mind, quick to find expedients; that masterful grasp of material things, lacking in the artistic but powerful to effect great ends; that restless, nervous energy; that dominant individualism, working for good and for evil, and withal that buoyancy and exuberance which comes with freedom – these are traits of the frontier, or traits called out elsewhere because of the existence of the frontier.
>
> *(1893, 9)*

Our argument is that the 'Wild West' rocket ship in the interview, the ranch myth of Bezos's origin, the 'day one' culture's continuous return to the point of origin, even *Star Trek* – all of these tropes found repeatedly in Bezos's celebrification (Driessens 2013) – are drawing on and embedded in the semantic structures of the frontier settlerism that runs deep in the ideological veins of Silicon Valley, and indeed American culture in general.

But these fragments from his story do not tell us everything about Bezos the man-myth, and his possible affinity to the philosophy of the frontier. None of these biographical details on its own explains the promotional strategy that places these particular elements at the centre of his corporate celebrity. For a fuller understanding, we need to explore in more depth a further aspect of Bezos's persona – his connections to 1960s counterculture – an aspect of Bezos's celebrity that is part of the wider paradigm of West Coast tech. In order to do that we turn now to a different point of connection – with a man who is a key figure in the crossover between the counterculture and tech culture, Stewart Brand.

The counterculture and the posthuman frontier

The relationship with Brand provides an important part of Bezos's legitimacy within the more outwards-facing, seemingly progressive dimensions of the

Silicon Valley ideology. Brand is a key figure in the establishment of tech institutions like *Wired* magazine, and is linked to the home of tech liberalism (or arguably libertarianism) – the Electronic Frontier Foundation; but he is also the founder of the 1960s hippy lifestyle magazine the *Whole Earth Catalog* (WEC). This was a magazine and mail-order catalogue that offered the aspiring countercultural nomad-settler everything they needed to start a life off-grid – from books on philosophy and farming, through tools and implements for life off the land, to early home computers. It sported a picture of the Earth from space on its cover and opened with the line 'We *are* as gods and might as well get used to it.' That is followed a few lines later with: 'The WHOLE EARTH CATALOG functions as an evaluation and access device.' This is not dissimilar in presumptuous form – especially given the grandiose title – to what Amazon would eventually become.

Shel Kaphan, Amazon's first employee, and the original developer of its website, worked at the WEC as a teenager and introduced Brand to Bezos in the late 1990s (Stone 2014, 85). They shared a number of interests not least their admiration for Gerald O'Neill, a physicist and space exploration enthusiast famous for his book *The High Frontier* which set out the principles of space colonisation. O'Neill had taught Bezos at Princeton and Brand had edited a book called *Space Colonies* in the 1970s in his honour (Brand 1977). So we can see that Amazon's origins, though it was geographically located far to the north of San Francisco, were still tied, through Kaphan initially, and later through Bezos's direct relationship with Brand, to one of the key myth makers that legitimate the Silicon Valley culture. In this section we explore these in some detail before returning to the Axel Springer Award and Bezos's framing of the colonisation of space.

Critical scholarship on the formative history of West Coast tech culture has some key points of contestation. Westminster University hypermedia scholars, Richard Barbrook and Andy Cameron, famously declared in 1995 that a 'Californian Ideology' had taken over the world with little to oppose it. This influential essay stated that tech culture, built on an alliance of 'hippies and squares,' saw itself as having the potential to reboot 'Jeffersonian democracy' – and believed that, through the use of technology, power structures (both government and capitalist) would soon dissolve, leaving a society where each individual would be able to 'express themselves freely within cyberspace' (Barbrook and Cameron 1995, 2). The article cites the American New Left, *Wired* magazine, Marshall McLuhan's technological determinism, and Republican senator Newt Gingrich's 1990s New Right. What is really interesting about it, for our purposes, is the way it points to unresolvable contradictions in the Californian Ideology that it names for the first time.

These are twofold. Firstly, there is a persistent obfuscation of the central role of the state in the formation of the West Coast tech industry. Acknowledging this openly runs hard up against the narrative of brilliant individual minds breaking free from the constraints of an oppressive bureaucracy and producing socially transformative technologies that liberate their users from the state (among other things). The second is the strong racist undercurrent that permeates the ideological culture of a tech industry that sees itself as a bastion of liberal values. This is particularly visible in the still present history of American slavery and the dispossession of Hispanic, Latinx, and indigenous populations in the American West. Barbrook and Cameron directly address these points. They insist that 'the development of successive generations of computers has been directly or indirectly subsidised by the American defence budget' (6); and on the issue of race they remind us that: 'In "Jeffersonian democracy," freedom for white folks was based upon slavery for black people' (9), adding: 'In this hi-tech [variant], the difference between masters and slaves endures in a new form' (10).

Fred Turner's book on Stewart Brand, subtitled 'From Counterculture to Cyberculture' is a partial rebuttal of Barbrook and Cameron's overall narrative while also offering more nuanced evidence for some of these key claims. Turner is critical of Barbrook and Cameron's glib summary of tech culture, and their later followers, as overly simplistic and too close to Silicon Valley's own professed utopianisms:

> By confusing the New Left with the counter-culture, and the new communalists with both, contemporary theorists of digital media have often gone so far as to echo the utopians of the 1990s and to reimagine its peer-to-peer technologies as the rebirth in hardware and software of a single, 'free' culture that once stood outside the mainstream and can do again.
> (Turner 2008, 33–34)

In unpicking some of these issues, Turner starts by challenging the links between tech culture and the 1960s New Left, arguing that there were several strands to the counterculture that fed into contemporary Silicon Valley that were largely separate – philosophically and in terms of core membership.

To substantiate this claim Turner focuses on Brand, as a maven and serial entrepreneur who was present at many of the key moments in the development of the Silicon Valley culture. He shows that it was the back-to-the-land movement and psychedelic culture that inspired most of the early technologists, rather than the explicitly political movement of the New Left. These new communalists were both less and more radical than their more directly political counterparts in the Yippies (Youth International Party) and other alternative formations. They were also closer to the military-industrial research and development infrastructure that was growing in the Northern California Bay Area at the time.

Turner argues that the communes that sprouted across the USA in the late 1960s recreated the middle-class suburban values which their residents tended to bring with them. This was particularly the case with gender: 'many communes ... did not so much leave suburban gender relations behind as recreate them within a frontier fantasy' (2008, 71). Overt racism would be considered abhorrent in these commune spaces, but issues around race pervaded them and they were almost exclusively white. The establishment of communes was also seen as a form of gentrification, pushing usually Hispanic people out of desirable areas by increasing the cost of land (77).

Turner's book implies that the 1960s communards represented a continuation of white settler traditions in the US – in their combination of radical split with the societies left behind and a transposition of their values to new contexts. There were strong continuities with the ideas of the religious non-conformists of the early settlement of the New World, with their fantasy of 'Terra Nullius' (Couldry and Mejias 2019, 9) offering both the physical space for a new society and the political space for social experimentation. There are similarities too in the notion that existing residents were not equals in this endeavour, but were a problem to be resolved (for the early settlers by either missionary conversion, exploitation, or extermination), while also usefully providing exotic colour to be fetishised and incorporated into the radical myths of frontier settlement. Bezos repeats their principles explicitly in the epigraph to this chapter: 'Missionaries are cool … Explorers are cool.'

'Stewart Brand' appears 163 times in 20 books in the concordance. He is most prominent – at 68 references – in *Valley of Genius*, which uses quotations from key Silicon Valley figures to construct a discursive history (in 9 of the 20 books he is only mentioned once). These references are sometimes brief, but they also sometimes initiate an extended discussion of his life and works (i.e. through the use of 'he' and the use of only one of his names 'Stewart' or 'Brand,' with the referent made clear through context and initial use of the full name). These references are for the most part positive and sometimes reverential. For instance, in *Abundance* he is referred to as 'one of the most potent forces for abundance the world had yet seen' (Diamandis and Kotler 2014, 119); Po Freeman sees him as a heroic guru figure for technology: 'Stewart Brand had lent the early technology this incredible gravitas and nobility and high-mindedness. The ultimate thing was your mind – mind expansion' (cited in Fisher 2018, 246). Alan Kay of the influential Xerox PARC laboratory saw him as a key inspiration: 'he was the guy who was giving us the early warning system about what computers were going to be' (Foer 2017, 21). Franklin Foer mentions him from a critical perspective: 'The big tech companies present themselves as platforms for personal liberation, just as Stewart Brand preached' (2017, 56).

Turner's book on Brand is also referenced as a source in some of the books, but the tone tends to the positive: Brand's accomplishments are usually listed as the *Whole Earth Catalog, Wired Magazine*, being Ken Kesey's LSD sidekick, and the establishment of pioneering pre-Web bulletin board *The Whole Earth 'Lectronic Link* or *WELL*. He is also credited with coining the phrases 'personal computer' and 'information wants to be free' and identified as a key figure in the establishment of the Electronic Frontier Foundation that promotes hackerism and defends 'free speech' online. He is cited in *Valley of Genius* from his 1972 article in *Rolling Stone* on the game *Space War* as predicting that: 'When computers become available to everybody, the hackers take over.'

Turner repeatedly presents the role of Brand, in his various guises from the 1960s to the 1990s, as a legitimating figure who was able to transfer the kudos of one group of people to another, as for instance in this discussion of the promotion within the WEC of certain kinds of systems theory principles: 'Together [these principles] offer a way for members of the New Communalist movement to claim some of the legitimacy of the American research community. They also work to legitimate mainstream forces of consumption, technological production, and research, as hip' (Turner 2008, 84).

As part of Turner's discussion of the WEC, he offers us composite characters such as the 'Cowboy nomad,' who is described thus:

> He is to reject the middle-class consumer culture (the feminised 'Mother country'), though not the process of consumption. Mobile, flexible, masculine, he is to consume knowledge and information and carry it with him on his migrations ... In short, despite talk of cowboys and Indians, he is to become a member of an information-orientated, entrepreneurial elite.
>
> *(88)*

This figure is ultimately destined to transcend its Earthly rebellion and head to space. Turner quotes from Brand himself, who saw the future of technological innovation as 'out-law country, where rules are not decree or routine so much as the starker demands of what's possible' (Brand 1972, cited in Turner 2008, 117).

Turner continues:

> To the extent that the *Whole Earth Catalog* serves as a guide [to the sort of world this new elite would build], it would be masculine, entrepreneurial, well-educated, and white. It would celebrate systems theory and the power of technology to foster social change. And it would turn away from questions of gender, race, and class, and toward a rhetoric of individual and small-group empowerment.
>
> *(97)*

The digital cowboy is, of course, only part nomad. He is also responsible for and to the homestead, the place where wife and children await the cowboy's return with his herd from the far pastures (i.e. Rheingold 1993). Sometimes the cowboy – like Bezos perhaps – goes on to become a 'private statesman' (Turner 2008, 120) – the unelected visionary who shapes society through money, technology, and ideology. Slowly, in Turner's telling of Brand's life, the cowboy goes fully corporate: in this new world, corporate executives could 'see further, plan more effectively, and perhaps manage their firms "as gods"' (Turner 2008, 205). A God's eye view was invoked in the opening epigraph to the *Whole Earth Catalogue*; more recently, ride-share company Uber's 'God View' function (which was able to identify any user of their software's location through their app's backend) would become a scandal, as they used their software to spy on celebrities at corporate parties. It is to another God's eye view, the one from space that we now turn.

From time to space: the next frontier

Brand and Bezos have now been good friends for around 20 years. Indeed, Brand is a key advocate for the Clock of the Long Now, a 10,000-year mechanical clock being built on Bezos's West Texas property, on which, in one of his purportedly rare acts of extravagance, he has spent $42 million. Though this is intended as a monument to the value of long-term thinking, it is also easy to see this as a weird vanity project that has emerged out of the intersection of tech and counterculture – Brand himself has called it an 'ambitious folly' (Brand 2004). But we can also read it as a key philosophical symbol for this ideological movement.

Political scientist David Karpf describes the clock eloquently in *Wired* magazine:

> There is a clock being constructed in a mountain in Texas. The clock will tick once a year, marking time over the next 10,000 years. The clock is an art installation. It is intended as a monument to long-term thinking, meant to inspire its visitors to be mindful of their place in the long arc of history.
>
> The clock was conceived by a tech millionaire. It is funded by the world's richest man, a tech billionaire. It is being built adjacent to his private spaceport, inside a mountain that he owns. You can visit the clock in the mountain in Texas someday. You can walk through its jade doors, climb the staircase up to the sapphire dome. You can turn the clock's winding mechanism and hear one of Brian Eno's chimes. Just ask Jeff Bezos for an invite when you see him at Davos, or ask a board member of the Long Now Foundation for an introduction.
>
> If you can't get in touch with Bezos through your personal networks, you shouldn't worry about the 10,000-Year Clock. They wouldn't say it so bluntly, but this art installation isn't for you.
>
> You have more pressing concerns in the here and now.
>
> *(Karpf 2020)*

The philosophical premise of this installation is that through a tick just once every year – and a cuckoo every millennium – it will encourage visitors to 'conjure with notions of generations and millennia' (longnow.org). Its intention is to shift our moral compass from the present into the distant future, so that we think not in human terms – as the individual and collective inhabitants of the present – but in species terms, about the question of how are we going to survive and perhaps flourish on a civilisational timescale. It is a spectacularly convenient symbol for excusing present iniquities in favour of a narrative of long-term benefit for the species.

Bezos expresses this long-term view in the Döpfner interview when he describes his space company Blue Origin as 'the most important work I'm doing.' He pursues this work not because of his passion for *Star Trek* or space in general, but, drawing on the teachings of Gerard O'Neill, because of the risk posed by a 'civilisation of stasis' for his 'great grandchildren's great grandchildren.' The generational/civilisational frame is very clear. He goes on to describe the increasing energy crisis in terms again established by O'Neill, not in terms of global warming, but in terms of increasing energy consumption: 'In just a few hundred years you need to cover the entire surface of the Earth in solar cells. That's the real energy crisis and it's happening soon … in just a few hundred years'[6] (Döpfner 2018; O'Neill 2019[1976]). He then makes the case for expansion into the solar system with unlimited resources and a trillion people – with 'a thousand Einsteins and a thousand Mozarts.' Later in the interview, he says: 'I have a mission driven purpose with Blue Origin, that I think is incredibly important for civilisation long term and I'm going to use my financial lottery winnings from Amazon to fund that.'

Part of Bezos's celebrity story is precisely this emphasis on long-term thinking, and this is what the philosophical message of the Clock of the Long Now legitimates. It was long-term thinking that underpinned his tax avoidance strategy, and long-term thinking that made the exploitation of staff acceptable,[7] and this same long-term thinking now means that his wealth will be invested in his long-standing obsession with space ships rather than used for more immediate human good. But the clock is also a specific celebrified manifestation of the wider posthuman ideology that suffuses the tech industry. Time-keeping is an originary form of standardised measurement that draws its metrics from a natural phenomenon (the rotation of the Earth). The Clock of the Long Now, in contrast, is a timepiece that keeps time in a way that has no practical use at all for humans in organising their lives. It is a shrine to the posthuman. It is also more tangibly a set of social, political, and political practices for which Amazon provides an important infrastructural basis. The tech-culture ideology of dataism, like the clock, is also posthuman in orientation: it places emphasis on the flow of information, not the corporeal 'carcass,' mere human users, (Zuboff 2019, 377) that provide the conduits for it. Brand wants 'long term thinking to be automatic and common, instead of difficult and rare' and sees that as the clock's primary message (Brand 2004). In essence, the clock points to a solution to the tech industry's devaluing of human subjectivity in favour of the 'objective' data that is only legible to machines: that is, we shouldn't worry about it, in the long run we'll thank them for the transformations of society wrought by their technologies.

At an earlier phase of the development of the tech sector, political theorist Eran Fisher describes what being a human in this transformed world would look like through the lens of his comprehensive discourse analysis of *Wired* magazine:

> Being part of the network, humans shift swiftly and easily between multiple tasks: they are flexible and can engage with reality based on only

superficial, temporary, and fleeting encounters. The spirit of networks upholds humans as informational: they are coreless (or unessential), comprised of a network of components, which could be disassembled, distributed, and reassembled in order to create a new whole.

(Fisher 2010, 216)

The clock is there as a proving ground for these new humans – for those determined or privileged enough to have access to it. It is designed for a quest of sorts – for those deserving, interested, and wealthy enough (see Brand's 2004 TED Talk). It is a mark of the permanent frontier – Stuart Brand's Long Now Foundation is building its own version of the Clock of the Long Now in Nevada and it is hours from an airport requiring a long hike to get to. But Bezos's Clock is different: it marks the point of access to the next frontier, his private space port where he tests his Blue Origin rockets – and which one day, if all goes to plan, will be our portal to outer space. As paying customers queue up to explore the stars, they will be able to arrive a few hours or a day earlier and go and see the clock, a monument to the long-term thinking that enabled Jeff Bezos to run Amazon at a loss for over a decade and still succeed in creating a new digital infrastructure for consumption. This is how Jeff Bezos chooses to tell his celebrity, how he legitimates his incredible wealth and power: this same long-term thinking will open up a new frontier in the vast empty beyond of space. And this is a frontier that will remake the human beings who can afford to pay into a new space-faring species, as surely as the Western frontier remade Europeans into Americans, network technologies turn humans from organic to informational subjects and the United States of Amazon makes citizens into customers.

Notes

1 The ALSA (Amyotrophic Lateral Sclerosis Association) campaigns on and conducts research into Amyotrophic Lateral Sclerosis (also known Lou Gherig's disease, and, in the UK, motor neurone disease).
2 One of the mechanism's for reducing Amazon's tax payments is through paying its employees partly in shares. This is conveniently a key part of Bezos's ideology – see below.
3 Interestingly, *Star Wars* has also been identified as continuing in the tradition of the American Western (McVeigh 2007, 193). Zuckerberg, like Thiel, is also a Star Wars rather than Star Trek guy – his Bar Mitzvah was themed for the former, although he has been compared unflatteringly to the character 'Data' from the latter. (Pfeffer 2017)
4 According to an incorrectly referenced source on Wikipedia, Bezos sold his remaining Insider Inc. shares to Axel Springer in 2018 (https://en.wikipedia.org/wiki/Insider_Inc.).
5 Bezos's philosophy is demonstrably influential more generally. In our database, the lemma 'customer' as a word appears 447 times per million words. This is more than double the 192 times per million words frequency in the control corpus. The reason this is significant is that most of the time, tech companies refer to their client base as

users, it is Bezos, who started in retail, who prefers to use customer. Furthermore, a biography of the Google founders identifies Bezos as the ideal CEO that they used as a model when they were looking for someone to help run their company: their choice was Eric Schmidt (Brandt 2011).

6 O'Neill writing in the aftermath of the 1974 oil crises sees this looming power crunch in almost Malthusian terms, although his figures may strike some in the environmental movement as eerily prescient even if his timescales for space exploration were highly inaccurate.

7 Their rewards would come in time through stock increases.

References

Amazon (2014) 'Jeff Bezos Accepts the ALS Ice Bucket Challenge' *YouTube*. www.youtube.com/watch?v=DFVezzjAhFY Last accessed 03/05/2020.

Amazon (2018) 'Amazon Raises Minimum Wage to $15 for All U.S. Employees' *Amazon Day One Blog*, 2nd October. https://blog.aboutamazon.com/working-at-amazon/amazon-raises-minimum-wage-to-15-for-all-us-employees Last accessed 03/05/2020.

Amazon Webservices (2019) 'Public Sector Sales' https://aws.amazon.com/government-education/government/ Last accessed 03/05/2020.

Axel Springer Award (2019) http://axel-springer-award.com/ Last accessed 3/05/2020.

Barbrook, Richard and Andrew Cameron (1995) 'The Californian Ideology' *Mute* 1(3). www.metamute.org/editorial/articles/californian-ideology Last accessed 03/05/2020.

Beeman, Richard R. (2015) *The Old Dominion and the New Nation : 1788–1801*. Lexington: University Press of Kentucky.

Bernardi, Daniel (1997) 'Star Trek in the 1960s: Liberal-Humanism and the Production of Race' *Science-Fiction Studies*, 24(2), 209–225.

Bezos, Jeff (2017) 'Jeff, What Does Day 2 Look Like?' *SEC Archives*. www.sec.gov/Archives/edgar/data/1018724/000119312517120198/d373368dex991.htm

Bezos, Jeff (2017) 'Letter to Shareholders' www.sec.gov/Archives/edgar/data/1018724/000119312517120198/d373368dex991.htm Last accessed 03/05/2020.

Blodgett, Bridget and Anastasia Salter (2018) *Toxic Geek Masculinity in Media: Sexism, Trolling, and Identity Policing*. Basingstoke: Palgrave.

Bloodworth, James (2018) 'I Worked in Amazon Warehouse. Bernie Sanders is Right to Target Them' *Guardian*, 17th September. www.theguardian.com/commentisfree/2018/sep/17/amazon-warehouse-bernie-sanders Last accessed 03/05/2020.

Booker, M. Keith (2008) 'The Politics of Star Trek' in Telotte, J. P. (ed.) *The Essential Science Fiction Television Reader*. Lexington: University Press of Kentucky.

Brand, Stewart (1977) *Space Colonies*. Menlo Park: CoEvolution Quarterly.

Brand, Stewart (2004) 'Stewart Brand: Building a Home for the Clock of the Long Now' *TED YouTube*[uploaded 2008]. www.ted.com/talks/stewart_brand_the_long_now#t-64177 Last accessed 03/05/2020.

Brandt, Richard (2011) *Google Guys: Inside the Brilliant Minds of Google Founders Larry Page and Sergey Brin*. London: Portfolio.

Burgess, A., V. Miller, and S. Moore (2018) 'Prestige, Performance and Social Pressure in Viral Challenge Memes: Neknomination, the Ice-Bucket Challenge and SmearForSmear as Imitative Encounters' *Sociology*, 52(5), 1035–1051.

Butler, Sarah (2019) 'Amazon Accused of Handing over "Diddly-Squat" in Corporation Tax' *Guardian*, 3rd September. www.theguardian.com/technology/2019/sep/03/am

azon-accused-of-handing-over-diddly-squat-in-corporation-tax-despite-tripling-payment Last accessed 03/05/2020.
Chander, Anupam (2012) 'Facebookistan' *North Carolina Law Review*, 90, 1807–1842.
CNN. https://edition.cnn.com/specials/tech/united-states-of-amazon
Cohen, Noam (2019) *The Know It Alls: The Rise of Silicon Valley as a Political Powerhouse and Social Wrecking Ball*. London: Oneworld.
Couldry, Nick and Ulises Mejias (2018) 'Data Colonialism: Rethinking Big Data's Relation to the Contemporary Subject' *Television and New Media*, 20(4), 336–349.
Couldry, Nick and Ulises A. Mejias (2019) *The Costs of Connection: How Data is Colonizing Human Life and Appropriating it for Capitalism*. Stanford: Stanford University Press.
Diamandis, Peter H. and Steven Kotler (2014) *Abundance: The Future is Better than You Think*. New York: Free Press.
Döpfner, Mathias (2018) 'Jeff Bezos Talks Amazon, Blue Origin, Family, and Wealth' *Business Insider. YouTube*. www.youtube.com/watch?v=SCpgKvZB_VQ Last accessed 03/05/2020.
Driessens, Olivier (2013) 'The Celebritization of Society and Culture: Understanding the Structural Dynamics of Celebrity Culture' *International Journal of Cultural Studies*, 16(6), 641–657.
English-Lueck, J. A. (2017) *Cultures@SiliconValley*, Second Edition. Stanford: Stanford University Press.
Enloe, Cynthia (2017) The Big *Push: Exposing and Challenging the Persistence of Patriarchy*. Oxford: Myriad Editions.
Evans, Will (2019) 'Ruthless Quotas at Amazon Are Maiming Employees' *Atlantic*, 5th November. www.theatlantic.com/technology/archive/2019/11/amazon-warehouse-reports-show-worker-injuries/602530/ Last accessed 03/05/2020.
Fichau, Tabb (2016) 'Door Desk – A Start-Up's Best Friend' *Every Axis. Medium*, 23 December. https://everyaxis.com/door-desk-a-startups-best-friend-20c3a54cbe9f Last Accessed 03/05/2020.
Fisher, Adam (2018) *Valley of Genius: The Uncensored History of Silicon Valley, as Told by the Hackers, Founders, and Freaks Who Made It Boom*. New York: Hachette.
Fisher, Eran (2010) *Media and New Capitalism in the Digital Age: The Spirit of Networks* New York: Palgrave MacMillan.
Foer, Franklin (2017) *World Without Mind: The Existential Threat of Big Tech*. London: Jonathan Cape.
Gartner.com (2019) 'Gartner Says Worldwide IaaS Public Cloud Services Market Grew 31.3% in 2018' www.gartner.com/en/newsroom/press-releases/2019-07-29-gartner-says-worldwide-iaas-public-cloud-services-market-grew-31point3-percent-in-2018 Last accessed 03/05/2020.
Geraghty, Lincoln (2003) 'Homosocial Desire on the Final Frontier: Kinship, the American Romance, and Deep Space Nine's "Erotic Triangle"' *Journal of Popular Culture*, 36(3), 441–465.
Ging, Debbie (2017) 'Alphas, Betas, and Incels' *Men and Masculinities*, 22(4), 638–657.
Google (2014) 'Ice Bucket Challenge Accepted by Larry & Sergey' *YouTube*. www.youtube.com/watch?v=HDIzL61H4aY Last accessed 03/05/2020.
Guthey, Eric, Timothy Clark, and Brad Jackson (2009) *Demystifying Business Celebrity*. London: Routledge.
Hall, Sarah-Marie, Kimberley McIntosh, Eva Neitzert, Laura Pottinger, Kalwinder Sandhu, Mary-Ann Stephenson, Howard Reed, and Leonie Taylor (2017) *Intersecting Inequalities: The Impact of Austerity on Black and Minority Ethnic Women in the UK*.

London: Runnymede Trust. www.runnymedetrust.org/uploads/publications/Intersecting%20Inequalities.pdf Last accessed 03/05/2020.

Jackson, Frederick Turner (1893) 'The Significance of the Frontier in American History' *National Humanities Centre*. http://nationalhumanitiescenter.org/pds/gilded/empire/text1/turner.pdf Last accessed 03/05/2020.

Jones, K. R., and J. Wills (2009) *American West: Competing Visions*. Edinburgh: Edinburgh University Press.

Karlinksy, Neal, and Jordan Stead (2018) 'How a Door Became a Desk, and a Symbol of Amazon' *Day One Blog*, 17th January. https://blog.aboutamazon.com/working-at-amazon/how-a-door-became-a-desk-and-a-symbol-of-amazon Last accessed 03/05/2020.

Karpf, David (2020) 'The 1000 Year Clock Is a Waste of Time' *Wired*, 29th January. www.wired.com/story/the-10000-year-clock-is-a-waste-of-time/ Last accessed 03/05/2020.

Khan, Lina (2018) 'Amazon – An Infrastructure Service and Its Challenge to Current Antitrust Law' in Martin Moore and Damian Tambini (eds) *Digital Dominance The Power of Google, Amazon, Facebook, and Apple*. Oxford: Oxford University Press, 98–129.

Kirchgaessner, Stephanie (2020) 'Bezos Hack: UN to Address Alleged Saudi Hacking of Amazon Boss's Phone' *The Guardian*. 22nd January. www.theguardian.com/technology/2020/jan/22/un-investigators-to-address-alleged-saudi-hacking-of-jeff-bezos-phone Last accessed 03/05/2020.

McVeigh, Stephen (2007) *The American Western*. Edinburgh: Edinburgh University Press.

Mills, Charles (1997) *The Racial Contract*. New York: Cornell University Press.

Moore, P., and A. Robinson (2016) 'The Quantified Self: What Counts in the Neoliberal Workplace' *New Media & Society*, 18(11), 2774–2792.

Newport News (n.d.) 'CVN 80: The Next Generation of USS Enterprise' *Ford Class Aircraft Carriers*. www.thefordclass.com/cvn80/ Last accessed 03/05/2020.

Ni Michael Y., Brandford H. Y. Chan, Gabriel M. Leung, Eric H. Y. Lau, and Herbert Pang (2014) 'Transmissibility of the Ice Bucket Challenge among Globally Influential Celebrities: Retrospective Cohort Study' *British Medical Journal*, 349, g7185.

O'Connor, J. E., and P. C. Rollins (2005) *Hollywood's West: The American Frontier in Film, Television, and History*. Lexington: University Press of Kentucky.

O'Neill, Gerard K. (2019 [1976]) *The High Frontier: Human Colonies in Space*. North Hollywood: Space Studies Institute.

Ortner, Sherry B. (2014) 'Too Soon for Post-Feminism: The Ongoing Life of Patriarchy in Neoliberal America' *History and Anthropology*, 25(4), 530–549.

Pashkoff, Susan (2014) 'Women and Austerity in Britain' *New Politics*, 14(4). https://newpol.org/issue_post/women-and-austerity-britain/ Last accessed 03/05/2020.

Pateman, Carol (1988) *The Sexual Contract*. Stanford: Stanford University Press.

Perry, Imani (2018) *Vexy Thing: On Gender and Liberation*. Durham: Duke University Press.

Pfeffer, Anshel (2017) 'Shallow and Evasive' *Haaretz*, 4th October. www.haaretz.com/opinion/zuckerbergs-curated-jewish-conscience-is-shallow-and-evasive-1.5455322 Last accessed 03/05/2020.

Princeton Academics (2010) 'Amazon Founder and CEO Jeff Bezos Delivers Graduation Speech at Princeton University' *YouTube*. www.youtube.com/watch?v=vBmavNoChZc Last accessed 03/05/2020.

Punit, Itiki Sharma (2020) 'Jeff Bezos' Surprise Visit to India Did Not Go Well' *Quartz*, 18th January. https://qz.com/1787217/amazon-founder-jeff-bezos-surprise-visit-to-india-didnt-go-well/ Last accessed 03/05/2020.

Rakusen, India, Julia Carrie Wong, and Jim Waterson (2019) 'Jeff Besoz and the United States of Amazon' *The Guardian*. www.theguardian.com/news/audio/2019/jul/29/amazon-25-powerful-jeff-bezos-podcast

Rheingold, Howard (2000 [1993]) *The Virtual Community: Homesteading on the Electronic Frontier*. Cambridge, MA: MIT Press.

Ries, Eric (2011) *The Lean Startup: How Constant Innovation Creates Radically Successful Businesses*. London: Portfolio.

Rojek, Chris (2014) '"Big Citizen" Celanthropy and Its Discontents' *International Journal of Cultural Studies* 17(2), 127–141. doi:10.1177/1367877913483422.

Schlosser, Kurt (2018) 'Want to "Be Peculiar" in Your Office? Build the Scrappy, Iconic Amazon Door Desk in 6 Easy Steps' www.geekwire.com/2018/want-peculiar-office-build-scrappy-iconic-amazon-door-desk-6-easy-steps/

Schmidt, Eric and Jonathan Rosenberg (2017) *How Google Works*. Grand Central Publishing.

Shaxson, Nicholas (2012) *Treasure Islands: Tax Havens and the Men Who Stole the World*. London: Vintage.

Star Trek: Beyond (2016) Lin, Justin (dir) Paramount.

Star Trek: The Original Series. (1966–69) NBC.

Star Trek: The Original Series (1968) 'Plato's Stepchildren' 22nd November, NBC.

Star Wars (1977) George Lucas (dir) Lucasfilm.

Stone, Brad (2014) *The Everything Store: Jeff Bezos and the Age of Amazon*. London: Corgi.

Thiel, Peter (2009) 'The Education of a Libertarian' *Cato Unbound*, 13th April. www.cato-unbound.org/2009/04/13/peter-thiel/education-libertarian Last accessed 03/05/2020.

Turner, Fred (2008) *From Counterculture to Cyberculture: Stewart Brand, the Whole Earth Network, and the Rise of Digital Utopianism*. Chicago: University of Chicago Press.

Van Dijck, José, Thomas Poell, and Martijn de Waal (2018) *The Platform Society Public Values in a Connective World*. Oxford: Oxford University Press.

Vettel-Becker, Patricia (2014) 'Space and the Single Girl: Star Trek, Aesthetics, and 1960s Femininity' *Frontiers: A Journal of Women Studies*, 35(2), 143–178. doi:10.5250/fronjwomestud.35.2.0143

Whitaker (2014) 'Former CIA CTO Speaks Out on Snowden Leads, Amazon's $600m Cloud Deal' *ZDNet*, 24th April. www.zdnet.com/article/former-cia-cto-speaks-out-on-snowden-leaks-amazons-600m-cloud-deal/ Last accessed 03/05/2020.

White, R., Grossman, J. R., Limerick, P. N., and Newberry Library (1994) *The Frontier in American Culture*. Chicago: University of California Press.

Zuboff, Shoshona (2019) *The Age of Surveillance Capitalism: The Fight for a Human Future at the New Frontier of Power*. London: Profile Books.

4

MARK ZUCKERBERG'S CORPORATE HOUSEHOLD

Mark Zuckerberg is, at the time of writing, a very different figure from when we started this project in 2017. At that time, he was seen as having – and traded on – a reputation for being a 'boy wonder,' a genius who was making our lives better through good ideas well implemented in software. Now, few tech watchers would have that opinion of him. Scandals like Cambridge Analytica's intervention in elections using Facebook data, as well as unconvincing Senate Committee appearances in the USA and parliamentary addresses in the EU, have led to him being associated with the political turmoil of the last few years in a manner that appears either cynical or incompetent. Since we started our research Zuckerberg has lost some control over his celebrity brand. According to a year-long YouGov survey published recently, in the UK the people who hold negative views of him are roughly twice as numerous as his fans, with a popularity rating only marginally better in the USA (YouGov 2020a; YouGov 2020b).

Yet this wasn't always the case, and, for our purposes, Zuckerberg's curated celebrity *before* he fell from grace gives us a clear insight into the processes of legitimation used to institute digital capitalism. In contrast to the traditional reliance of celebrity CEOs on the mainstream and specialist media (Littler 2007), Zuckerberg usually spreads information via his own Facebook platform, which is then taken up as material for newspapers, blogs, and online journals (many of which will recirculate through Facebook itself). For example, the widely discussed spat in July 2017 between Zuckerberg and Elon Musk over the future of artificial intelligence, used a video that Zuckerberg made in his backyard while having a barbeque (Solon 2017a) – as we shall see, the barbeque is a recurring feature of the Zuckerberg-Facebook promotional repertoire.

Typically, business leaders who become celebrities (e.g. Richard Branson) go through a fairly complex process of celebrification (Driessens 2013). The assemblage that must form around the CEO-turned-celebrity has certain standard features. These elements include 'corporate representatives, cultural entrepreneurs and third-party go-betweens that include talent agents, managers, publicists, marketers and advertising executives, public relations departments, newspaper editors and journalists, television producers, book publishers, talk-show hosts, photographers, stylists, bloggers, and many others' (Guthey et al. 2009, 32). This is largely, as Guthey et al. note, a collection of gatekeepers: these are not just in-house personnel but also third-party mediators, who bring their own values and priorities to the practice of constructing celebrity businesspeople. For the Zuckerberg-Facebook celebrity assemblage the balance is different: the dynamics of control are simplified. By using the Facebook platform itself, Zuckerberg's celebrity eliminates many of the gatekeeping functions of the roles external to a corporation as listed above. Certainly, there are publicists, PR, and corporate intermediaries working with Zuckerberg, but they carry the values and intentions of the Facebook brand rather than bringing their own agendas. This meant that, at least until the Cambridge Analytica scandal, Zuckerberg had a celebrity profile that he retained an unusual amount of control over – free from the agendas of publishers, journalists, and editors.

Significantly, of all the patriarchs we use as subjects of case studies, Zuckerberg is one of the most celebrified (as we saw in Chapter 1, where he is the most referenced figure in our concordance after Bill Gates and Steve Jobs – although Tesla's Elon Musk is gaining on him in second place). He is also the one most filtered through the optics of American politics. In this chapter we analyse the construction of Zuckerberg's celebrity in the pre-scandal period, including posts on his 2016 and 2017 Facebook Timeline. More specifically, we look at a number of images and videos uploaded just before and after the election of Donald Trump, especially a video officially called 'Grill Talk.' This is a video of Zuckerberg about to watch the US presidential 2016 debates, before Trump was elected. We also look at an offshoot of Zuckerberg's Timeline, a 2017 page called 'The Year of Travel,' which represents Zuckerberg performing as a celebrity statesman as he travels American states, talking and eating with American households, workforces, and communities.

We argue that Zuckerberg exploits his location in a traditional family structure to naturalise his masculine authority in the public realm. In the period we are looking at here his persona is more that of the settled master of the corporate homestead rather than the pioneer-hacker-in-the-electronic-frontier image of his earlier days (Rheingold 2000 [1993]). More specifically, in the representations of his domestic family household Zuckerberg performs a variant of what Hannah Hamad calls postfeminist paternalism (Hamad 2014). These performances of paternal masculinity are a means to legitimate not only Zuckerberg's sovereignty over the Facebook corporation, but also over its users' data. In the Year of Travel, Zuckerberg is deliberately set up in opposition to Trump, through appearing to be a connective and cohesive figure, who is open to 'the other.' We argue that this opening to 'the other' is partly represented through the optics of hospitality. However, in accepting the invitation extended to us to join the

Zuckerberg-Facebook assemblage, our own households then become party to the processes of data relations, and thus fall within the ambit of digital colonialism driven by men such as Zuckerberg (Couldry and Mejias 2019). In the words of Robin Murray, Facebook plays 'host to the attention economy,' but as we will see, this hospitality is at least partly a trap (Gilbert and Goffey 2015).

This chapter is primarily based on textual analysis of Zuckerberg's Facebook page and content uploaded to his account. Our approach to this analysis is informed by assemblage thinking (Featherstone 2011), and we occasionally supplement this with supporting evidence datamined from our corpus of popular technology books. Textual analysis is the classical way of making sense of texts in media and cultural studies. And, as Bev Skeggs and Simon Yuill point out, Facebook 'works with traditional forms of narrative and discourse to produce a particular genre of self-revelation' (Skeggs and Yuill 2015). By this they mean that Facebook is a platform employed by users to tell their network of followers and friends things about themselves that have a general affect of 'authenticity' (Banet-Weiser 2012). Facebook as a platform relies on these affects both as the primary draw for users to the site (a simulation of intimate connection with others) and for advertisers (this is what your market is really like, what they really want). Zuckerberg is performing an idealised user in the posts we analyse – hence the higher level of (constructed) intimacy that we find in his media performances than the other subjects of this book (Sandberg excepted). This means that the posts on Zuckerberg's feeds need to be read with the particular modes of production and consumption, that his Facebook pages model, in mind (Skeggs and Yuill 2015, 7).

Facebook-Zuckerberg corporate household

Facebook is the most used social network in the world with 2.27 billion monthly active users worldwide. Every 60 seconds 510,000 comments are posted, 293,000 statuses are updated and 136,000 photos are uploaded to the platform (Naughton 2019). As we noted previously, Facebook meets at least two of the four requirements of being a nation-state (according to the Montevideo Convention on Statehood) and Zuckerberg has set up a diplomatic corps to represent Facebook's interests in various countries and regions (Chander 2012; Partzsch 2017). By talking to people about 'how they're living, working and thinking about the future,' Zuckerberg gives the illusion of democratic accountability. He may have been voted for by no one (he exercises absolute control of the corporation on a minority shareholding), but the images and posts on his profile are curated to give the impression that his power and reach have a political legitimacy, not just a corporate one. Zuckerberg and his family alongside Sheryl Sandberg as a senior Facebook executive embrace this complexity and its representational burdens. They perform the public face of the corporation: when Facebook is publicly seen to hurt people, they personify it by acknowledging that they have 'made mistakes,' for instance around the Cambridge Analytica scandal (Vanian 2018).

By making these corporate activities personal and simply taking the consequences on the chin, they use their celebrity to deflect from the structural problems underlying their corporate role and indeed the wider business models that digital capitalism relies on.

We consider this Zuckerberg-Facebook assemblage as a more-than-human configuration of organic and inorganic elements (Braidotti 2013; Massumi 2015). The Zuckerberg we see on his Facebook Timeline is not 'merely' a man in his backyard but an assemblage that incorporates both textual elements and contextual factors that shape how we approach the material. While we cannot read Zuckerberg's posts as 'ordinary,' we can still deploy some of the same tools for interpreting it. By using this assemblage thinking we are able to analyse Zuckerberg and Facebook together, including the politico-cultural dimensions of their influence; and this approach also helps to clarify precisely what is at stake in interrogating them as a case study. The wider Zuckerberg-Facebook assemblage includes (among other things): Zuckerberg as the chief executive, founder and chairman; his immediate family, other executives, shareholders, and board members such as Sheryl Sandberg, Sean Parker, and Peter Thiel; a media platform (covering advertising, social networking, news circulation, representation, and audiences/users); data collection, storage, transmission and retrieval, both local and global, and interacting with laws and regulations in different territories; a corporation with a hierarchical but unevenly gendered, classed, and raced workforce (including content moderators, engineers, cleaners, outsourced staff); an organisation with political clout disproportionate to its economic role, because of its reach and power over data as well as its lobbying budget; an imperialist instrument of US soft-power; a similar set of interlinked elements for WhatsApp, Instagram, and other acquisitions; a philanthrocapitalist foundation; ideological mission statements and manifestos; and so on.

Aside from being mooted for a presidential run (as we discuss in the next section), Zuckerberg also regularly meets heads of state (e.g. presidents and prime ministers from Brazil, China, Russia, and Israel) as a seeming equal; and he has hired former UK deputy prime minister Sir Nick Clegg as his Vice-President, Global Affairs. Yet it is in domestic spaces rather than on his geopolitical soapbox that we have found him to be most revealing. Images of the American household – both Zuckerberg's and the households that he visits – recur on Zuckerberg's Facebook Timeline. For example, to mark Halloween in 2016 there is a photograph of the Zuckerberg-Chan family on the steps of their house. Zuckerberg stands on the top step above his wife and daughter. They are all dressed as characters from the animated film and TV series *How to Train Your Dragon?* (Timeline 1 November 2016). The optics of this image is interesting for our purposes: the PR team has decided to locate him in paternal terms, on the steps of his family home, the threshold of the household. On Zuckerberg's Facebook Timeline there are many such images of his domestic life, whether these are of his dog, Beast, his wife Priscilla Chan, or his daughters Maxima and August. Zuckerberg is often framed at the centre or head of the family. The relationship between Zuckerberg and Chan is also romanticised by photographs posted on Valentine's day or anniversaries. These images and posts work not only to reveal the Zuckerbergs' strong family bonds and emotional structure, but also to centre Zuckerberg as the paternal head of his family.

The patriarchal household, centred on the strict father, is at the heart of the American conservative imaginary (Lakoff 1996). Part of the way that Zuckerberg tempers his patriarchal role in the family (cf bell hooks: 'patriarchy as learnt in the household' (hooks 2010)) is to adopt a postfeminist, future-focused fatherhood that capitalises on the millennial 'boy genius' tropes that proliferate around him, as emerges in our concordance.[1] For example, there is a video of Zuckerberg working out in his home gym with his oldest daughter Max in a sling on his back (31 March 2017). There is the open letter written by him and Chan to Max on the occasion of her birth posted to his Timeline (1 November 2015) and which was used to announce the launch of the family's philanthropic wing – the Chan-Zuckerberg initiative – tying a major family event to a public display of wealth and generosity; and a photograph of him hugging Max as they watch the 2016 presidential election results come in, again linking his paternal role, the platform, and his personal investment in high politics (10 November 2016). Hamad notes that postfeminist fatherhood is conventionally 'emotionally articulate, domestically competent, skilled in managing the quotidian practicalities of parenthood' (Hamad 2014, 2). And we can see this being enacted in his celebrification. Zuckerberg is explicitly constructed as the paternal head of the family, and this paternalism is suffused with a postfeminist sensibility (Gill 2007). As we will demonstrate in this chapter, masculinity and patriarchy are mutually constituted and reconstituted by the reconfiguration of the household and the power relations therein. Furthermore, his celebrification as millennial father resolves (as brands are supposed to do) many of the contradictions latent and explicit in the assemblage.

'Live grilling in my back yard': Zuckerberg-Facebook's hospitality

'Grill Talk' is a 30-minute video posted on 10 October 2016, partly created in order to promote Facebook's live video feature, which was relatively new at the time (Figure 4.1). The video has received over eleven million views. It models Facebook's affective brand strategy: it represents Zuckerberg sitting in the domestic space of his backyard with his wife, daughter Max, and dog, as well as two close friends, while talking to his global followers. It was made during the presidential election, which suggests that Zuckerberg wants his platform to be a vehicle for discussing politics and elections (indeed Facebook was a key component of Trump's electoral strategy – see Bartlett 2018). In addition, Zuckerberg uses this opportunity to talk about his philanthropic work in the Chan-Zuckerberg Initiative. It is important to note how he uses Facebook (both in terms of profits and reach) to promote his brand of 'philanthrocapitalism'

FIGURE 4.1 'Live Grilling' Mark Zuckerberg (right), Sam Lessin (centre), and Joe Green (left), October 2016

(Edwards 2009; Aschoff 2015). As this video encapsulates, Facebook is a location that presents his celebrity persona holistically and comprehensively.

Grill Talk is part press release, part interview, part social-influencer live-streamed video, part reality-television segment, part home video, and part advert. Zuckerberg is performing not only the way this feature works for ordinary users, for communication, but also – through its heavy emphasis on branded goods – its potential as a way for showcasing products for advertisers. Posted next to Grill Talk is the text, 'Live grilling in my backyard.' The video starts with Zuckerberg sitting on one of two supermarket-style patio chairs, and the camera is angled so that we can only see the chairs and the barbeque equipment directly behind. His barbeque equipment includes the brand Big Green Egg and The General by MakGrill, and these provide talking points with his friends, family, and followers. As well as these brands, Zuckerberg mentions Sweet Baby Rays Sauce, Volkswagen, and AT&T. We cannot get a sense of how big the yard is and we cannot see the house, which downplays Zuckerberg's wealth and reinforces his ordinariness, as does the choice of middle-market brands.

He begins the video by talking about smoking meats, the triathlon he started that morning, killing animals for food, and the Facebook company. About 13 minutes into the video Chan and Max enter the screen and sit in the empty chair. Zuckerberg holds Max up to the camera for a few seconds and talks to Chan about their daughter eating her first rib. Chan and Max then inspect the smoking meats and stay off camera or in its periphery for the rest of the video. Subsequently, Zuckerberg picks up the dog Beast and talks about him briefly. Finally, Zuckerberg's two friends – Sam Lessin and Joe Green – arrive. Lessin sits in the chair next to Zuckerberg and Green squats behind. During the rest of the video, they look at meats, talk about cooking, answer some of the commenters' questions, and drink beer. The video ends with Lessin, Green, and Zuckerberg saying goodbye to the camera before Zuckerberg needs to take a call for work. The apparently everyday American heteronormativity of the scene – 'there's nothing more American than a barbeque and a presidential debate,' says Joe – including its gender division, is crucial for understanding the mediated paternalism being curated here.

The themes that emerge in the comments below the video are instructive: simple questions about the products being used; criticism of meat-eating; pleas for money and/or support; 'shout-outs' asking for recognition for a place or team; job requests; comments on the backyard setting, and more. Zuckerberg responds to a (very limited) number of the positive comments. These casual encounters with Zuckerberg, while he smokes meats and answers questions from his followers, are the equivalent within digital capitalism of F. D. Roosevelt's fireside chats, and while they occur at irregular intervals, they form part of Zuckerberg's repertoire of direct encounter with his userbase. Zuckerberg's Facebook posts – particularly after the election of Trump – follow a similar pattern: they promote a new Facebook feature, reveal part of Zuckerberg's intimate life, and make an ideological statement about American or global politics. His holding of toddler Max and talking to her – 'Yes Max, it's a screen' – generates considerable capital, as can be noted by the comments ('Max says hi as well,' responds Zuckerberg). Although Zuckerberg keeps his emotional articulation to a minimum apart from a general affective enthusiasm (here he returns to alpha-male soundbites: 'everyone likes ribs' and 'smoking meats'), his interaction with Max reveals his participation in the domestic sphere and gives the impression of care.

What is also significant about this video is Zuckerberg's ability to demonstrate that he is, in Hamad's words, 'adept at negotiating a balance and/or discursive confluence of private sphere fatherhood and public sphere paternalism' (Hamad 2014, 2). As he sits in his backyard, he slips easily between the family dynamic and his work in terms of Facebook. In fact, his private sphere fatherhood is key to the way that he operates and legitimates his public sphere paternal sovereignty. This is not just because he cut short a triathlon for work, or because he must take a five-minute work call at the end of Grill Talk, but also because he is intimate with his family while doing this promotional work. Indeed, modelling this familial connection *is* his promotional work; it is what he wants his platform to be used for. Zuckerberg enacts what Gregg calls 'presence bleed,' where work and home life blur (2011). And more than this, he models digital capitalism's entrepreneurial and self-governing individuality, where work-life is rendered intimate (Moore and Robinson 2015). Through this video, the affective shift that this blurring of work and private life produces filters through to comments, audiences, and social media practices. Zuckerberg's performances of the private-in-public demand an emotional engagement with what is primarily a promotional activity. The mise-en-scène manifest through the video shows him enjoying his life as he works, and asks his followers to reciprocate that and reproduce it themselves in their own social media use. It is also demonstrating a pathway for advertisers into valuable intimate – and, importantly, trusted – domestic spaces through the platform.

The other intimate relationship that is being enacted in this video is Zuckerberg's friendship with Lessin and Green – both Harvard graduates (Zuckerberg himself dropped out of Harvard to pursue Facebook but has since received an honorary degree). As Ortner (2014) and others have pointed out, homosociality is a key way through which patriarchy recoups its power, and looking at the relationships between men is therefore useful for understanding the way that patriarchy operates and how it is connected to masculine performativities. Lessin was formerly a Facebook executive after his platform was bought out by Zuckerberg. He is now a CEO of Fin, a worker analytics platform that enables managers to monitor customer service representatives, and a venture capitalist. Green helped Zuckerberg create the misogynistic Facemash at Harvard that scraped the pictures of students from campus websites without their permission and invited users to say which of two images was more attractive.[2] Green is also co-founder of Causes, a Facebook app that encourages philanthropy. He has worked with Zuckerberg on lobbying initiatives around immigration and education. The Harvard links, as well as the Silicon Valley contexts and connections to politics, give some insight into the homosocial networks of the digital capitalists, and the way they function around patronage as well as friendships that are both public and private. These personal-professional connections are revealing both of the wider hinterlands across the tech sector, and of the politics of the Zuckerberg-Facebook assemblage; and here they serve to mitigate the dominating role that the figure of Zuckerberg himself plays within it. Both men, though presenting as equals here in the horizontal social cultures of Silicon Valley, are in fact beneficiaries of Zuckerberg's patronage. They are trusted members of Zuckerberg's extended corporate household, and their role is to legitimate the practice in which they are collectively engaged – that is to make Zuckerberg look like a credible leader figure, but one when in the domestic space is a magnanimous and generous host. His hospitality, as we will discuss later, although it necessarily appears relaxed, carries with it a need for the performance of patriarchal fealty.

From hacker to paternal statesman

Zuckerberg is unusual in placing so much emphasis on fatherhood in his celebrity profile. Elon Musk, for instance, has five sons, and, while he shares custody of them with his ex-wife, and talks about making sure to spend time with them, excepting paparazzi media they are almost entirely absent from his celebrified assemblage. (However, Musk's most recent child X Æ A-12, with musician Grimes in 2020 has been more directly part of his celebrity.) Jeff Bezos, Larry Page, and Sergey Brin's children barely register in their celebrity. This is reflected in the concordance: there are only four mentions of 'fatherhood' in toto (compared to 25 of motherhood) – and one of them is in the title of a referenced article about how women are severely punished financially for having children. While the others all make heavy reference to their fathers and indeed grandfathers – albeit in different ways for each – Zuckerberg focuses instead on his immediate family. This positions him primarily as a father rather than as a son, and is an important marker of difference in the wider network of competition and collaboration that distinguishes the tech-founder networks. That is, the figure who was the quintessence of the boy genius disruptor of Silicon Valley myth now works hardest among all his peers to disavow that label.

Earlier in his career, Zuckerberg performed a very different sort of public identity as a 'hacker,' and even ensured that the word 'hack' – written in big letters across Facebook's Menlo Park campus – was visible from space (or at least through Google Earth). Whereas fatherhood barely makes an appearance, hacker is 11 times more likely to appear in our concordance than in the control web sample. Thus the harnessing of this particular postfeminist masculinity does a lot of work in counteracting the portrayal of Zuckerberg as arrogant, for example in the 'wildly inaccurate biopic,' *The Social Network* (Zadie Smith 2010). He is working to offset the associations between being a 'hacker' and 'toxic geek masculinity' (Salter and Blodgett 2018) that have been linked to his founding of Facebook, in popular texts in our concordance like *The Boy Kings* (Losse 2014).

The hacker is the tech equivalent of the Wild West's cowboy. He (traditionally a 'he') is able to navigate the wilds of cyberspace and make possible new worlds, carving out new ways of living in the space between silicon chips. As we saw in Chapter 3, the hacker has been invoked by figures like Stewart Brand since the 1970s aiding in the concatenation of the 'empty' spaces of the West, space travel (both fictional and real), and technology. Similarly, for Elon Musk, some element of the hacker mystique feeds into how he sells high-end electric cars – i.e. to (mostly) men with disposable income and a fascination with the cowboy-meets-counterculture narrative in the vein of Stewart Brand and the Electronic Frontier Foundation.

Hackers are a core concept in the development of new companies in Silicon Valley. From a random sample of 50 uses in our concordance we learn that hackers are 'individualistic and anti-authoritarian' and 'immortal superheroes'; they find 'power outside its normal channels'; and 'being a hacker is defined by skill, knowledge and mindset alone'; it is also 'descriptive of a talent set.' Who these hackers are is perhaps harder to work out in relation to other vectors. In one example the author states: 'I think it's fantastic that now in high schools people can be themselves whether they are gay or a hacker, right?' In Randall Stross's 2012 book on tech entrepreneur finishing school Y-Combinator, where investors invite young people to develop new companies under their mentorship, he notes that they look for companies to invest in that are usually made up only of hackers. Stross tries hard in his book to make the case that it's not really Y-Combinator's fault that their startups end up being founded almost exclusively by white and Asian men: 'Paul Graham and the other partners with technical backgrounds were ideologically committed to a gender- and race-blind view of merit' (Stross 2012, 49). But it is very hard to see the hacker identity as anything other than culturally coded as masculine. Indeed Stewart Brand explicitly genders them in a tradition of masculine explorers and inventors: 'hackers were not mere "technicians," but a mobile new-found elite, with its own apparat[us], language and character, its own legends and humour. Those magnificent men with their flying machines, scouting a leading edge of technology' (Brand cited in Turner 2008, 117).

Zuckerberg's initial celebrity persona was utterly focused on these tech mythologies and its masculinities: Facebook's original motto was 'move fast and break things,' explicitly referencing Silicon Valley's countercultural aim to be disruptive of staid institutions and practice (Turner 2008). As Brand puts it: 'Once a new technology rolls over you, if you're not part of the steamroller, you're part of the road' (cited in McNamee 2019, 177). The hacker identity was an important brand asset initially: it gave Zuckerberg cachet in tech and venture capital circles, and Facebook's early growth strategy sought to target students at elite universities who would appreciate both its underground cool as well as the high economic value of the skills required to be a hacker. But the social network now has two billion users worldwide, and the 'hacker mystique' has a limited charm for most of them. Facebook today is a platform that wants to be integrated into every element of daily life, and thus needs to be essential, ordinary, intimate, reliable, and universal. A heavy emphasis on fatherhood, invoking the basic essentials of social reproduction, does a much better job at projecting that image than the elite and subversive figure of the hacker. More than this, the paterfamilias identity lends a form of masculinist authority, and this legitimates Zuckerberg's (postfeminist or otherwise) patriarchal status. In addition, the universality of 'fatherhood' can be stretched to help reconcile other masculinities within a single motif – something that Zuckerberg attempts to do, with limited success, during this period.

P. David Marshall's work on celebrity and politics helps in understanding the wider implications of Zuckerberg's performance of postfeminist fatherhood. Marshall investigates how politicians like Ronald Reagan and George Bush Snr have invoked the familial as a key component of their bid to masculine authority and leadership. Because masculinity 'continues to connote power, control, and mastery,' political leaders must demonstrate these qualities in order to establish their legitimacy: '[l]ayered onto the construction of leadership as a form of masculinity is the division of power in the family itself. The political leader, then, is generally painted as the father figure for the nation and its people' (Marshall 2013, 217). This has resonances with the Lockean portrayal of the household that we discussed in Chapter 1 where the social contract theorist John Locke outlines the ideal colonial structure of the heteronormative family, headed by a patriarch. Although Locke notes the differences between the private homestead and the political sphere, he does make connections (Pateman 1988).

Marshall uses Bush's 1988 presidential campaign to illustrate the ways that representing a leader with his family 'operates symbolically' as an acceptable feminised version of masculine power. Because the 'family patriarch' is depicted as benevolent, as a consequence of his responsibilities or care for others, his power appears tempered (Marshall 2013, 217). This is a technique that certainly seems to hold true for understanding 'Grill Talk.' In the video, and throughout Zuckerberg's Facebook Timeline, we can see the attempt to temper his power through the depiction of his intimate role in the family. Indeed, his mediated fatherhood is crucial for understanding how his patriarchal power is naturalised. Zuckerberg's performance of paternity is the emotional glue which works to provide a common bond with his users. Focusing primarily on television as the site where this paternalism plays out, Marshall argues that:

> [t]he homologous relationship between the familial and the nation, the father and the political leader, is a form of affective transference: the acceptability and the 'warmth' conveyed by a 'good' and 'strong' family structure become a legitimate model for structuring the organization of the political sphere.
>
> *(218)*

In this way, the 'unknown-ness of the electorate' is shaped to a certain political meaning that is connected to the leader.

Zuckerberg is not running for president, he is not bidding for an electorate, and his family is not represented on television in the same way as the politicians who are being examined by Marshall; rather, Zuckerberg utilises his digital platform. Nevertheless, in both cases, we can see parallels in the imaginary of the heteronormative household headed by a benevolent father. By representing himself as part of an intimate sphere, Zuckerberg aims for a solidarity with the people; he is like them, he is part of a wider collective of 'common' people (Marshall 2013, 220). This is the work the assemblage we've discussed here is doing: bringing Zuckerberg and his users closer together to legitimise his role as the 'leader' of Facebook. In the next section, we examine the ways that he attempts to intervene in the political sphere through his 'Year of Travel.' This intervention is also framed by his intimate paternalism, where the strong organisation of the household provides justification for his leadership in the public realm. In both cases the optics of hospitality are primary.

Mark's Year of Travel: family, community, liberalism

From 2009 to 2019 Zuckerberg shared his annual personal challenge 'to learn something new' with his Facebook followers. As part of these challenges he has built AI for his home (discussed below), run 365 miles, read 25 books, and learned Mandarin. One year he only ate meat that he had killed himself. In 2017, his personal challenge was to visit every US state. In January 2017 he posted: 'After a tumultuous last year, my hope for this challenge is to get out and talk to more people about how they're living, working and thinking about the future' (Zuckerberg, 8 January 2017a). He updated his subsequent travels on Instagram, his personal Facebook page, and a Facebook Group called 'Mark's Year of Travel':

> The trips will all take different forms – road trips with Priscilla, stops in small towns and universities, visits to Facebook offices across the country, meetings with teachers and scientists, and trips to fun places the community will recommend along the way.
>
> *(Year of Travel, 15 January 2017)*

These images and text are not only for his followers and users of the platform, but also for mainstream media circulation. Using the features of the platform, followers are encouraged to join a Facebook Group devoted to the challenge, and 'share your own story of travel.' Of course these posts are curated by a PR team, as part of the Year of Travel project. In addition – something that isn't highlighted in any of the Facebook presentation of the tour – Charles Ommanney, former photographer to presidents Barack Obama and George W. Bush, is part of the travelling team, as well as David Plouffe, Obama's former campaign manager. But why is a White House photographer following Zuckerberg, and why is his tour of the US being organised like a political campaign?

The Year of Travel photographs are located in culturally significant American settings such as, for example, Vicksburg National Military Park and Mother Emanuel African Methodist Episcopal Church. Many of the photographs include food, signifying patriotic hospitality. Zuckerberg might be sharing a meal with a Trump-voting family in Ohio, gutting fish in Alaska, eating cheesesteak in Philly, chatting at a truck stop in Iowa, or drinking a milkshake with a resident at a diner (also in Iowa). He could be sharing a plate of biscuits, a takeaway or pizza in a workplace setting, or sitting down for a meal in a restaurant or community centre, as when he shared an Iftar dinner with Somali migrants in Minneapolis. He might promote a Facebook feature, such as in May 2017, when he uses the recommendation feature for brats. One obvious inference from all this is that Zuckerberg is being represented in the Year of Travel Timeline as a viable leadership alternative to Donald Trump. Significantly, we see divisions that have been appropriated and emphasised by Trump being apparently bridged and resolved through the mediated presidential figure of Zuckerberg. During this period speculation was mounting that he was about to run for president. This was evidenced not only in the comments on Zuckerberg's Facebook Timeline, but also in a 2016 rewrite of the legal terms of the Facebook stock structure that gave Zuckerberg absolute control of the company while still allowing him time out for up to two years should he choose to run for office (Bilton 2017; Lafrance 2017, Leswing 2017). Zuckerberg has publicly denied his political ambitions (Kantrowitz and Tiku 2017). However, his increasingly politicised posts, as well as his commitment to visiting every state in America and sharing meals with traditional Democrat voters who had voted for Trump, reveal that he was at the very least threatening an intervention into formal politics (Solon 2017b).

At a rally in Minnesota in November 2016, Trump denounced Somali migrants as a 'disaster,' claiming that some Somalis were 'joining ISIS and spreading their extremist views all over our country' (Jacobs and Yuhas 2016). In deliberate contrast, and to promote Zuckerberg's more liberal values, the Year of Travel portrays Zuckerberg apparently accepting hospitality from Somali hosts, and then reciprocating digitally, by conveying his hosts and the meal through his platform, thus extending his hospitality to them. In this way, Zuckerberg promotes his brand as welcoming of diversity (implicitly Democrat tropes). Such posts model Facebook's blending of community, commercial promotion, and digital sociality. They are interspersed with yet more pictures of Zuckerberg cooking or eating with his wife and two daughters at home, in an attempt to give the heavily curated page the illusion of organic authenticity, and extend his branded paternalism.

The tour can be seen as functioning to perform Facebook's role as the foundational infrastructure of what Antonio Gramsci called 'civil society.' Churches, unions, community groups, membership organisations, and so forth are collective, civil society, spaces that, crucially, are independent from the capitalist profit motive or the state (Gramsci 1971). Throughout the tour, Zuckerberg makes the case that Facebook is the contemporary space for these things to occur, bridging the gap between atomised citizen and the material infrastructure of nations. Historically, the ideological space of nation was collectively imagined through shared media – newspapers and later TV; now Facebook provides that as well (Anderson 1983; Debray 2007). Consequently, the representation of the tour is much more than PR, just as Facebook is much more than a corporation. This is not just a rebranding exercise. The optics of the tour – as revealed on the platform – tell us much about the corporation's reach and ambition. Interspersed with the photographs, Zuckerberg announces policy, and comments on the socioeconomic and affective states of the people that he meets. When he guts fish in Alaska he advocates a universal basic income – a policy popular in Silicon Valley tech culture, and one advocated by failed 2019 Democrat presidential candidate Andrew Yang (his book is in our corpus). In South Dakota, Zuckerberg discusses fracking and notes that despite his commitment to renewable energy, it was important to hear the views of presumably Republican voting workers in the fossil fuel sector (Yeo 2017). This tour – and especially being hosted at meals by former-Democrat-turned-Trump-voters as well as refugees – works to emphasise the corporation's critical role in civil society; Zuckerberg is depicted as working to connect the world rather than reap immense profit from it. Facebook and its founder are co-deployed through the Year of Travel to each legitimate the other.

America's historical and intergenerational trauma in connection to race, migration, and socioeconomic deprivation is implied throughout the tour. For example, Zuckerberg visits Blackfeet Reservation in Montana, as well as Black men who have been 'wrongly incarcerated' (Zuckerberg 2017a). Significantly, the Facebook platform attempts to visually resolve the complexities of these inequalities through the recurring figure of Zuckerberg and patriotic optics. The welcoming of diversity is visually conveyed through images of food and mediated hospitality, making Facebook the host of connections in Trump's divided America.

Sharing food across cultural difference can contribute to an appreciation of the other (Narayan 1997). It can also, in Amanda Wise's words, be a form of 'low-level cosmopolitanism,' as well as producing 'cultural anxiety and disjuncture ... disgust and desire' (Wise 2011, 84). Food and food cultures are seen as particularly important in Silicon Valley, so it is interesting that Zuckerberg focuses on them here. English-Lueck argues that: 'Bay Area identity is marked by the range of cuisines and the importance of good food.' So we can also see that Zuckerberg's consumption of traditional American food types is putting taste distinctions of tech culture aside in favour of a more 'everyman' ordinary persona. English-Lueck again:

> In the United States, food is tied to upward mobility; being a 'foodie' both excludes those with different tastes and creates a sense of belonging with those whose tastes are elevated ... The Bay Area's haute cuisine is local, fresh, wholesome, and exquisitely presented. The cuisine captures global flavors, and should be source sustainable. It also marks the consumers of the cuisine as educated, discerning, and, in the words of Bourdieu, 'distinct.'
>
> *(English-Lueck 2017, 134)*

It is key to the rebuttal to Trump, therefore, that Zuckerberg is pictured eating with Republican voters as well as Somali migrants. The Year of Travel exploits this to promote Zuckerberg's 'presidential' brand-building; it harnesses the tropes of a typical Democrat who is open to liberalism and diversity – at least in the optics. The sharing of food – in person but then later as pictures on the platform – reveals Zuckerberg and Facebook as being both invited guest and hospitable host.

In February Zuckerberg is photographed having lunch with white members of the fishing community in Bayou La Batre. He posts:

> One of the families we met were the Zirlotts – they run an oyster farm and are succeeding by using Facebook and Instagram to show their product directly to chefs. The fishing industry is more than a job to these folks – it's their community and a way of life.

Zuckerberg is pictured at the centre of the photograph, listening and looking at the other people who mainly have their back to the camera. This post, combined with the photograph of sharing a meal, is significant for its promotion of Facebook as the key facilitator of civil society. Its repetition of the word 'community' – 'I'm looking at more of the world through the lens of building community these days' – reveals the PR team working hard to legitimate Facebook as a hospitable location for civil society.

Interestingly, 'politics' and 'democracy' have no special emphasis in our corpus: they occur at almost identical rates as in our baseline Web TenTen 2015 corpus. 'Community,' on the other hand, shows up less than a quarter as often in our corpus as in the baseline (190/mw as opposed to 824/mw). In other words, although it is a key word for Facebook (i.e. it is what Zuckerberg and his PR team want the platform to be understood as supporting – which in fact it does, albeit in a fashion heavily mediated by 'data relations'), community appears not to be a significant concept for tech culture in general. This finding is surprising, and goes against anthropological studies of tech culture at the level of the tech social imaginary. English-Lueck, for instance, sees 'community' as a central point of focus for people working in technology but mediated by the technology itself: 'Community is "designed," "invented," "reinvented" and "refreshed,"' she says (English-Lueck 2017, 45). Likewise, for Stewart Brand and the countercultural technologists inventing new forms of community – something that is inherent to Turner's definition of the tech pioneers as 'The New Communalists' – it was absolutely key for their philosophy. However, in this case, the interest wasn't in community in general, but always in an elite community of what became technology workers. Whatever the evidence and interpretation of community may be elsewhere in the tech world, Facebook is now definitely unusual in wanting to create a *general* community, for everyone, rather than specific groups clustered by status or interest (even though, when it started in elite universities, this was exactly what the company was doing).

It must be noted, however, that once you're part of the big Facebook community – that is on the platform as a user – the company profits from the careful distinctions it makes. It employs personal data to categorise users into algorithmic groups, with one of the kinds of relevant data being identifications with communities. Thus 'community' has no natural, straightforward, or single concept in this milieu. More than this, as we discuss below, users are by no means seen as equivalent, and all of them are subject to some extent to Zuckerberg's sovereignty. As Skeggs and Yuill argue:

> Facebook argues that it embodies connectivity as a universal right, and that it does so in a way that gives this equally to all. Such claims of equivalence must be questioned, for there is a history of how such rights and values have been constructed and whose interests they serve, which such claims ignore.
>
> *(Skeggs and Yuill 2019, 97)*

This is the history of liberalism, the household, and personhood that we have been mapping in this book, and which we investigate further below.

In this instance, however, the Year of Travel functions to make the hosting of a general community become a proxy for political leadership: the range of specificities is used to produce a universality. That is, diversity of place and race are intended to stand for a larger whole, the nation. The images produced in the Timeline attempt to integrate monopoly tech capitalism as a supporter of local communities, and curate Zuckerberg as a viable 'president.' Yet they are also revealing of lines of division, and of the constructed and specifically liberal nature of this claim to a putative universal, albeit national, community. For example, when Zuckerberg is photographed at the iconic truck stop, Iowa 80 Kitchen (Figure 4.2), he posts:

> I asked the truckers what's changed over the last few decades. When the truckers I met started driving, you logged your driving hours on pieces of paper. Now it's electronic and automatic, which makes it harder to drive more hours than you're supposed to. Some people said they want to work longer, but they feel like regulations are getting in the way of their freedom and doing what they want to do. It's tough because those regulations try to keep people on the road safe.
>
> *(Zuckerberg, 24 June 2017a)*

Here we can see Zuckerberg triangulating like a politician, trying to find the balance between both sides, to speak for, and to a constructed majority. This triangulation continues in the optics. Accompanying this post is a picture of Zuckerberg eating apple dessert and ice-cream on a diner counter next to a Black man with a headpiece. In the background, to the right of the photograph, is an unsmiling white man in a stars and stripes baseball hat that reflects the light of

FIGURE 4.2 Mark Zuckerberg at Iowa 80 Kitchen, 2017

the ceiling lamp, thus illuminating its patriotic symbolism. Zuckerberg is located at the centre of the photograph, listening and talking to the Black trucker. They are both smiling. In the visual triangle between the three men, we can see once more how The Year of Travel represents Zuckerberg as a cohesive figure, bridging divides. The framing of the photograph means that the image of Zuckerberg works to bridge race and class – through the man in the stars and stripes hat – in ways that are normally freighted with racism. And indeed, this is picked up by the commenters who discuss Trump, Obama, and the politics of race in America. The comments below the image reflect the global plurality of the users of the platform – and are evidence that the platform really does host a multiplicity of different voices and opinions. However, the fact that Facebook is host is key.

In June, The Year of Travel announces: 'Mark had his first Iftar dinner' (the evening meal which ends the Ramadan fast at sunset), and he is pictured with a group of Somali refugees in Minneapolis. Explicitly contesting Trump's denigration of the community (as mentioned above), a grey t-shirted Zuckerberg is photographed ostensibly participating in a meal in a community centre that he has been invited to. He is in the centre of the photograph bathed in the light of a ceiling window. He is flanked by four Somali women, and they appear to be engaged in conversation; Zuckerberg and two of them are smiling. There are 'Speak English' posters on the left-hand side of the photograph, and the two posters behind Mark conjugate the verbs 'To Be' and 'To Do.' We can read these optics as what Elaine Swan calls 'strategies of containment' which are a means to contain any potential threat to the racial hierarchies and stratifications of the social field (Swan 2009). Zuckerberg posts:

> As a refugee, you often don't get to choose which country you end up in. When I asked one man, who had spent 26 years in a refugee camp, whether America now felt like home, he gave a simple and profound answer:
>
> 'Home is where you are free to do what you want. Yes, this feels like home.'
>
> There are few places in the world he felt comfortable to be who he is: the country he was born, and our country that values freedom.
>
> What a beautiful tribute to America.
>
> Thanks to my hosts for being so gracious at the very end of Ramadan. I left impressed by your strength and resilience to build a new life in an unfamiliar place, and you are a powerful reminder of why this country is so great.

The figure of Zuckerberg appears to accept difference but also resolves any potential conflict through patriotic assimilation, centring America as host. Moreover, although he offers the position of host to the Somali community, it is he who has the last word. He incorporates this visit into his celebrity assemblage, employing it as means to emphasise his platform as the liberal site for civil society.

Migration, and its histories, provides a number of sites where Zuckerberg's leadership qualities can be contrasted with the xenophobia of Trump. Zuckerberg's Jewishness – which he started to re-assert at this time – and the Chinese and Vietnamese heritage of his spouse – are marshalled to criticise Trumpian policy. In January 2017 he posts:

> My great grandparents came from Germany, Austria and Poland. Priscilla's parents were refugees from China and Vietnam. The United States is a nation of immigrants, and we should be proud of that.
>
> Like many of you, I'm concerned about the impact of the recent executive orders signed by President Trump.

Immigration, migration, and hospitality are represented as cornerstones of American identity. Skilfully, the Year of Travel brings policy, personal and familial history, and the platform, together. Zuckerberg's criticism of Trump is significant, especially as he is such an influential figure. However, we need to examine these claims as part of Zuckerberg's celebrity which itself is located as a component of the Zuckerberg-Facebook assemblage. The 'strategies of containment' (Swan 2009), the technologies of patriotic assimilation, as well as the representation of the postfeminist paternalist family disrupt a straightforward reading of Zuckerberg's claims. As we argue below, the Facebook platform reinforces taxonomies of race, gender, and class which cannot be resolved by Zuckerberg's Facebook Timeline.

The traditional American family meal

One of the strategies of Zuckerberg's mediated hospitality is to represent the corporation as treating people as citizens rather than the collection of data points intrinsic to Facebook's business model. In the images of Zuckerberg in people's homes there are no phones, laptops, or computers. Signifiers of the traditional American household are highlighted. Facebook is represented not as a cornerstone of 'surveillance capitalism' and its processes of capital accumulation through data (Zuboff 2019), but as an invited guest. In the photographs we examine in this section, Zuckerberg visits two white families who formerly voted Democrat and then campaigned for Trump (Wier 2017). These are the blue-collar workers that Trump courted through his rhetoric of the 'working class' (which deliberately omitted any reference to Black and other ethnic minority working-class constituents), and who, having been 'left behind' by the long decline of heavy industry and manufacturing, have not managed to successfully transition to digital capitalism. The only photographs of Zuckerberg sharing meals in familial homes are in the households of white people; and the tour thus invokes the white nostalgia of Trumpian rhetoric. Bygone sentiment pervades these photographs, and this is something that is picked up by many of the commenters, who note the lack of any digital media in the frame – as well as the old-fashioned nature of gathering together for family meals.

One meal is hosted on a farm in Wisconsin in April 2017. Zuckerberg, dressed in a plain dark jumper, is taking a plate of brownies and ice-cream from (we assume) the mother and grandmother of the family. Behind him is a fridge covered in children's pictures, magnets, coupons. The domestic intergenerational scene signifies ordinariness, authenticity, tradition, locality – all tropes the Year of Travel project is keen to link to Facebook and Zuckerberg. Indeed, many of the comments pick up on these themes. Zuckerberg demonstrates respect for the family – and the demographic which they symbolise – by appreciating their hard work, but also in highlighting his ability to share and listen at the dinner table. He posts:

> Family 'dinner' at noon. When you wake up at 4am, I guess your schedule is shifted up a bit.
>
> *(Zuckerberg, 30 April 2017a)*

From the photographs and the posts, it appears that Zuckerberg has been invited into these families' homes, and they all seem to be eating the same food. They are presented as respectable people worth listening to and making visible, as well as being invested with agency.

A photograph is also posted of a meal Zuckerberg shares with a family in Newton Falls, Ohio: 'Just got into Ohio. Thanks to Dan and Lisa Moore for welcoming me into your home for a wonderful dinner!' he posts (Zuckerberg, 29 April 2017a). Ohio is a key state that turned Republican in 2016, and the members of this family were former Democrat voters who campaigned hard for Trump (Wier 2017). Again, this seems to be another blue-collar family, suggested by the wallpaper trim, presentation cabinet, the colours of the room, the decoration hanging from the lamp, and the clothes of the family at the table. In this photograph no one is smiling apart from Zuckerberg; indeed, the meal appears awkward. The comments pick up on this, and there are ongoing discussions of why the family hosts Zuckerberg with paper plates and plastic cutlery, to the point that Zuckerberg has to wade in with 'It was a great meal and great conversation. I appreciate their hospitality!' (Zuckerberg, 29 April 2017a). Although he is framed at the centre, in neither photograph is he at the head of the table; other men are given more presence – through body language (including facial expressions), hair and attire, their connections with the other members (i.e. father), or location at the table. Zuckerberg is smiling, talking, or listening to another person, rather than looking at the camera. Zuckerberg projects soft leadership by making the people he visits visible to a global audience; he is extending Facebook's arm of hospitality to former Democrat Trump voters.

The normative view of the household as white is a key dimension of the founder cultures we have identified and it is also reflected in this Year of Travel. Overall the journey may have the optics of diversity, but in fact Zuckerberg only visits traditional white American households: when he is photographed with people of colour it is at community centres, diners, or churches. It appears to be that the white family is the marker against which others are measured; it is also the means by which a heteronormative, racialised patriarchy reproduces itself. This is long-standing in American culture more generally as illustrated, for example, in Patricia Hill Collins's 1989 critique of the Moynihan report of 1965 on 'the negro family.' As Hill Collins argues, the white middle-class household is upheld in the report as having moral value, and contrasted to the morally suspect African-American family.

To reinforce this point, all is not what it seems in the Newton Falls photograph. According to *The Vindicator* – a local Ohio news outlet – the family had no idea that Zuckerberg was coming to visit until 20 minutes before he showed up; and the visit had been organised by the Year of Travel team (Wier 2017). This goes some way to explaining the paper plates. Although the family have extended their hospitality and agreed to the photographs being taken, uploaded, and commented upon, their agency in the scenario has been circumscribed, as they are framed in such a way as to work towards the main intention of the Year of Travel – that is, for Zuckerberg to appear as a viable alternative to Trump's leadership.

Indeed, it is not insignificant that Zuckerberg is represented in people's homes and workplaces observing private behaviours and relationships – and sharing this information with users and media. It replicates what the corporation does – as part of the wider tech industry – as it surveils people and hoovers up data, before aggregating it according to algorithmically determined demographics. Facebook inserts itself into intimate life and monetises it. We can therefore read this Year of Travel as visually rendering Zuckerberg-Facebook's settlement of the intimate frontier. As Zuckerberg is pictured crossing America visiting households and communities, his power as host is tempered or obfuscated as an invited guest. What is also interesting here is the way that this scenario might replicate how we extend our own hospitality to Facebook. As part of the assemblage ourselves, we agree to its terms and conditions (although we might not agree to them wholeheartedly, or even understand the implications of them): we agree to its capturing and sharing of data, and tracking of activities online and offline (see Couldry and Mejias 2018; Carmi 2018). However, this agreement is lopsided and unequal. One could call it – and perhaps this was what it was like for the family in Newton Falls – being coerced. Although we have agency – we can (almost) leave Facebook – we don't have control over the terms of 'data relations'(Couldry and Mejias 2019): the data they have, or the ways they might still be tracking us, or information about us is stored and sold. These signifiers of hospitality, food, and benevolence are attempts to humanise, legitimate, and render benign the deliberately mysterious and powerful reach of digital capitalism. But they also, unwittingly, reveal the extent of the corporation's power. In short, Zuckerberg 'the surprise guest' is a good metaphor for how Facebook enters our homes and thus how we enter into the ambit of datafication through his platform.

'I can control the gates': AI and the household patriarch

Jacques Derrida's work on hospitality helps make sense of the way that hospitality pivots on the notion of difference. Derrida makes a distinction between 'the foreigner and the absolute other' (Derrida 2000, 23), as well as between the hospitality contract and 'absolute hospitality' – the latter of which means I will 'give up my home' to the absolute, unknowable, other (Derrida 2000, 25). He argues that, according to the hospitality contract, hospitality can only be offered 'to a foreigner "as a family," represented and protected by his or her family name' (Derrida 2000, 23). That is, the hospitality contract is only extended to someone who can be known and identified by their patrilineal name. And the person who accepts the hand of hospitality then enters into a contract where they have obligations. During the Year of Travel, hospitality was offered to Zuckerberg by workplaces and families because he is a known celebrity, and because there were donations involved (Wier 2017). Entering into the hospitality contract in this way surrounds Zuckerberg with the aura of a politician's responsibility; one might expect him to now have an obligation to those who he visited – and this expectation runs through the comments. And yet the question of what it is that Zuckerberg offers in return for all the hospitality that is afforded to him, particularly by the non-white and working-class communities he visited, remains.

In 2016 journalists found Facebook to be illegally allowing housing advertising to target customers according to their race. Facebook was using 'ethnic-affinity targeting,' so that even though users are not asked their race when creating an account, their data reveals 'interest in race-related content.' In an interview Noble states: 'We are being racially profiled by a platform that doesn't allow us to even declare our own race and ethnicity … What does that mean to not allow culture and ethnicity to be visible in the platform?' (cited in Wachter-Boettcher 2017, 113). Facebook has evaded responsibility for these practices by citing Section 230 of the Communications Decency Act (1996) to defend its advertising platform. Section 230 protects intermediaries from liability for distributing third-party user content. This means that social media companies are seen as tech companies rather than media companies, and so they are not liable for content that is uploaded on their sites. Facebook argues for immunity because it is the advertisers' responsibility. These practices around housing continue (Sylvain 2018). In her critique of the way that Silicon Valley's private decisions influence public policy, Ruha Benjamin suggests an alternative motto for Facebook: 'Move Fast, Break People, and Call It Progress' (Benjamin 2019, 13). Siva Vaidhyanathan has also written extensively and passionately on the way that Facebook undermines democracy: 'the problem with Facebook is Facebook' (Vaidhyanathan 2018, 1).

To give another example of Facebook inhospitality, and the way that it perpetuates the paradigm of the conservative household, we can turn to the work of Rena Bivens. As we discussed in Chapter 1, even though Facebook offered users a 'custom' option in addition to 'male' and 'female' in 2014, these non-binary possibilities of identification only exist at the surface level of the software. Deeper into the database, non-binary users are re-classified in order to meet the needs of advertisers and marketers (Bivens 2017). Therefore, it is not insignificant that hospitality is extended to what Derrida defines as the 'foreign other' only once a user can be identified in a Western-style and heteronormative patrilineal lineage. Facebook's product design means that those who deviate from the patriarchal norm are denied the recognition of personhood by the platform. In addition, Facebook will only give us an account if we agree to pay with our data from offline and online spaces. As long as the platform can thoroughly 'know' its users through their data, it will continue to extend hospitality and thus *retain* sovereignty. As Benjamin points out, because Facebook is advertising-driven, 'users *get used*' (Benjamin 2019, 14). These are just a few examples of the ways that Facebook reinforces oppressions along the lines of race, class, gender: see, for example, the open letter from Civil Rights groups to Zuckerberg (The Leadership Conference Civil and Human Rights 2019). It is to further questions of personhood, property, and sovereignty that we now turn.

As we mentioned earlier, one of the annual challenges that Zuckerberg set himself was to build AI for his home. Jostling with Sergey Brin and Elon Musk for the association with Marvel's most popular superhero, he tells his followers in a post on Facebook that, 'You can think of it kind of like Jarvis in Iron Man.' (Jarvis is the AI butler.) Enacting the tropes of geek masculinity and postfeminist fatherhood he posts on his Facebook Timeline:

> I'm going to start by exploring what technology is already out there. Then I'll start teaching it to understand my voice to control everything in our home – music, lights, temperature and so on. I'll teach it to let friends in by looking at their faces when they ring the doorbell. I'll teach it to let me know if anything is going on in Max's room that I need to check on when I'm not with her. On the work side, it'll help me visualize data in VR to help me build better services and lead my organizations more effectively.
>
> *(Russell 2016)*

Zuckerberg is describing being in control of the technology of his home, including in his tasks as father and gatekeeper of the household. In a corporate question and answer session in Rome six months later, he is seen discussing his progress:

> 'I got it to this point where now I can control the lights, I can control the gates, I can control the temperature – much to the chagrin of my wife, who now cannot control the temperature because it is programmed to only listen to my voice ... I'll give her access once I'm done ... So it's getting there. And it's starting to be able to do some pretty fun things, and I'm looking forward to being able to show it to the world.'
>
> *(Welch 2016)*

On one level this is a more respectable version of the home voice assistant: he models his voice-activated assistant on Tony Stark's male AI butler rather than the sexy voiced digital secretary in *Why Him?* that we discussed in Chapter 1. But we are obviously interested in the gendered joke here, coming as it is from someone who has been so carefully curated through the optics of paternalism. It is significant that he performs control over his home – 'I control the gates' – and that he will gift his wife access to this control in his own time.

Interestingly, we can see how this paternalist representation reinforces how the 'platform family' technology (e.g. Amazon Household and Google Families – see Chapter 1), reinvents the family where roles are 'ascribed largely by gender, the husband in the instrumental role as wage earner, the wife in the affective role of family carer' (Goulden 2019, 4). Although Amazon Household and Google Families – as Murray Goulden notes – are not intrinsically gendered, they effectively take their gendered dimensions from normative assumptions. Because 'Google's Family Manager derives ultimate authority from being the first adopter in the family' then the fact that the associated technologies are 'designed by and for men' will have 'deep implications for how agency is distributed within the platform family' (Goulden 2019, 12). In addition, the design interpellates a specific kind of normative family 'as being of a certain size, as co-located, as isolated, and as stable and enduring, in which authority over others is formally vested in one, or perhaps two, key roles.' According to Goulden, the digital households offer a technical, but normative, account of what home is, and what the family does. We can see this being enacted by Zuckerberg here as part of his celebrity assemblage.

Significantly though, in being control of the AI around his home, Zuckerberg is also in control of its data. This begs the question, why might Zuckerberg want to create his own AI for his home, rather than using, for example, Amazon Household or Google Families or other technologies available for households? We suggest that this is a question of authority and sovereignty. Zuckerberg cannot be seen to submit management of his household to devices like Google's Nest thermostat or Amazon's voice-activated operating system Alexa, which are owned by rival billionaires. It is a matter of competition. More than this, however, it is also connected to digital personhood and who is offered proper personhood under the rule of the West Coast Tech corporate households.

Questions of domestic sovereignty, technology, and patriarchy are strongly linked. Goulden's (2019) work on 'the platform family' that is being created by the smart home is again helpful for understanding these connections. The home and its people make the household, and once technology comes to mediate between this domestic economy and the wider culture, it starts to be able to reshape or reinforce social relations inside the household in fundamental ways. We can understand this history of attitudes to the normative family as constituting the longer-term context that frames the imaginary of the contemporary smart home that Zuckerberg playfully celebrates in regards to his AI butler. As Couldry and Mejias argue, the smart home plays a role in the erasure of cultural heterogeneity; through the disciplinary logics of data, a single reality is imposed, denying agency to those whose lives do not conform to its framings:

> The smart home, and the code running through it, can be read as such – as not merely a landgrab, but a concerted effort to rewrite the lives situated within it, such that they are permanently in the service of the platform and its generation of surplus value.
>
> *(Couldry and Mejias 2019, 15)*

It is a site of the intimate frontier to be settled and controlled.

Continuing with our parallel analysis of the metaphorical and literal Zuckerberg-Facebook households, we suggest that, by building a proprietary AI for his own household, Zuckerberg is also locating his sovereign power outside the normal ambit of data relations. Because of the relationship that Zuckerberg – as part of the Zuckerberg-Facebook assemblage – has with data colonialism, his personhood is significantly different from, for example, those of the ordinary users investigated by Skeggs and Yuill (2019) in relation to Facebook. Skeggs and Yuill (2019) note that the liberal subject, which once 'hinged property to propriety in the making of personhood' has now been 'unhinged' from this connection, because the patriarchs of digital capitalism extract and aggregate data from those middle-class white people who (also) benefit from the cultural and social capital that the monopoly platforms can offer them. As we argue in Chapter 6, using the work of Skeggs and Yuill, the proper subject – who 'relied on the de-legitimation, de-valuation, de-grading and de-personalizing of others in order to claim power' has now 'had their propriety propertised for them.' Even the head of the household loses power in data colonialism. Those who once could inhabit proper personhood 'have become subject to the expropriation that was long the condition of their constitutive others' (Skeggs and Yuill 2019, 96). This means that it is only a very few men who hold the position of proper personhood under digital colonialism.

In the building of his own AI for his home, Zuckerberg maintains this sovereignty as part of the patriarchal network of digital capitalism. Moreover, it is no accident that he associates this power with the butler of the superhero Ironman. He harnesses the tropes of geek masculinity in making the AI, but also in the invocation of Iron Man. He also connects these motifs to his authority as the husband and father in his household. In short, as we discussed in Chapter 2, these superhero motifs are a means to justify and legitimate immense disparities in power and wealth. They both reveal and obfuscate patriarchy as a superpower.

Notes

1 Zuckerberg explicitly defines him as a millennial. For example, in his 2017 Harvard commencement speech he states: 'Today I want to talk about purpose. But I'm not

here to give you the standard commencement about finding your purpose. We're millennials. We'll try to do that instinctively. Instead, I'm here to tell you finding your purpose isn't enough. The challenge for our generation is creating a world where everyone has a sense of purpose' (Zuckerberg 2017b).

2 Facemash also provides part of Zuckerberg's narrative about meeting Priscilla. From the Harvard Commencement speech cited above: 'But my best memory from Harvard was meeting Priscilla. I had just launched this prank website Facemash, and the ad board wanted to "see me." Everyone thought I was going to get kicked out. My parents came to help me pack. My friends threw me a going away party. As luck would have it, Priscilla was at that party with her friend. We met in line for the bathroom in the Pfoho Belltower, and in what must be one of the all time romantic lines, I said: "I'm going to get kicked out in three days, so we need to go on a date quickly"' (Zuckerberg 2017b).

References

Anderson, Benedict (1983) *Reflections on the Origin and Spread of Nationalism*. London: Verso.

Aschoff, Nicole (2015) *The New Prophets of Capital*. London: Verso.

Banet-Weiser, Sarah (2012) *Authentic: The Politics of Ambivalence in a Brand Culture*. New York: New York University Press.

Bartlett, J. (2018) *The People vs Tech: How the Internet is Killing Democracy (and How We Save It)*. London: Penguin.

Benjamin, Ruha (2019) *Race after Technology: Abolitionist Tools for the New Jim Code*. Cambridge: Polity.

Bilton, Nick (2017) 'Will Mark Zuckerberg Be Our Next President' *Vanity Fair*, 24 July. www.vanityfair.com/news/2017/01/will-mark-zuckerberg-be-our-next-president.

Bivens, Rena (2017) 'The Gender Binary Will not Be Deprogrammed: Ten Years of Coding Gender on Facebook' *New Media and Society*, 19(6), 880–898.

Braidotti, Rosi (2013) *The Posthuman*. London: Polity Press.

Carmi, Einor (2018) 'Do You Agree?: What Me Too Can Teach Us about Digital Consent' *Open Democracy*. www.opendemocracy.net/en/digitaliberties/what-metoo-can-teach-us-about-digital-consent/

Chander, Anupam (2012) 'Facebookistan' *North Carolina Law Review*, 90, 1807; *UC Davis Legal Studies Research Paper No. 295*. https://ssrn.com/abstract=2061300.

Collins, Patricia Hill (1989) 'The Social Construction of Black Feminist Thought' *Signs*, 14(4), 745–773.

Couldry, Nick and Ulises Mejias (2018) 'Data Colonialism: Rethinking Big Data's Relation to the Contemporary Subject' *Television and New Media*, 20(4), 336–349.

Couldry, Nick and Ulises A. Mejias (2019) *The Costs of Connection: How Data is Colonizing Human Life and Appropriating it for Capitalism*. Stanford: Stanford University Press.

Debray, Régis (2007) 'Socialism: A Lifecycle' *New Left Review*. https://newleftreview.org/issues/II46/articles/regis-debray-socialism-a-life-cycle

Derrida, Jacques (2000) *On Hospitality*. Stanford: Stanford University Press.

Driessens, Olivier (2013) 'The Celebritization of Society and Culture: Understanding the Structural Dynamics of Celebrity Culture' *International Journal of Cultural Studies* 16(6), 641–657.

Edwards, Michael (2009) 'Gates, Google, and the Ending of Global Poverty: Philanthrocapitalism and International Development' *Brown Journal of World Affairs*, 15(2), 35–42.

English-Lueck, J. A. (2017) *Cultures@SiliconValley*. Second Edition. Stanford: Stanford University Press.
Featherstone, D. (2011) 'On Assemblage and Articulation' *Area*, 43, 139–142. doi: 10.1111/j.1475-4762.2011.01007.x
Gilbert, Jeremy and Andrew Goffey (2015) 'Post-Post-Fordism in the Era of Platforms: Robin Murray Talks to Jeremy Gilbert and Andrew Goffey' *New Formations*, 84, 184–208.
Gill, Rosalind (2007) 'Postfeminist Media Culture: Elements of a Sensibility' *European Journal of Cultural Studies*, 10(2), 147–166.
Goulden, Murray (2019) '"Delete the Family": Platform Families and the Colonisation of the Smart Home' *Information, Communication & Society*. doi: 10.1080/1369118X.2019.1668454
Gramsci, Antonio (1971) *Selections from the Prison Notebooks*. London: Lawrence and Wishart.
Gregg, Melissa (2011) *Work's Intimacy*. Cambridge: Polity.
Guthey, Eric, Timothy Clark, and Brad Jackson (2009) *Demystifying Business Celebrity*. London: Routledge.
Hamad, Hannah (2014) *Postfeminism and Paternity in Contemporary U.S. Film: Framing Fatherhood*. London: Routledge.
hooks, bell (2010) 'Understanding Patriarchy' *No Borders*. http://imaginenoborders.org/zines/#UnderstandingPatriarchy.
Jacobs, Ben and Alan Juhas (2016) 'Somali Migrants Are "Disaster" for Minnesota, Says Donald Trump' www.theguardian.com/us-news/2016/nov/06/donald-trump-minnesota-somali-migrants-isis.
Kantrowitz, Alex and Nitasha Tiku (2017) 'Mark Zuckerberg Says He's Not Running for President' (2 July 2017) Web. 24 Jan 2017. www.cnbc.com/2017/01/24/mark-zuckerberg-says-hes-not-running-for-president.html.
Lafrance, Adriene (2017) 'Zuckerberg 2020?' *Atlantic*. Web. 19 Jan 2017 www.theatlantic.com/technology/archive/2017/01/zuckerberg-2020/513689/.
Lakoff, George (1996) *Moral Politics: What Conservatives Know that Liberals Don't*. Chicago: University of Chicago Press.
Leswing, Kif (2017) 'There's an Alternative Theory about Why Mark Zuckerberg Looks Like He's Running for President' Web. 26 June 2017. http://uk.businessinsider.com/mark-zuckerberg-presidential-trip-every-state-product-focused-ceo-2017-6.
Littler, Jo (2007) 'Celebrity CEOS and the Cultural Economy of Tabloid Intimacy' in Su Holmes and Sean Redmond (eds) *Stardom and Celebrity: A Reader*. London: SAGE, 230–224.
Losse, Kate (2014) *The Boy Kings: A Journey into the Heart of the Social Network*. New York: Simon and Schuster.
Marshall, P. David ((1997) 2013) *Celebrity and Power: Fame in Contemporary Culture*. Minneapolis: University of Minnesota Press.
Massumi, Brian (2015) *Politics of Affect*. Cambridge: Polity Press.
Moore, Pheobe and Andrew Robinson (2015) 'The Quantified Self: What Counts in the Neoliberal Workplace' *New Media & Society*, 18(1), 2774–2792.
Narayan, Uma (1997) *Dislocating Cultures: Identities, Traditions & Third World Feminism*. London: Routledge.
Naughton, John (2019) 'Facebook's Burnt-Out Moderators Are Proof that Facebook is Broken' *The Guardian*, 6 January. www.theguardian.com/commentisfree/2019/jan/06/proof-that-facebook-broken-obvious-from-modus-operandi.

Ortner, B. Sherry (2014) 'Too Soon for Post-Feminism: The Ongoing Life of Patriarchy in Neoliberal America' *History and Anthropology*, 25(4), 530–549.

Partzsch, Lena (2017) 'Powerful Individuals in a Globalized World' *Glob Policy*, 8, 5–13. doi: 10.1111/1758-5899.12367

Pateman, Carol (1988) *The Sexual Contract*. Stanford: Stanford University Press.

Rheingold, Howard (2000 [1993]) *The Virtual Community: Homesteading on the Electronic Frontier*. Cambridge, MA: MIT Press.

Russell, John (2016) 'Mark Zuckerberg is Building a Real-Life Version of Iron Man's Digital Assistant "Jarvis"' 4 January 2016. https://techcrunch.com/2016/01/03/iron-zuck/

Salter, Anastasia and Bridget Blodgett (2018) *Toxic Geek Masculinity in Media: Sexism, Trolling, and Identity Policing*. Basingstoke: Palgrave.

Skeggs, Beverly and Simon Yuill (2015) 'The Methodology of a Multi-Model Project Examining How Facebook Infrastructures Social Relations' *Information, Communication & Society*. doi: 10.1080/1369118X.2015.1091026

Skeggs, Beverly and Simon Yuill (2019) 'Subjects of Value and Digital Personas: Reshaping the Bourgeois Subject, Unhinging Property from Personhood' *Subjectivity*, 12, 82–99. doi: 10.1057/s41286-018-00063-4

Smith, Zadie (2010) 'Generation Why?' *New York Review of Books*. 24 July 2017. Web. 25 November 2010. www.nybooks.com/articles/2010/11/25/generation-why/.

Solon, Olivia (2017a) 'Killer Robots? Musk and Zuckerberg Escalate Row Over Dangers of AI' *The Guardian*. 25 July 2017. www.theguardian.com/technology/2017/jul/25/elon-musk-mark-zuckerberg-artificial-intelligence-facebook-tesla.

Solon, Oliva (2017b) 'Mark Zuckerberg's 2017 Plan to Visit All US States Hints at Political Ambitions' *The Guardian*, 3 January 2017. www.theguardian.com/technology/2017/jan/03/mark-zuckerberg-facebook-2017-resolution-visit-us-states.

Stross, Randall (2012) *The Launch Pad: Inside Y Combinator Silicon Valley's Most Exclusive School for Startups*. London: Penguin.

Swan, Elaine (2009) 'Commodity Diversity: Smiling Faces as a Strategy of Containment' *Organization*, 17(1), 77–100.

Sylvain, Olivier (2018) 'Discriminatory Designs on User Data' *The Knight First Amendment Institute's Emerging Threats Series*. https://knightcolumbia.org/content/discriminatory-designs-user-data.

The Leadership Conference on Civil and Human Rights (2019) 'Letter Urging Facebook to Protect Civil Rights' October 21. https://civilrights.org/resource/letter-urging-facebook-to-protect-civil-rights/.

Turner, Fred (2008) *From Counterculture to Cyberculture: Stewart Brand, the Whole Earth Network, and the Rise of Digital Utopianism*. Chicago: University of Chicago Press.

Vaidhyanathan, Siva (2018) *Anti-Social Media: How Facebook Disconnects Us and Undermines Democracy*. Oxford: Oxford University Press.

Vanian, Jonathan (2018) 'Facebook CEO Mark Zuckerberg Admits 'Huge Mistake' but Will Not Step Down' 4 April. https://fortune.com/2018/04/04/facebook-mark-zuckerberg-data-cambridge-analytica/.

Wachter-Boettcher, Sara (2017) *Technically Wrong: Sexist Apps, Biased Algorithms, and Other Threats of Toxic Tech*. New York: Norton.

Welch, Chris (2016) 'Mark Zuckerberg Built an AI that Controls His House, and He'll Demo it Next Month' *The Verge*, 29 August. www.theverge.com/2016/8/29/12691608/mark-zuckerberg-artificial-intelligence-smart-house-demo.

Wier, Justin (2017) 'Zuckerberg Pays Surprise Visit to Falls Family' *Vindicator*, April 29. www.vindy.com/news/2017/apr/29/facebook-founder-pays-surprise-visit-newton-falls-/.

Wise, Amanda (2011) 'Moving Food: Gustatory Commensality and Disjuncture in Everyday Multiculturalism' *New Formations*, 74(26), 82–107.

Year of Travel (2017) www.facebook.com/YearofTravel.

Yeo, Sophie (2017) 'What Mark Zuckerberg Was Doing in the Middle of North Dakota' *Washington Post*, July 2017. www.washingtonpost.com/news/energy-environment/wp/2017/07/13/what-mark-zuckerberg-was-doing-in-the-middle-of-north-dakota/.

You Gov (2020a) 'Mark Zuckerberg' https://today.yougov.com/topics/politics/explore/public_figure/Mark_Zuckerberg.

You Gov (2020b) 'The Most Famous Business Figures in America' https://today.yougov.com/ratings/politics/fame/business-figures/all.

Zuboff, Shoshona (2019) *The Age of Surveillance Capitalism: The Fight for a Human Future at the New Frontier of Power*. New York: Public Affairs.

Zuckerberg, Mark (2016) 'Mark Zuckerberg Timeline' www.facebook.com/zuck.

Zuckerberg, Mark (2017a) 'Mark Zuckerberg Timeline' www.facebook.com/zuck.

Zuckerberg, Mark (2017b) 'Mark Zuckerberg's Commencement Address at Harvard' *The Harvard Gazette*. https://news.harvard.edu/gazette/story/2017/05/mark-zuckerbergs-speech-as-written-for-harvards-class-of-2017/.

5
PETER THIEL'S TECHNOLOGICAL FRONTIERS

> The hero Silicon Valley needed.
>
> (Milo Yiannopoulos, Breitbart, 2016)

In the last ever episode of *Halt and Catch Fire* (AMC 2014–2017), the two female leads, Donna and Cameron, have breakfast in a diner. It is 1994, and they debate splitting the bill. Because Donna is a venture capitalist and significantly richer than Cameron, who is a games developer, she pays. As she counts her dollars, she looks around the diner at the transactions taking place: the jukebox, people ordering, people paying. The scene then cuts to her running out to Cameron, who is in the carpark looking at a map. 'I have an idea,' says Donna breathlessly. Cameron looks dismayed and then excited. They drive off, the tropes of the map and the journey signifying a new frontier. This scene plays out as the penultimate scene of the show, rewriting history in its portrayal of two women about to embark on the development of a new social technology. *Halt and Catch Fire* tracks the personal computer revolution of the 1980s and the growth of the internet in the early 1990s. In the second season, the two female characters who have so far played romantic (technologically smart) partners to the male protagonists, Joe and Gordon, develop an online community start-up, managing young male geeks. Although their relationships with Joe and Gordon are still central to the plot, by the end of the final season Gordon is dead and Joe (modelled partly on Steve Jobs) has opted for the tranquil life of a university lecturer in the Humanities. In many ways this programme is a revisionist account of Silicon Valley: in this world women are not only welcome and celebrated, but are the pioneers of digital capitalism.

We start the chapter with this scene because of the way that *Halt and Catch Fire* centres white, cis, heterosexual women in its representation of the history of West Coast Tech. In the show's portrayal of Silicon Valley, the men fade into the background and the women become the power brokers. The focus on the exchange of money in this scene hints at the potential seeding of a female version of the PayPal Mafia – a key male network in Silicon Valley. The show reworks many significant moments in the development of West Coast Tech. Therefore, it seems that the TV show is invoking the moment when Peter Thiel and Max Levchin 'hatched the idea for PayPal' over breakfast in Hobee's (Chang 2018, 48). According to Reid Hoffman (another Mafia member and founder of LinkedIn), Thiel and Levchin came up with the idea of a 'digital wallet' – 'an encryption platform that allowed you to store cash and information securely on your mobile phone': 'That soon evolved to software that allowed you to send and receive digital cash wirelessly and securely via a Palm Pilot (the first of several iterations) so that two friends could split a dinner tab using their PDAs' (Hoffman and Casnocha 2013, 65). In this reading of the show, the skewed gender ratios of the West Coast Tech's workforces are re-imagined. As we have noted in this book, West Coast Tech, disproportionately hired male workers as the tech industry became hegemonic (Chang 2018; Broussard 2019). Marie Hicks argues in *Programmed Inequality*, there is a 'masculine ideal for computer workers.' And this professional identity is tied to a history of structural discrimination that has nothing to do with skill (Hicks 2017, 235).

The suggestion that Donna might come up with the idea of PayPal is an ironic and knowing wink at the audience – because the founding of PayPal has been overtly portrayed as a story of male domination, and its original workers mythologised, semi-ironically given their professed geekiness, by toughguy imagery. This patriarchal network was visually enshrined in a famous 2007 *Fortune* Magazine photograph that depicts 13 men – all originally PayPal workers and founders – ironically imitating a gangster aesthetic; the men are shown wearing gold chains, smoking cigars, and drinking Maker's Mark (O'Brien 2007) (Figure 5.1).[1] Elon Musk, another PayPal founder, is not in this picture – he is collecting an award elsewhere – and was photographed separately for the issue. There is also a gap at the back of the photograph, where Steve Chen and Chad Hurley (who went on to co-found YouTube) may have been; apparently they refused to be included in the published photograph after Google objected to the gangster connotations. In the foreground of the photograph is Peter Thiel.

Before PayPal, Thiel was a graduate of Stanford and Stanford Law School. In the late 1990s Thiel left a career in law to set up PayPal, along with other friends and 'like-minded' people from Stanford and the University of Illinois at Urbana-Champaign (O'Brien 2007). In 2003 he founded the big data analytics company, Palantir, which took antifraud technology from PayPal and now participates in 'intelligence gathering.' Palantir is partly funded by the CIA and also does work for the government; its two main products are named Gotham and Metropolis, after Batman and Superman respectively. Here we can see Thiel's company engaging with superhero mythologies partly tied to geek masculinities. His corporations stay true to the US military origins of the internet, thus continuing the links between geek masculinity and patriarchal dominance that we

FIGURE 5.1 The 'Paypal Mafia' from *Fortune.com* 2006

discussed in relation to Musk (see Chapter 2). Thiel was Facebook's first major investor, and is now one of the nine people on the Facebook board. In 2005 he started Founders Fund with two partners from PayPal and they went on to fund, among others, Airbnb, Spotify, and also several financial rounds in Facebook.

Thiel is not a key founder of the 'Big 5 Infrastructure companies' (Van Dijck et al. 2018). He is not the head of the corporate household in the same way as the other founders we are looking at. He does not have the wealth or reach of Bezos, and does not fit the boy genius moniker in the same way as Zuckerberg, Page, or Brin (although he was reportedly a chess prodigy). He also departs from the identities of the other patriarchs – and the heterosexual household metaphor that we have been working with – because he is a gay man. He was outed by Gawker in 2007, but his sexuality was apparently public before this. Thiel formally outed himself at the 2016 Republican National Convention, and we discuss the significance of this below.

We have included Thiel in our study because, importantly, he is a key part of the network we set out in Chapter 1, as well as being ideologically influential. In his 2016 commencement speech at Hamilton College, Thiel focuses on the importance of friendship and forging networks, and this emphasis on creating and sustaining networks is articulated in other writings, as well as interviews that Thiel has given (cf 2007). We argue in this chapter that he is a key broker in the patriarchal networks that we are mapping. He is a broker between the men in West Coast tech, but also between these men and the racialised patriarchal structures of the Trump administration as evidenced by the Trump Tech Summit. Thiel appears as a negotiator – between Trump, who he supports, and West Coast Tech, within which he is a major ideologue and funder.

Thiel is widely understood to be the 'the philosopher-king of Silicon Valley' (Chang 2018, 41). His books include *The Diversity Myth: 'Multiculturalism' and the Politics of Intolerance at Stanford* (co-authored with David O. Sacks), published in 1995 by the conservative think tank the Independent Institute, and the 2014 New York bestseller, *Zero to One: Notes on Startups, or How to Build the Future* (written with Blake Masters). He has also written agenda-setting blog posts and given high-profile talks and keynotes in conservative political arenas. In this chapter we spend time analysing his two published books, especially *The Diversity Myth*. Although this book was written before he co-founded PayPal and before he became a tech billionaire, it is here that Thiel's conservative thinking finds a voice. We situate this book within the postracial and postfeminist landscape of the 1990s; part of the conservative backlash against social justice movements and coinciding with the rise of neoliberalism. What is significant about this book is the way that its critique of multiculturalism, anti-racist activism, and feminism has now exploded onto the internet with the emergence of the alt-right. We do not make explicit links between Thiel and the alt-right here. Rather, we note the conceptual links between the patriarchal networks of West Coast Tech and the hubs bidding for racialised patriarchal alliances online. Nevertheless, it is worth noting that Thiel and Milo Yiannopoulos are mutual fans. Yiannopoulos was part of a new wave of ultra-right-wing internet celebrities centred on a number of platforms and outlets like Breitbart News and YouTube in the build-up to the 2016 US Presidential election and its aftermath. Thiel endorsed Yiannopoulos's 2017 book, *Dangerous* with: 'If you don't use your freedom of speech, one day you might find that it's gone. Buy this book while it's legal' (Thiel, quoted on Yiannopoulos 2017). To provide some context, Thiel has not endorsed any of the books in the concordance. Yiannopoulos wrote of Thiel in Breitbart:

> Facebook needs Thiel – the only man who leans to the right in a company hopelessly biased against the right. But they're not the only ones. It seems that all of Silicon Valley, and indeed, all of the internet needed Peter Thiel.
> *(Yiannopoulos, Breitbart, 2016)*[2]

Thiel's celebrity provides cement for the patriarchal networks in West Coast Tech. Not only is he able to bring men into networks, and make connections between them and the American conservative right; his well-known positions also reveal the underlying coherence across digital capitalism in terms of its production of inequalities. As Jonathan Taplin points out, these founders are under the political protection of the right-wing Koch brothers, without whom none of these monopolies would exist 'at [their] current scale': it was the Kochs who 'financed the rise of the libertarian political framework that Peter Thiel, Larry Page, Jeff Bezos and Mark Zuckerberg used to get rich' (Taplin 2017, 193). As a vocal supporter of American conservative values and a billionaire, Thiel was a keynote at the 2019 National Conservatism conference (along with Fox News presenter Tucker Carlson). National Conservatism is a conservative organisation attempting to influence the Trump administration, seeking 'to recover and reconsolidate the rich tradition of national conservative thought' (National Conservatism 2020). Thiel was introduced by Christopher deMuth, former President of conservative think tank American Enterprise Institute (crucial to the younger Bush administration), as a disseminator of 'philosophy masquerading as how-to-succeed business advice,' as well as a purveyor of 'original Nietzsche-esque social theory' (Thiel 2019). Given these overt conservative alliances, Thiel is the face in the mirror that the other founders do not want to see. Whereas Zuckerberg might strategise his celebrity status around his difference from conservatives and Trump as we saw in the previous chapter, Thiel makes these connections visible.

Contrarian thinker

Thiel's intellectualism is celebrated in Ryan Holiday's book *Conspiracy: Peter Thiel, Hulk Hogan, Gawker, and the Anatomy of Intrigue*, which is replete with literary and philosophical references. The book provides an account of the bankruptcy of Gawker Media – a gossip outlet which earned Thiel's enduring animosity for outing him; the company eventually had to file for bankruptcy in 2016, after Thiel helped fund a number of celebrities (including Hulk Hogan) in their lawsuits against it. The book opens with a description of Thiel's library in his New York City apartment – 'paperbacks and ancient hardcovers about economics, chess, history and politics' – and focuses on *Discourses on Livy* by Niccolò Machiavelli (Holiday 2018, 4). Throughout the book Thiel is depicted as a well-read strategist and genius. The author takes great pains in representing Thiel as serious, secretive, and intellectual – presumably a figure that Thiel (who participated in the book through interviews) has been involved in co-constructing. The book closes with a scene depicting a dinner party 'with the spirit of a limitless tab' that Thiel is hosting at his home in Los Angeles:

> Peter was the quietest. At the end, he walked out past his fire pit, onto the balcony with its sweeping views of the city in every direction. In a few minutes he would be leaving, though it was late, to take his plane back to San Francisco for meetings in the morning, and the car was, as always, already running in the driveway. For the moment he was still, standing there, alone, reflecting. Or more likely, his mind had already moved on and he was pondering some trade in oil futures or the company he might fund the next day or some new conspiracy already under way.
>
> *(Holiday 2018, 288)*

The author quotes lines from *Hamlet* – mimicking Thiel's love of 'the bard' as discussed further below, as he stands behind the billionaire Thiel.

Not only is Thiel a philosopher; he is consistently described as a contrarian one. Indeed, this is also central to his celebrification. Throughout his *New York Times* bestseller *The Power of One* a self-help guide for start-up entrepreneurs – he adopts the posture of the contrarian. The book is premised on the question that Thiel apparently always asks whenever he interviews someone for a job: "'What important truth do very few people agree with you on?" The best answers take the following form: "Most people believe in x, but the truth is the opposite of x'" (Thiel 2014, 5–6). He was interviewed in 2018 by the libertarian Dave Rubin (Rubin 2018) who calls him the 'ultimate contrarian thinker.' In contrast, Thiel's friend Musk has said that they 'are not directly aligned philosophically ... "Peter's philosophy is pretty odd. It's not normal"' (O'Brien 2007).

Portraying Thiel as a contrarian also fits with the disruptor or hacker ethos of Silicon Valley (Hasinoff and Levina 2017). In addition, depicting Thiel as idiosyncratic, or a secretive loner, has the advantage of positioning him as different from the founders and CEOs who brand themselves as progressive. For example, Zuckerberg and Thiel employ distinct self-branding strategies, even though their business regarding corporate monopolies overlap. Constructing himself in opposition has the effect of disguising the hegemony of the ideals that Thiel stands for; it implies that he is an underdog. In the context of Silicon Valley, Thiel is partly understood to be different because he is a Republican. His support for Trump, for example, has apparently alienated him from what he calls 'the monoculture' of Silicon Valley, and this encouraged his move to Los Angeles. Thiel gave a $1.25 million contribution to Trump super PACS and the presidential campaign, subsequently giving a speech at the Republican National Convention. (Streitfeld 2016). It is certainly significant – both in the context of the Silicon Valley founders and the Republican Party – that when he states that he is gay at this convention he says: 'I am proud to be gay. I am proud to be a Republican.' But he also uses this opportunity to dismiss the rolling debate about trans rights: 'When I was a kid, the great debate was about how to defeat the Soviet Union. And we won ... Now we are told that the great debate is about who gets to use which bathroom. This is a distraction from our real problems. Who cares?' (Drabold 2016).

We can understand Thiel's strategy here as a form of what Lisa Duggan calls 'homonormativity,' as well as what Jasbir Puar terms 'homonationalism.' Duggan and Puar argue in different ways that some white gay men can be included in centres of power at the expense of those who are deemed 'other.' Duggan argues that homonormativity is 'a politics that does not contest dominant heteronormative assumptions and institutions, but upholds and sustains them, while promising the possibility of a demobilized gay constituency and a privatized, depoliticized gay culture anchored in domesticity and consumption' (Duggan 2003, 58–59). Her argument is partly based on examining the neoliberal intertexts and lobbying groups of the 1990s. For example, the Independent Gay Forum which positioned itself against antigay conservatism and queer progressive politics. In her words, this was a highly visible influential 'center-libertarian-conservative-cla ssical liberal formation in gay politics' that aimed to 'contest and displace' the politics of progressive activists, and was 'a crucial new part of the cultural front of neoliberalism in the United States' (Duggan 2003, 57–58). It is against this backdrop that Thiel is able to come out at a Republican conference (Figure 5.2). And is entirely consistent with his public degradation of the issues raised by trans people as the wrong sort of queer activism.

In *Terrorist Assemblages Homonationalism in Queer Times*, Puar invokes 'homonationalism' (short for 'homonormative nationalism') to illustrate the ways that homonormative queer subjects are disciplined and normalised to US national citizenship (Puar 2007). In this way they are rehabilitated away from 'other' bodies, sometimes designated as terrorists. Trump, for example, used the mass shooting at the gay Pulse Night Club in Orlando for his anti-immigration and Islamphobic agenda. At his Republican Nomination Speech in July 2016 he appropriated this shooting to state: 'I will do everything in my power to protect our LGBTQ citizens from the violence and oppression of a hateful foreign ideology.' Part of this protection was to halt immigration from 'any nation that has been compromised by terrorism' and to 'have the best intelligence gathering operation in the world' (Trump 2016). Again, Thiel's support of the Trump administration is concomitant with being an out gay white man who works in the tech industry. Thiel's company Palantir is a data analytics company that analyses data that has already been gathered by other organisations. It does so with the aim of 'building trust'; or of identifying troublemakers. Its work has included participating in the immigration deportation policies championed by Trump (and which were decried by Zuckerberg). In 2020 it secured another contract with the Department of Defence (worth $823 million), thus revealing the deep

FIGURE 5.2 Peter Thiel giving a speech at the 2016 Republican Convention in Cleveland

integration of West Coast Tech with American militarism. The US military origins of the tech industry come to fruition in Palantir; its product Gotham was rumoured to have 'found' Osama Bin Laden (Forsten 2019).

Cyberspace frontiersman

Like Jeff Bezos, Thiel's celebrity is partly constructed through his invocation of the American frontier. In his 2016 commencement speech mentioned above, Thiel tells the audience that: 'Our whole continent is a new world. The founders of this country set out to create what they called "a new order for the ages." America is the frontier country. We are not true to our own tradition unless we seek what is new' (Thiel 2016a). This frontier spirit – including its raced, classed, gendered structures – suffuses all his books and much of his other work too. In a 2009 blog post for the conservative outlet *Cato Unbound*, Thiel advocates cyberspace and outer space as sites of freedom to escape contemporary politics. In his 2014 book *Zero to One: Notes on Startups, or How to Build the Future* the frontier spirit haunts through nostalgia for the figure of the colonialist:

> There are no blank spaces left on the map anymore. If you grew up in the 18th century, there were still new places to go. After hearing tales of foreign adventure, you could become an explorer yourself. This was probably true up through the 19th and early 20th centuries; after that point photography from National Geographic showed every Westerner what even the most exotic, underexplored places on earth look like. Today, explorers are found mostly in history books and children's tales.
>
> *(Thiel 2014, 97)*

Zero to One was originally a series of talks given by Thiel at Stanford University in 2012 and eventually written up by a former student, Blake Masters and published by Random House in 2014. It is publicised as a business self-help book for entrepreneurs. However, it is not so much an advice book about the practicalities of making a start-up. Instead its abstract tone makes it an exercise in glorifying the monopoly cultures of Silicon Valley, the importance of networks, and the significance of Thiel's role as a contrarian in this milieu. It is an opportunity for Thiel to extend the electronic frontier motif that we discussed in Chapter 1. His work, as well as that of other libertarian defenders of cyberspace, has been influential for those who see themselves as tech pioneers working to extend its boundaries. This should be understood as part of the wider libertarian – and postracial and postfeminist – disavowal of structural inequalities that is endemic to the tech patriarchs' view of society. This is an ideology of freedom that enables its proponents to appear as champions of liberty even as they continue to pursue patriarchal domination and control.

Thiel represents the technological frontier as blossoming through the corporate household. Remarkably, Thiel employs the metaphor of the patriarchal household to describe corporate tech monopolies, as well as the ideal kind of relationship between powerful men. He imagines a production based on *Romeo and Juliet* (in line with his Shakespearean literary celebrification) called Gates (of Microsoft) and Schmidt (of Google):

> The House of Montague built operating systems and office applications. The House of Capulet wrote a search engine. What was there to fight about? Two great families, run by alpha nerds, sure to clash on account of their sameness.
>
> *(Thiel 2014, 38)*

Thiel is talking about the sameness of products here: 'Windows v. Chrome OS, Bing vs. Google Search, Explorer vs. Chrome, Office vs. Docs, and Surface v. Nexus' (Thiel 2014, 39). His argument is that monopolies should be left to do what they are good at, and that competition isn't good for business; it destroys it. A monopoly is 'the kind of company that's so good at what it does that no other firm can offer a close substitute.' He offers Google as an exemplar (Thiel 2014, 25). According to him, monopolies drive progress, give more choice, and are powerful engines to make the world better and more innovative. Monopolies are ideal corporate forms for patriarchy – they form and entrench it. As Zuboff, among others, has argued, after neoliberalism there was a 'turn towards oligarchy' (Zuboff 2019, 43). In Thiel's celebration of tech monopolies we can see these ideologies at work. More than this, however, he is evidencing the importance of the patriarchal network; each household, headed by a man, doing something complementary but different in order to achieve social control.

Although *Zero to One* is a bestseller addressed to a global corporate audience, it is also about people in Silicon Valley. In his metaphor of the household, Thiel is not just describing and supporting the paternalistic structure of the corporation: he is describing how patriarchal networks need to work. Aware of the need of patriarchs to collaborate as well as compete (see our discussion of Ortner 2014 in Chapter 1), Thiel explains that to succeed in Silicon Valley you need to monopolise a specific field, not to compete over it. He tells the story of rivalry between him and Musk when he was co-running Confinity and Musk X.com before they merged to become PayPal. By 1999, as he tells it, the two companies were at all-out war, though he concedes that in February 2000 other tactical concerns came to the fore:

> Elon and I were more scared about the rapidly inflating tech bubble than we were about each other: a financial crash would ruin us both before we could finish our fight. So in early March we met on neutral ground – a café almost equidistant to our offices – and negotiated a 50-50 merger. De-escalating the rivalry post-merger wasn't easy, but as far as problems go, it was a good one to have. As a unified team, we were able to ride out the dot-com crash and then build a successful business.
>
> *(Thiel 2014, 42)*

This movement from competition to collaboration was necessary to maintain and entrench the male-dominated networks coalescing around PayPal. We return to the PayPal Mafia below, but first we examine race, gender, and *The Diversity Myth*.

The Diversity Myth

We can evidence the incredible absence of thinking about race in the concordance – even though it is a primary social division in the USA: 'African-American' appears in only 29 books – with the most frequent usage being in Peter Thiel's right-wing attack on multiculturalism in *The Diversity Myth*; and almost all critical discussion of race happens in books we coded as polemic (i.e. challenging Silicon Valley on the grounds of its racial hierarchies). The aim of the authors of *The Diversity Myth* is to produce a critique of affirmative action, multiculturalism, anti-racist activism, and feminism. The book is used as an opportunity for the authors to push back against decolonising the curriculum changes which were expected to take place at Stanford in 1989 (Sacks and Thiel 1995, 15).

We spend time examining this book because it reveals so much about Thiel's conservative agenda, at least how it manifested in the 1990s. Thiel's co-author on *The Diversity Myth*, David Sacks, was also a contributor to the provocative and right-wing student paper *The Stanford Review* that Thiel co-founded. And he was also later involved with a number of key tech companies. Sacks authored several pieces for *The Stanford Review* criticising the new awareness about date rape and sexual assault, and he also used the now widely used term 'feminazis.' In one editorial he wrote, 'If you're male and heterosexual at Stanford, you have sex and then you get screwed' (cited in Chang 2018, 45). Thiel said of *The Stanford Review*: 'In hindsight, we were preaching mainly to the choir – even if this had the important side benefit of convincing the choir's members to continue singing for the rest of their lives' (Thiel 2009).[3] Significantly, many of the book's (and *The Review's*) rhetorical strategies, in both form and content, are ongoing in reactionary online spaces. And the book is also important, because there are professed continuities between its rhetoric and the self-proclaimed PayPal Mafia discussed at the beginning of this chapter.

The Diversity Myth's postracial framing centres the claim that 'there are almost no real racists at Stanford or, for that matter, in America's younger generation' (Sacks and Thiel 1995, 140). They argue that, given that 'real racism' has already been eradicated, the decolonised curriculum and 'the multiculture' are now the hegemonic ideologies at Stanford. The book extensively quotes feminists and other campaigners, but they are presented in such a way as to appear self-evidently ridiculous. And because feminism and 'multiculture' are seen as hegemonic, the proponents of these causes are portrayed as Orwellian, as in denial about their own dominance. They have sneering subheads such as 'The Victims' Curriculum' and 'The Empty Curriculum.' And they dismiss descriptions of individuals' experiences of racism and of institutional racism. Using debating style bullet points they gleefully expound what they see as the rhetorical downfalls of people's accounts of racial discrimination. For example, they state that the students' arguments are 'circular' (143). The authors misuse or quibble with the ideas of 'diversity' and 'multiculturalism' so that they become meaningless.

Although *The Diversity Myth* was published before Thiel became a tech billionaire, we can see that this book contributes to an (albeit uneven) set of postracial and postfeminist discourses emerging and consolidating in the 1990s, and which coincided with the rise of the internet. In *Digitizing Race: Visual Cultures of the Internet*, Lisa Nakamura, notes how US political cultures in the 1990s disavowed race by ignoring racial injustices and inequalities (Nakamura 2008, 2). As Roopali Mukherjee wrote in 2011: 'We have entered the "postracial" era, some suggest a historical moment in which neither cultural practices nor political solidarities cohere predictably along racial lines' (178). This brings us to Sara Ahmed's understanding of postracial discourse 'as a fantasy through which racism operates: as if racism is behind us because we no longer believe in race, or as if racism would be behind us if we no longer believed in race' (Ahmed 2017, 5). Nakamura argues that this wilful 'colorblindness' coincided with the Clinton administration's 'identification of the Internet as a privileged aspect of the national political economy' (3). In particular, the administration linked it to a corporate culture and deregulation.

Sacks and Thiel's rhetoric draws its power both from the canonisation and authority of Western texts, which shore up their sense of entitlement, and from the contemporary harnessing of postracial tropes, which serve to transmogrify critiques of racist structures into individual expressions of victimisation and complaint. The lone colonial explorer of *Zero to One* cited above had already appeared in *The Diversity Myth* in the form of Christopher Columbus, 'The First Multiculturalist' (also the title of the book's introduction). The authors paint Columbus as a man weary of 'the growing complexity of European life' (xxv) and in search of Eden (as opposed to new markets which can be violently opened up). The colonial enterprise is figured in the book as a moral quest as Columbus meets 'Taino natives' who 'dwelt in a state of preternatural grace.' The authors then turn to Montaigne and the figure of 'the Noble Savage.' They argue that Columbus took sides with the Taino people against 'The warlike Caribs' – 'and the rest is history':

> Stripped of his initial illusions, Columbus would return to Europe at the end of his quest with a more balanced impression of the world outside the West. The explorer who first depicted the 'noble savage' also had discovered the Carib tribe, whose name later would provide the basis for the word 'cannibal.' For Columbus at least, the once-lustrous appeal of multiculturalism had dulled.
>
> *(xxvi)*

This cynical avoidance of the realities of the butchery and genocide of the indigenous populations is typical of the authors' provocative stance. Their equation of colonialism with multiculturalism is also deliberatively provocative: we can see the seeds of online trolling (Whitney Phillips 2015) being sown here. But it is also crucial to understand that this disavowal of the violence of racialised capitalism (Bhattacharyya 2017) – encapsulated in the phrase 'the rest is history' – is fundamental to their aim in this book, which is to protect it from Stanford's decolonising initiative.

The authors scaffold their book with weaponised binaries (primitive/civilised; irrational/rational), and, by operating within this structure, they implicitly frame a large range of sets of ideas as opposed to each other, associating positives (e.g. ideas) with those things that men like them have, while negatives (e.g. unruly bodies) are associated with otherness. The political thrust of the book is reflected in their comment that: 'Real diversity requires a diversity of ideas, not simply a bunch of like-minded activists who resemble the bar scene from Star Wars' (Sacks and Thiel 1995). The bar scene from the 1977 film is revealing of Thiel and Sacks' fears. The film features a varied collection of aliens, which the authors presumably see as standing in for difference in multiculturalism: the racialised signifiers of the scene – including smoking hookahs and jazz music – are offset against the luminous whiteness of Luke Skywalker. It is the alien others in this Tatooine cantina who are represented as threatening, but by the end at least two of them are dead at the hands of Skywalker's posse.

Sacks and Thiel recognise that the authorities they marshal in support of their arguments – figures such as Columbus and 'the Bard' – and the lexicon of western philosophy they deploy (tautology, sufficient conditions, etc.) are rooted in historically specific structures of power – but they claim them as universal. Equally, they turn away from a historical reading of the present, and any recognition of the continuities of the interlocking structures of oppression that maintain them in their privilege (Hill Collins 1989; Crenshaw 1989). Even though they mobilise philosophical terms, they are not interested in the logic of arguments. Rather, they are interested in the rhetorical performance of logical arguments. They have denied history on the one hand, and yet continue to weaponise it on the other. And this rhetorical move produces an affect of confusion. The two authors perform reason; and they deny the presence of emotion by projecting it onto an Other.

Part of the racialised patriarchal self-help strategy of *The Diversity Myth* is its modelling of how to gaslight, how to debate postracial power, using the same ideology of white supremacy that circumscribed the rights to personhood in the first place. We can see this strategy at play in one of the techniques we have already noted Sacks and Thiel employing in the book – the scornful retelling of anecdotes. They tell a story about two white students who vandalise a flier that depicts Beethoven by scrawling on it a 'brown face, curly black hair, enlarged lips.' The two white students then post the defaced flier on a noticeboard next door to the room of a Black student (B. J.) who had previously stated – according to Sacks and Thiel – that 'all music is black.' Sacks and Thiel performatively perceive these acts as equivalent – 'B. J.'s words and the two white students' drawing had said precisely the same thing' – and in so doing they re-harness the colonial trope of rational white men and irrational Black man (all the while overlooking the racism of the 'blackface' Beethoven caricature). Frantz Fanon exposes the 'crushing objecthood' that is imposed on Black men (Fanon 2008, 82). It is not only that Black men are denied proper personhood; they are also appropriated as part of its construction: 'not only must the black man be black; *he must be black in relation to the white man*' (Fanon 2008, 83). The proper (white) person is partly constituted by 'excluding blacks from the self-other dynamics of subjectivity itself' (Tyler 2013, 42). Following the racist incident Sacks and Thiel describe, there is an emergency house meeting at the university. The authors state that there were conflicting accounts of what happened, but then make the decision – in line with their racial structuring – to describe B. J. as 'emotional': 'he started to gesticulate wildly, lunged violently at the two white freshman, and, seeming to have lost his mind, collapsed on the floor' (Sacks and Thiel 1995, 42–43). They then repeat other reports about the emergency house meeting, amplifying the stories of 'hysteria' and 'pandemonium.'

Charles Mills's book *The Racial Contract*, published in 1997 (two years after *The Diversity Myth*), parallels the work of Carole Pateman on the sexual contract – each writer explores the seventeenth-century social contract as being a contract drawn up between white men. Instead of reading the 'crucial human metamorphosis' from 'natural' man to 'civil/political' man as told by social contract theorists like Locke or Hobbes, Mills argues that there was a conceptual partitioning as between white and non-white men. The story of the social contract theorists is constructed in such a way as to justify and legitimate the white settler state: the creation of the state is dependent upon an understanding of non-white men as being in a permanently 'prepolitical state' – uncivilised, barbaric. Because non-white men are regarded as not having developed the capacity of rationality they are kept out of the public sphere. Mills argues that in order to maintain the 'racial contract,' there are 'white mythologies, invented Orients, invented Africas, invented Americas, with a correspondingly fabricated population.' These were 'countries that never were, inhabited by people who never were – Calibans and Tontos, Man Fridays and Sambos' (Mills 1997, 18–19). All of these myths – being repudiated by decolonising the curriculum at Stanford – are re-inscribed in *The Diversity Myth*. And here we should note Mills's argument that: 'these phenomena are in no way *accidental*, but *prescribed* by the terms of The Racial Contract, which requires a certain schedule of structured blindnesses and opacities in order to establish and maintain the white polity' (19). The Racial Contract functions to construct the 'individual' or proper person as unraced, while simultaneously racialising others. It also plays a key part in the frontier mythology, where the Others of the white man are necessary for the constitution of his white settler identity as the sovereign individual; the proper person of the household. As we discuss in Chapter 7 in relation to the predominance of dataism, this is also the data that contributes to the contemporary algorithmic architecture.

Invested in their own form of identity politics, their book is driven by fear of losing socio-economic privilege through a struggle over culture and by their heroic desire to protect patriarchy in that same struggle. (These are strategies that, we will later argue, are also harnessed in contemporary digital capitalism, for example by James Damore and the alt-right hubs that support him.) *The Diversity Myth* is a trolls' handbook, both deliberatively provocative, and deliberately obfuscatory; it is a plea to retain racialised patriarchal structures, through a strategy of discursively performing reason, as well as white male victimhood (Carroll 2011). We return to *The Diversity Myth* later in this chapter in relation to postfeminism, sexual violence, and online misogyny. However, first we conclude this section by making connections between *The Stanford Review*, work cultures in Silicon Valley, and the ways that racial discrimination is baked into platforms.

In *Algorithms of Oppression* Noble critiques algorithms as value-laden propositions. She interrogates the political economy of Silicon Valley platforms and the ways that they influence representative discourses that surround racial and gendered discourses (Noble 2018, 171). (Algorithms are a keyword in the concordance occurring 147/mw as compared to 30/mw in the enTenTen15.) Noble concludes the book with a focus on Yelp, and an interview with Kandis an owner of an African-American hair salon near a prestigious college town in the US (173). Kandis' business was directly impacted by the shifts away from affirmative action since the 1980s which impacted on the recruitment of Black students (as argued for in *The Diversity Myth*). But her business has also suffered under the value-laden algorithms of platforms like Yelp. Yelp's 'colorblind' algorithms meant that Kandis was not in control of her representation and the representation of her business which is dependent on being recognised in terms of race and gender. Yelp was founded by Jeremy Stoppelman and Russel Simmons; it was funded by Levchin, who later joined as chairman. All three were part of the PayPal Mafia.

Although these men were not part of *The Stanford Review*, it is significant that this platform was seeded in the PayPal Mafia because of how this culture could impact on the design of later digital products i.e. Yelp's interface as well as its algorithms. In the 2007 *Fortune* article which coined the term 'PayPal Mafia,' its author Jeffrey O'Brien points out that PayPal 'wasn't exactly welcoming toward women' (O'Brien 2007). As Rabois says, 'We were very network-driven in hiring. And they were weird networks' (Chang 2018, 49). Apart from one woman programmer who quit after six months, the only woman in the early PayPal team was the office manager, which mirrors the roles that we have seen allocated to women in popular culture texts as discussed in Chapter 2. Levchin and Rabois argue that the people they hire have to be ideologically similar (Chang 2018, 50). This network-driven hiring is still true for Silicon Valley, as Chang and Wachter-Boettcher have argued. Chang conveys other stories of how men get jobs and opportunities in the tech industry through their connections: 'their relationships became the currency in which they traded. They joined one another's companies, funded one another's ventures, defended one another's controversial public statements, and more' (Chang 2018, 54). This has impacts on the digital products that are then made and monopolise the internet.

Personhood on the technological frontier

Thiel's views from *The Diversity Myth* continued to prevail even after PayPal had been founded and sold. In 2009 he wrote an essay for the libertarian journal *Cato Unbound*, run out of the Cato Institute, entitled 'The Education of a Libertarian,' in which he outlines his pioneering visions of sea steading, cyberspace, and 'efforts to commercialize space.'[4] These are 'new worlds' that 'will impact and force change on the existing social and political order' (Thiel 2009). 2009 is the year that Barack Obama became president. However: 'I do not despair because I no longer believe that politics encompasses all possible futures of our world.' Instead, he visions 'technological frontiers' that are beyond politics:

> The critical question then becomes one of means, of how to escape not via politics but beyond it. Because there are no truly free places left in our world, I suspect that the mode for escape must involve some sort of new and hitherto untried process that leads us to some undiscovered country; and for this reason I have focused my efforts on new technologies that may create a new space for freedom.

In this article, Thiel dreams of an escape beyond politics to an as yet 'undiscovered country,' a new 'space for freedom' – echoing that first 'multiculturalist' Columbus and pre-empting those maps from *Zero to One*. This will be the place from which to change public and political life. Thiel marshals freedom, which is a key motivating force of the frontier spirit; framed as freedom from European rule, or as freedom from government as in the work of Perry Barlow. But it is also the freedom of impunity.

In this vision the internet as a site of freedom is not for everyone: it is a space for a specific kind of politics – one presumably in line with that outlined in *The Diversity Myth*. Thiel's frontier imaginary comes to a standstill, or cannot be made sense of, in the face of multiculturalism because the frontier is constructed by coercion and domination. Thiel is concerned that rights to personhood might be extended through the internet, presumably something particularly worrying at a time of potential social justice reforms being ushered in by a Black president:

> The future of technology is not pre-determined, and we must resist the temptation of technological utopianism – the notion that technology has a momentum or will of its own, that it will guarantee a more free future, and therefore that we can ignore the terrible arc of the political in our world.

This is why it is of utmost importance that the libertarian frontiers are weaponised to protect men like Thiel:

> A better metaphor is that we are in a deadly race between politics and technology. The future will be much better or much worse, but the question of the future remains very open indeed. We do not know exactly how close this race is, but I suspect that it may be very close, even down to the wire. Unlike the world of politics, in the world of technology the choices of individuals may still be paramount. The fate of our world may depend on the effort of a single person who builds or propagates the machinery of freedom that makes the world safe for capitalism.

A world safe for capitalism is presumably one of monopoly companies and patriarchal networks, where 'the multiculture' has been transformed into racialised domination. It isn't until Trump becomes a candidate that the possibility of politics returns for Thiel. It is interesting here that Thiel locates technology or the internet as a battleground over politics. As so many critics have argued, that the digital is precisely the site which is changing politics.

In Thiel's vision, who is this space of freedom for? Bewailing the extension of suffrage to women, as well as 'the vast increase in welfare beneficiaries,' he perceives the extension of proper personhood (see discussion over personhood in Chapter 1) – in the form of suffrage and state benefits – as a threat to 'freedom':

> Since 1920, the vast increase in welfare beneficiaries and the extension of the franchise to women – two constituencies that are notoriously tough for libertarians – have rendered the notion of 'capitalist democracy' into an oxymoron.

Exclusions from personhood based on race, class, disability, gender, and age are implicit in this statement, not only in its dismissal of women's rights to personhood, but also in its denigration of people dependent, or partially dependent, on state support. It also seems to say that the sphere of care in the household should be the preserve of disenfranchised women (because what else will they be doing?). And women should not be allowed entry into the world of politics. All this begs the question, who are the agents of the technological frontier called upon by Thiel to change politics? We return briefly to *The Diversity Myth* as well as the work of Eugenia Siapera to help make sense of what might be happening in Thiel's vision of the future.

The Diversity Myth is also part of the postfeminist intertexts proliferating in the 1990s. Key to these discourses is the way that racism and sexism are disavowed, and framed as belonging to the past (McRobbie 2009). What is relevant here, is how scholars have made links between postfeminist discourses and the rise of online misogyny. And as Debbie Ging argues, postfeminism's key features include: 'individualism, bio-essentialism, the commodification of intimacy, the myth of equality achieved, a renewed focus on heteronormativity and war-of-the-sexes tropes, and the turn towards a cultural politics of emotion.' She also argues that these have 'both facilitated and provided justifications' for some of the online misogyny that is so pervasive on the internet (Ging 2019, 59).

Other books that similarly harnessed reactionary arguments against victimisation similar to *The Diversity Myth's* and were published in and around the same year included: Katie Roiphe's *The Morning After: Sex, Fear and Feminism on Campus* (1994); Christina Hoff Summers's *Who Stole Feminism* (1994); and Rene Denfeld's *The New Victorians: A Woman's Challenge to the Old Feminist Order* (1995). Seemingly taking up the argument from Roiphe's *The Morning After*, Sacks and Thiel describe as 'controversial' a 'new policy on sexual harassment, which concluded that "psychological coercion" (a euphemism for verbal seduction) might be equivalent to rape' (27). This slighting dismissal of coercion is followed by the argument:

> But since a multicultural rape charge may indicate nothing more than belated regret, a woman might 'realize' that she had been 'raped' the next day or even many days later. Under these circumstances, it is unclear who should be held responsible. If the alcohol made both of them do it, then why should the woman's consent be obviated any more than the man's? Why is all blame placed on the man?

And:

> Although [the alleged perpetrator] was clearly guilty of serving alcohol to an underage woman and taking advantage of her resulting lack of judgement, there was no sexual assault.

These claims echo Sacks' writing for *The Stanford Review* as noted above. The book's refutation of potential rape charges marshals the discourses of law, especially the lexicon, or mode, of cross-examination and word games. Rhetorically, they stake their position in institutionalised (legal) frameworks that assume the perpetrator's innocence. And while proof of guilt is necessary in a legal justice system, here the principle is used to reverse the terms of assault and the victim becomes the perpetrator of a crime (for a powerful analysis of how this logic plays out in other contexts, see Anita Biressi (2019) on the case of elite politician Dominique Strauss-Kahn and hotel cleaner Nafissatou Diallo). It is precisely these logics that intimidate women out of coming forward after rape or sexual assault charges. Far from being contrarian, here Sacks and Thiel are absolutely conventional.

Sexual violence is one of the ways that patriarchal structures have sought to perpetuate oppressions (Manne 2018). Thus, to disavow the multiple ways that sexual violence is perpetrated, as the authors do in this book, is, in effect, to defend it on the grounds of patriarchal rights. Discussions about alleged 'witch trials' of men accused of harassment or assault have been used for some time as a means to undermine feminist campaigning around sexual assault.[5] The feminist campaigners or accusers are portrayed as hysterical, and the accused men are depicted as victims. This is a way of disavowing violence against women, while simultaneously invoking the affective charge of witchery to produce an undercurrent of misogyny. In the 1990s Sardar made connections between the electronic frontiers of, for example, The Well and sexual violence against women (Sardar 1995). And because sexual violence is so embedded in the realities and the mythologies of the electronic frontier, it is perhaps not surprising that part of Sacks and Thiel's diatribe invokes property rights to women's bodies (it is entirely contingent with the saloon brothel as a paradigmatic location for civilisation in the mythical 'Wild West').[6]

In her discussion of online misogyny, Siapera links the sexual humiliation and degradation of women to Silvia Federici's analysis of the witch hunts where misogyny and violence were unleashed against women in the transitional period between feudalism and capitalism (Federici 2004). Siapera argues that there is increased 'social competition imposed by neoliberal informational capitalism' and as a consequence of this 'misogyny resurfaces as part of struggles over a new division of labour':

> The specific attacks against prominent women are telling: if technology is part of our common future, if the political and public sphere is where our future will be decided, then banning or scaring women away from participating in making technology and from speaking out in the public sphere means that women are excluded from having any say in the direction of this future and from sharing it equitably.
>
> (Siapera 2019, 38)

Certainly in 2009 Thiel perceived the internet as a site where politics could be changed so that women were less able to participate; so they would have less of a say in the direction of the future. Silvia Federici argues that the violence against women that was enacted in the shift from feudalism to modernity was a struggle over property and personhood, where women (mostly peasant women) who were economically autonomous were publicly murdered. The bodies of women were and are the territory on which these political battles over capitalism are fought because they are responsible for producing soldiers and workforce; they are consigned to unpaid labour to satisfy the needs of ascendant capitalism. In Federici's words, '"the struggle for the body of women [is] the last frontier of capitalism"' (Lyons 2019). Women are a problem if they exceed their subordinate position in the household and seek participation in the public sphere. From this space of personhood they are in the position to make demands from the government that are at odds with libertarian philosophies, thus making in Thiel's words 'capitalist democracy an oxymoron.' Siapera extends Federici's argument to explain the intensity of online misogyny as a gendered struggle over the ownership of digital technology. And this is why, for Thiel, cyberspace should be a site free of women, in order to properly forge and then actualise a future run by a male-dominated patriarchal network.

Conclusion

In a keynote address at the National Conservatism Conference in 2019, an event intending to reformulate nationalism in the era of the Trump administration, Thiel pursued many of the themes that we have mapped thus far in this chapter, and for this he received a standing ovation. Thiel uses this platform to issue a warning to Silicon Valley for its 'insane left wing politics,' as well as to attack universities. Again, we see paranoid echoes of *The Diversity Myth* and a perceived threat to the frontier household. Thiel suggests starting a criminal investigation into universities, likening Harvard, Stanford, and Yale to the Studio 54 night club (a now closed but once notorious disco venue). He also takes the opportunity to try to humiliate the Obamas, to the loud laughter of the National Conservatism audience. He claims that Silicon Valley is 'like a one-party state,' and that: 'there's some kind of soft totalitarianism that is creating an incredible conformity.' He particularly takes issue with Google. Gone is his admiration of Google as the ideal monopoly corporation. Instead, he compares Google to the 'communist' *Star Trek*. He questions Google's 'treasonous decision' to work with the Chinese government rather than the US military. He poses three questions that should be asked of Google, which, he says, 'need to be asked by the FBI, by the CIA': 'and I'm not sure quite how to put this, I would like them to be asked in a not excessively gentle manner.' [7] The suggestion to deploy militarist surveillance management techniques is in keeping with the militarism of Thiel's philosophies – and of the company that he founded, Palantir.

One of the key charges levelled at Silicon Valley, by Peter Thiel and indeed by political scientists like Broockman et al. whose work we discussed at length in Chapter 1, is that it is remarkably politically homogenous: it is consistently liberal in outlook and affect, with a deep belief in sexual and gender liberation. Ethnographies of the actual Bay area also note this is the case (Lueck-English 2017). However, Lueck-English also identifies that at the level of everyday life this diversity is unevenly experienced at the level of race and ethnicity. Moreover, research suggests that West Coast Tech's products and its social impacts are profoundly conservative (Vaidhyanathan 2012). There is no straightforward answer for why this is so, but there are clearly identifiable factors. The specific demographic groups that are recruited to prestigious engineering jobs is one; the racial hierarchies inherited through the histories of the American West and similar are undoubtedly at play. But equally important is the prominent networks found around Peter Thiel and the Paypal Mafia.

Notes

1 The 'PayPal Mafia' photographed at Tosca in San Francisco, October 2007. Text underneath image in original publication reads: 'Back row from left: Jawed Karim, co-founder YouTube; Jeremy Stoppelman, CEO Yelp; Andrew McCormack, managing partner Laiola Restaurant; Premal Shah, Pres president of Kiva; second row from left: Luke Nosek, managing partner The Founders Fund; Kenny Howery, managing partner The Founders Fund; David Sacks, CEO Geni and Room 9 Entertainment; Peter Thiel, CEO Clarium Capital and Founders Fund; Keith Rabois, VP business development BIz Dev at Slide and original YouTube Investor; Reid Hoffman, Founder LinkedIn; Max Levchin, CEO Slide; Roelof Botha, partner Sequoia Capital; Russel Simmons, CTO and co-founder of Yelp.'
2 He is followed and celebrated on Twitter by alt-right accounts (although his Twitter account only has one Tweet advertising his 2014 book). For example, when Gawker lost, alt-right accounts started trending, sharing the hashtag '#ThankyouPeter' (Holiday, 2018, 253). The comments under his YouTube interviews and other Thiel content also bear witness to his popularity in these conservative and male-run networks.
3 Many of Thiel's friends at *The Stanford Review* were subsequently hired by him to work at Paypal, where, presumably – in his words – they went on singing. For example Ken Howery (former managing editor of *Stanford Review*) was co-founder of PayPal and the Founders Fund; Sacks was COO at Paypal when Thiel was CEO and has also funded Facebook, Palantir, and SpaceX; he is a co-founder of Yammer and Angel Investor; Keith Rabois, (former Opinion Editor) was COO of Square and is now a venture capitalist; Joe Lonsdale (former EIC) is co-founder of Palantir; Stephen Russell (former section editor) is co-founder of Prism Skylabs; Stephen Cohen (former EIC) is a co-founder of Palantir; Erik Jackson (former EIC) is CEO of Caplinked and wrote *The Paypal Wars*; Gideon Yu (former business manager) is former CFO of YouTube and Facebook; Bruce Gibney (former EIC) is a former venture capitalist at Founders Fund. This all fits pretty neatly with Ortner's delineation of a patriarchal network (Ortner 2014).
4 Duggan notes that the Independent Gay Forum includes David Boaz, executive vice president of the Cato Institute and author of *Libertarianism: A Primer* (Free Press 1997).
5 The idea of a witch trial was also invoked by Brett Kavanaugh and his conservative supporters (e.g. Newt Gingrich and Tucker Carlson) when he was accused of sexual assault by Christine Blasey Ford and others after being nominated by Trump as Associate Justice of the Supreme Court. It is perhaps worth noting that Kavanaugh's friend Joel Kaplan, who sat behind Kavanaugh throughout his appearance before the Senate Judiciary Committee, is Facebook's VP of global public policy; the two had worked together during the last George W. Bush administration. It is also worth noting that there was anger around Kaplan's overt support of Kavanaugh by some workers at Facebook.
6 See for instance *West World* starring Talulah Riley, Musk's second wife.
7 Thiel is introduced by Christopher DeMuth at the National Conservatism Conference as 'A social visionary' and an 'ardent American nationalist.' Thiel states: 'Number one, how many foreign intelligence agencies have infiltrated your Manhattan Project for AI? Number two, does Google's senior management consider itself to have been thoroughly infiltrated by Chinese intelligence? Number three, is it because they consider themselves to be so thoroughly infiltrated that they have engaged in the seemingly treasonous decision to work with the Chinese military and not with the US military ... because they are making the sort of bad, short-term rationalistic [decision] that if the technology doesn't go out the front door, it gets stolen out the backdoor anyway?' (Thiel 2019).

References

Ahmed, Sara (2017) *Living a Feminist Life*. Durham: Duke University Press.
Bhattacharyya, Gargi (2018) *Rethinking Racial Capitalism: Questions of Reproduction and Survival*. New York: Rowman and Littlefield.
Biressi, Anita (2019) 'Following the Money: News, Sexual Assault and the Economic Logic of the Gendered Public Sphere' *European Journal of Cultural Studies*, 22(5–6), 595–612.
Broussard, Meredith (2019) *Artificial Unintelligence: How Computers Misunderstand the World*. Cambridge, MA: MIT Press.
Carroll, Hamilton (2011) *Affirmative Reaction: New Formations of White Masculinity*. Durham: Duke University Press.
Chang, Emily (2018) *Brotopia: Breaking Up the Boys' Club of Silicon Valley*. New York: Penguin Random House.
Collins, Patricia Hill (1989) 'The Social Construction of Black Feminist Thought' *Signs*, 14(4), 745–773.
Crenshaw, Kimberle (1989) 'Demarginalizing the Intersection of Race and Sex: A Black Feminist Critique of Antidiscrimination Doctrine, Feminist Theory and Antiracist Politics' *University of Chicago Legal Forum*, 8. https://chicagounbound.uchicago.edu/uclf/vol1989/iss1/8
Denfeld, Rene (1995) *The New Victorians: A Woman's Challenge to the Old Feminist Order*. New York: Warner Books.
Drabold, Will (2016) 'Read Peter Thiel's Speech at the Republican National Convention' *Time*, 21 July 2016. https://time.com/4417679/republican-convention-peter-thiel-transcript/
Duggan, Lisa (2003) *The Twilight of Equality: Neoliberalism, Cultural Politics, and the Attack on Democracy*. Boston: Beacon Press.
English-Lueck, J. A. (2017) *Cultures@SiliconValley*, Second Edition. Stanford: Stanford University Press.
Fanon, Frantz (2008) *Black Skin, White Masks*. New York: Grove Press.
Federici, Siliva (2004) *Caliban and the Witch: Women, the Body and Primitive Accumulation*. Brooklyn: Autonomedia.
Fortson, Danny (2019) 'Palantir, the Tech Spooks Who Found Bin Laden Are Helping BP Find Oil' *The Times*, October 27 2019. www.thetimes.co.uk/article/palantir-the-tech-spooks-who-found-bin-laden-are-helping-bp-find-oil-9qddfpv2r#
Ging, Debbie (2019) 'Bros v. Hos: Postfeminism, Anti-feminism and the Toxic Turn in Digital Gender Politics' in Debbie Ging and Eugenia Siapera (eds) *Gender Hate Online: Understanding the New Anti-Feminism*. Basingstoke: Palgrave Macmillan, 45–68.
Ging, Debbie and Eugenia Siapera, eds. (2019) *Gender Hate Online: Understanding the New Anti-Feminism*. Basingstoke: Palgrave Macmillan.
Halt and Catch Fire (AMC 2014–2017)
Hasinoff, Adele Amy and Marina Levina (2017) 'The Silicon Valley Ethos: Tech Industry Products, Discourses, and Practices' *TV and New Media*, 18(6), 489–495. doi: 10.1177/1527476416680454
Hicks, Marie (2017) *Programmed Inequality: How Britain Discarded Women Technologists and Lost Its Edge in Computing*. Cambridge: MIT Press.
Hoff Summers, Christina (1994) *Who Stole Feminism: How Women Have Betrayed Women*. New York: Simon and Schuster.
Hoffman, Reid and Ben Casnocha (2013) *The Start-Up of You: Adapt to the Future, Invest in Yourself, and Transform Your Career*. New York: Currency.

Hoffman, Reid with Chris Yeh (2018) *Blitzscaling: The Lightning-Fast Path to Building Massively Valuable Companies*. London: Penguin, Random House.
Holiday, Ryan (2018) *Conspiracy: Peter Thiel, Hulk Hogan, Gawker, and the Anatomy of Intrigue*. London: Profile.
Lyons, Sarah (2019) 'Silvia Federici on Witch Hunts, Body Politics, and Rituals of Resistance' 15 February 2019. www.pmpress.org/blog/2019/09/15/silvia-federici-on-witch-hunts-body-politics-rituals-of-resistance/
Manne, Kate (2018) *Down Girl: The Logic of Misogyny*. Oxford: Oxford University Press.
McRobbie, Angela (2009) *The Aftermath of Feminism: Gender, Culture and Social Change*. London: SAGE.
Mills, Charles (1997) *The Racial Contract*. New York: Cornell University Press.
Mukherjee, Roopali (2011) 'Bling Fling: Commodity Consumption and the Politics of the "Post-Racial"' in Michael G. Lacy and Kent A. Ono (eds) *Critical Rhetorics of Race*. New York: New York University Press, 178–193.
Nakamura, Lisa (2008) *Digitizing Race: Visual Cultures of the Internet*. Minneapolis: University of Minnesota Press.
National Conservatism (2020) 'About' http://nationalconservatism.org/about/.
Noble, Safiya Umoja (2018) *Algorithms of Oppression: How Search Engines Reinforce Racism*. New York: New York University Press.
O'Brien, Jeffrey M. (2007) 'The PayPal Mafia' *Fortune*, November 13. https://fortune.com/2007/11/13/paypal-mafia/ Last accessed 04/05/2020.
Ortner, B. Sherry (2014) 'Too Soon for Post-Feminism: The Ongoing Life of Patriarchy in Neoliberal America' *History and Anthropology*, 25(4), 530–549.
Phillips, Whitney (2015) *This Is Why We Can't Have Nice Things: Mapping the Relationship between Online Trolling and Mainstream Culture*. Cambridge, MA: MIT Press.
Puar, Jasbir (2007) *Terrorist Assemblages Homonationalism in Queer Times*. Durham: Duke University Press.
Roiphe, Katie (1994) *The Morning after: Sex, Fear and Feminism on Campus*. New York: Little Brown and Co.
Rubin, Dave (2018) 'Trump, Gawker, and Leaving Silicon Valley' 12 September. www.youtube.com/watch?v=h10kXgTdhNU.
Sacks, David O. and Peter A. Thiel (1995) *The Diversity Myth: Multiculturalism and Political Intolerance on Campus*. Oakland: Independent Institute.
Sardar, Ziauddin (1995) 'alt.civil izations.faq Cyberspace as the Darker Side of the West' *Futures*, 27(7), 717–794.
Siapera, Eugenia (2019) 'Online Misogyny as Witch Hunt: Primitive Accumulation in the Age of Techno-capitalism' in Debbie Ging and Eugenia Siapera (eds) *Gender Hate Online: Understanding the New Anti-Feminism*. Basingstoke: Palgrave Macmillan, pp. 21–44.
Star Wars (1977) George Lucas (dir.) Lucasfilm.
Streitfeld, David (2016) 'Peter Thiel to Donate $1.25 Million in Support of Donald Trump' *The New York Times*, 15 October 2016. www.nytimes.com/2016/10/16/technology/peter-thiel-donald-j-trump.html.
Taplin, Jonathan (2017) *Move Fast and Break Things: How Facebook, Google and Amazon Have Cornered Culture and What It Means for All of Us*. London: Macmillan.
Thiel, Peter (2009) 'The Education of a Libertarian' *Cato Unbound*. 13 April. www.cato-unbound.org/2009/04/13/peter-thiel/education-libertarian.
Thiel, Peter (2016a) 'Peter Thiel Commencement Speech, Hamilton College, May 2016 (Transcript)' *Entrepreneur*, May 23.

Thiel, Peter (2019) 'The Star Trek Computer is Not Enough' National Conservatism Conference. https://youtu.be/7JRyy2MM-rI

Thiel, Peter with Blake Masters (2014) *Zero to One: Notes on Startups, or How to Build the Future*. London: Penguin.

Trump, Donald (2016) 'Full Text: Donald Trump 2016 RNC Draft Speech Transcript' Politico, 21 July 2016. www.politico.com/story/2016/07/full-transcript-donald-trump-nomination-acceptance-speech-at-rnc-225974.

Tyler, Imogen (2013) *Revolting Subjects: Social Abjection and Resistance in Neoliberal Britain*. London: Zed Books.

Wachter-Boettcher, Sara (2017) *Technically Wrong: Sexist Apps, Biased Algorithms, and Other Threats of Toxic Tech*. New York: W.W.Norton & Company.

Westworld (2016–present) HBO.

Vaidhyanathan, Siva (2012) *The Googlization of Everything*. Berkeley: University of California Press.

Van Dijck, José, Thomas Poell, and Martijn de Waal (2018) *The Platform Society Public Values in a Connective World*. Oxford: Oxford University Press.

Yiannopoulos, Milo (2016) 'How Peter Thiel Saved Free Speech on the Web' www.breitbart.com/social-justice/2016/05/31/peter-thiel-free-speech/

Yiannopoulos, Milo (2017) *Dangerous*. Dangerous Books.

Zuboff, Shoshona (2019) *The Age of Surveillance Capitalism: The Fight for a Human Future at the New Frontier of Power*. London: Profile Books.

6
ENDORSED BY SANDBERG
Resilience not resistance

On 4 December 2017, Sheryl Sandberg was the first interviewee on media mogul Oprah Winfrey's podcast SuperSoul Conversations (Figure 6.1). The episode, titled 'Sheryl Sandberg: How to Build Resilience and Find Joy after Loss,' is a promotional exercise for Sandberg's 2017 bestselling book *Option B: Facing Adversity, Building Resilience and Finding Joy* (written with psychologist Adam Grant). Sandberg did extensive international publicity for this book, for example a tearful appearance on the BBC radio show Desert Island Discs. *Option B* is part autobiography and part self-help book. Following the sudden death of her husband in 2015, Sandberg and her co-author detail the trauma of grief and offer dataist solutions to building resilience and finding joy. The SuperSoul Conversations episode also makes mention of Sandberg's previous 2013 bestseller *Lean In: Women, Work and the Will to Lead* (written with television writer and producer Nell Scovell). This book is similarly based on personal experience, and advises women on how to succeed in leadership positions in a corporate world. The diagnosis as to why women are excluded from leadership positions largely boils down to a lack of confidence and insufficient *leaning in* to the male-dominated workplace. During the interview, Winfrey and Sandberg co-create what Lauren Berlant (2008) calls 'intimate publics' through a feminine heterosexual narrative. Their conversation is framed as personal and revealing. Sandberg performs significant 'emotion work' (Nunn and Biressi 2010) by detailing her grief over the loss of her husband and the impact that this has had on her and her family, often weeping. We understand this podcast, as well as Sandberg's books and other official media appearances as part of the construction of her celebrity. As we stated in the introduction, we interrogate the patriarchs' celebrification as deeply entwined with the companies that they work for, as well as being ideological proponents of digital capitalism; rather than making claims about the people themselves.

168 Endorsed by Sandberg

FIGURE 6.1 Sheryl Sandberg and Oprah Winfrey *SuperSoul Conversations*, 2017

Nicole Aschoff in her 2015 book *The New Prophets of Capital* argues that Winfrey and Sandberg are part of an elite set of storytellers (which includes Bill Gates) who masquerade as progressive thinkers. The stories that they tell – as Winfrey and Sandberg do in this podcast – are cleaved to free-market capitalism: 'Their visions carry within them a systemic and coherent meaning that seems possible, safe, and achievable within capitalism' (Aschoff 2015, 11). For the purposes of this chapter we also locate Sandberg's storytelling within the context of the household metaphor – both Zuckerberg's corporate household and Sandberg's domestic household as mediated through her books and interviews. These two structures are not always distinct. We have been arguing that the stories these patriarchs tell about themselves and their companies and the social power they exercise are deeply entangled. Sandberg has been instrumental in monetising the services offered by Facebook; but her wealth is less than 2% that of her boss and work partner Zuckerberg. Her position within the company is also starkly at odds with Zuckerberg, as she is not its founder and it is Zuckerberg who has majority voting rights on the board. Part of Sandberg's argument in *Lean In* is that through successfully managing the private household and balancing this with one's place in a corporation, a woman can achieve happiness. Indeed, this is *the* way to achieve happiness. The household in *Lean In* is emphatically a heterosexual one inhabited by a heterosexual couple and their children. She later critiques this perspective in the interview with Winfrey, apologising over her previous lack of understanding regarding single mothers.

Because our book specifically looks at the patriarchal networks of digital capitalism, we position Sandberg's storytelling within the celebrity assemblages that we have identified. In particular, we use Deniz Kandiyoti's work to show that Sandberg models how to bargain with patriarchy, both in the home and in the corporate household. Concomitant with this modelling, Sandberg advises on how to negotiate these bargains. Her advice is to be resilient in the context of male domination, rather than resistant. And the resilient subject that is celebrated is also the subject who shares and shares, who connects extensively; who turns her private and public lives into commercial property for the corporate households of digital capitalism. We also argue that Sandberg makes her own bargain with the patriarchal networks by demonstrating how to monetise the data produced by women, thus forging the female data subject of value – who is also the imagined (and real) audience for her books. In order to make these claims we offer a textual analysis of her two books, as well as Facebook posts. We also use the concordance to provide ideological context to the field that Sandberg is working in. Before we turn to the concordance we look more deeply at the patriarchal bargaining that Sandberg models.

Bargaining with patriarchy

Describing Google's Sergey Brin and Larry Page as 'true visionaries' (Sandberg and Scovell 2013, 60), Sandberg and Scovell begin *Lean In* with a story about Sandberg bringing 'pregnancy parking' to Google:

> The next day, I marched in – or more like waddled in – to see Google founders Larry Page and Sergey Brin in their office, which was really just a large room with toys and gadgets strewn all over the floor. I found Sergey in a yoga position in the corner and announced that we needed pregnancy parking, preferably sooner rather than later. He looked up at me and agreed immediately, noting that he had never thought about that before.
>
> *(Sandberg and Scovell 2013, 4)*

Not only are the founders of Google likened to children in a playroom, but they are reasonable, listen to women, and keen to help around issues of childcare in the workplace. The story shows us that all you need to do is 'announce' to men what women need, and then it will appear. In another anecdote, this time from *Option B*, Elon Musk bonds with Sandberg and her children over grief (Musk had a son who died as a baby) as they watch a SpaceX rocket successfully launch (Grant and Sandberg 2017, 143). We can see this anecdote as one of Musk's cameos rather than a celebration of Sandberg's and Musk's relationship, as we have found little else to connect them in the concordance. But we can read it also as a portrayal of Sandberg's elite position in the networks we are mapping, as well as providing some useful marketing for Musk. Sandberg's intimacy with the main patriarchs is key to her celebrification. She endorses them and their books, and they endorse her.

Depicting the patriarchs of US West Coast Tech as benign visionaries, willing to listen to what women want, is one of the ways that Sandberg's celebrity negotiates her hypervisibility. Another way is to deflect attention from the leaders in the leadership positions (apart from through poignant anecdotes) and instead focus on women's culpability for not being in those leadership positions. *Lean In* matter-of-factly discusses the discrepancy in the 'leadership ambition gap' between men and women, but sees women as being the driver for its solution. At one point Sandberg states that 'in addition to facing institutional obstacles, women face a battle from within,' as if the two bear equal weight – and, indeed, as if this inner battle is the most problematic. Sandberg's celebrity brand fuses the household performances of wife, mother, daughter, with female corporate leadership; it is a version of corporate womanhood that patriarchy can be hospitable to. We suggest that digital capitalism's conservative understanding of what a woman 'is' partly accounts for why Sandberg employs this gendered position as a significant component of her celebrification. She is given many platforms from which to speak to women about leadership, precisely because her brand acknowledges but then obfuscates so much about the axes of oppression that structure digital capitalism's power. We can see these strategies as part of the patriarchal bargains that Sandberg's celebrity models.

There is a conspicuous dissonance when reading Sandberg's celebrifying texts alongside the critiques levelled against her, Facebook, and Silicon Valley. Whereas critics such as Emily Chang, Kate Losse, and Ellen Pao track a terrifying terrain of deep inequalities and prejudice against a backdrop of white supremacy and bro culture, Sandberg is positive, upbeat, and solution-oriented. (Not unrelatedly, she also comes across as personable and charming.) When *Lean In* was published in 2013, one did not get a sense of the ravaging inequalities and misogyny pervasive in the industry that she describes – which, for example, forced Ellen Pao to quit her job in Kleiner Perkins, a venture capital firm that was one of the first to invest in Facebook (Pao 2017). In her book *Reset*, Pao describes herself using Sandberg's invocation to 'lean in' on a private jet with her male colleagues. She makes a point of sitting with the men, to which they respond by discussing their favourite ethnicity of stripper in order to deliberately alienate her and render Pao uncomfortable (Pao 2017, 78). Pao also faced sustained abuse in her position as CEO of Reddit (Pao 2017) from misogynist and racist users, forcing her to quit there too. There is no inkling of this in *Lean In* or *Option B* – indeed misogyny is only mentioned once and as a joke (Sandberg and Scovell 2013, 154). Unlike Pao, Sandberg has chosen not to resist the cultures of Silicon Valley – though it is worth noting that she worked for Google and Facebook rather than a venture capitalist organisation. Sandberg is also a white woman, whereas Pao is Asian American. From the position of whiteness, Sandberg is in the location to bargain along the lines of class, race, and sexuality, in her privileging and reiteration of the household (see hooks 2013).

At the beginning of *Lean In*, the authors state that 'men still run the world' (Sandberg and Scovell 2013, 5). Sandberg has acknowledged that she has been criticised for 'letting our institutions off the hook' (Sandberg and Scovell 2013, 11), and putting the emphasis on individual women. Rather than examining these men in more detail, and revealing how to resist them, Sandberg models and advises on patriarchal bargaining. Deniz Kandiyoti argues that women strategise within the constraints and internal logics of a society's gender ideology (Kandiyoti 1988). And that these strategies can be understood as contributing to a 'patriarchal bargain': 'Women's strategies are always played out in the context of identifiable patriarchal bargains that act as implicit scripts that define, limit, and inflect their market and domestic options' (Kandiyoti 1988, 285). Although Kandiyoti locates her analysis in sites of what she calls 'classic patriarchy,' we have found this concept very productive in identifying Sandberg's role in the patriarchal network. It helps make sense of her privileged position, but also why her celebrity texts are so popular. Her books and interviews offer advice which is potentially possible to achieve for an elite group of women who already benefit from the patriarchal structures in place.

These bargains are also constantly renegotiated and contested, both in Sandberg's celebrity and by those who follow her work. Kandiyoti states that the patriarchal bargains made 'indicate the existence of set rules and scripts regulating gender relations, to which both genders accommodate and acquiesce.' We turn to the concordance in the next section to give us an insight into the kinds of rules and scripts that regulate gender relations in West Coast tech, relations that Sandberg is working within. It is from this analysis that we locate Sandberg's gendered ideological storytelling. However, we recognise that we are working with complexity and what we called in our introduction 'assemblage thinking.' As Kandiyoti states, gender relations can 'be contested, redefined, and renegotiated' (286, note 1). And we can see Sandberg renegotiating, for example, in her inclusion of single mothers who she omitted in *Lean In*. It helps make sense of the Page and Brin allowing pregnancy parking or Zuckerberg extending compassionate leave. Gender relations are to some extent resisted and renegotiated in different contexts.

Gender and the concordance

Acknowledgements and endorsements in our concordance of 95 books on tech culture are a key way that networks are made visible. For example, Sandberg's 'closest adult friends' in her acknowledgements for *Lean In* include Silicon Valley guru Larry Brilliant and former Facebook employee and serial investor Chamath Palihapitiya, and both her books are peppered with appearances from key Silicon Valley players. Sandberg endorses five books in the concordance, a figure which is only beaten by Bill Gates, who endorses six (one of which is *Option B*). For a comparison, Brin, Page, and Thiel do not endorse any books in the concordance (although Page does write a foreword to one of Eric Schmidt's books). Sandberg sees the brand value in engaging in the economy of book endorsements. Performing this role involves connecting to traditional forms of legitimacy and gatekeeping among entrepreneurs, celebrities, and the publishing industry. Endorsing books by Reid Hoffman (twice), Larry Brilliant, Klaus Schwab, and Eric Ries garners social capital for Sandberg and for the authors, as well as building bridges between Sandberg, Facebook, and the organisations affiliated with the authors (e.g. with the World Economic Foundation founded by Schwab). It signals Sandberg as a key cultural figure in tech's patriarchal networks. Sandberg's books are also endorsed by a variety of women, including Oprah Winfrey, Alicia Keys, Chelsea Clinton, Condoleeza Rice, Malala Yousef, and Melinda Gates. When Sandberg endorses others, however, she is a component in a mainly male endorsement network, including Bill Gates, Eric Schmidt, Jack Dorsey, Marc Andreessen, and Michael Bloomberg. This demonstrates the woman-centred address of her books, as does the fact that she seeks to market her books outside the genre of tech 'how-to' manuals and biographies; it is also notable that her celebrification is partly constituted through appearing to be endorsed by high-profile women of colour, perhaps obfuscating the raced and classed dimensions of the patriarchal bargaining that Sandberg endorses.

Some clues from the concordance as to the terrain on which Sandberg is staking her claim can be seen in the occurrences of the binary pronouns she/he, and conservative homestead divisions such as husband/wife, son/daughter, he/she. (Neo-pronouns such as xe and ve do not appear at all.) Because we have included books specifically about women in the concordance, the difference between the number of times *man* and *woman* are mentioned per million words is not insignificant: *man* appears 541 times per million words (/mw) and *woman* 414/mw. However, if we take out the books explicitly about women (nearly 20% of the total), the difference becomes much starker: 465/mw for *man* to 153/mw for *woman* (we discuss this in more detail below). *Wife* appears considerably more than *husband* in the concordance (90/mw to 31 /mw) and *daughter* significantly less than *sons*. Baker states that in general, wife is typically more used than husband, 'because it implicitly refers to a man' (2014, 92). That is, women are discussed more in relation to their marital status, whereas men are seen in relation to other men; while *sons* are more interesting than *daughters*. On the other hand, *girl* appears proportionally more often than *daughter* in relation to its dyad term (*boy*), presumably as it is a term that can refer to sexually available young women as well as children. It is clear that the gendering of these texts is part of their ideological construction (regardless of the relationship to the real bodies that these representational texts take as referents). As Laura Mandell argues of data mining: 'the gender binary is not really about gender'; it is about '"textual gender," the stylistic and textual features associated with gendered genres' (Table 6.1).[1]

We suggest that Sandberg's celebrification is based in these 'gendered genres.' This is her way of leaning into the patriarchal terrain. And the nature of this terrain is further elucidated when we look at other patterns in the occurrences of gendered words in our concordance data. Thus, for example (drawing on the methodologies of corpus linguistics scholar Paul Baker (2014)), we can look at collocations with *man* and *woman*. In doing so we see that *woman* is strongly associated with race, minorities and the family in ways that *man* is not. This suggests that the perspective of the books that we have included about and by women – for example, *Lean Out, Brotopia, Reset, Technologically Wrong* – all focus on the ways that the category of woman intersects with race and class, among other interlinking factors.

TABLE 6.1 A gendered genre: pronouns and gender terms in the concordance

Word (simple)	Tech concordance (books about women excluded)/million words	Internet text control corpus: English web 2015 ten/million words	Books in English control corpus Google Ngram 2008/million words
Man	541 (465)	404	594
Woman	414 (153)	421	210
Husband	31 (22)	60	85
Wife	90 (87)	84	126
Boy	101 (86)	96.8	102
Girl	68 (45)	157.2	110
Son*	111 (102)	108.58	150
Daughter	42 (31)	69.27	77
He	5,479 (5,626)	N/A (too many hits)	4,946
She	1,012 (776)	N/A (too many hits)	2,208

* This figure is perhaps slightly exaggerated in our concordance due to a common optical character recognition error in the reading of the word 'reason' as 'rea' and 'son.'

Adjective use reinforces these results. Although *gay* is used exclusively to describe men, *queer* is exclusively applied to women. More tellingly perhaps, *white* is used to describe men far more frequently than women (69 to 9) and *black* collocates three times more with women than men. Men are exclusively described as *rich*, *wealthy*, *wise*, *mad*, *self-made*, or *great*; women exclusively as *trans*, *successful*, *pregnant*, *naked*, or *beautiful*. This is unsurprising perhaps in general terms of the social organisation of gender, and indeed the exclusive appellation of the adjective *family* to *man* is largely due to the fact, as Baker indicates, that all women are considered to be self-evidently 'family' orientated. It is also important to remember that *man* occurs far more frequently in the concordance than *woman*, so the ratios or exclusions are in fact more pronounced than the numbers here might express. So, for instance, *Asian* appears twice as often for women than men, but given that *man* is roughly four times as frequent as *woman* we can say that *Asian* is associated with *woman* at a frequency of roughly eight times that of *man*.

Exclusive collocations of verbs produce some interesting results. For instance, according to Sketch Engine, *man* is exclusively the subject of verbs such as *invent*, *dominate*, *found*, and *drive*; whereas *woman* collocates much more strongly with *feel* (22 to 5), and exclusively for *appear*, *complain*, and *experience*. The former indicates quite clearly the status afforded to men as leaders, while the latter presents women as in general objects that endure the vicissitudes of their environment. Indeed *experience* in a concordance setting tends to indicate that women have endured something negative, rather than a positive experience indicative of growth. For instance: 'These are the subtle slights that women experience daily, sometimes five to ten times per day' (*Brotopia*). Likewise the formulation *man/woman of* produces only two results: *man of the year* appears 14 times; while *woman of color* appears 22 times.

We placed no emphasis on the gender of authors in our selection criteria, so the spread of gender was revealing if unsurprising (see Appendix for more details about the methodology and gender breakdown). Tech is a male-dominated sector, and books about tech companies and their founders no less so it seems. Out of the 119 named authors on the books, 20 (17%) were identifiable as women.[2] These were unevenly spread across the thematic coding. Twenty-seven per cent of biographical-coded texts were written by women, while only 12% of ideological texts were. These sorts of figures are reflected throughout the concordance content itself, as we can see in Table 6. However, some of these proportions reflect perhaps either divisions in English language writing in general or are specific to the difference between books and the web. Google Ngram presents an interesting comparison: the most recent year for comparison – 2008 – which suggests that books in English themselves have a masculine orientation: albeit less than our gender-adjusted figures.

Much of this could be dismissed as symptomatic of a generalised culture of sexism. But we should understand what we're seeing here as significantly more extreme than normal trends. One major finding from the concordance is the much greater recurrence of *he* as compared to *she*. *He* appears 5479 per million words, while *she* appears only 1012 times. If we take out the woman-centred books then it is 5626 against 776. The significance of this is that *he* and *she* indicate the gendering of the *continuous active subject* in these books: they are pronouns that indicate a continuous actor once someone has been introduced by proper name. The dominance of 'He' in this context recalls gendered binaries in relation to ideas about who is active and who is passive. For example, the work of Hélène Cixous, who explored the ways in which men are seen as active, desiring subjects, while women are passive receptacles. What is absolutely remarkable here is firstly that these figures show an imbalance that is double the rate found in the books from Google Ngram and secondly that books about *women* also reproduce an emphasis on men as active subjects: 5,560 per million words for *he* vs. 4586/mw for *she*. Even in books about women, men remain the dominant active subject. It is within this gendered context that we situate Sandberg and analyse her celebrity.

Pioneer woman: managing the homestead

Feminist critics have named Sandberg's brand of feminism 'trickle-down feminism' (Grant 2013), 'faux feminism' (hooks 2013), 'neoliberal feminism' (Rottenberg 2018), 'popular feminism' (Banet-Weiser 2018), and 'Davos Feminism' (Shulevitz 2013). In general, these critics argue that because Sandberg is not interested in tackling women's oppression through government intervention or agitating collectively at the level of state policy, her feminism (if it is one at all) is a very limited one. More than this, her solutions are individual and her vision is magnificently elitist. Her version of feminism is seen as sabotaging long histories of feminist visioning and campaigning as she re-routes the mainstream feminist conversation so that it becomes one about individualist entrepreneurial psychology. As bell hooks argues:

> Sandberg's definition of feminism begins and ends with the notion that it's all about gender equality within the existing social system. From this perspective, the structures of imperialist white supremacist capitalist patriarchy need not be challenged. And she makes it seem that privileged white men will eagerly choose to extend the benefits of corporate capitalism to white women who have the courage to 'lean in.' It almost seems as if Sandberg sees women's lack of perseverance as more the problem than systemic inequality. Sandberg effectively uses her race and class power and privilege to promote a narrow definition of feminism that obscures and undermines visionary feminist concerns.
>
> *(hooks 2013)*

We follow hooks's line of thinking: Sandberg is not interested in subverting the patriarchal networks. Rather she is an ideological storyteller for the patriarchal networks, modelling how to make patriarchal bargains.

For the purposes of this chapter, we are looking at her celebrification not as a feminist, but as a cis, heterosexual daughter, mother, and wife. And we also locate her explicitly in the patriarchal networks of West Coast Tech, rather than feminism more widely. We do this because Sandberg is explicit about her role as a woman in Silicon Valley, but does not call herself a feminist; indeed she is coy about using this term. *Lean in* is described as being:

> not a self-help book, although I truly hope it helps. It is not a book on career management, although I offer advice in that area. It is not a feminist manifesto – okay, it is sort of a feminist manifesto, but one that I hope inspires men as much as it inspires women.
>
> *(Sandberg and Scovell 2013, 10)*

This ambivalence is not surprising given the hostility to feminism in some quarters in Silicon Valley. Antonio Garcia Martinez, who wrote a well-reviewed insider account (which is in our concordance) of working under Sandberg at Facebook had this to say on the topic of feminism:

> Most women in the Bay Area are soft and weak, cosseted and naive despite their claims of worldliness, and generally full of shit. They have their self-regarding entitlement feminism, and ceaselessly vaunt their independence, but the reality is, come the epidemic plague or foreign invasion, they'd become precisely the sort of useless baggage you'd trade for a box of shotgun shells or a jerry can of diesel.
>
> *(2016, 57)*

Feminism is not mentioned in *Option B*: instead this book is grounded in the ideology of resilience and positive psychology. Consequently, we do not locate Sandberg's books as contributions to feminist discourse. Rather, we are looking at them as interventions in the ideologies and visions of West Coast Tech. These books can be seen as frontier guides by a woman to other women (and men) who are interested in how more women can 'lean in' to patriarchal networks.

Kate Manne discusses how misogyny is employed as a way of policing gendered behaviour to make sure that women continue to adhere to their role as care-givers (Manne 2018). Indeed, by framing herself as wife, widow, mother, and daughter, Sandberg is careful not to provoke men's 'aggrieved entitlement' (Kimmel 2013). As she states in a 2016 Facebook post: 'Being a mother is the most important – and most humbling – job I've ever had' (Sandberg 6 May 2016). Sandberg was number 12 on the Forbes list of self-made women for 2018; her $1.6 billion fortune mostly comes from the millions of shares of Facebook stock she owns (Forbes 2 May 2020). In spite of this, she repeatedly locates herself within a domestic patriarchal hierarchy. Although her expertise as a businesswoman is unassailable, her role as woman, daughter, wife, widow, and fiancé are key to her self-brand. Sandberg dedicates *Lean In* 'TO MY PARENTS for raising me to believe that anything was possible AND TO MY HUSBAND for making everything possible.' Motherhood is intrinsic to her celebrity storytelling as evidenced in her interview with Winfrey. On Mother's Day she also celebrates motherhood through Facebook posts. For example:

> On Mother's Day, we celebrate all moms. This year I am thinking especially of the many mothers across the country and the world who are raising children on their own.
>
> People become single parents for many reasons: loss of a partner, breakdown of a relationship, by choice. One year and five days ago I joined them.
>
> For me, this is still a new and unfamiliar world. Before, I did not quite get it. I did not really get how hard it is to succeed at work when you are overwhelmed at home. I did not understand how often I would look at my son's or daughter's crying face and not know how to stop the tears.

In 2017 she wrote:

> Being a mother is the most rewarding – and hardest – job many of us will ever have. The day you become a mom, you also become a caregiver, teacher, nurse, and coach. It's an all-in-one kind of role that comes with no training.
>
> *(14 May 2017)*

Not only is motherhood, and this location in the household, key to her celebrity, but the home is an important site of advice for the women she is addressing. A considerable part of *Lean In* discusses the gendered organisation of the household, which the authors see as key to questions of gender and the corporation. We are told that Sandberg's mother did most of the household work when she was growing up (116). The authors' advice is to aim for 50–50 parity. Sandberg states:

> Our division of household chores is actually pretty traditional. Dave pays bills, handles our finances, provides tech support. I schedule the kids' activities, make sure there is food in the fridge, plan the birthday parties. Sometimes I'm bothered by this classic gender division of labor. Am I perpetuating stereotypes by falling into these patterns? But I would rather plan a Dora the Explorer party than pay an insurance bill, and since Dave feels the exact opposite, this arrangement works for us. It takes continual communication, honesty, and a lot of forgiveness to maintain a rickety balance. We are never at fifty-fifty at any given moment – perfect equality is hard to define or sustain – but we allow the pendulum to swing back and forth between us.
>
> *(Sandberg and Scovell 2013, 112)*

What is obscured from this description of the gendered division of labour within the Sandberg household is who the other members of the household are: who is picking up the children from school, taking them to their activities, and putting them to bed? And, significantly, who is managing the household volunteers (extended family and friends) and employees (babysitters, nannies, cooks, cleaners, tutors, gardeners)?

In her book *Meritocracy*, Jo Littler, drawing on the work of Nancy Fraser, notes that Sandberg encourages women to embrace 'corporate working culture and succeeding in the workplace rather than leaving it and returning to the home' (Littler 2017, 184). As Fraser shows, precisely because the question of social reproduction and the home has not been interrogated, 'privileged women lead lives that are socially male, while abandoning other women' (Fraser 2013, 22). Care is outsourced by privileged women and thus rendered irrelevant in neoliberal discourse, but this means that the women who carry out the labour of care are then denied a stake in the patriarchal rewards that Sandberg is claiming for women. Catherine Rottenberg argues that many feminist claims are made from an understanding of the public/private divide, and the role of social reproduction in the private realm: it follows from this that if the private realm is disavowed, the women doing the private-realm work will be neglected in the claims being made to power, property, and personhood. Although there is mention of childcare providers in Sandberg's books, we are not told who hires them or pays them, what their working conditions are like, where and how they live, or who in the management of the household has discussed their working and living conditions. The advice given in both books, therefore, is somewhat baffling (Sellgson 2017). On the one hand, the advice is to better manage the household (to make the domestic bargain) in order to have the opportunity to lean in at work. However, being too explicit about what this management will look like will presumably reveal the classed and racialised hierarchies of the household (see Roberts 1993), as well as the elitism of the intended audience.

Before arriving in Silicon Valley Sandberg worked for Larry Summers, who was US Secretary of the Treasury under President Bill Clinton. In this role she assisted work on forgiving global debt. Simultaneously, she oversaw the deregulation of the US banking industry (Vaidhyanathan 2018, 126). This two-pronged wielding of power is typical of Sandberg. On the one hand she fights hard to circumscribe the ways that tech companies are regulated, thus supporting the erosion of social justice in public space. At the same time, she enjoys visibly spreading her philanthrocapitalist work. For example, at Google she helped to set up its philanthropic arm Google.org, while being key to the process of monetising surplus behavioural data. She is also vocal about the work that she has done to help promote women. Sandberg is a promoter of women's leadership day; and her Ted Talks, speaking circuit engagements, interviews, and books are ostensibly aimed at encouraging women into corporate leadership roles. Currently she is Board Chair for the Sheryl Sandberg and David Goldberg Family Foundation, which aims to 'build a more equal and resilient world' through the initiatives Leanin.org and OptionB.org. Alongside other feminist critics of these initiatives, we see them as functioning together to play a part in maintaining the structures of racialised and patriarchal power under digital capitalism, as well as constituting a keystone of her benevolent brand. Philanthrocapitalism is an important part of the way that Silicon Valley legitimates and justifies its concentration of wealth, as with The Bill and Melinda Gates Foundation and The Chan-Zuckerberg Initiative.

Aschoff argues against Sandberg's perspective that more women in leadership means a more equitable world. She uses an example from Sandberg's *Lean In* to illustrate her point. Sandberg makes links between the gendered division of the household and access to corporate success, but for her the two are mirrored. She tells the story of a woman friend who was struggling with the gendered division of labour with her husband, including the sharing of childcare. Sandberg recommended this friend for a job at Startup:Education (part of the Chan-Zuckerberg Initiative). In order to accept this the woman has to negotiate care with her husband, which she succeeds in doing. She has effectively bargained in the patriarchal home. However, this is at the expense of other women. As Aschoff argues, the aim of Startup:Education was 'to institute a merit pay program for Newark's teachers.' In reality, and unsurprisingly, the programme had the effect of weakening the tenure rights of teachers – many of whom are women attempting to improve their schools in difficult and complex environments (Aschoff 2015, 37–38). So the solution for the individual woman came at the expense of other women in the workforce. Here, as elsewhere, Sandberg is keen to be recognised for her philanthropy, especially for helping women. But her philanthropic initiatives are reflective of her deep and committed support for neoliberal initiatives and Silicon Valley ideologies, as well as her commitment to being seen as a benefactor, and because of this they become forms of economic and social control. Like the pioneer woman of the frontier imaginary, Sandberg seeks ways to control spaces already claimed by the male colonisers. She may want to support women, but only corporate women.

Sandberg does not overtly use the frontier spirit as part of her celebrification (the words pioneer, frontier, settler hardly appear in her books). 'Pioneered' appears once in *Option B*; 'Settlers' appears in the name of a board game. In fact, her celebrification pivots on intimacy, authenticity, and womanhood. However, we can identify some of the ways that the frontier spirit suffuses her celebrity assemblage. Resilience is an important part of her message, and this is also a key part of the frontier imaginary; it is connected to facing the elements, including nature, humans, and scarcity, and it is part of the myth of becoming American. Resilience is key to Sandberg's self-brand and we read her idea of resilience as a standpoint to be taken in order to accept the status quo. That is, resilience rather than resistance (Diprose 2014; Gill and Orgad 2018). As Kristine Diprose points out, resilience is urged on people who are suffering as a means to 'tame the troublesome,' who might otherwise rebel. She links the term to the injunctions that were publicly stated after the UK 2011 riots, when, she argues, resilience became 'the preferred means of maintaining business as usual' (44); it was 'deployed as an inducement to putting up with precarity and inequality and accepting the deferral of demands for change, and as a means of relocating responsibility' (45). We return to questions of resilience later in this chapter. But first we investigate Sandberg's entanglement in Zuckerberg-Facebook household.

Work wife: mediating the brand

There is a striking moment in *Option B* when Sandberg describes hosting a dinner party in her home for Facebook 'clients.' This is one of the many stories that Sandberg tells about grief and the deep pain of widowhood. In this anecdote, we see her crying upstairs as the party starts; still deep in the process of grieving she is too distraught to greet her guests. Her son consoles her, and, using his mother's guidance, advises 'just be yourself.' Following this intimate familial moment, Sandberg is able to join the work party (Grant and Sandberg 2017, 126). This anecdote brings together some of the key themes that we are examining in relation to Sandberg: her celebrity entanglement in the Facebook brand; the significance of managing the private homestead as well as the corporate household; and the way that these two merge, much like Zuckerberg's own branded 'presence bleed' (Melissa Gregg 2011) into the gendered data subject, and thus generating capital for patriarchs. It is also of interest because of its obfuscation of the hierarchies of the household. We are not told who let the guests in, who made the food, who served the food, where the food was prepared, who eventually put the children to bed.

Enmeshed in Sandberg's ideological storytelling, are some of Facebook's key corporate values: intimacy, connection, and sharing – as discussed in Chapter 4 in relation to Zuckerberg. We can see the presence of these themes throughout her mediatisation, whether this is manifested in the personal address of her books, or her tears in interviews, such as Winfrey's podcast above. Her brand, like Zuckerberg's, leans heavily on the tropes of hospitality. One example that springs to mind here are her women circles and the monthly dinners for women at her home – which morphed into the global Lean In circles (Heffernan 2018). She has cultivated a direct, personal, and emotional address, whether this is expressed in her books, or posts, or interviews. And she encourages this from others too.

There is a professed deep intimacy between Sandberg and Zuckerberg (Helft 2010). Zuckerberg has numerous cameos in both Sandberg's books, and they appear together in promotional images and videos on Facebook. When Sandberg talks about Facebook she always says 'we.' According to *Option B*, Zuckerberg came to see Sandberg as soon as she came home after her husband's death and has talked to her every day since. He also planned the funeral. They are depicted as having an excellent working relationship (Hempel 2017). Just as Sandberg emphasises the importance of telling your male boss what you need in the case of Page and Brin, so with Zuckerberg she gives him credit for his flexibility in the way that, for example, compassionate leave has been increased at Facebook. She credits Zuckerberg with thoughtfulness and an ability to work with women. In interviews she repeatedly insists on Zuckerberg's compassion. For example, in one interview in *The Guardian* she says, 'Mark is why I'm walking [...] When I felt so overwhelmed and so isolated and just needed to cry, I would grab him into his conference room and he would just sit there with me and be like, "We're going to get through this and we want to get through it with you." He did it over and over' (Topping and Aitkenhead 2017). It is almost as if Sandberg is performing the 'corporate wife' as described by Judy Wajcman in *Managing Like a Man* (in the book the 'corporate man' is dependent on his stay-at-home wife to provide the care and hospitality that mediates his private and public life). Sandberg is able to resolve this gendered division of labour, and gendered exclusions from the workplace, by appearing to play both corporate manager and wife.

Sandberg's representations of grief and familial intimacy lend her authenticity and show her qualities of empathy. A further example of how these are deployed is seen in a story told in *Wired* as part of the promotional campaign for *Option B*:

> Thirty days after Goldberg's funeral marked sheloshim, the end of the Jewish period of mourning for a relative. The night before, Sandberg penned a Facebook post to mark the day. She did it in haste, without overthinking her words, intending it primarily for people she knew – colleagues, casual friends, other parents. Reading it over, she decided it was too personal to post.
> The next morning, she woke up feeling awful. She reconsidered posting her essay. 'I was like, "It can't get worse. It might get better,"' she remembers.
> So she clicked the blue 'Post' button.
>
> (Hempel 2017)

Sandberg has a considerable online following and is a key public representative of the platform on which she posts so it is somewhat disingenuous to cast herself as an ordinary user, and the platform as one of potential salvation. Entangling her celebrification in the platform – and with Zuckerberg – is also of importance on the occasions when Sandberg has to publicly apologise for Facebook's multiple scandals: it is often Sandberg who is called upon to be the public face of corporate shame. Marshalling to her aid both the intimate style of her address and her own personal griefs, she often personifies the corporation's ruthlessness with statements such as: 'these are difficult decisions and we don't always get it right' (Reuters 2016); or she focuses on 'earning the trust of the people who use our service' (CBSN 2018). What we can see Sandberg doing here, and in the Oprah interview, as well as elsewhere is modelling how to give value to the corporate household. This is what we can identify as Sandberg's second patriarchal bargain. Indeed, the bargaining within the domestic realm is crucial to this second bargain: commitment and devotion to the corporate household.

Posttraumatic growth: gendered data solutions

We can also see Sandberg's fidelity to Facebook in the ways that the platform – as well as its use of psychology and data – are linked to her self-brand. Siva Vidhyanathan notes that 'if not for Sandberg and her formidable vision and management skills, Facebook might be a broke and trivial company today' (Vidhyanathan 2018, 57). Sandberg is credited with 'discovering' how to monetise people's data, or in Zuboff's words 'behavioural surplus' (Zuboff 2019). The things that people do on the internet, other than their direct searches, can be captured, extracted, and aggregated for use by marketing and advertising companies. Zuboff has called Sandberg 'Typhoid Mary' – after Mary Mallon, a historical figure who was believed to have spread typhoid while having no symptoms herself. This is because of Sandberg's crucial role in the development of surveillance capitalism. According to Zuboff, when Sandberg became Google's vice president of global online sales and operations, she 'led the development of surveillance capitalism through the expansion of AdWords and other aspects of online sales operations' (Zuboff 2019, 92). And when Sandberg joined Facebook in 2008, she was able to bring to them the knowledge that she had garnered and implemented at Google. Facebook's surplus behavioural data was able to give real information about the gender, age, and location of its users – as opposed to inferred information, as in the case of Google. Facebook's quality of information represented billions of dollars of resource. As Kirkpatrick states in *The Facebook Effect* (in the concordance):

> Facebook would learn to track, scrape, store, and analyse UPI to fabricate its own targeting algorithms, and like Google it would not restrict extraction operations to what people voluntarily shared with the company. Sandberg understood that through the artful manipulation of Facebook's culture of intimacy and sharing, it would be possible to use behavioural surplus not only to satisfy demand but also to create demand. For starters, that meant inserting advertisers into the fabric of Facebook's online culture, where they could 'invite' users into a 'conversation.'
>
> *(266, cited in Zuboff 92)*

We see Sandberg as a pioneer woman, not just managing the homestead and corporate household but sharing her resilient spirit, and seeking out the ground that has been colonised in order to more effectively control it. The ground that she seeks to control is data and its possibilities of monetisation. In her vision, there is a place for some women in digital capitalism. This might be in corporate households, but it is also through their value as data subjects.

Rottenberg argues that neoliberalism *needs* a specific kind of feminism as articulated by Sandberg in order resolve its contradictions, particularly around care: 'As an economic order, neoliberalism relies on reproduction and care work in order to reproduce and maintain human capital.' At the same time, however: 'as a political rationality neoliberalism has no lexicon that can recognize let alone value reproduction and care work.' Part of the reason for this is the 'infiltration of a market rationality into all spheres of life, including the most private ones' (Rottenberg 2018, 16). We can see this infiltration being modelled by Sandberg. Sandberg represents her work life as deeply entangled in her domestic one – not just in relation to her home, but also her family and her subjectivity as mother and grieving widow.

Her emotions and psychological state are depicted to the reader of her books as well as her Facebook posts. These stories ostensibly reveal her inner world – an inner world that she then shares with her colleagues and clients as she encourages herself and us to 'be yourself.' Although Sandberg seems to argue that we should be more emotional at work – and indeed she is credited for introducing this management style to the tech industry – she also blurs the lines between the traditional public and private domains (Wiggers 2019). But it is precisely through such blurring, as Rottenberg argues, that market rationality begins to erode all aspects of life:

> [Privileged people in particular] are increasingly being hailed as generic human capital, as part of a process that strips them of any value (or identity markers) except market ones. This interpellation helps produce subjects who are informed by a cost-benefit metric and who, in order to remain viable, let alone thrive, just carefully sequence their lives while making smart self-investments in the present to ensure enhanced returns in the future.
>
> *(Rottenberg 2018, 17)*

It is to the monetisation of people's intimate life that we now turn.

In the interview with Winfrey, Sandberg exclaims that people might talk about posttraumatic stress 'but no one' talks about 'posttraumatic growth.' It is worth dwelling on Sandberg's language here. This focus on growth mimics the corporate language of the entrepreneur and the start-up (e.g. Reid Hoffman's *The Start-Up of You* endorsed by Sandberg). It uses the West Coast tech language of scalability: Trauma can make us more productive and more profitable under digital capitalism! Ros Gill and Shani Orgad call Sandberg's posturing here, 'the bounce-backable woman' in their research on *Option B* (Gill and Orgad 2018). Interpellating the self as a business that effectively negotiates at home and in corporate life, who overcomes adversity and the abjection or non-productivity that adversity might generate, are important for what Rottenberg identifies as the female subjectivity that Sandberg's 'neoliberal feminism' marshals. More than this, however, rendering non-patriarchs as individual enterprises is a strategic way of making sense of persons and their location within the meritocratic and patriarchal logics of digital capitalism. In other words, people (especially privileged women) can be made legible through dataism. We can link Rottenberg's observation that people are rendered specks of human capital under neoliberalism, with recent work published on Facebook and the data subject.

In Skeggs and Yuill's work on Facebook, they map how users are tracked on the basis of class and gender. For example, middle-class women, trading on their cultural capital, benefit significantly from the professional networks and social capital of Facebook. Skeggs and Yuill's research showed that one middle-class woman they tracked was considered 'to be a person of interest and certainly of value' for Facebook: 'They are ever present on her browser, extracting and placing information, not just on the Facebook platform but across her other sites, and trading her on to advertisers who compete in real-time bidding auctions to place adverts on her browser.' Facebook and women like her are 'a perfect match' (Skeggs and Yuill 2019, 83). These are the women being interpellated by Sandberg. Using Facebook to model to women how to be more valuable to digital capitalism Sandberg's gendering of the data subject provides significant value for the founder patriarchs. It is significant here that the elite women that Sandberg addresses, who themselves negotiate their personhood through patriarchal bargains made in the domestic and corporate households, are now offered up as another patriarchal bargain.

We have mapped in this chapter the way that Sandberg is given a platform precisely because she replicates the traditional household at different scales in the Zuckerberg-Facebook celebrity assemblage. Furthermore, part of the patriarchal bargain that is made through the figure of Sandberg is the way that privileged women in particular can also provide value to the patriarch founders through sharing the data accumulated in their private and public spaces.

Drawing together Chapters 5 and 6, we can see that both Thiel and Sandberg are ideological storytellers performing different but similar functions in relation to the patriarchal networks we are mapping. Whereas Sandberg offers advice for corporate women wanting to succeed in patriarchal sites, Thiel offers self-help for men wanting to entrench patriarchal corporate interests; Thiel's books are self-help books for aspiring patriarchs, masquerading as philosophical business advice. Although Thiel does not have the celebrity profile that Sandberg enjoys, his celebrity captures the attention of a different market, one that is more amenable to reactionary ideas regarding gender, race, and patriarchy. Whereas Thiel's audience and admirers include fans of alt-right journalists such as Yiannopoulos, Sandberg addresses elite women. Indeed, we can see Thiel and Sandberg as reconciling the patriarchal networks to markets that are not automatically interpellated by them. The alt-right feel excluded at a cultural level as we explore in more detail in relation to Google in Chapter 7. Women are overtly excluded, and the visibility of Sandberg functions more or less effectively to obfuscate patriarchal power. It is useful here to recall Sarah Banet-Weiser's funhouse mirror of popular feminism and misogyny. Banet-Weiser argues that popular feminism's politics is its visibility (Banet-Weiser identifies Sandberg as a proponent of this brand of feminism). In reaction to this visibility, popular misogyny is weaponised, often marshalling injury and vulnerability in a distorted mimicry of the strategies of popular feminism. We can understand these loose online factions as bidding for a stake in the rewards of patriarchal digital capitalism. Thiel and Sandberg function as ideologues for these different groupings, attempting to reconcile them to the founder networks and their corporate households.

Notes

1 See Mandell (2019). We also need to think carefully about sexuality and how that is represented in our concordance as Baker argues, 'words relating to homosexuality are much more frequent than words for heterosexuality … because heterosexuality is

seems to be the default norm and preferred state not needed to be mentioned because it is so pervasive' (Baker, 2014, 75).
2 We are not 100% sure of the gender identities of all the participants and do not know how many of them are cis gendered. We have done some basic internet checking however, to ensure we were not making false assumptions based on presuming name from gender. Julian Guthrey presents as a woman while Ashlee Vance as man for instance. As a result of these checks we are confident that these figures are broadly accurate, while also acknowledging that the binarisation of gender for the purposes of data collection would be more problematic in other contexts. We are comfortable with its uses here, given that part of what we are trying to point to is the way in which gender binaries are rigidly enforced in the material we are looking at.

References

Aschoff, Nicole (2015) *The New Prophets of Capital*. London and New York: Verso.
Baker, Paul (2014) *Using Corpora to Analyse Gender*. London: Bloomsbury.
Banet-Weiser, Sarah (2018) *Empowered: Popular Feminism and Popular Misogyny*. Durham: Duke University Press.
Berlant, Lauren (2008) *The Female Complaint: The Unfinished Business of Sentimentality in American Culture*. Durham: Duke University Press.
CBS (2018) 'Facebook's Sheryl Sandberg Apologises for "Breach of Trust"' www.cbsnews.com/video/sheryl-sandberg-apologizes-facebook-breach-of-trust/
Diprose, Kristina (2014) 'Resilience is Futile' *Soundings*, 58, 44–56.
Fraser, Nancy (2013) *Fortunes of Feminism*. London: Verso.
Gill, Rosalind and Shani Orgad (2018) 'The Amazing BounceBackable Woman: Resilience and the Psychological Turn in Neoliberalism' *Sociological Research Online*, 23(2), 477–495.
Grant, Melissa Gira (2013) '"Like" Feminism' *Jacobin*, 4 March 2013. www.jacobinmag.com/2013/03/like-feminism/
Gregg, Melissa (2011) *Work's Intimacy*. Cambridge: Polity.
Heffernan, Virginia (2018) 'The Empress of Facebook: My Befuddling Dinner with Sheryl Sandberg' *Wired*. www.nytimes.com/2010/10/03/business/03face.html
Helft, Miguel (2010) 'Mark Zuckerberg's Most Valuable Friend' *The New York Times*, October 2. www.nytimes.com/2010/10/03/business/03face.html
Hempel, Jessi (2017) 'Sheryl Sandberg's Accidental Revolution' *Wired*, 24 April. www.wired.com/2017/04/sheryl-sandbergs-accidental-revolution/
hooks, bell (2013) 'Dig Deep: Beyond Lean In' *The Feminist Wire*, 28 October. https://thefeministwire.com/2013/10/17973/
Kandiyoti, Deniz (1988) 'Bargaining with Patriarchy' *Gender & Society*, 2(3), 274–290.
Kimmel, Michael (2013) *Angry White Men: American Masculinity at the End of an Era*. New York: Nation Books.
Kirkpatrick, David (2011) *The Facebook Effect: The Real Inside Story of Mark Zuckerberg and the World's Fastest Growing Company*. London: Virgin Books.
Littler, Jo (2017) *Against Meritocracy: Culture, Power and the Myths of Mobility*. London: Routledge.
Mandell, Laura (2019) 'Gender and Cultural Analytics: Finding or Making Stereotypes?' https://dhdebates.gc.cuny.edu/read/untitled-f2acf72c-a469-49d8-be35-67f9ac1e3a60/section/5d9c1b63-7b60-42dd-8cda-bde837f638f4#ch01
Manne, Kate (2018) *Down Girl: The Logic of Misogyny*. Oxford: Oxford University Press.

Nunn, Heather and Anita Biressi (2010) '"A Trust Betrayed": Celebrity and the Work of Emotion' *Celebrity Studies*, 1(1), 49–64. doi: 10.1080/19392390903519065

Pao, Ellen (2017) *Reset: My Fight for Inclusion and Lasting Change*. New York: Random House.

Pechenick, E. A., C. M. Danforth, and P. S. Dodds (2015) 'Characterizing the Google Books Corpus: Strong Limits to Inferences of Socio-Cultural and Linguistic Evolution' *PLoS ONE*, 10(10), e0137041. doi: 10.1371/journal.pone.0137041

Reuters (2016) 'Facebook's Sheryl Sandberg on "Napalm Girl" Photo: "We Don't Always Get it Right"' *The Guardian*, 12 September 2016. www.theguardian.com/technology/2016/sep/12/facebook-mistake-napalm-girl-photo-sheryl-sandberg-apologizes

Roberts, Dorothy E. (1993) 'Racism and Patriarchy in the Meaning of Motherhood' *Faculty Scholarship*, Paper 595.

Rottenberg, Catherine (2018) *The Rise of Neoliberal Feminism*. Oxford: Oxford University Press.

Sandberg, Sheryl (2016) *Facebook*. May 6 2016. www.facebook.com/sheryl.

Sandberg, Sheryl (2017) May 14 2017. www.facebook.com/sheryl

Sandberg, Sheryl and Adam Grant (2017) *Option B: Facing Adversity, Building Resilience and Finding Joy*. New York: Knopf.

Sandberg, Sheryl and Nell Scovell (2013 [2015]) *Lean In: Women, Work, and the Will to Lead*. London: Penguin Random House.

Sellgson, Hannah (2017) 'The True Cost of Leaning In' *The Daily Beast*, April 21. www.thedailybeast.com/the-true-cost-of-leaning-in

Shulevitz, Judith (2013) 'The Corporate Mystique: Sheryl Sandberg and the Folly of Davos-Style Feminism' *New Republic*, 10 March. https://newrepublic.com/article/112610/sheryl-sandberg-and-lean-folly-davos-feminism

Skeggs, Beverly and Simon Yuill (2019) 'Subjects of Value and Digital Personas: Reshaping the Bourgeois Subject, Unhinging Property from Personhood' *Subjectivity*, 12, 82–99. doi: 10.1057/s41286-018-00063-4

Stainback, Kevin, Sibyl Kleiner, and Sheryl Skaggs (2016) 'Women in Power: Undoing or Redoing the Gendered Organization?' *Gender and Society*, 30(1), 109–135. doi: 10.1177/0891243215602906

Topping, Alexandra and Decca Aitkenhead (2017) 'Sheryl Sandberg Credits Mark Zuckerberg with Saving Her Life' *The Guardian*, 15 April. www.theguardian.com/technology/2017/apr/15/sheryl-sandberg-credits-mark-zuckerberg-with-saving-her-life

Vaidhyanathan, Siva (2018) *Anti-Social Media: How Facebook Disconnects Us and Undermines Democracy*. Oxford: Oxford University Press.

Wajcman, Judy (1998) *Managing Like A Man: Women and Men in Corporate Management*. Penn: Penn State University Press.

Wiggers, Kyle (2019) 'AI Classifies People's Emotions from the Way They Walk' *Venture Beat*, July 1. https://venturebeat.com/2019/07/01/ai-classifies-peoples-emotions-from-the-way-they-walk/

Winfrey, Oprah (2017) 'Super Soul – EP.#1: Sheryl Sandberg: How to Build Resilience and Find Joy After Loss' 4 December. www.youtube.com/watch?v=VpCakrNdC-U

Zuboff, Shoshona (2019) *The Age of Surveillance Capitalism: The Fight for a Human Future at the New Frontier of Power*. London: Profile Books.

7

THE LIMITS OF LIBERALISM

Google's Larry Page and Sergey Brin

Liberal librarians

The celebrity personae of Google's Larry Page and Sergey Brin draw on some key tropes of the paradigmatic Silicon Valley founders' narrative, particularly that of the visionary boy genius. Both are from academic families, and both learned intellectual independence at an early age through their Montessori schooling. Both are Jewish by background, but secular in practice. Brin's family fled anti-semitism in Russia, while Page's family has a history of left-wing and trade union activism. They established their apparent brilliance as teenagers. Page made a functioning ink-jet printer out of Lego, while Brin started his undergraduate studies a year early (Batelle 2005b). They were both early users of the internet, absorbing the cultures of the electronic frontier, including 'the world of Dungeons & Dragons and MUDs, and the free software on offer' (Brandt 2011, 33). Brandt's *The Google Guys: Inside the Brilliant Minds of Google Founders Larry Page and Sergey Brin* depicts the two founders as having a sense of adventure. It tells the story of how two young PhD students developed an algorithm in the course of their research which would change the course of human history (i.e. more specifically, they developed a dynamic search engine that worked by providing an algorithmically determined index of all the content on the world wide web and made it intuitively accessible by key-word search). In Brandt's telling, this was too precious a discovery to hide away in fusty academia and too important to be sold off to the corporate world who would ruthlessly exploit it for profit, so the two young men formed Google to make sure the benefits of their discovery would be shared as widely as possible without cynical exploitation of its value for shareholder profit.[1]

This origins narrative is an important structuring force in both the corporate branding and the celebrification of its founders. We can see some commonalities with Amazon here, for example in the narrative of domestic 'lean' beginnings. But there are also some core differences. Like Bezos, they set up in a garage (as it happens in the garage of Susan Wojcicki, current CEO of YouTube and Brin's future ex-sister-in-law); and, copying Amazon, they made desks out of cheap doors to save money. Unlike Bezos, however, whose early investment helped get Google off the ground, the frontier mythology is very much in the background for Page and Brin. Although they start in a house, it is not theirs – they do not assume the patriarchal head of a household position; indeed, the house is owned by a woman: the relationship between Susan Wojcicki and the founders does not neatly fit the pattern of a frontier homestead. Instead the relationships are far more cosmopolitan. And while faith in data and a belief in science are shared with Bezos, the ruthlessness that characterises Amazon's formative years is notably absent from Google, at least at the beginning. The emphasis was on 'making the world a better place,' as well as preserving and making available knowledge as opposed to forging new frontiers in the manner of Bezos or Thiel.

The central role of universities in their biographies meant that the founders' story reflects core values of liberal academia: equality, universalism, and intellectual freedom. These values are also reflected in Google's stated mission regarding access to knowledge and the universal benefits of intellectual endeavour, as well as in their investment in the laid-back campus culture of elite US universities, which they see as fostering creativity and curiosity. Brandt frames the founders' story within a discussion of the Great Library of Alexandria, but rather than generations of scholars it is solely Brin and Page who created 'the great library of the Internet,' thereby becoming the joint embodiment of 'world's head librarian' (Brandt 2011, 3). Indeed, the Google Search Engine is predicated on academic publishing and library cataloguing. According to John Batelle, Brin and Page appropriated the principles of citational practices, peer review, and annotation to develop PageRank. This algorithm took into account the number of links to a particular site, as well as the number of links into each of the linking sites, thus mirroring 'the rough approach of academic citation counting' (Batelle 2005a, 75) while adding a level of complexity.

These origin stories provide legitimating principles that have a profound effect on the sort of company that they underpin. But it is important to interrogate the relationship between this legitimation and actual corporate behaviours – not least in the story we are looking at here. Google ended up becoming the very opposite of what Brin and Page once insisted a search engine should be: 'not for profit' (Brandt 2011, 39), making $34 billion in 2020 according to Fortune.com. Moreover, while search was once supposed to be a universal tool for finding information sorted by quality and utility, it is now highly personalised to meet the needs of advertisers and based on algorithmic assumptions of the interests of users. AdWords, search engine optimisation, crawling, and algorithmic indexing all mean that the knowledge served to users is commercially driven (Noble 2018, 150). Perhaps this helps us to understand some of the contradictions that have emerged over time in Google's self-presentation – and why the two men have now withdrawn from their roles as celebrity founders, and in effect from public life (as of December 2019) (Page and Brin 2019).

Google's responsibility to the world

One place where we can see, empirically, how these West Coast tech founding narratives relate to actual corporate practice (for Google and for other companies) is through the initial public offering (IPO) documents they have issued to potential investors as their companies have been floated on the stock market. *IPO* appears a staggering 1,418 times in the concordance, or nearly 120 times per million words. It is found in 56 of the 95 books we scanned, with a median number count of 9. In the control EngTenTen15 corpus it appears 2.7 times per million words, or around 45 times less frequently. In short, the IPO is a lexically significant term for understanding the technology sector. In ideological terms, it is best understood as the mythical transition moment that turns a geek genius into a billionaire founder.

Google went public in 2004, with its original slogan 'Don't Be Evil' appearing as a heading in Larry Page's 4,000-word IPO letter to potential shareholders. This stated that their 'mission' was 'to organize the world's information and make it universally accessible and useful' (Page and Brin 2004).[2] 'World' appears 17 times in the document; the 'world' being subject to the founders' belief that they will make it 'a better place.' Aligning with America's global humanitarianism, they have a self-declared 'responsibility' to this world. Unlike Bezos and some of the other tech pioneers, their approach to celebrity is not based on the myth of the cowboy or the colonial explorer. Instead, their celebrification is curated through a paternal American imperialism, where their intentions are philanthropic, for the 'better,' and against 'evil.' The founders' brilliance and their belief in American technology as a global value legitimates these claims.

Inspired by billionaire and philanthropist Warren Buffet, Page opened the letter to shareholders with the sentences 'Google is not a conventional company. We do not intend to become one.' He emphasises equality of access to end-users in order to 'significantly improve the[ir] lives' (this is why it was funded by ads, to ensure no-one was excluded by the cost of subscriptions). Just as Bezos rhapsodises to his shareholders, Page presents the company as focused on long-term thinking, not quarterly returns. The core argument legitimating this unconventional approach rests on the unique qualities of the executive level management team at Google (the two founders and then CEO Eric Schmidt). Under this logic, it makes it all the more fortunate that its dual-class voting structure will ensure that control of Google as a company will rest with the founders, who will hold preferential shares that command ten times the voting power of a normal share. As they put it, 'new investors will fully share in Google's long term economic future but will have little ability to influence its strategic decisions through their voting rights' (Page and Brin 2004).

The Google IPO thus institutionalised two key elements of the company's structure by reference to its celebrity founders' 'exceptional' motivations in setting it up. Firstly, there was the argument that Google was not a conventional company and should therefore not be held to normal standards of oversight by shareholders (or regulation by government). In this way – just like the other corporate households – they set themselves up as a site where normal oversight would be suspended. This is the particular way in which Google marshals some aspects of the frontier spirit: it creates an indeterminate zone that is ruled by the founders, who in this case are imbued with extraordinary capability and judgement and thus do not require oversight. The second element institutionalised in the IPO was that the founders themselves should retain the right to determine the future direction of their company since they had not only Google's interests at heart, but also those of the wider 'public good.' Much like Facebook's Zuckerberg, who would learn the value of reiterating his company's belief in fostering 'community,' so Page and Brin emphasised the social mission at the heart of their company, and took personal responsibility for it:

> We believe a well functioning society should have abundant, free and unbiased access to high quality information. Google therefore has a responsibility to the world. The dual class structure helps ensure that this responsibility is met. We believe that fulfilling this responsibility will deliver increased value to our shareholders.

In the IPO letter they also state the importance of their staff. These staff are rewarded well in terms of shares and benefits – 'We provide many unusual benefits for our employees, including meals free of charge, doctors and washing machines' – but they also see the staff as finding reward in terms of the moral mission that Google affords them. The letter signs off with: 'Sergey and I, and the team will do our best to make Google a long term success and the world a better place.' The librarians marshal paternal liberalism to maintain control over the company and determine its direction.

In its shareholding strategies, combined with its extensive lobbying against regulation (Taplin 2017), we can see that Google, like Facebook and others, is a domain that evades conventional laws, such as, for example, those that oversee media companies. Protected by Section 230 of the Communications Decency Act (1996), they are immunised from state tort liability, at least if they do not participate in the creation of content. When this is combined with the Digital Millennium Copyright Act (1998), they are also protected from issues arising from copyright infringement. Armed with these immunities, the founders are enabled to seek dominance over the 'world's information,' and determine how knowledge is produced, found, and shared. The celebrification of the founders is marshalled to justify their shareholder status; and, as we examine later in this chapter, it is also used to legitimate their embargo on unionisation. Above all, it is used as their justification for forging ahead with their belief that they are providing 'unbiased, accurate and free access to information for those who rely on us around the world' (Page and Brin 2019).

In fact, Google is a monopoly company 'indexing knowledge' that to some extent structures our daily life (Vaidhyanathan 2012). The politics that Page and Brin ostensibly espouse thus seem to be at odds with many of their actual corporate practices. Most notably, their expropriative practices in relation to data extraction have been exposed by Shoshana Zuboff (and others), their attitudes to their workforce and unionisation are a paradigmatic example of post-class industrial relations, and the racial bias baked into their algorithms has been highlighted by Safiya Umoja Noble. It is this tension that occupies much of this chapter rather than the role of their celebrity per se. Yet it is worth sketching briefly how their celebrity personae functioned – at least until very recently.

Celebrity and post-class politics

For the first 15 or so years of Google's life, Page and Brin were effective celebrified leaders of this emerging global brand. As Google's product offering expanded and their share price rocketed, so too did their celebrity rise. Brin, like Musk and Zuckerberg, was compared to superhero Iron Man, although in his case in an extended profile in *Vanity Fair*, where he and ex-wife Anne Wojcicki are described in frontier terms as 'pioneers' (Grigoriadis 2014). Page got married on Richard Branson's private island, with the iconic billionaire as his best man (although a medical problem with his vocal cords has led to him being the less outspoken corporate leader than Brin, if in the main more hands-on with their business). Despite occasional cracks in the ethical veneer (as when emails revealed a 2006 lawsuit, in which Schmidt had to referee a dispute between the two founders about the size of the beds on their party plane) (Vance 2006), the two managed to retain their positive celebrity reputations for being motivated by public good.

An analysis of a video of Larry Page's commencement speech at the University of Michigan in 2009 (posted by Google to its YouTube platform) gives some clues as to how the progressive image was already beginning to falter. Being asked to give a commencement address at a degree-conferring ceremony is both a ritual accolade and a key location for the exposition of a celebrity persona. Zuckerberg gave one at Harvard in 2017, Bezos at Princeton in 2010, and Brin at Maryland in 2003.[3] Other tech leaders have given similar speeches at their alma maters. These commencement addresses are something the speech-giver does have control over, but it is also a rhetorical genre, constrained by the particularities of the university graduation event (in a not too dissimilar way to the structures demanded by the Ice Bucket Challenge discussed in Chapter 3). In particular, the speeches are seen by rhetoricians and others as key places for the exploration of elite cultural values (Rutherford 2004). The genre rules seem consistent among the tech elite (especially following Jobs's 2005 speech at Stanford): you must provide an inspiration for graduating students, while telling a compelling story about life and success. As Heracleous and Klaring note, the audience for these speeches is dual: an immediate one in the form of the physical audience of graduating students, and a wider one, far less fleeting, through the publication of the speech online through platforms like TED or YouTube (2017).

Page's 2009 speech fits this pattern. He proceeds with the required stories, including one that recurs in his celebrity biography – much like Bezos recalling his childhood on the Texas ranch – the tale of Page's grandfather's 'Alley Oop' strike hammer (Figure 7.1). This is the home-made cudgel that was used by striking factory workers in Flint, Michigan to resist the police. Page waves it to the crowd of graduating students, emphasising how lucky it is that people don't need these at work anymore and explaining his generous attitude to his workforce. However, this serves to immediately, and somewhat perversely, draw attention to the complete absence of trade unions in Google itself. In tech culture, to make unions core to one's identity and a key point of reference is almost an act of sectoral sacrilege. As Broockman, Ferenstein, and Malhotra state, opposition to unions is one of the key features of tech founder ideology, in a key point of divergence from mainstream liberal political values in America (2019). Page's post-class position here appears to be simultaneously pro- and anti-union: the contradiction is resolved by the idea that unions are no longer needed – an idea that is not common in progressive circles outside the tech industry. Jo Littler's discussion of post-class and meritocracy is useful here. Littler makes connections between postfeminist, postrace, and post-class discourses, discussing how the 'desires and impulses' of liberation movements are hijacked and commodified by neoliberal capital. This is exactly what we can see happening in Page's speech (Littler 2017, 67) (Figure 7.1).

In our concordance this tech opposition to unions partly manifests itself in the infrequency of 'trade union,' which appears at about 12% of the frequency of the background EngTenTen2015 (about 1.2/mw as opposed to 10/mw). At a glance, 'labor union' as a phrase fares better, appearing 2.7/mw as opposed to 1.9/mw in the control. But this is deceptive – over half the references are in one section of a single book, *Conscious Capitalism*, which was co-authored by John Mackey, founder of Whole Foods, a company that was recently bought by Amazon (Mackey and Sisodia 2014). The passage in question makes a similar post-class argument that with a more caring form of capitalism the need for unions can be obviated (this has long the position of many tech companies, including Amazon and Facebook as well as Google). With that single section of a single book removed, the figures look far lower. Given that these are books largely about corporations (indeed we have coded over half the books as part of a 'corporate/how-to' genre), this is a remarkable absence. One would expect that industrial relations would be a key theme in books about corporate management, and that workplace unions – entities recognised by law in the US – would be an important part of that.

To return now to the speech: after recounting the 'Alley Oop' incident, Page continues by giving the students sincere, if clichéd advice. 'When a really

FIGURE 7.1   Larry Page with his grandfather's 'Alley Oop' Hammer, 2009

great dream shows up, grab it'; 'have a healthy disregard for the impossible'; 'always work hard on something uncomfortably exciting'; and so on.[4] He then says something particular about technology: 'three people can write something that millions can use and enjoy' (i.e. himself, Brin, and Schmidt presumably). By doing so he frames the core technology of Google as resulting from an elite practice for social and technological advancement. This framing allows him to argue for the possibility of 'laziness' – in Google's world, where 'work' has become a form of idle pleasure, and wage labour and industrial conflict have been relegated to the past. We can see the mobilisation of an ideology of classlessness here where 'neoliberal, entrepreneurial, corporate market-based logic' offsets and rectifies inequalities of class, race, and gender (Littler 2017, 67).

Business celebrity, as well as having the straightforward function of legitimating the actions of a company, usually also plays a role in resolving contradictions between corporate brands and corporate actions (Guthey et al. 2009). Think of the way Bezos's repeated insistence on a long-term timeframe distracts attention from labour abuses in Amazon's warehouses. In the case of Google, however, particularly as it has matured and spawned Alphabet, the public images of the do-gooding founders have stopped functioning as they needed to. Page and Brin stepping down from Alphabet and out of public life thus makes sense. Google is under intense scrutiny as befits a hugely influential monopoly, and the progressive image that the Google Guys projected is not only unsustainable: it seems at odds (on the face of it at least) with the activities of the corporation they founded.

Liberal brand, neoliberal corporation

Liberalism in America is contested and contradictory. Julie Wilson (2018) and others have noted that liberal hegemony has never been a coherent, unified project. Wendy Brown argues that twentieth-century liberalism 'sustained an interval and a tension between a capitalist political economy and a liberal democratic political system': and this meant that it was necessary for there to be a 'relative autonomy of certain institutions from one another and from the market – law, elections, the police, the public sphere.' This has the consequence that non-market rationalities have the possibility of prevailing in 'institutions, venues and values'; and: 'while liberal democracy encodes, reflects, and legitimates capitalist social relations, it simultaneously resists, counters, and tempers them' (Brown 2005, 46). But this tension does not mean that liberal democracy is by any means divergent from capitalist values; most notably, it converges in relation to questions such as 'property rights, individualism' (Brown 2005, 46).

The New Deal settlement of the 1930s and 1940s – and the following gains made by Civil Rights, feminist, and queer activists – provides a baseline for many US liberals today (we are calling this 'social democratic liberalism' here). And it is the form of liberalism that Google marshals at the level of branding and celebrity in the waving of the 'Alley Oop' hammer. But it is important to point out that, as we have been discussing in this book, liberalism itself is rooted in the idea of property: liberal freedom is originally linked to owning property including the owning of other people as property. We see these liberal tenets being contested and fought over in the nineteenth and twentieth centuries with the introduction of laws to protect people's rights to personhood. Over time, because of changing economic and social conditions, and also because of challenges made to the status quo by those who were excluded from personhood at the foundation of liberalism, possibilities for proper personhood have expanded considerably from the definitions of the frontier days of the seventeenth to nineteenth centuries. For example, in the US and Europe suffrage has gradually been extended to all its national citizens (though there have been, and continue to be, many battles over this). As these changes happened, they opened up splits within liberal thought between those supporting the old ways and those supporting the extension of rights. In the US in the 1930s, in response to the Depression, a new kind of liberalism was espoused by Roosevelt: the New Deal extended certain legal and material rights to a range of unpropertied persons, and a number of laws were passed to give protections to working- and middle-class Americans. For example, the Glass-Steagall Act of 1933 set up regulatory agencies to oversee the banks. The 1935 National Recovery Administration and the National Labor relations Act recognised labour unions and the rights of workers to organise. Several other Acts were also passed to protect workers in employment and beyond. Finally, a range of programmes, policies, and agencies were established to provide pathways to home-ownership to the poor and homeless (see Julie Wilson 2018, 26). Following the second world war there were many more welfare reforms, although the US was still extremely limited by institutional and federal racism. Indeed, Brown understands liberalism to be 'compromised by a variety of economic and social powers from white supremacy to capitalism.' Others have always had 'to pay' – 'politically, socially, economically' for liberal societies to function (Brown 2005).

In locating the struggle for labour rights in the past, Brin and Page embrace a mode of leadership that reconciles good working conditions with corporate efficacy at the expense of democratic rights. Indeed, in their paternalistic monopoly company they mimic earlier industrialists like Henry Ford who put great emphasis on obviating the need for unions by improving working conditions.[5] More than this, Google has achieved hegemonic status precisely through the space created by the rollback of the social democratic gains of the twentieth century. They have become a global monopoly company due to the neoliberal forces of deregulation, free markets, the weakening of anti-trust legislation, as well as the dominance of the financial markets.

In Zuboff's framing, the US corporation during most of the twentieth century was a social and liberal institution with long-standing reciprocities with employees and customers. These companies made money as the producers of profitable goods (Zuboff 2019, 40). The role of the public firm changed under the neoliberal settlement forged by Margaret Thatcher and Ronald Reagan in the 1980s and made unassailable by Bill Clinton, Tony Blair, and others in the 1990s as they reconciled previously social democratic political parties to 'increasingly exotic forms of financial speculation' as the primary driver of growth in advanced economies. This meant, among other things, that the cult of the entrepreneur 'would rise to near-mythic prominence as the perfect union of ownership and management' offering 'a single glorified template of audacity, competitive cunning, dominance, and wealth' (Zuboff, 41). As the speculative markets came to dominate in the long boom of the 1990s and 2000s, so we see the introduction of Google's Gmail in 2004 scanning private emails in order to extract data to better serve their users advertisements through real-time auction platforms; the loss of privacy for users' data was the price to be paid for access to Google's 'free' services. While the founders were professing a commitment to the social democratic liberal values, Google's early monetisation strategy, under the careful watch of Sheryl Sandberg, was rooted in the erosion of the fundamental rights that enable a society to live by the very values they publicly committed to.

Zuboff argues neoliberalism and more specifically surveillance capitalism is a form of feudalism. However, she also observes that people are not willing to erase the progress of the twentieth century to subsume themselves to feudal relations in exchange for free email and a search engine (44). What we see happening in Google's celebrity assemblage discussed above is the Google founders playing this 'double shuffle' (Hall 2003). On the one hand, they take full advantage of neoliberal economic forces in the domination of the company by three men, hiring union busters to deal with staff walkouts (Scheiber and Wakabayashi 2019), and extracting data for speculation on the financial markets. On the other hand, Page waves his grandfather's hammer, thus performing social democratic liberalism as part of their celebrification. And they have presented these values in a very particular way. As a corporation they have incorporated liberal values – 'don't be evil' – through paternalistic policies for staff – a washing machine, free meals, a dentist.

Diversity and Google's workforce

As we discussed in Chapter 1, what is distinctive about the American West in the frontier imaginary is the stratification of the workforce according to race and gender producing a particularly racialised class structure. In theory at least, unions and labour organising give workers protection from racism, sexism, and poor working conditions through legal knowledge and industrial relations expertise. In relegating union organising to the past and adopting the paternalism of nineteenth-century corporations while hiding behind the façade of social democratic liberal values, so Google replicates (like many Silicon Valley companies) the racial and gender hierarchies of the West in their workforces.

In the early days, Google arguably did do more to address gender inequality than any other Silicon Valley company. With processes in place to encourage the recruitment of female programmers and executives, the early Google managed to produce three of the most powerful women in the tech industry: Marissa Mayer, Sheryl Sandberg, and Susan Wojcicki. After offering Brin and Page room in her garage, Wojcicki eventually became the sixteenth employee at Google, in 1999. The company has also prided itself on good maternity and childcare policies. Since 2014 it has made publicly available an annual Diversity Report, as part of its bid to transparency.

Nevertheless, the inclusion of women in leadership positions proved to be unsustainable in the increasingly masculine work cultures of Silicon Valley, and with the aggressive, competitive nature of the businesses. Emily Chang reports that, as Google grew, 'it defaulted to recruiting methods that were more standard in the industry,' and began outsourcing recruitment. This strategy focused on hiring according to the archetype of the 'brogrammer' – a 26-year-old, socially awkward coding savant (Chang 2018). Similarly, confrontation – framed as robust debate ('you need dissent' says Schmidt) – became seen as a key leadership skill: Chang's interviewees suggest that the company developed a reputation for an aggressive work environment, and many women simply stopped applying for jobs there (Chang 2018, 85–86). Google is currently being sued for ageism and sexism by women employees and the government. In addition, Google mainly hires from prestigious universities like the ones the founders went to: Stanford, Berkeley, MIT, and this reinforces a classed and raced dimension to their recruitment, in that it reflects the racialised make-up of American elites more broadly (Loudenback and Baer 2015).[6]

Google's diversity programme has consistently tried to address these fundamental imbalances. There are very different stories in circulation about the programme's effectiveness: buzzy PR pieces by journalists such as *Fortune*'s Ellen McGirt conflict with significantly less-glowing insider accounts (see for instance surveys done by Christian Fuchs on work–life balance (Fuchs 2014, 165–169)). Other promotional writing is also contradictory, for example stating both that the founders wanted to hire clones of themselves, and that they wanted more women employees (Brandt 2011). But these workforce imbalances are largely paradigmatic of the industry as a whole and are similarly reflected at Facebook. Across the tech sector it is evident that white and Asian people take the lion's share of the senior roles, including in the investment firms that support the industry. These investors believe deeply in the cult of the founder, which, as we have argued, forms the primary legitimating feature of the sector's financial and proprietary organisation: and these genius founders have tended to come from a limited pool that is primarily white or Asian and male. Insiders to this founder culture are aware of the problem but typically disavow it, or argue that there is nothing they can do about it, given that the pool from which they are fishing is made up of those who 'are playing with computers when they are thirteen years old.' Their line is that it is the problem of the education system or the parents of the 13-year olds (Stross 2012, 55). Google is heavily invested in this culture: literally, in terms of a financial stake, and ideologically, in relation to their own founders – and to the aspirations of many of their staff to set up their own billion-dollar start-ups (perhaps eventually to be acquired by Google). This deep cultural orientation towards a specifically raced and gendered employee sits uncomfortably alongside the stated desires for diversity. But as Sara Ahmed argues, using the language of diversity does not 'translate into creating diverse or equal environments.' Indeed, there is often 'a gap between a symbolic commitment and a lived reality' (Ahmed 2017, 90).

The diversity of the workforce has partly come under scrutiny because of the ways that forms of oppression are baked into their products under the ideology of dataism (which we discuss in the next section). The company itself recognises that lack of diversity within the staff can lead to problematic algorithmic outcomes: a vision statement on Google's diversity page quotes CEO Pichai as saying, 'A diverse mix of voices leads to better discussions, decisions, and outcomes for everyone' (Riel 2017). And there is also acknowledgement of the specifics of the problem, for example, in the discussions about Google's image-search algorithm that started marking pictures of gorillas as Black people. As McGirt reports:

> Bradley Horowitz who led Google Photos at the time … explains that if the team had been more diverse, it would have noticed the problems earlier in the process: 'To the degree that the data is sexist or racist, you're going to have the algorithm imitating those behaviors … It's the world we all live in, but it's Google's job to put its finger on the scale to make it level.'
> *(McGirt 2017)*

Google here, following its Don't Be Evil mantra, is taking personal responsibility for the baked-in racism of an emerging technology, and failing. At the very least, Google acknowledges it should hire more Black employees as engineers, and we know from the diversity statistics that Google is not succeeding even at that. But Google is also building on data sets that have been produced primarily by white and Asian programmers in a context of white supremacy for decades. Kate Crawford in her talk at the Royal Society points out that the Faces in the Wild database which most facial recognition software has been trained on is not only predominantly white but near to 30% of the photos in the database are of George W. Bush (Crawford 2018). Here too we come up against the limits of Google's post-class, post-race, postfeminist brand in its disavowal of the always ongoing struggles for equality and liberation. Indeed, the gap between the company's professed values and its practices towards its employees has become ever more evident, and in 2018 there was a spate of staff walkouts, protesting against sexual harassment by senior men. Certain key figures were paid off or resigned. Following this, the organisers of the walkouts were punished. This was in keeping with the company's continued denial of access to unionisation, and therefore is a further way of entrenching patriarchal management cultures in the company.[7]

Privatisation of knowledge

What holds together the celebrity narratives of Google's founders and corporate contradictions around liberalism is the ideology of dataism. Here we again follow José Van Dijck's definition of dataism (discussed in Chapter 1) as the 'widespread belief in the objective quantification and potential tracking of all kinds of human behavior and sociality through online media technologies' (Van Dijck 2014). Dataism is a form of scientism – i.e. a belief system that states the world can be reduced to and understood by the rigorous application of the scientific method. But dataism is different from previous variants of scientism in that it posits that digital technologies have enabled a paradigm shift so that the social can now be appertained scientifically, at scale and speed, and driven by algorithms. This new techno-ideological construct lays claim to the idea that a different quality of social 'truth' can be accessed, rendering the contradictions between liberalism and neoliberalism moot. Dataism smooths these tensions by allowing a datafied market in personal preferences to become the route to social justice and progress – all the while meeting the needs of advertisers and financial speculators. That is, we can identify our social, material, and political needs much faster through Google's algorithmic applications, while corporations profit from the same deepened understanding and connection.

Yet the inability of data to exhaust the possibilities of human interaction and shared culture, or to meaningfully process history (or most notably, for our purposes, any idea of oppression as a historical force) is clear to most critics (cf O'Neil 2016; D'Ignazio and Klein 2020). Data is a potent tool under neoliberalism. Not least because it is a tool for managers to quantify and govern workforces;

marketers and political consultants to micro-target voters and consumers; and the financial services industry to legitimate risk (Eubanks 2017). Combined with the decontexualisation of knowledge and the belief in the unbiased neutrality of the results – they simply reflect the underlying data – means that the feudal structure of Google is also extended to the kinds of knowledge that are privatised and produced through its search engine. We demonstrate how this works in practice by building on Siva Vaidhyanathan's work on Google and the university.

Vaidhyanathan observes that state and public institutions have been deeply hampered by the neoliberal assault on their social roles. Consequently, Google has been able to take advantage of the potential of digital technologies in their fields when universities have been unable to take proactive steps themselves. The Google founders' celebrification harnesses the trope of the young male genius: they have presented themselves as natural allies to the university as a normative institution – even as their platform is apparently seeking to supersede it. In such a way the so-called 'democratisation of knowledge' immanent in the advent of the digital era also becomes the privatisation of knowledge (Crouch 2011).

In our concordance, 'university' produces an astonishing 414 results per million words, which is approximately double the baseline found in the EngTenTen15 from sites from the '.edu' top-level-domain that is reserved exclusively for schools and university. That is, 'university' is twice as likely to be referenced in our concordance as it is in websites specifically about education.[8] The university is a central institution for tech culture, especially through the well-documented relationship between Stanford (where Page, Brin, Musk, and Thiel all studied and/or dropped out) and the entrepreneurial origins of the Bay Area of Northern California (Cohen 2019). And yet, as we have seen, the university is a site of ambivalence for many, and of hostility for some (such as Thiel). There is very often a downplaying of the support founders have been given by university or other state-funded research to actually produce their products. And, in the case of Google, there is an apparent drive to colonise or replace the university through a process of datafication. Once knowledge and information are seen as both a commodity produced through data extraction and the lever by which to extract even more data, the logical step within the digital economy is to maximise the profit to be gained from this process.

Some advocates of a digital knowledge economy now barely even recognise universities as having a research or social function. Technologist and educational theorist Ryan Craig, in his 2015 book *College Disrupted*, sees universities as a sector ripe for the disruptive application of dataism. He sees them as institutions that need 'unbundling,' separating out their various social, educational, and consumer functions to reduce costs and ensure that student 'return on investment' is maximised by only selling them the parts of the college experience they desire, and thus ensuring that their educational purchases can align with their desired career trajectory. Data is the means to do this. Craig argues that courses simply do not measure student learning adequately, and that the solution is to organise universities in such a way that activities can become fully measurable – in a similar way as they are, say, in baseball. Ultimately, for the 'disrupter,' universities are simply inefficient vendors of labour market training.

Google is heavily implicated in this. Under such logics, the flattening of the variety and complexity of higher education (HE) into a set of comparable data points makes perfect sense. Google makes this possible through its search, books, and scholar websites, which provide an architecture to displace the university library, but also through its YouTube site, which offers the digital simulacrum of the lecture. Other companies are now jostling to provide more specialist and tailored versions of these platforms (particularly around lecture capture), but this is as much to profit from the defensive budgetary allocations of HE providers as it is to compete with Google in its core areas of business. Moreover, as they are 'unbundled,' the formerly public spaces of libraries and universities are themselves becoming private profit-making entities where commercial imperatives are entangled with both research and learning – thus compromising the very 'product' universities are supposed to offer.[9]

Google privileges an engineering perspective on the world – one which is undoubtedly important but also necessarily incomplete. According to Schmidt and Rosenberg, Google conducts itself in a way that is 'solution-orientated,' with 'a bias towards data' in its decision-making processes (Schmidt and Rosenberg 2017, 152–155). At Google, 'data' is seen as providing unexpected answers to difficult questions. In their advice to prospective hires, Schmidt and Rosenberg summarise its importance thus: 'Data is the sword of the twenty-first century, those who wield it well, the samurai. So start sharpening that blade, *uruwashii*, and take statistics' (138). (Google's search engine can itself answer any questions here about the gender dimensions of this statement. In a Google image search for 'samurai,' we had to scroll through four pages before a picture of a woman appeared, and that was for a female martial artist and Ted Talk coach from Southern California.)[10] Furthermore, in most Google conference rooms there are two screens, 'one of them is for ... meeting notes. The other is for data' (152). A lack of awareness of these limitations, however, extends to Google's philanthropy, which is 'Data-driven, human-focused philanthropy' – a striking oxymoron. For 'data' can be put to many uses, but it is rarely sufficient in a human context. In spite of this, data-driven culture is central to Google's 'visionary' founders Brin and Page, who, it is claimed, have 'a very disciplined, scientific approach to solving problems ... [which means that] "information is the basis for almost all the decisions anybody makes"'(Brandt 2011, 61). Indeed, a failure to interrogate the assumptions underpinning dataism is one of the ways in which the limits of the liberal subject is revealed: seemingly neutral data is produced in contexts that privilege certain sorts of subjects (i.e. the imbalanced workforce make-up of Silicon Valley) and the values that buttress those privileges are then reproduced in the data themselves. In so doing Google perpetuates the privilege of particular categories, thereby basing itself upon and promoting a particular form of epistemology (Ahmed 2007). This is particularly important when we think about the role Google plays in transforming public institutions and particularly universities. Universities may have been complicit institutions in perpetuating hierarchies of oppression throughout their history, but they were also a key node in the movements to both challenge those oppressions and institutionalise the knowledge that emerged from those struggles (for instance through postcolonial thinking, Women's Studies, queer theory).

Google dominates the digital realm; it is 'the victor in the winner-take-all race to serve as the chief utility for the World Wide Web' (Vaidyanathan 2012, 17).[11] And for all the public good it may seem to produce, the overall effect of Google's presence in the digital sphere is: 'inherently conservative ... winners keep winning' (Vaidyanathan, 60). As we have seen, the basic principle of its search algorithms rewards not some intrinsic value or arbitrary measure of quality, but popularity, as measured by the number of links to the sites that link to a given page. While corporations can spend vast amounts of money on search engine optimisation consultants to make sure that they come at the top of search results lists, Google has many other ways of influencing the results. For example, it applies measures of quality designed to facilitate the filtering out of low-quality academic articles (the PageRank algorithm and its descendants). While in the abstract this might seem as if it would produce a relatively value-neutral system, in practice the search algorithm embeds a highly conservative epistemic architecture at the heart of the world wide web's knowledge distribution mechanisms. This is because, through using popularity as a proxy for quality in assigning significance to digital content, Google's algorithms reinforce the pre-existing dominance of 'common sense' ideas about, for instance, race, class, and gender. Thus, this architecture reinforces patriarchal and racially hierarchised ways of configuring the social.

Vaidhyanathan states that any idea of Google as neutral can only be based in an almost religious trust in the company to deliver reliable results:

> The University of Google lacks accreditation, to be sure ... Poor searches by faithful Google users are only part of the problem with the Googlization of knowledge ... Google structures, judges, and delivers knowledge to exacerbate our worst tendencies to jump to erroneous conclusions and act on them in ways that cause harm.
>
> *(Vaidhyanathan 2012, 78)*

He goes on to argue that universities and Google already have a very close relationship, but that Google has 'taken the lead and set the terms of the relationship' (Vaidhyanathan 2012, 186). Vaidhyanathan also points to research that suggests that, for students in the US, the internet had replaced the university library as the first place to check for information as early as 2002. He states that, as with the other areas Google 'disrupts,' the company steps in to fill gaps created by 'public failure.' Google's transformation of the internet's indexing function is assisted by the commercial imperatives that have been placed on the university system. These imperatives have reshaped the organisation of knowledge *within* universities to better serve commercial interests and further embed dataist logics in education and research. Google enables different sorts of universities to emerge by lowering the costs of entry (as seen in online-only courses that depend heavily on Google's architecture or indeed are run by Google themselves on the Coursera platform), but it remains to be seen whether this will lead to a pluralistic educational commons, to the deeper commodification of education or simply that education will be a subsidised corporate activity to develop specific and specialised workforces. And if, as seems probable, it does lead to deeper commodification and corporate takeover, this will deepen inequalities and intersecting oppressions in the social field tied to economic class as well as its intersections with race and gender. Education, rather than the individual and social good of twentieth-century democratic liberalism, returns to being an expression of a form of class privilege (as it was until around the 1960s). Or an extension of what Zuboff sees as the refeudalisation of society under surveillance capitalism as, for example, Google delivers training for specific qualification-gated roles within organisations.

James Damore's memo

In these final sections, we bring together our discussions of dataism, liberalism, and the workforce to consider a significant flashpoint in Google-Alphabet's mediatisation: a memo shared by Google engineer, James Damore, which critiqued Google's diversity initiatives, arguing that women are biologically less suited to high-stress, high-status technical employment. We discuss how the dataism of Damore's memo reveals the irreconciled tension between Google's social democratic branding and their neoliberal logics, but also how dataism in both contexts can perpetuate patriarchal inequalities. In addition, we focus on Susan Wojcicki's role as CEO of YouTube and how the potentially feminist power of women in leadership roles in companies like Google is circumscribed.

Following the memo's leak, Damore was sacked by Google, its CEO Pichai deeming its views 'not okay.'[12] In the media furore that followed, a survey indicated widespread support for Damore's position within the tech industry.[13] For example, one poll of 441 Google staff indicated that 50% of respondents thought he shouldn't have been fired (Bort 2017). Until April 2019, Damore was in the process of suing Google (with the aid of Republican lawyers) as part of a class-action suit, alleging discrimination against white male conservatives. He has since moved his case into arbitration, a process which often leads to a financial settlement under specific conditions (e.g. a non-disclosure agreement). Damore was subsequently taken up by the alt-right as a kind of right-wing 'influencer,' and a large part of the story was played out across YouTube, where the alt-right has gained significant traction, especially in their mimicry of the university lecture format. Damore's memo is presumably compelling because of the way it taps into (and thus reveals) prevailing populist commonsense about questions of power and its supposed relationship to inherent difference. More than this, though, the kinds of knowledge that he retrieves mirror the racialised patriarchal structures of the culture within which it is located. The assertion that these structures are not in any way biased is appealing to those who benefit from it: one reason that Damore is so invested in forms of knowledge that give biological justification for discrimination on the basis of gender is that they suggest that he is rightfully positioned in a site of privilege.[14]

Although Damore's critique is of 'diversity,' his evidence base is primarily linked to the differences between men and women. His main argument is that '[o]n average, men and women biologically differ in many ways,' and that these 'differences may explain why we don't see equal representation of women in tech and leadership':

These [biological] differences aren't just socially constructed because:

They're universal across human cultures
They often have clear biological causes and links to prenatal testosterone
Biological males that were castrated at birth and raised as females often still identify and act like males
The underlying traits are highly heritable
They're exactly what we would predict from an evolutionary psychology perspective.

(Damore https://firedfortruth.com/)

More than this, he argues, diversity initiatives are disingenuous: 'Discriminating just to increase the representation of women in tech is as misguided and biased as mandating increases for women's representation in the homeless, work-related and violent deaths, prisons, and school dropouts.' He goes on to argue that diversity initiatives comprise an 'ideological echo chamber' that excludes conservatives and dissenting voices who presumably prefer their highly paid workforce white, middle-class, and male. Throughout the memo, he hyperlinks to internet sources, in an attempt to provide scientific evidence that gendered differences 'aren't just socially constructed.' His sources range from Wikipedia, to blogs, conservative internet outlets, and academic psychology journals that are sympathetic to popular renderings of evolutionary psychology – a discipline that has been subject to feminist critique (McKinnon 2005, O'Neill 2016; Meyers 2012, 1–2).

Damore has stated in a media interview that his memo and his intention were within the stated cultural expectations of Google (Lee 2018). He has some justification for this claim. Damore is a self-declared Google fanboy, and a product of Google in more than one way. Given a slightly different chronology, there is no reason why Damore couldn't have become part of the Paypal Mafia (see Chapter 5), or a founder of Google or Facebook. Most importantly, however, his memo is also in line with Google's ideology of dataism: that is, the belief that the world can be reduced to decontextualised information and subject to quantifiable logics. For example, drawing on texts seemingly sourced through Google itself, he constructs an argument that presents a datafied approach to evolutionary science: he seems to view it as a sort of 'primary' social science – which is a radical extension of the sorts of claims the underpinning research can sustain. Furthermore, in a sort of parody of the way in which data can be insensitive to context Damore makes an equivalence between wanting to increase the number of women in leadership roles at Google and wanting more homeless women and prisoners.

As we argued above, Google harnesses the ideology of dataism to reconcile their social democratic values at the level of culture with their neoliberal economics: dataism is virtuous, rendering social truth objective. This means that the struggle over labour rights (for example) is located in the past and has been resolved historically revealing a post-class terrain. At Google, where there are inequalities in the data this can be addressed by, for example, corporate policy such as a diversity programme. This data practice dovetails with the neoliberal fostering of the hyper-competitive individual subject as forms of collective action are no longer needed. Not only does Damore extrapolate from the inequalities evident in Google's workforce and then frame them as natural, but he also reveals that the data is malleable to political views; that different data sets can be used to support different political positions. He exposes that what is key is the assumptions made when collecting the data as well as the context and interpretation through which they are understood: data is not neutral, it is a political tool. But what he said was culturally incompatible with the Google founders' celebrity.

Unprotected by a union and subsequently sacked, Damore was appropriated by a number of different figures across emergent right-wing subcultures, from evolutionary psychologists to alt-right celebrities to YouTube anarcho-capitalists. Significantly, he was interviewed by three key figures of the alt-right: Milo Yiannopoulos, Stefan Molyneux, and Jordan Peterson. Damore describes himself as a 'huge fan' of Peterson as well as Molyneux, and as such he reflects their views, values, and rhetoric in his memo (although he doesn't cite them directly, preferring to use Wikipedia) (Levin 2017). The alt-right is a digital-era phenomenon that Annie Kelly describes as 'a network of smallish digital social hubs whose ideological position can be understood as the natural conclusion of neo-conservative logics surrounding liberalism, manhood and national security' (Kelly 2017, 69). Forms of 'popular misogyny' can also intersect with these hubs (Banet Weiser 2018). Damore became a visible symbol of their reach outside of their alt-right circles on YouTube. Overall, the extent of the alt-right and its influence is difficult to judge – it is too recent a phenomenon to make a big splash in either our concordance or the EngTenTen15. However, in the 24 times 'alt-right' does appear in our concordance, the authors' tone is consistently hostile to them. Where it does appear it is usually in association with either Thiel or Facebook, though neither is credited with endorsing it. It is never mentioned alongside Google.

How (not) to break up the Silicon Valley boy's blub: Susan Wojcicki

In response to Damore's memo, YouTube CEO Susan Wojcicki, once described as 'the most important person in advertising' (Peterson 2013), penned an opinion piece for *Fortune*. YouTube, was founded in 2005 by Chad Hurley, Steve Chen, and Jawed Karim, who were members of the PayPal Mafia discussed in Chapter 5. YouTube was assimilated as part of Google in 2006, and rapidly became the most popular entertainment site in the USA (Burgess and Green 2018). Wojcicki is identified in the media as 'a reluctant public ambassador' (Bergen 2019). She tweets and re-tweets YouTube-related content on Twitter, and has posted publicly on Facebook only a handful of times; her media spotlights are limited. Nevertheless, she has written op-eds on gender issues – for example, on the boys' network in Silicon Valley (Wojcicki 2017a) and on James Damore (Wojcicki 2017b), as well as on the importance of maternity leave and generational reproduction (Wojcicki 2014). She is an advocate for refugees, and for women in tech. For example:

> At YouTube, we still have a long way to go toward improving our diversity, but we've made some progress. We've supported underrepresented groups, established a ... Leadership Diversity Council, and ramped up our female hiring – since I joined in 2014, we've gone from a company that is 24 percent women to one that's nearly 30 percent.
> *(Wojcicki 2017a)*

Here, we focus on the op-eds that she wrote in 2017, as well as a 2018 interview for Recode, where she spoke to Kara Swisher, a prominent tech journalist and lesbian (Swisher 2018).

In her article for *Vanity Fair* from 16 March 2017, headlined 'Exclusive: How to Break Up the Silicon Valley Boy's Club,' Wojcicki demonstrated her support for Susan Fowler at Uber and A. J. Vandermeyden at Tesla, both of whom have spoken out about sexual harassment in the workplace. (This op-ed was also posted on Facebook by Sandberg: 'Great and important piece from my friend Susan Wojcicki.') Wojcicki suggests hiring more women as the solution as this 'has been proved to address gender discrimination in all its forms.' Her argument fits in with the data-oriented corporate logics predominant at Google; she argues that 'greater diversity leads to better outcomes, more innovative solutions, less groupthink, better stock performance and GDP growth.' Hiring more women is good for business. Moreover: 'Improving diversity, like any priority, requires dedicated resources, clear goals, comprehensive analytics, and company-wide transparency.' She has a three-pronged solution. First, give paid family leave (Google offers 18 weeks – good from an American perspective, but well below norms in many European countries). Second, some companies should give money and staff to groups that support female 'or any underrepresented' employees. Third, those in management positions should 'extend their privilege' to 'elevate women in the workplace.' She tells a story of how she was not on a guest list due to being a woman, which had meant that YouTube would not be represented at a key 'important invitation-only conference convening most of the top leaders in tech and media.' To address this she needed to turn to Bill Campbell, her mentor, to 'work his magic.'[15] In her rebuttal of Damore, Wojcicki again names men who have supported her career in tech: Page, Brin, Schmidt, Rosenberg, Campbell.

In another article from 2017 Wojcicki frames her critique of Damore within a conversation with her daughter about the supposed biological inferiority of women. Like other people in leadership positions she condemns the memo, but there are also a number of problems with her critique when it comes to the discussion of race and Google:

> what if we replaced the word 'women' in the memo with another group? What if the memo said that biological differences amongst Black, Hispanic, or LGBTQ employees explained their underrepresentation in tech and leadership roles? Would some people still be discussing the merit of the memo's arguments or would there be a universal call for swift action against its author? I don't ask this to compare one group to another, but rather to point out that the language of discrimination can take many different forms and none are acceptable or productive.
>
> *(Wojcicki 2017b)*

There is a strange equivalence made here as if women cannot be Black – that these categories don't intersect. But in making this equivalence Wojcicki inadvertently points to how small, for example, the number of Black women at Google actually is. Like the Google founders, Wojcicki adopts a postrace rhetoric (Mukherjee 2011): this could have been an opportunity to ask why Black, Hispanic, and LBGTQ+ employees are underrepresented (more so than women), and why Google's ideology of dataism has discriminatory effects (Benjamin 2019).

But in other public content Wojcicki seems less concerned about these issues, for example in relation to questions of 'free speech.' Thus, in the interview with Swisher, Wojcicki consistently uses the language of branding and free speech when questioned about content and content moderation. When she states that 'we want our brand to be a place where they want to build their brand,' she is, in effect, signalling an acceptance that the site is policed extensively through the corporate values of companies like Proctor and Gamble. More than this, though, the conversation discusses an apparent line between 'censorship' and 'freedom of speech,' rather than discussing pressing questions of social justice, including racism, sexism, homophobia, and transphobia; and instead of linking these issues to historical and contemporary forms of campaigning around social liberation and equality, the conversation resorts to the language of the brand, and to adjectives such as 'offensive,' 'egregious,' 'distasteful.' This means that the issue is reduced to personal emotions and matters of taste, rather than having any sense of a political consensus in a civil society. In addition, Wojcicki bases her argument on an appeal to 'experts,' rather than to civil rights legislation, or policies that have been put in place to protect people from discrimination. YouTube's global monopoly also avoids questions of civil rights and social justice across the world, on the grounds that there are 'different values in different countries' (Swisher 2018). All these issues are connected to YouTube's role as a platform that itself becomes the foundation, generator, and site of a specific system of values: in a platform society, YouTube and other corporations are forging the ways that public value is created online, including the way that decisions, debates, and discourse are articulated in public space (cf Van Dijck et al. 2017).

The way that content moderation is framed here is particularly alarming because the comments section under the video of the interview is filled with anti-semitism and misogyny. The comments are almost completely abusive, with the commenters calling Wojcicki a 'fascist jew.' Here is one comment:

> Both women are Feminist Jews. Karen [sic] is a lesbian. So 3 Strikes and your account is deleted ... according to who? ... a SJW snowflake who was triggered by the content or a comment? The rules are so vague they can censor whomever they want. Karen is ultra left. If she were CEO the account deletions would be thru the roof. Sad that in today's world, these type of women are in positions of power where their 'feeling' rule over logic. They both are power hungry fascists ... very dangerous.
>
> *(comment on Swisher 2018)*[16]

Anti-semitism and online misogyny are not niche practices. Misogyny is a key part of the contemporary political terrain and, as Debbie Ging argues, it is the inevitable outcome of postfeminism – which was itself a response to feminist struggle (Ging 2019). Hate speech of all kinds is widespread on the internet, and it is clear that the tech companies do not have sufficient will to address it. As many critics have argued, misogyny functions to control women and keep them out of public space by doing them harm (Ging and Siapera 2018, Keller, Mendes and Ringrose 2016; Jane 2014). This should mean that online content moderators who claim to be progressively liberal would be keen to stamp it out, but this is not what has happened. It is also well established that YouTube – and Google search – spreads anti-semitism (Noble 2018) – another one of the contradictions that the Google founders have been unable to resolve. The recourse by Wojcicki to branding language and her support for the obscure rules pertaining to content moderation exacerbates these problems.

The prevalence of hate speech reveals problems in how YouTube implements its community guidelines (which are accepted by agreeing to its Terms of Service); these state that 'Hate speech is not allowed on YouTube.' The site also claims that: 'We remove content promoting violence or hatred against individuals or groups' (based on, e.g., ethnicity, race, and gender). There is in fact some recourse to the language of social justice and civil rights in the way that YouTube content is moderated, but there is no transparency around how this is enforced. Sarah T. Roberts's scholarship on the limits of content moderation, including the brutal labour conditions of the workers, is deeply sobering (Roberts 2019). There has also been a recent spate of journalistic exposés of some of the low-wage, low-status sites in the US and the Philippines where moderation work is carried out. Content on YouTube may be flagged (i.e. reported) as including hate speech by users, but the process that then ensues is opaque to say the least. The site is not obligated to honour the flags it receives, and, indeed, because 'flags remain open to interpretation and can be readily gamed,' platforms prefer to ignore them (Crawford and Gillespie 2016). Corporations like Google and Facebook have little reason to lobby *for* the kind of regulation of content that would require their moderating practices to be more robust. They are more than happy for the internet to remain outside the sphere of regulation that has legislatively enforced non-discriminatory values and practices in the media throughout the twentieth century. Google is responsible for its own moderation practices, and, given that it is permeated with dataism, and allied at an economic level to the anti-regulation doctrines of neoliberalism, it is unsurprising that these have not proved adequate.

The fact that there are a few women in key leadership roles such as Wojcicki and Sandberg, even if they actively advocate for more women in such roles, can do little to alleviate the patriarchal practices of West Coast Tech. The Google founders have fought for an autonomous space, including freedom from unions and regulation, and for control of voting rights on their corporate boards; and they also perform the arbiters of good and evil, hubristically, placing themselves on the side of good. They have lobbied hard for a site of juridical suspension where the regulation of their sites is indeterminate and opaque (see Chapter 1). Yet for all this personal responsibility in exchange for abnormal shares of wealth and power: the misogyny, the anti-semitism, the hate speech they promised to protect us from is not absent or even hidden but directly on view. For instance, underneath a video of the CEO of YouTube herself, the woman whose garage hosted Google on its very first day, and a family member (by ex-marriage at least) of Sergey Brin. That, at least, is relatively transparent.

Conclusion

Google and the alt-right are very different kinds of entities, and there are few explicit links between them. One is a corporation, and the other is a loose online network that uses, among other technologies, Alphabet-Google's platforms (especially YouTube) to disseminate, share and collaborate over so-called conservative viewpoints. Our argument here, however, is that, although it seems as if the alt-right and Google are at odds, they are not as polarised as they might appear on the surface. The founders' Judaism, early experiences of migration, and exposure to radical progressive politics mark them as natural opponents of the alt-right. Yet their company is at the centre of a dominant strand within the politics of tech culture – a strand that has facilitated the rise of radical reactionary politics online. As we have seen, Damore shares many values with the men who own and run the companies of Silicon Valley, including the apparent belief that the world can be understood and altered through the continuous application datafied approaches. And as Damore draws on legitimated bodies of knowledge like evolutionary psychology, we see how the core belief structures of Silicon Valley, when decontextualised and transferred to the cultural and social domain, can reproduce the sort of misogynistic 'rationalism' that fuels the alt-right.

If we return to the IPO discussed at the beginning of this chapter, we can see how Brin and Page owned their particular and special responsibilities to Google's impact on the world. They issued themselves special Class B shares with ten times the normal voting rights to ensure that they and a few others would retain control of the company no matter how many ordinary shares they sold. But their companies' impacts have been far from universally positive. It is through the YouTube platform (owned by Alphabet) that the alt-right has been able to mainstream their racist, misogynistic, and transphobic discourses: sometimes claiming, as does Damore, that they are simply 'classical liberals' (Brooks 2020; Finlayson 2020). Through the algorithmic logics of personalisation that Google pioneered in their rush to monetise the free internet, race, class, and gender have calcified as social categories and racism, classism and sexism flourish online. It is true that other more progressive activisms also find space to organise online carrying views that the Google's founders perform agreement with (for instance the pro-migration protests of 2017 that Sergey Brin participated in), but these happen in spite of, not through, the epistemic architectures of commercial data-ism that Google developed. The facilitation of reactionary politics is a conscious decision made by corporations like Google all too aware of its presence on their platforms. Its continued presence on these platforms is permitted by a corporate commitment to a business model that enables its spread.

In the face of this irreconcilable contradiction between their performed views and the activities of their company, the founders may have given up their public roles, but they have not given up their privileged voting shares. They might proclaim the liberal values of social democracy but the rise of Google is thanks to the cultural and economic shift to neoliberalism. More than this, though, the founders of Google are beneficiaries of an old boy's club: the patriarchal network that we have been mapping in this book. And hiring women for some leadership roles is not going to break this network up. As Brin and Page told the world when they invited the public to share in the great wealth they would generate, the buck stops with them on moral and political issues: and until they return to company to a more conventional ownership mode (or break it up) it always will. We should hold them accountable to it.

Notes

1 See also Reid Hoffman's generic version of this story in *Blitzscaling*: 'A brilliant entrepreneur discovers an incredible opportunity. After dropping out of college, he or she gathers a small team who are happy to work for equity, sets up shop in a humble garage, plays foosball, raises money from sage venture capitalists, and proceeds to change the world—after which, of course, the founders and early employees live happily ever after' (Hoffman and Yeh 2018, 16–17).

2 'Don't Be Evil' was withdrawn as an official motto in 2018, and replaced with 'Do the right thing.'

3 Brin begins by humouring his audience, encouraging them to stretch. Then he states:

> 'I see now that in my undergraduate days I made a very important oversight. Now what is this programme over here at the front that has about 100 women in it and 3 men?'

Everyone laughs. Brin studied computer science and mathematics, and this is partly a reference to the recurring trope in popular culture that geeks find it hard to have heterosexual sexual relationships. It is straight out of *Big Bang Theory* (see Chapter 2). But this statement, in its disingenuous reference to the maleness of Brin's world – as if it represented disadvantage rather than power – also brings together some key issues for our consideration of the difficulties facing women working in tech and the patriarchal networks that circumscribe this work. Marie Hicks (2017), Emily Chang (2018), Ellen Pao (2017), and others have pointed out that women were systematically and specifically discouraged or prohibited from studying computer science. Brin is on home territory, with his father a professor at Maryland and seems not to be thinking about the various present and future audiences for the speech. It is not surprising then, that even though the speech was televised by CSpan, it does not appear on YouTube and is instead hosted on the lesser known video platform *The Daily Motion* where it has only been viewed 73 times (at the time of writing) in the six years it had been online (as opposed to Page's speech garnering 305,000 views on YouTube).

4 'Uncomfortably exciting' is a repeated term tied to Brin and Page's celebrification that reappears in Alphabet CEO Sundar Pichai's response to Page and Brin standing down from Alphabet (Page and Brin 2019).

5 While Ford did bestow genuine largesse to his workers by implementing low working hours and leisure benefits, it is important to remember he spent his later life promoting antisemitic politics.

6 Their own diversity report for 2019 shows that women make up only 31.6% of Google's global workforce. In the United States, 54.4% of the workforce is white, 39.8% is Asian, 3.3% is Black, 5.7% is Latinx, and 0.8% is Native American. In leadership positions, women make up 26.1% of the roles. 66.6% are white, 28.9% Asian, 3.3% Latinx, 2.6% Black, 0.7% Native American. (Brown and Parker 2019). This is against a baseline of 60.1% white (non-Latinx or Hispanic); 18.5% Hispanic or Latinx; 13.4% Black; 1.3% Native American; 5.9% Asian and 2.8% other two or more racial identities (census.gov 2020a) in the US as a whole. In California, the state where Google is based, this is 36.5% white; 39.4% Hispanic or Latinx; 6.5% Black; 15.5% Asian; 4% two or more racial identities and 2.1% Native American or Hawaiian. Whichever way you might choose to cut it, white and Asian people are overrepresented. We discuss this further in Chapter 1.

7 For more on the Google Walk Outs, their demands, and retaliation see Catherine D'Ignazio and Lauren F. Klein, (2020) *Data Feminism*. Cambridge, Mass: The MIT Press. pp. 205–208.

8 As we saw in the Thiel chapter, the university is a contested space. We can still see Stanford's apparent 'multiculturalism' being assaulted in *The Stanford Review* today, and the university plays a key part in the American culture wars. Jaron Lanier in *Who Owns The Future?* States: 'The list of top company runners who dropped out of college

is commanding: Bill Gates, Steve Jobs, Steve Wozniak, and Mark Zuckerberg, for a start. Peter Thiel, of Facebook and PayPal fame, started a fund to pay top students to drop out of school, since the task of building high tech startups should not be delayed' (Lanier, 2013, 85).
9 As we go to press the coronavirus pandemic is rapidly accelerating these trends as universities look to spend a year primarily engaged in online teaching.
10 See https://strategicsamurai.com/ Recall too the significance of the samurai sword in Musk's interview with Joe Rogan.
11 And it shows in the concordance: Google appears 1400/mw, as compared to 701/mw for Facebook and 75/mw for Tesla.
12 www.blog.google/topics/diversity/note-employees-ceo-sundar-pichai/
13 His personal website is called www.firedfortruth.com and @fired4truth was James Damore's Twitter handle in the aftermath of the sacking.
14 Interestingly while evolution is an important term in the corpus appearing at double the baseline EnTenTen2015, 'evolutionary psychology' is not present at all.
15 A woman's influence is constrained by the amount of women on a board combined by the amount of women directly managing in the workplace (Stainback, Kleiner, and Skaggs, 2016). Sandberg's power is constrained by Zuckerberg and the others on the Facebook board – including Thiel and Andreesson. Wojcicki's power is constrained by the board of directors for Google: Eric Schmidt, Sundar Pichai, Larry Page, Sergey Brin.
16 We note that this comment was removed by YouTube or deleted by the user sometime in 2020. What is interesting about this is not just that it was allowed to stay up for at least a year, but that misogynistic comments still remain. Deeper in the comments there are still calls for Wojcicki's execution and antisemitic conspiracy theory.

References

About (2020) *Google.com*. https://about.google/intl/en-GB/ Last accessed 03/05/2020.
Ahmed, Sara (2007) 'A Phenomenology of Whiteness' *Feminist Theory*, 8(2), 149–168.
Ahmed, Sara (2017) *Living a Feminist Life*. Durham: Duke University Press.
Banet Weiser, Sarah (2018) *Empowered: Popular Feminism and Popular Misogyny*. Durham: Duke University Press.
Barbrook, Richard and Andrew Cameron (1995) 'The Californian Ideology' *Mute*, 1(3). www.metamute.org/editorial/articles/californian-ideology Last accessed 03/05/2020.
Batelle, John (2005a) *The Search: How Google and Its Rivals Rewrote the Rules of Business and Transformed Our Culture*. London: Nicholas Brealey.
Batelle, John (2005b) 'The Birth of Google' *Wired*. www.wired.com/2005/08/battelle/ Last accessed 03/05/2020.
Beer, David (2018) *The Data Gaze: Capitalism, Power and Perception*. Basingstoke: Palgrave.
Benjamin, Ruha (2019) *Race after Technology: Abolitionist Tools for the New Jim Code*. Cambridge: Polity.
Bergen, Mark (2019) 'YouTube Executives Ignored Warnings, Letting Toxic Videos Run Rampant' *Bloomberg*, 2nd April. www.bloomberg.com/news/features/2019-04-02/youtube-executives-ignored-warnings-letting-toxic-videos-run-rampant Last accessed 03/05/2020.
Bock, Laszlo (2016) *Work Rules! Insights from Inside Google Which Will Transform How You Live and Lead*. London: John Murray.
Bolsover, Gillian and Philip Howard (2017) 'Computational Propaganda and Political Big Data: Moving Toward a More Critical Research Agenda' *Big Data*, 5(4), 274–276.
Bort, Julie (2017) 'Over Half of Google Employees Polled Say the Web Giant Shouldn't Have Fired the Engineer Behind the Controversial Memo' *Business Insider UK*, 10

August 2017. http://uk.businessinsider.com/many-google-employees-dont-think-james-damore-should-have-been-fired-2017-8 Last accessed 03/05/2020.

Brandt, Richard (2011) *Google Guys: Inside the Brilliant Minds of Google Founders Larry Page and Sergey Brin*. London: Portfolio.

Broockman, David E., Gregory Ferenstein, and Neil Malhotra (2019) 'Predispositions and the Political Behavior of American Economic Elites: Evidence from Technology Entrepreneurs' *American Journal of Political Science*, 63(1), 212–213.

Brooks, Michael (2020) *Against the Web: A Cosmopolitan Answer to the New Right*. Alresford: Zer0 Books.

Broussard, Meredith (2019) *Artificial Unintelligence: How Computers Misunderstand the World*. Cambridge, MA: MIT Press.

Brown, Danielle and Melonie Parker (2019) 'Google Diversity Annual Report 2019' https://diversity.google/annual-report/.

Brown, Wendy (2005) *Edgework: Critical Essays on Knowledge and Politics*. Princeton: Princeton University Press.

Burgess, J. and J. Green (2018) *You Tube*. Cambridge: Polity.

Carroll, Hamilton (2011) *Affirmative Reaction: New Formations of White Masculinity*. Durham: Duke University Press.

Chang, Emily (2017) 'Fired Engineer James Damore: I Feel Google Betrayed Me' *bloomberg.com*, 10 August. www.bloomberg.com/news/videos/2017-08-10/fired-engineer-damore-i-feel-google-betrayed-me-video Last accessed 03/05/2020.

Chang, Emily (2018) *Brotopia: Breaking Up the Boys' Club of Silicon Valley*. New York: Penguin Random House.

Cheney-Lippold, John (2017) *We Are Data: Algorithms and the Making of Our Digital Slaves*. New York: New York University Press.

Cohen, Noam (2019) *The Know It Alls: The Rise of Silicon Valley as a Political Powerhouse and Social Wrecking Ball*. London: Oneworld.

Couldry, Nick and Ulises A. Mejias (2019) *The Costs of Connection: How Data is Colonizing Human Life and Appropriating it for Capitalism*. Stanford: Stanford University Press.

Craig, Ryan (2015) *College Disrupted: The Great Unbundling of Higher Education*. Basingstoke: Palgrave.

Crawford, Kate (2018) 'You and AI: Machine Learning, Bias and Implications for Inequality' https://royalsociety.org/science-events-and-lectures/2018/07/you-and-ai-equality/.

Crawford, Kate and Tarleton Gillespie (2016) 'What is a Flag for? Social Media Reporting Tools and the Vocabulary of Complaint' *New Media & Society*, 18(3), 410–428.

Crouch, Colin (2011) *The Strange Non-Death of Neoliberalism*. Cambridge: Polity.

D'Ignazio, Catherien and Lauren F. Klein (2020) *Data Feminism*. Cambridge, MA: MIT Press.

Damore, James. 'Fired for Truth' https://firedfortruth.com/ Last accessed 03/05/2020.

Daniels, Jessie (2015) '"My Brain Database Doesn't See Skin Color": Color-Blind Racism in the Technology Industry and in Theorizing the Web' *American Behavioral Scientist*, 59(1), 1377–1393.

Diamandis, Peter H. and Steven Kotler (2014) *Abundance: The Future is Better Than You Think*. New York: Free Press.

English-Lueck, J. A. (2017). *Cultures@SiliconValley*. Second Edition. Stanford: Stanford University Press.

Eubanks, Virginia (2017) *Automating Inequality: How High-Tech Tools Profile, Police, and Punish the Poor*. New York: St Martins Press.

Finlayson, Alan (2020). 'YouTube and Political Ideologies: Technology, Populism and Rhetorical Form' *Political Studies*. doi: 10.1177/0032321720934630

Fuchs, Christian (2014) *Social Media: A Critical Introduction*. London: SAGE.
Ging, Debbie (2019) 'Bros v. Hos: Postfeminism, Anti-feminism and the Toxic Turn in Digital Gender Politics' in Debbie Ging and Eugenia Siapera (eds) *Gender Hate Online: Understanding the New Anti-Feminism*. Basingstoke: Palgrave Macmillan, pp. 45–68.
Ging, Debbie and Eugenia Siapera (2018) 'Editorial to Special Issue on Online Misogyny' *Feminist Media Studies*, 18(4), 515–524.
Grigoriadis, Vanessa (2014) 'O.K., Glass; Make Google Eyes' *Vanity Fair*, March 12. www.vanityfair.com/style/2014/04/sergey-brin-amanda-rosenberg-affair Last accessed 03/05/2020.
Guthey, Eric, Timothy Clark, and Brad Jackson (2009) *Demystifying Business Celebrity*. London: Routledge.
Hall, Stuart (2003) 'New Labour's Double Shuffle' *Soundings*, 24, 10–24.
Hasinoff, Adele Amy (2017) 'Where Are You?: Location Tracking and the Promise of Childhood Safety' *TV and New Media*, 18(6), 1–17.
Hasinoff, Adele Amy and Marina Levina (2017) 'The Silicon Valley Ethos: Tech Industry Products, Discourses, and Practices' *TV and New Media*, 18(6), 489–495.
Heracleous, Loizos and Laura Klaering (2017) 'The Circle of Life: Rhetorical of Identification in Steve Jobs' Stanford Speech' *International Journal of Business Research*, 79, 31–40.
Hicks, Marie (2017) *Programmed Inequality: How Britain Discarded Women Technologists and Lost Its Edge in Computing*. Cambridge, MA: MIT Press.
Hoffman, Reid and Chris Yeh (2018) *Blitzscaling: The Lightning-Fast Path to Building Massively Valuable Companies*. London: Harper Collins.
Jane, Emma Alice (2014) '"Back to the Kitchen, Cunt": Speaking the Unspeakable about Online Misogyny' *Continuum*, 28(4), 558–570.
Jefferson, Thomas (1982) *Notes on the State of Virginia* (Peden W., Ed.). Chapel Hill: University of North Carolina Press.
Keller, Jessalynn, Kaitlynn Mendes, and Jessica Ringrose (2016) 'Speaking "Unspeakable Things": Documenting Digital Feminist Responses to Rape Culture' *Journal of Gender Studies*, 27(1), 22–36.
Kelly, Annie (2017) 'The Alt-Right: Reactionary Rehabilitation for White Masculinity' *Soundings*, 66, 68–78.
Lanier, Jaron (2013) *Who Owns The Future?* London: Penguin.
Lee, Timothy B. (2018) 'Google Fired James Damore for a Controversial Gender Memo – Now He's Suing' *arstechnica*, 9 January. https://arstechnica.com/tech-policy/2018/01/1 awsuit-goes-after-alleged-anti-conservative-bias-at-google/ Last accessed 03/05/2020.
Levin, Sam (2017) 'James Damore, Google, and the YouTube Radicalization of Angry White Men' *The Guardian*, 13 August. www.theguardian.com/technology/2017/aug/13/james -damore-google-memo-youtube-white-men-radicalization Last accessed 03/05/2020.
Littler, Jo (2017) *Against Meritocracy: Culture, Power and the Myths of Mobility*. London: Routledge.
Loudenback, Tanza and Drake Baer (2015) 'The 20 Schools with the Most Alumni at Google' *Business Insider UK*, 4 September. http://uk.businessinsider.com/schools-wi th-the-most-alumni-at-google-2015-10?r=US&IR=T Last accessed 03/05/2020.
Lowe, Lowe (1996) *Immigrant Acts on Asian American Cultural Politics*. Durham: Duke University Press.
Mackey, John and Raj Sisodia (2014) *Conscious Capitalism: Liberating the Heroic Spirit of Business*. Boston: Harvard Business Review Press.
Manne, Kate (2018) *Down Girl: The Logic of Misogyny*. Oxford: Oxford University Press.
Massaro, Rachel (2020) 'Silicon Valley Index' *Institute for Regional Studies*. https://jointve nture.org/images/stories/pdf/index2020.pdf Last accessed 02/05/2020.

McAndless, David (2017) 'Diversity in Tech' *Information is Beautiful*. https://informationisbeautiful.net/visualizations/diversity-in-tech/ Last accessed 03/05/2020.

McGirt, Ellen (2017) 'Google Searches for Its Soul' *Fortune*, 1 February 2017. http://fortune.com/google-diversity/ Last accessed 03/05/2020.

McKinnon, Susan (2005) *Neo-Liberal Genetics: The Myths and Moral Tales of Evolutionary Psychology*. Chicago: Prickly Paradigm Press.

Meyers, D. T (2012) 'FEAST Cluster on Feminist Critiques of Evolutionary Psychology – Editor's Introduction' *Hypatia*, 27, 1–2.

Morozov, Evgeny (2014) *To Save Everything Click Here: The Folly of Technical Solutionism*. New York: Public Affairs.

Mukherjee, Roopali (2011) 'Bling Fling: Commodity Consumption and the Politics of the "Post-Racial"' in Michael G. Lacy and Kent A. Ono (eds) *Critical Rhetorics of Race*. New York: New York University Press, 178–193.

Nakamura, Lisa (2008) *Digitizing Race: Visual Cultures of the Internet*. Minneapolis: University of Minnesota Press.

Noble, Safiya Umoja (2018) *Algorithms of Oppression: How Search Engines Reinforce Racism*. New York: New York University Press.

O'Neil, Cathy (2016) *Weapons of Math Destruction: How Big Data Increases Inequality and Threatens Democracy*. London: Penguin Random House.

O'Neill, Rachel (2016) 'Feminist Encounters with Evolutionary Psychology' *Australian Feminist Studies*, 30(86), 345–350.

Page, Larry and Sergey Brin (2004) 'Google IPO Founder's Letter' https://abc.xyz/investor/founders-letters/2004-ipo-letter/ Last accessed 03/05/2020.

Page, Larry and Sergey Brin (2019) 'A Letter from Larry and Sergey' 3rd December. https://blog.google/inside-google/alphabet/letter-from-larry-and-sergey/ Last accessed 03/05/2020.

Pao, Ellen (2017) *Reset: My Fight for Inclusion and Lasting Change*. New York: Random House.

Perry, Imani (2018) *Vexy Thing: On Gender and Liberation*. Durham: Duke University Press.

Peterson, Tim (2013) 'Is this the Most Important Person in Advertising?' *Adweek*, 25th February. www.adweek.com/brand-marketing/most-important-person-advertising-147489/ Last accessed 03/05/2020.

Riel, Jennifer (2017) 'Tolerance is for Cowards' *Quartz*, 27 October 2017. https://qz.com/work/1111746/tolerance-is-for-cowards/.

Roberts, Dorothy E (1993) 'Racism and Patriarchy in the Meaning of Motherhood' *Faculty Scholarship*. Paper 595. https://scholarship.law.upenn.edu/faculty_scholarship/595/ Last accessed 03/05/2020.

Roberts, Sarah T (2019) *Behind the Screen: Content Moderation in the Shadows of Social Media*. New Haven: Yale University Press.

Robertson, Adi (2019) 'Google Will Confirm that Employees Can Discuss "Workplace Issues" as Part of a Settlement' *The Verge*, 12th September. www.theverge.com/2019/9/12/20862845/google-nlrb-settlement-employee-workplace-speech-kevin-cernekee Last accessed 03/05/2020.

Rutherford, Markella B. (2004) 'Authority, Autonomy, and Ambivalence: Moral Choice in Twentieth-Century Commencement Speeches' *Sociological Forum*, 19(4), 583–609.

Scheiber, Noam and Daisuke Wakabayashi (2019) 'Google Hires Firm Known for Anti-Union Efforts' *New York Times*, 20th November. www.nytimes.com/2019/11/20/technology/Google-union-consultant.html Last accessed 03/05/2020.

Schmidt, Eric and Jonathan Rosenberg (2017) *How Google Works*. London: John Murray.

Stainback, Kevin, Sibyl Kleiner and Sheryl Skaggs (2016) 'Women in Power: Undoing for Redoing the Gendered Organization' *Gender and Society*, 30(1), 109–135.

Stross, Randall (2012) *The Launch Pad: Inside Y Combinator, Silicon Valley's Most Exclusive School for Startups*. London: Penguin.

Surgey, Nick (2013) 'The Googlization of the Far Right: Why is Google Funding Grover Norquist, Heritage Action and ALEC?' *PR Watch*. www.prwatch.org/news/2013/11/12319/google-funding-grover-norquist-heritage-action-alec-and-more Last accessed 03/05/2020.

Swisher, Kara (2018) 'Full Interview with Susan Wojcicki, CEO of YouTube, at Code Media' *Recode YouTube*. www.youtube.com/watch?v=klQZLssoyl4 Last accessed 03/05/2020.

Taplin (2017) 'Why is Google Spend Vast Sums Lobbying Washington?' *The Guardian*, 30th July. www.theguardian.com/technology/2017/jul/30/google-silicon-valley-corporate-lobbying-washington-dc-politics Last accessed 03/05/2020.

Turner, Fred (2006) *From Counterculture to Cyberculture: Stewart Brand, the Whole Earth Network, and the Rise of Digital Utopianism*. Chicago: University of Chicago Press.

Vaidhyanathan, Siva (2012) *The Googlization of Everything*. Berkeley: University of California Press.

Van Dijck, José (2014) 'Datafication, Dataism and Dataveillance: Big Data between Scientific Paradigm and Ideology' *Surveillance & Society*, 12(2), 197–208.

Van Dijck, José, Thomas Poell, and Martijn de Waal (2018) *The Platform Society Public Values in a Connective World*. Oxford: Oxford University Press.

Vance, Ashlee (2006) 'Google Founders Spar Over Party Plane' *The Register*. www.theregister.co.uk/2006/07/07/google_bed_plane/ Last accessed 03/05/2020.

Wilson, Julie (2018) *Neoliberalism*. London: Routledge.

Wojcicki, Susan (2014) 'Paid Maternity is Good for Business' *Wall Street Journal*, 16th December. www.wsj.com/articles/susan-wojcicki-paid-maternity-leave-is-good-for-business-1418773756 Last accessed 03/05/2020.

Wojcicki, Susan (2017a) 'How to Break Up the Silicon Valley Boy's Club' *Vanity Fair*, 16th March. www.vanityfair.com/news/2017/03/how-to-break-up-the-silicon-valley-boys-club-susan-wojcicki Last accessed 03/05/2020.

Wojcicki, Susan (2017b) 'Read YouTube CEO Susan Wojcicki's Response to the Controversial Google Anti-Diversity Memo' *Fortune*, 9 August. http://fortune.com/2017/08/09/google-diversity-memo-wojcicki/ Last accessed 03/05/2020.

Wong, Julia Carrie (2017) 'Segregated Valley: The Ugly Truth about Google and Diversity in Tech' *The Guardian*, 7 August 2017. www.theguardian.com/technology/2017/aug/07/silicon-valley-google-diversity-black-women-workers Last accessed 03/05/2020.

Young, Cathy (2017) 'An Interview with James Damore' *Reason: Free Minds and Markets*, 14 August. https://reason.com/2017/08/14/an-interview-with-james-damore/ Last accessed 03/05/20202.

Zuboff, Shoshona (2019) *The Age of Surveillance Capitalism: The Fight for a Human Future at the New Frontier of Power*. London: Profile Books.

CONCLUSION

What this book adds to the academic analyses of West Coast Tech is the understanding of a group of powerful celebrity founders as a racialised patriarchal network. Patriarchy is a useful concept for two reasons. It is, in Maria Mies' words, a 'struggle concept' – a powerful tool of resistance; a means to locate resistance to the men who own the big tech companies in sociocultural hierarchies in which sex and gender, as well as race and class, play important roles. But it can be a blunt instrument if we don't investigate what is particular about this patriarchal system. To understand who the patriarchs are, what is specific about their formation, and how they legitimate and wield dominance, is to also forge a resistance, including what this might look like at a granular level.

In this book we identify how this racialised patriarchal system comprises a network of white men who buttress and support each other. We built a ten million word concordance of 95 popular books on Silicon Valley to empirically investigate the ideologies that these men (and West Coast Tech culture more broadly) have marshalled as part of their stratospheric rise to dominance. Using traditional forms of textual analysis alongside corpus linguistics, we developed a rigorous and meticulous method for exploring the ideological practices of this extremely powerful group of economic elites. As a result, this book has presented the most complete interrogation of these men as mediated figures that we believe is possible in a time-limited academic study. There are limitations in the method due to the fast pace of events surrounding the men. Nevertheless, this account and its findings should inform readers' engagement with the vast quantities of journalistic writing on the founders. Much of this journalism is obfuscatory: it can posit rivalries which are also friendships and presents discord where there is often harmony. This all works well for the men, for the media companies who can better sell drama to their audiences, and for the sector overall which can appear dynamic. But the sector as manifest through this network of founders is largely committed to an ideology, a business model, and a set of political values that are reasonably static.

Our early findings suggested that the means by which this network of founders has risen to prominence shares enough similarities to speak of a pattern. Indeed, the members of the network we have identified have supported each other in this pattern's development: sharing ideas, techniques, and financial resources to grow each other's businesses. The rough pathway (on an ideological level according to the concordance but also on a practical level as this is what these men actually did) to becoming a tech patriarch then goes something like this:

- Start 'lean' – in a garage preferably or small office.
- Develop a celebrified public persona drawing on 'Boy Genius' and founder myths and rooted in the idea of changing the world.
- Keep overheads very low by paying staff as little as possible and using small amounts of equity to keep them loyal.
- Ignore or avoid regulations: from having safe furniture, to hate speech, to copyright. These regulations add expense, that can be ill afforded at the start.
- Suppress any sort of challenge to authority from trade unions, shareholders, or state oversight. Rather than acquiesce to any legitimate challenge, lobby hard against state interference whether it's around workplace rights or immigration or monopoly.
- If a competitor company emerges, crush it by copying its technology or buy it and scrap it or incorporate it.
- When forced to face lawmakers, obfuscate and confuse.
- Be connected to others who have done, or are doing, the same thing.

We have mapped this network and its effects through our concordance while looking through the lens of our case studies' public profiles. What we found was that the head of the corporate household, having become the patriarch by virtue of his authority over others, is strongly networked with other patriarchs in the public sphere. These relationships may be based on rivalries, friendships, and collaborations, but they are primarily a means to maintain control over the corporation-as-household-as-property – away from other patriarchs. Because it is not enough to merely follow this pattern. Not all white men from Ivy League universities who followed this path ended up becoming billionaires. Indeed, since Facebook's acquisition of Instagram in 2012 it has been clear that the most that wannabe founders can hope for is to be bought up by one of these patriarchs, rather than to become one on the same scale.

It should also be noted that this network is the product of a specific sectoral context at a specific moment in history. The network has been and continues to be supported and nourished by neoliberalism which has centred speculative markets, deregulation, and the rise of a necessarily small group of billionaires. We have also argued – crucially – how the legitimating ideologies of the founders are profoundly gendered (e.g. the boy genius), raced (e.g. identifying a post-racial discourse where racism is of the past, while presiding over profoundly racialised hierarchies), and classed (e.g. through the privileging of meritocracy). But these ideologies are also specifically American. They harness the language and affect of the colonial frontier in legitimating the will to dominate the 'terrain' of digital capitalism, including owning other people's data. American exceptionalism and the imperial drive to identify and then solve problems on a global scale are also evident.

How the categories of race, class, and gender intersect in the men's celebrity biographies – and in the concordance - helps us to locate how the legitimation of this patriarchal network is rooted in the imaginary of the American frontier. More specifically, it is also provided by a long history of liberalism. This liberalism is rooted in America's white settler colonial period and its imaginary of the household headed by a white patriarch. In this, the founders can be seen to reproduce the man of the homestead on the American frontier: a man who accrues power through his ability to lay claim to territory (in this case the territories of cyberspace and more specifically personal data) and then to control that space through property relations. Historically, this would have been through the indigenous people that he has dominated, as well as the servants, slaves, labourers, children, and his wife – all of whose claims to personhood were constituted as a property relation to the head of the household, but with different qualities, freedoms, and responsibilities. In the digital era there are parallels to be made between the patriarchs and their workforces, users, customers, shareholders, and government in the metaphor of the household. This form of early 'household liberalism' (sometimes celebrated as 'classic liberalism' by the alt-right and other right-wing groups) has been historically contested, both from within liberal thought and from other political tradition, such as socialism. People have campaigned collectively to be recognised as full persons through legislation, including democratic suffrage so the conception of a person has expanded. Nevertheless, the neoliberal context that has turned these founders into billionaires armed with a global reach has been at the expense of many of the gains made by labour activists and other campaigners. Most of the founders we look at display a kind of social democratic liberalism as part of their public branding. However, the accelerated drive to global market domination means that in practice their corporations – and the systems of power they wield – entrench inequalities and systems of oppression.

The tech founders hold a unique form of power through their businesses (often buttressed through majority voting arrangements on shares, as well as the mythic status invested in the idea of the founder in tech culture). The control of these patriarchs over workforces and users is through monopolistic dominance of a key area of the digital economy: online sociality for Facebook, architectures of knowledge for Google, online retail for Amazon, and so forth. We have become 'data subjects' in this new world, but we are still organised on familiar raced, classed, and gendered lines by the cudgel of dataism, which means inequalities are reproduced as natural through the belief that data sets are neutral (and not, for example, informed by the hyper-surveillance of people of colour, the poor, and the working class). We can identify the founder's control (with their exotic shareholding rights), not only over the workforce (who have limited organising rights) and product design in their corporation, but also over the data that is extracted and aggregated from the users of their products. This puts these patriarchs in a unique position when it comes to extracting value from internet users, and this new kind of value extraction has also been associated with colonialism by a number of scholars on whose work we have drawn: our data subjectivity is not ours. Even those who once could inhabit liberal personhood as a consequence of race, gender, citizenship, 'have become subject to the expropriation that was long the condition of their constitutive others' (Skeggs and Yuill 2019, 96). Only a very few men hold the position of proper or full personhood under digital capitalism. And this is why patriarchy is such an important concept; it helps explain this property relation and its outcomes.

Using assemblage thinking has helped us to make sense of resistance to these forms of power, because it gives agency to the components of assemblages. Such resistance might be in the form of Sandberg's bargaining role for women under digital capitalism. Or it might be in the form of James Damore and the alt-right, who see these corporate households as discriminating against white male conservatives. Assemblage thinking has also helped us to recognise the contextual and fluid nature of patriarchy. Patriarchy is relational: it inaugurates and organises relationships to itself, but it also circumscribes the kinds of relationships others can form under its sovereignty – for instance the relationship of the worker to the union movement, or the extent to which women experience sexual harassment. But it is always possible to contest and resist those relationship structures. Thus we see resistance in the form of the Google Walk-Outs, and the Amazon workers' attempts to strike. And we see it in the multiple valuable protests that take place on social media, in journalism, in academia.

Yet, the network of founders has proved a surprisingly agile formation able to absorb and deflect much of the criticism levelled at them. We should be wary of thinking that there are any easy solutions to the problems we present. For instance, in the Netflix documentary *The Social Dilemma* (2020), Silicon Valley reckons with itself by representing key engineers in the growth of surveillance capitalism expressing anxiety – or even regret – about the power of their products. However, the documentary holds tightly to the ideologies of American exceptionalism and the boy genius. By underplaying the wider neoliberal contexts, it suggests the Silicon Valley milieu holds the solution to the problems it has created. The white men of West Coast Tech will save us yet again, but this time from their own brilliance.

Similarly, consumer-based solutions (boycotts and account deletions) are unlikely to be sufficient on their own. We are, after all, talking about monopolistic corporations who have inaugurated new forms of social and economic life while extinguishing the spaces of previous socio-technological formations. The high streets and shopping malls are closing as Amazon flourishes, social life is conducted on Facebook and Instagram, and to look up a fact or an idea is 'to Google.' Thus, boycotts or account deletions are more performative kinds of protest for raising awareness rather than challenging the dominance of the companies' hegemonic position.

Legislative solutions are more promising but they need to be international in at least some dimension and the USA needs to play a central role. (The EU has done much good here but lacks the juridical authority or geopolitical clout to really force through the changes needed.) As we produce this conclusion in October 2020 the US Congress and Department of Justice looks like they are starting to bare their teeth in the struggle against the hegemony of big tech, but whether they can withstand the lobbying tsunami that is likely to follow any serious threat to the tech companies remains to be seen. And the political outlook is uncertain even under a Biden administration.

But even if the US government did break up Google or Facebook, or support unionisation at Tesla or Amazon, the network would remain, as would the model for monopoly. The men themselves would keep their wealth. (After 1916, J. D. Rockefeller's net worth grew with the breakup of the Standard Oil monopoly as the successor companies Exxon, Chevron, and so forth rapidly grew in value). They might find new sectors to rule: biotech or genesplicing, robotics or aviation, health care or education. Or they might just sit back and enjoy their wealth, perhaps with a nice view from an orbital space capsule. Would such a break up stop the exploitation of factory workers in China manufacturing devices? Would it stop the use of child labour in cobalt mining in the Democratic Republic of Congo? And another generation might cotton on to the formula, start a new network, a new PayPal mafia, with their own Peter Thiel and Sheryl Sandberg. Most likely the frontier will form the basis of their legitimation or they will find a new way of reworking the racial and sexual contracts of liberalism to underpin a new pathway to dominance.

There are snippets of hope at the margins however: we can have inclusive design in terms of interfaces and imagery, we can have better algorithms and databases, more diverse workforces in content moderation and systems architecture. There are a multiplicity of more radical suggestions, practices, and points of resistance here (for example, see Benjamin 2019; D'Ignazio and Klein 2020). But really what is at the heart of the greatest wealth acquisition network of our age is the transposition of liberal property relations from the material, legal and ideological planes to a new digital reality where many of us conduct large aspects of our lives.

Liberal capitalist property relations place the patriarchal household at the centre and then modifications are made to expand the parameters of who counts, who gets to own things, who can approximate the proper person of liberalism. These simply do not produce equitable outcomes in an age of great technological expansion such as ours. Algorithms and data subjects produce exciting possibilities for new ways of living and connecting, but as currently formulated they are a dispossessing force, without adequate regulation, they erode the gains of social democracy and reinstate the property-owning household as the primary economic and social actor, but at the level of the multinational corporation. And this is to the benefit of a small class fraction, which is in turn dominated by a small group of men, including the men we have identified here.

The challenge we must make to these new patriarchs is on all the levels outlined above – in workforces and union organising, to combat harassment, racism, and sexism in the companies and online, at the level of markets and competition as consumers and through legislation – but there is another deeper task at hand. And that is to fundamentally rethink the property relations inherited through liberalism for a digital age. We need to find a way to think about owning things in common which make the potential of contemporary economic transformations work for all of us not just a few men on the Pacific Coast. If patriarchy is a struggle concept then this is where we should direct the energies of that struggle. We need a model of ownership which is not based on a group of white men drawing boundaries round pieces of land, kicking out or dominating the previous group, and then setting up households over which they are sovereign. Instead we need property relations that do not have to correct for the subordinate positions of women, people of colour, queer people, children, or those without wealth, but starts with them having equal stakes in the legal and philosophical foundations of how we can all prosper. Only then will we avoid the gross distortions at the level of culture, politics, and economics that the digital age has thrown up and that can be clearly seen through the celebrity biographies of the tech founders.

Bibliography

Benjamin, Ruha (2019) *Race after Technology: Abolitionist Tools for the New Jim Code*. Cambridge: Polity.

D'Ignazio, Catherien and Lauren F. Klein (2020) *Data Feminism*. Cambridge, MA: MIT Press.

Mies, Maria (1986/1998) *Patriarchy and Accumulation on a World Scale: Women in the International Division of Labour*. London: Zed Books Ltd.

Skeggs, Beverly and Simon Yuill (2019) 'Subjects of Value and Digital Personas: Reshaping the Bourgeois Subject, Unhinging Property from Personhood' *Subjectivity*, 12, 82–99 doi: 10.1057/s41286-018-00063-4

The Social Dilemma (2020) Netflix.

APPENDIX

A concordance of popular books on digital capitalism

1. Overview

The book relies for evidence on a 95-book scanned digital corpus produced specifically for this project by the authors. The 95 books are all popular mass-market texts on the tech sector and digital capitalism more broadly, that is written for a wide general audience but with a specialist subject and lexicon. Concordancing has a long history in textual analysis emerging in the middle ages as a tool for biblical study. We use digital concordancing: a modern variant of this method that dates back to the 1960s and the first applications of computing to textual analysis (for example Burton 1968). At a basic level it provides a comprehensive list of examples of how words are used in a body of writing (a corpus). Using digital tools this becomes a partially automated approach to literary study and the techniques used are a form of data mining for 'distant reading' (Moretti 2000). The discipline most associated with this approach is called 'corpus linguistics' which in our case becomes a kind of literary computational analysis (Baker 2014).

2. Software

We have used two standard pieces of software to navigate the concordance.

For generation of most of the quantitative and concordance data we have used the Sketch Engine software. The key benefit is the ease by which two corpora can be compared against each other (see the section on Validity below). This software also has a number of useful functions embedded which are specifically designed for this sort of research.

Additionally, we have used the NVivo 12 software. This has primarily been used for text searches where we want full access to the broad context of word use. It has also functioned as a general library of books. We have used this in a limited number of cases to produce or check numbers produced by the Sketch Engine Software.

3. Validity

Our concordance is a 'specialist corpus' and we often use a 'reference corpora' to produce baseline statistics for comparison (Baker 2014, 10). The most frequently used general corpus is the enTenTen15 corpus on Sketch Engine (Sketch Engine, ND). This is produced in the same year as the median publication date for the books in our concordance and consists of nearly 17 billion words in English to compare to our primary corpus. The date is important because it indicates the currency of terms as compared to our texts and means that concepts and names that have risen to prominence relatively recently ('internet,' 'social media,' 'Mark Zuckerberg,' and so on) will appear at more appropriate levels than a traditional reference corpus such as a selection of Brown corpora or the British National Corpus, neither of which would have as recent vocabulary for comparison.

The use of an internet sample for comparison is not perfect, as webpages are extremely varied lexically and nearly all are a qualitatively different kind of text to a book, but the sheer volume of text being used as a control sample will correct that to some degree. In general we have settled on the enTenTen15 as the most appropriate reference corpus available.

4. Methods

Our concordance is used to test the readings we produce from a range of celebrity texts about Silicon Valley founders. We do that through several methods:

a. Comparative word frequency indicated by ## per million words or ##/mw rounded to nearest whole number. This is produced through Sketch Engine's concordance function. It usually consists of a comparison of the simple (i.e. plain) form of the word in the Digital Capitalism to the same figure in the enTenTen15. Sometimes the lemma form has been preferred to the simple form. The lemma form produces all the variants of the word in question from a shared stem for instance: 'board, boards, boarded, boarding, boardings,' with further capacity to distinguish between, for instance, a word's use as a noun or a verb. The simple form produces results which just contain the word and its plural usages, but will also produce lemma results if the lemma itself is the search term (i.e. 'board').
b. Total number of uses of a word. This is sometimes used by itself, but more often in a comparative way when the number of uses is more directly interesting than frequency. An example of this is our search of proper names where comparison between the raw numbers within the concordance produce more legible results than 'per million words' would have (see Introduction).

c. Concordance sample results through Sketch Engine. This produces a range of different uses of a particular keyword: for instance 'disrupt' or 'frontier.' These results will then be reproduced in our text as a list or as free text.
d. Collocations are used to show how a word is commonly associated with other words, for instance 'Man of' ... 'the Year' as compared to 'Woman of'... 'colour' as in Chapter 6. This is produced through the Sketch Engine 'Word Sketch' function.
e. As a library where we can read related materials by topic in broad (i.e. chapter) context. This provided a way of automating much of our background research.
f. As a way of tracking and checking particular textual elements, for instance the work done around book endorsements seen in Chapter 6.
g. Other methods sometimes combining one or more of the above – see for instance the reading of gender pronouns in Chapter 6.

5. Building the corpus

We selected our books for the concordance through a semi-structured process. Firstly, before we had designed our research to use concordancing and corpus linguistics, we sought out biographies of the tech founders, starting with the Google founders, Mark Zuckerberg, Jeff Bezos, and Elon Musk. Thus, we had a substantial starting selection once we committed to concordancing as a key evidence base. Through desk research we realised we were dealing with a wider ideological formation and began collecting more works to establish a concordance. This meant using published lists of books on tech culture online (for instance from www.goodreads.com/shelf/show/silicon-valley), Amazon bestseller charts under the 'technology' heading, and books which appeared promoted to us as our personalised online algorithms on Google and Amazon became trained to point us to books on a particular topic. We also tended to add books that had a publicity blitz in the middlebrow press (mainly *The Guardian*) around their launch and books that were heavily referenced by other books in the concordance, or whose author blurbed another author in the concordance. Because we are looking specifically at a popular and commercial book genre, these methods in combination are particularly apposite for our project as they reflect marketing practices for the genre's publishers.

As we have understood this is a 'fuzzy set' (see Introduction), with the celebrity founder biographies in the centre it means that we have included texts from the peripheries – for instance Michio Kaku's futurological *The Future of Humanity* or Yuval Noah Harare's *Homo Deus* as they are addressed at least in part to the tech industry.

6. Production

The concordance was produced through manually dismantling the books and scanning them to a local computer using a Fujitsu ScanSnap ix500 scanner and using the bundled ScanSnap software for image processing including optical character recognition. Books had their spines removed with a scalpel and were then fed into the scanner in batches of around 50 double-sided pages. Covers were scanned before the body of the book separately. The resulting .pdf was checked for rough accuracy of OCR by copy and pasting random selections of text into a word document. Files were then added to the NVivo database initially and then the Sketch Engine corpus.

7. Errors and inaccuracy

While the ScanSnap software has a high degree of accuracy typical of contemporary OCR software, errors persist. We lacked the specific expertise to correct the corpus via algorithmic means nor the time to correct files manually, which means that the text analysed is somewhere between 99 and 99.99% accurate.

Thus, to a limited degree some of the results may not precisely reflect the published material. Each book's typeface threw up specific and often different problems for the software and thus generated a different error rate per book. Taken as a whole, in a corpus of ten million words the size of the underlying database compensates for individual errors – even those that vary by degree between books.

However, where there are substantial repeated errors this became immediately apparent to the researchers dealing with a specific issue. For instance, the word 'reason' was frequently interpreted as 'rea' 'son' by the software across several different typefaces. This affected the reliability of a search in relation to gendered language that compared references to 'son' to those to 'daughter.' Similarly, 'Star Trek' was processed effectively when in normal font, but when italicised as '*Star Trek*' the software failed to parse the phrase, leading to a lower frequency rate in concordance searches.

In such cases we have attempted to allow for the error in our analysis of results, or discounted results that we felt were too inaccurate. This is a normal part of working with OCR texts, indeed 'dirty OCR' is something that often must be accounted for (Cordell 2017). While it would have been better to use official digital versions of the books, unfortunately copy-protection means that ebook formats are rarely appropriate for these methods, so we scanned all texts from physical copies to ensure consistency of production.

8. Coding

In the process of assembling the concordance, we noted four main sub-genres of book with significant overlap. Many books were thus coded under two genres. Our genres were:

- Polemic/Dystopian: 20
- Corporate/'How-To':   46

- Biography/Memoir: 41
- Ideology/Futurology: 42

In our book itself, we did not use this coding particularly often as we made the decision to keep this methodological work light, but coding is added to the complete list of texts at the end of this appendix, so the reader can get a sense of how we interpreted these texts at a macro-level.

9. General features of the concordance

Total books:	95
Total words:	9,933,113
Sentences:	490,996
Books with at least 1 female author:	17 out of 95 or 18%
Mean year of publication:	2013
Median year of publication:	2015
Mode year of publication:	2017
Published before or during 2008 financial crash:	16 books
Published after 2008 crash:	79 books

10. Genre and gender

We did not select texts based on the gender of the author, but on the basis of relevance to the corpus. On this basis, we believe that the sample of author gender is representative of technology books of this sort.

Where the gender of the author was uncertain (from a unisex first name for instance, i.e. Ashlee Vance or Julian Guthree), we have sought their personal publicity pages online and used the gender they self-identify with.

There were no obviously trans or non-binary authors in our concordance, but we accept that this may simply be that we have not found a public statement of such.

TABLE A.1 Authors: gender and coding
(named authors/editors i.e. on masthead; counted per book, not per author – some authors occur two or three times)

	Total named authors	Male	Female	% of total that are women writers
Overall	119	99	20	16.81
Polemic/Dystopian	21	17	4	19.05
Corporate/'How-To'	59	46	13	22.03
Biography/Memoir	44	32	12	27.27
Ideology/Futurology	59	52	7	11.86

11. Distribution of authors

Table A.2 indicates the number of authors who wrote more than one book. (This is counted per author, not per book as above.)

TABLE A.2 Distribution of authors by number of books

	Total	Male	Female	% Women
Total	102	84	18	18%
More than 1 book*	12	10	2	18%
More than 2 books*	1			0%

*This is in our concordance – it is worth noting many have written several books, just not all of them are in our concordance.

12. Complete list of books in concordance (with genre coding)

TABLE A.3 Complete list of texts with genre coding

Genre code
Polemic/Dystopian   a
Corporate/'How-To'   b
Biography/Memoir   c
Ideological/Futurology   d

Author	Year	Title	Place published	Publisher	Genre
Randall Stross	1993	Steve Jobs & the Next Big Thing	New York	Atheneum (Macmillan)	c, b
Bill Gates, Nathan Myhrvold, and Peter Rinearson	1995	The Road Ahead	Harmondsworth	Penguin	c, d
Randall Stross	1997	The Microsoft Way: The Real Story of How the Company Outsmarts Its Competition	Reading, MA	Addison-Wesley	b
Kara Swisher	1998	Aol.com: How Steve Case Beat Bill Gates, Nailed the Netheads, and Made Millions in the War for the Web	New York	Random House	b, c
David O. Sacks and Peter A. Thiel	1998	The Diversity Myth: Multiculturalism and Political Intolerance on Campus, 2nd edition	Oakland, CA	The Independent Institute	a

(Continued)

TABLE A.3 Continued

Randall Stross	2000	*eBoys: The First Account of Venture Capitalists at Work*	London	Texere	c
John Cassidy	2002	*Dot.con: The Greatest Story Ever Sold*	London	Penguin	a
Richard Branson	2002	*Losing my Virginity: Richard Branson, the Autobiography*, 2nd edition	London	Virgin Books	c, b
Kara Swisher and Lisa Dickey	2003	*There Must Be a Pony in Here Somewhere: the AOL Time Warner Debacle and the Quest for the Digital Future*	New York	Crown Business	b
Jeffrey Young and William L. Simon	2005	*iCon: Steve Jobs, The Greatest Second Act in the History of Business*	Hoboken, NJ	Wiley	c
Ray Kurzweil	2005	*The Singularity: When Humans Transcend Biology*	London	Duckworth	d
Steve Wozniak and Gina Smith	2006	*iWoz: Computer Geek to Cult Icon*	London	Headline (Hachette)	c, b
John Battelle	2006	*The Search: How Google and Its Rivals Rewrote the Rules of Business and Transformed Our Culture*	London	Nicholas Brealey Publishing	b, c
Randall Stross	2007	*The Wizard of Menlo Park: How Thomas Alva Edison Invented the Modern World*	New York	Three Rivers Press (Penguin)	c
Randall Stross	2008	*Planet Google: How One Company Is Transforming our Lives*	London	Atlantic Books	b, c
Viktor Mayer-Schonberger and Thomas Ramge	2008	*Reinventing Capitalism in the Age of Big Data*	New York	Basic Books (Hachette)	d
Michael Strong (ed.)	2009	*Be the Solution: How Entrepreneurs and Conscious Capitalists Can Solve All the World's Problems*	Hoboken, NJ	Wiley	d, b
Meg Whitman and Joan O'C. Hamilton	2010	*The Power of Many: Values for Success in Business and in Life*	New York	Three Rivers Press	d, c

(*Continued*)

TABLE A.3 Continued

Nicholas Carr	2010	The Shallows: How the internet is changing the way we think, read and remember, 2nd edition	London	Atlantic Books	a
Paul Allen	2011	Idea Man: A Memoir by the Co-Founder of Microsoft	London	Portfolio (Penguin)	c, b
Steven Levy	2011	In The Plex: How Google Thinks, Works, and Shapes Our Lives	New York	Simon & Schuster	b, d
Walter Isaacson	2011	Steve Jobs	London	Little, Brown (Hachette)	c
David Kirkpatrick	2011	The Facebook Effect: The Real Inside Story of Mark Zuckerberg and the World's Fastest-Growing Company 2nd edition	London	Virgin Books (Penguin)	c, b
Eli Pariser	2011	The Filter Bubble: What the Internet Is Hiding From You	New York	Penguin	a
Richard L. Brandt	2011	The Google Guys: Inside the Brilliant Minds of Google Founders Larry Page and Sergey Brin, 2nd edition	New York	Portfolio (Penguin)	c, b
Eric Ries	2011	The Lean Startup: How Constant Innovation Creates Radically Successful Businesses	London	Portfolio (Penguin)	d, b
Douglas Edwards	2012	I'm Feeling Lucky: The Confessions of Google Employee Number 59	Boston, MA	Mariner (Houghton)	c
Lisa Rogak (ed.)	2012	Impatient Optimist: Bill Gates in His Own Words	Chicago	Agate	c, d
Katherine Losse	2012	The Boy Kings: A Journey into the Heart of the Social Network	New York	Free Press (Simon & Schuster)	c, b
Jon Gertner	2012	The Idea Factory: Bell Labs and the Great Age of American Innovation	New York	Penguin	b, d
Randall Stross	2012	The Launch Pad: Inside Y Combinator; Silicon Valley's Most Exclusive School For Startups	New York	Portfolio (Penguin)	b, d

(Continued)

TABLE A.3 Continued

Eric Jackson	2012	*The Pay Pal Wars: Battles with eBay, the Media, the Mafia, and the Rest of Planet Earth*, 3rd edition	Washington DC	WND Books	b
Reid Hoffman and Ben Casnocha	2012	*The Start-Up of You: Adapt to the Future, Invest in Yourself, and Transform Your Career*	New York	Random House	d, b
George Beahm (ed.)	2013	*Billionaire Boy: Mark Zuckerberg in His Own Words. Hacker. Drop Out. Ceo.*	Melbourne	Hardie Grant	c, b
Nick Bilton	2013	*Hatching Twitter: A True Story of Money, Power, Friendship, and Betrayal*	London	Sceptre (Hachette)	c, b
Nicholas Carr	2013	*The Big Switch: Rewiring the World, From Edison to Google; the Definitive Guide to the Cloud Computing Revolution*, 2nd edition	New York	Norton	b, d
Eric Topol	2013	*The Creative Destruction of Medicine: How the Digital Revolution Will Create Better Health Care*, 2nd edition	New York	Basic Books (Hachette)	d
Brad Stone	2013	*The Everything Store: Jeff Bezos and the Age of Amazon*	New York	Transworld (Penguin)	c, b
Jaron Lanier	2013	*Who Owns the Future?*	London	Penguin	d, a
Peter H. Diamandis, Steven Kotler	2014	*Abundance: The Future Is Better Than You Think*, 2nd edition	New York	Free Press	d
John Mackey and Raj Sisodia	2014	*Conscious Capitalism: Liberating the Heroic Spirit of Business*	Boston, MA	Harvard Business Review Press	d, b
Eric Schmidt and Jared Cohen	2014	*The New Digital Age: Transforming Nations, Businesses, and Our Lives*	New York	Vintage (Random House)	d
Peter Thiel and Blake Masters	2014	*Zero to One: Notes on Startups, or How to Build the Future*	London	Virgin Books (Penguin)	d, b
Ryan Craig	2015	*College Disrupted: The Great Unbundling of Higher Education*	New York	Palgrave Macmillan	b, d

(*Continued*)

TABLE A.3 Continued

Steve Lohr	2015	*Data-ism: Inside the Big Data Revolution*	London	Oneworld	d
Sophia Amoruso	2015	*#Girlboss*, 2nd edition	London	Penguin	c
Sheryl Sandberg and Nell Scovell	2015	*Lean In: Women, Work, and the Will to Lead*, 2nd edition	London	WH Allen (Penguin)	d, b
Elissa Shevinsky (ed.)	2015	*Lean Out: The Struggle for Gender Equality in Tech and Start-Up Culture*	New York	OR Books	a, b
Walter Isaacson	2015	*The Innovators: How a Group of Hackers, Geniuses, and Geeks Created the Digital Revolution*	London	Simon & Schuster	d
Martin Ford	2015	*The Rise of the Robots: Technology and the Threat of Mass Unemployment*	London	Oneworld	a, d
Lazlo Bock	2015	*Work Rules! Insights from Inside Google That Will Transform How You Live and Lead*	London	John Murray (Hachette)	b, d
Duncan Clark	2016	*Alibaba: The House That Jack Ma Built*	New York	Ecco (HarperCollins)	c, b
Antonio Garcia Martinez	2016	*Chaos Monkeys: Mayhem and Mania Inside the Silicon Valley Money Machine*	London	EBury Press	c
Dan Lyons	2016	*Disrupted: Ludicrous Misadventures in the Tech Start-Up Bubble*	New York	Atlantic Books	c
Ashlee Vance	2016	*Elon Musk: How the Billionaire CEO of SpaceX and Tesla is Shaping Our Future*, 2nd edition	London	Virgin Books	c
Yuval Noah Harari	2016	*Homo Deus: A Brief History of Tomorrow*	London	Vintage (Random House)	d
Julian Guthrie	2016	*How To Make a Spaceship: A Band of Renegades, an Epic Race, and the Birth of Private Space Flight*	London	Transworld (Penguin)	c, b
Nicholas Carson	2016	*Marissa Mayer and the Fight to Save Yahoo*	New York	Twelve (Hachette)	c, b
Larry Brilliant	2016	*Sometimes Brilliant: The Impossible Adventure of a Spiritual Seeker and Visionary Physician*	New York	HarperCollins	c, d

(Continued)

TABLE A.3 Continued

Kevin Kelly	2016	*The Inevitable: Understanding the 12 Technological Forces That Will Shape Our Future*	New York	Penguin	d
Erik Brynjolfsson and Andrew McAfee	2016	*The Second Machine Age: Work, Progress, and Prosperity in a Time of Brilliant Technologies*, 2nd edition	New York	Norton	d
Satya Nadella, Greg Shaw, and Jill Tracie Nichols	2017	*Hit Refresh: The Quest to Discover Microsoft's Soul and Imagine a Better Future for Everyone*	London	William Collins (HarperCollins)	b, d
Eric Schmidt, Jonathan Rosenberg, and Alan Eagle	2017	*How Google Works*, 2nd edition	London	John Murray (Hachette)	b
Max Tegmark	2017	*Life 3.0: Being Human in the Age of Artificial Intelligence*	New York	Allen Lane (Penguin)	d, a
Jonathan Taplin	2017	*Move Fast and Break Things: How Facebook, Google and Amazon Have Cornered Culture and What It Means for All of Us*	London	Macmillan (Hachette)	a
Sheryl Sandberg and Adam Grant	2017	*Option B: Facing Adversity, Building Resilience, and Finding Joy*	London	WH Allen (Penguin)	c, b
Ellen Pao	2017	*Reset: My Fight for Inclusion and Lasting Change*	New York	Spiegel & Grau (Penguin)	c, a
Robert Kyncl and Maany Peyvan	2017	*Streampunks: How YouTube and the New Creators Are Transforming Our Lives*	London	Virgin Books (Penguin)	b, d
Sarah Wachter-Boettcher	2017	*Technically Wrong: Sexists Apps, Biased Algorithms, and Other Threats of Toxic Tech*	New York	Norton	a
Leigh Gallagher	2017	*The AirBnB story: How to Disrupt an Industry, Make Billions of Dollars and Plenty of Enemies*	London	Virgin Books (Penguin)	b, c

(Continued)

TABLE A.3 Continued

Scott Galloway	2017	*The Four: The Hidden DNA of Amazon, Apple, Facebook and Google*	London	Transworld (Penguin)	b, d
Klaus Schwab	2017	*The Fourth Industrial Revolution*, 2nd edition	London	Portfolio (Penguin)	d
Brian Merchant	2017	*The One Device: The secret history of the iPhone*	London	Transworld (Penguin)	b
Eric Ries	2017	*The Start Up Way: How Entrepreneurial Management Transforms Culture and Drives Growth*	London	Portfolio (Penguin)	d, b
Brad Stone	2017	*The Upstarts: Uber, Airbnb and the Battle for the New Silicon Valley*	London	Transworld (Penguin)	b, c
Mark O'Connell	2017	*To Be a Machine: Adventures Among Cyborgs, Utopians, Hackers and the Futurists Solving the Modest Problem of Death*	London	Granta	d
Jeremy Ring	2017	*We Were Yahoo: From Internet Pioneer to the Trillion Dollar Loss of Google and Facebook*	New York	Post Hill Press	b, c
Adam Lashinsky	2017	*Wildride: Inside Uber's Quest for World Domination*	New York	Portfolio (Penguin)	b, c
Franklin Foer	2017	*World Without Mind: The Existential Threat of Big Tech*	London	Jonathan Cape (Penguin)	a
John Carreyrou	2018	*Bad Blood: Secrets and Lies in a Silicon Valley Startup*	New York	Picador	b, a
Reid Hoffman and Chris Yeh	2018	*Blitzscaling: The Lightning-Fast Path to Building Massively Valuable Companies*	New York	HarperCollins	b
Emily Chang	2018	*Brotopia: Breaking Up the Boys Club of Silicon Valley*	New York	Penguin	a
Ryan Holiday	2018	*Conspiracy: Peter Thiel, Hulk Hogan, Gawker, and the Anatomy of Intrigue*	New York	Profile Books	d, c
Tim Fernholz	2018	*Rocket Billionaires: Elon Musk, Jeff Bezos and the New Space Race*	Boston, MA	Houghton	c, d

(Continued)

TABLE A.3 Continued

Author	Year	Title	City	Publisher	Notes
Jaron Lanier	2018	Ten Arguments for Deleting Your Social Media Accounts Right Now	London	Bodley Head (Penguin)	a
Carl Miller	2018	The Death of the Gods: The New Global Power Grab	London	Heinemann (Penguin)	a
Michio Kaku	2018	The Future of Humanity: Terraforming Mars. Interstellar Travel, Immortality and Our Destiny Beyond Earth	London	Allen Lane (Penguin)	d
Jamie Bartlett	2018	The People vs Tech: How the Internet Is Killing Democracy (and how we save it)	London	Penguin	a
Christian Davenport	2018	The Space Barons: Elon Musk, Jeff Bezos and the Quest to Colonize the Cosmos	New York	Public Affairs (Hachette)	d, c
Andrew Yang	2018	The War on Normal People: The Truth About America's Disappearing Jobs and Why the Universal Basic Income is Our Future	New York	Hachette	a, d
Leslie Berlin	2018	Troublemakers: Silicon Valley's Coming of Age	New York	Simon & Schuster	c
Adam Fisher	2018	Valley of Genius: The Uncensored History of Silicon Valley as Told by the Hackers, Founders and Freaks Who Made It Boom	New York	Twelve (Hachette)	c, d
Scott Kupor	2019	Secrets of Sand Hill Road: Venture Capital and How to Get It	London	Virgin Books	b
Noam Cohen	2019	The Know It Alls: The Rise of Silicon Valley as a Political Powerhouse and Social Wrecking Ball	London	Oneworld	a
Roger McNamee	2019	Zucked: Waking Up to the Facebook Catastrophe	London	HarperCollins	a, c

Bibliography to Appendix

Baker, Paul (2014) *Using Corpora to Analyse Gender*. London: Bloomsbury.

Burton, D. M. (1968) 'Some Uses of a Grammatical Concordance' *Computational Humanities*, 2, 145–154.

Cordell, Ryan (2017) '"Q i-jtb the Raven": Taking Dirty OCR Seriously' *Book History*, 20, 188–225.

Moretti, F. (2000) 'Conjectures on World Literature' *New Left Review*, 1, 54–68.

SketchEngine (n.d.) 'TenTen Corpora' *SketchEngine.eu.* www.sketchengine.eu/documentation/tenten-corpora/ Last accessed 01/05/2020.

INDEX

Page numbers in **bold** reference tables. Page numbers in *italics* reference figures.

1935 National Recovery Administration 194
2008 financial crash 4

absolute hospitality 136
African-American 33, 135, 153, 157
Ahmed, Sara 154, 197
AI (artificial intelligence) 62, 137–139
Alexa 32–33
algorithms 157; Google 188, 197, 201
'Alley Oop' Hammer 192–193
Alphabet 39, 193; *see also* Google
alt-right 202, 204, 208
Amazon 10, 13, 15–16, 40, 48n5, 74, 87, 193; Alexa 32–33; door desks 100; employment practices 100–101; founding 100; frontier spirit 100–104; leanness 102–103; as state 90–92; taxes 91–92
Amazon Household 32, 138
Amazon Web Services (AWS) 89, 98
American culture 34
American frontier 218; *see also* frontier
American internet 45
American West 40, 46; Bezos, Jeff 98
Amyotropic Lateral Sclerosis Association (ALSA) Ice Bucket Challenge 85–87
anti-semitism 207
apparatus 13–14, 17, 45, 59, 72, 73
ARPANET 16, 35
Aschoff, Nicole 169, 179
Asians 41, 59
Asian-American 41, 57, 59

assemblage 12–13, 74; Amazon 98; Zuckerberg-Facebook 117, 119
assemblage thinking 172, 219
authors: distribution of **228**; gender and coding **227**
AWS (Amazon Web Services) 89, 98
Axel Springer Award 98

Baker, Paul 22, 173–174
Banet-Weiser, Sarah 184
Barbrook, Richard 40, 105, 106
bargaining with patriarchy, Sandberg, Sheryl 169–172
Barlow, John Perry 35–36, 94
Bartlett, Jamie 67
Batelle, John 188
Bay Area identity 129
behavioural surplus 182
Belson, Gavin 64
Benjamin, Ruha 30, 137
Berlant, Laurne 167
Berners-Lee, Tim 98
Betas 64
Bezos, Jeff 5, 11, 15, 40, 46, 48n5, 60, 65, 73, 85–87, 191, 193; Axel Springer Award 98; Blue Origin 110; Clock of the Long Now 109–111; Ice Bucket Challenge 87–90; laughter 85–86; life at the ranch 97–100; philanthropy and celebrity 87–90; relationships 10; *Star Trek* 92–96; state and 90–92; wealth 7; *see also* Amazon

Bezos, Mackenzie Scott 100
The Big Bang Theory (2007-2019) 63, 65
The Bill and Melinda Gates Foundation 179
Bivens, Rena 47n1, 136
Black men 155–156
black 42
Blodgett, Bridget 58, 63, 64
Blue Origin 10, 65, 98, 110
Bodega 47
book endorsements, Sandberg, Sheryl 172
Booker, M. Keith 94
The Boring Company 78
Botha, Roelof 163n1
boy genius trope 56–58, 187
boycotts 219–220
Boyle, Danny 61
Brand, Stewart 35, 104–109, 111, 124, 125, 130
branding 4, 149, 187, 194, 202, 206–207, 218
brands 206; mediating 180–181
Brandt, Richard 187–188
Branson, Richard 73
Brilliant, Larry 172
Brin, Sergey 60, 169, 209, 210n3; celebrity and post-class politics 191–193; Google 189–191; ice bucket challenge 88; wealth 7; *see also* Google
Brodkin, Karen 42
Broockman, David 14–16, 192
Brown, Wendy 194, 195
Buffet, Warren 39, 98, 189
Burgess, A. 87
Bush, George 125
business celebrities 72–73
business strategy, celebrity as 71–74

Californian Ideology 40, 105
Cambridge Analytica scandal 118–119
Cameron, Andy 40, 105, 106
Campbell, Bill 206
capitalism 21, 33, 34, 39–40, 46, 74, 101, 159, 161, 169, 192; digital capitalism 4, 16, 20, 35, 96, 98, 116, 119, 122, 135, 139, 144, 147, 157, 167, 182–184; neoliberal capitalism 92; patriarchal capitalism 14; philanthrocapitalism 120, 179; surveillance capitalism 3, 12, 19, 133, 182, 195
celanthropy 88
celebrification 31, 72; Musk, Elon 75–80; Sandberg, Sheryl 170, 172; Zuckerberg, Mark 116–118
celebrity 8; Bezos, Jeff 97–100; Brin, Sergey 191–193; as business strategy, Musk 71–74; Google founders 190; Musk, Elon 59–63, 66–71; Page, Larry 191–193; philanthropy 87–90; politics and 125
celebrity studies 72
censorship 206
CEOs: celebrity 72–74; tech CEOs 74
Chan, Priscilla 119–121, 140n2
Chander, Anupam 90
Chang, Emily 157, 196
Chan-Zuckerberg Initiative 31, 120, 179
Chen, Steve 145, 205
Chinese internet 45
Christie, Chris, Ice Bucket Challenge 87
Chuck 63
civil rights 207
civil society 128
class 29–32, 38, 41, 44, 58, 87, 94–95, 108, 132–133, 136, 139, 151, 171, 173, 175, 183
classic liberalism 218
classic patriarchy 171
Clegg, Nick 119
Clinton, Hillary 1
Clock of the Long Now 109–111
coercion 160
Collins, Patricia Hill 30, 135
colonialism (imperialism) 4, 28, 32, 38–39, 45–47, 119, 154–155, 175, 189, 218; *see also* settler colonialism
colonialists 151
Columbus, Christopher 154
commencement addresses 191–192
communes, gender 106
community 130
concordance 6, 21–22, 223; algorithms 157; alt-right 204; authors, genre and gender **227**; Brand, Stewart 107; building the corpus 225; coding 226–227; distribution of authors **228**; errors and inaccuracies 226; famous tech executives full name mentions **7**; fatherhood 123–124; features of 227; gender and 172–175; genre and gender 227; IPO (initial public offering) 189; list of books **228–235**; methods of testing 224–225; production of 225–226; pronouns 172–175; race 153; *Star Trek* 93; unions 192; university 199; validity 224
conjunctural analysis 12
Connell, R. W. 65
Conspiracy: Peter Thiel, Hulk Hogan, Gawker, and the Anatomy of Intrigue (Holiday) 148
corporate household 20, 27–28, 169, 217; Sandberg, Sheryl 180–182; Thiel, Peter 151–152; Zuckerberg, Mark 118–120
corporate wife 180–181

corpus linguistics 223
Couldry, Nick 4, 12, 31–32, 45, 96, 138–139
counterculture 104–106
Craig, Ryan 199
Crawford, Kate 198
cultural strategy 12
cyberspace 37; Thiel, Peter 151–153

Damore, James 202–204, 209
Daniels, Jessie 41
data colonialism 3, 45
databases 6, 47n1, 111n5, 137, 198, 220; *see also* concordance
datafication 43, 135
dataism 42–45, 198–202, 204, 218–219
Davis, Aeron 14
de Waal, Martijn 90
'The Declaration of the Independence of Cyberspace' 35–36
democratisation of knowledge 199
DeMuth, Christopher 148, 163n7
Denfeld, Rene 160
Derrida, Jacques 136
Diamandis, Peter 67
digital capitalism 4, 16, 20, 35, 96, 98, 116, 119, 122, 135, 139, 144, 147, 157, 167, 182–184
digital cowboy 108
digital media, frontier spirit 36
digital wallet 145
Diprose, Kristine 179
distant reading 223
diversity 205; Google 196–198, 202–205
The Diversity Myth (Thiel) 147, 153–160
domestic households 169
door desks 100
Döpfner, Mathias 97–98, 103
Driessens, Olivier 72
Duggan, Lisa 149

electronic frontier 36–37
Electronic Frontier Foundation 35
employment 16
employment practices: Amazon 100–101; Musk, Elon 70
English-Lueck, J.A. 42, 129
Enloe, Cynthia 29, 95
enTenTen15 corpus 224
entrepreneurial celebrity 59
entrepreneurs 62
ethnic-affinity targeting 136

Facebook 3, 10, 11, 13, 31, 47n1, 74, 117, 118, 217; Cambridge Analytica scandal 118–119; corporate household 118–120; gendered data solutions 181–184; race 136; statehood 90; values 180; *see also* Zuckerberg, Mark; Sandberg, Sheryl
Facemash 140n2
family, Zuckerberg, Mark 123–126
family meals, Zuckerberg, Mark 133–135
family patriarchs 126
famous tech executives, full name mentions in the concordance 7
Fanon, Frantz 156
fatherhood 123–125
Federici, Silvia 161
femininity 59
feminism: neoliberal feminism 183; popular feminism 184; Sandberg, Sheryl 175–176
Ferenstein, Gregory 14, 192
Fisher, Adam 33–34, 37
Foer, Franklin 107
food 129
foreign other 137
founders 6, 14–17
Fowler, Susan 205
Fraser, Nancy 178
freedom 158, 159
freedom of speech 206
friendships 10
frontier 33–40, 43, 45, 87; American frontier 34–35, 92–96; electronic frontier 36–37; homesteading 35, 37; households 31–33; patriarchal network 218; Thiel, Peter 151–153; Western frontier 40, 46, 94, 96, 103, 111, 151
frontier spirit 33–40, 92; Amazon 100–104; digital media 36; Sandberg, Sheryl 179–180
fuzzy set 21
FWD.us 15

Gabrielatos, Costas 22
Galloway, Scott 62
Gamson, Joshua 71
Gates, Bill 39, 87, 98, 172
Gates, Melinda 39, 87
Gawker Media 148
geek masculinity 57–58, 63–66
gender: communes 106; concordance 227; concordance and 172–175; households 31–33; Silicon Valley 144–145; textual gender 173
gender dynamics, superhero celebrity 60–61
gender inequality 196
gender relations 172

gender terms, concordance 172–175
gendered data solutions, Facebook 181–184
gendered division of labour 177–178
gendered genres 173
gendered hierarchies 30
genius, boy genius trope 56–58
Gilded Age 38–39
Gill, Ros 183
Gilmore, John 35
Gingrich, Newt 36, 105
Giving Pledge 39
Glass-Steagall act of 1933 194
Gmail 195
God's eye view 108–109
Google 10, 13, 152, 162, 187, 189–191, 208–209; algorithms 201; Damore, James 202–204; diversity 202–204; diversity in the workforce 196–198; Gmail 195; pregnancy parking 169–170; privatisation of knowledge 198–202; racism 38, 197–198; *see also* Brin, Sergey; Page, Larry
Google Families 32, 138
The Google Guys: Inside the Brilliant Minds of Google Founders Larry Page and Sergey Brin (Brandt) 187–188
Google Home 32
Google Ngram 174
Google Photos 197
Google.org 178
Goulden, Murray 32, 138
Graham, Paul 124
Gramsci, Antonio 14, 38, 64, 128
Grant, Adam 167
Grant, D. 61
Green, Joe 121–123
Gregg, Melissa 122
'Grill Talk,' Zuckerberg, Mark 120–123
Grimes 62
Grossberg, Larry 12
Guthey, Eric 73, 97, 117

hackers 124–125
Halt and Catch Fire (AMC 2014-2017) 144
Hamad, Hannah 117, 120
Hasinoff, Adele 44
Hastings, Reed 87
hate speech 207–208
HE (higher education) 200
Heard, Amber 62
hegemonic masculinity 58
hegemony 38
Heracleous, Loizos 192
Hester, Helen 32

Hicks, Marie 145
higher education (HE) 200
Hispanics 42
Hoffman, Reid 145, 163n1, 172
Holiday, Ryan 148
Hollywood 5, 62, 65, 71, 78, 97
home assistants 32–33
homestead 33, 35, 37
homonationalism 149–150
homonormativity 149
homosexuality 149–150
homosociality 123
hooks, bell 175
Horowitz, Bradley 197
hospitality 136; traditional American family meals, Zuckerberg 133–135; Zuckerberg-Facebook assemblage 120–123
household liberalism 218
households 29–33; colonial household 20, 35, 87; corporate households *see* corporate households; digital households 32, 138; domestic households 169; Facebook-Zuckerberg corporate household 118–120; gendered division of labour 177–178; patriarchal households 151–152, 220–221; Sandberg, Sheryl 177
Howery, Kenny 163n1
Hunt, Gus 89
Hurley, Chad 145, 205
hypervisibility 170

ice bucket challenge 87–90; Bezos, Jeff 85–86
identities 43–44; Bay Area identity 129; Facebook 136–137
ideology 15; Californian Ideology 40, 105
immigration 15
initial public offering (IPO), Google 189–191
Instagram 217
'The Intellectual Dark Web' (IDW) 77
internet 35–37
intimate publics 167
IPO (initial public offering), Google 189–191
Iron Man 59–60, 191
Iron Man 65
Iron Man 2 60, 61

Jackson, Frederik Turner 92, 102
Jefferson, Thomas 40
Jeffersonian democracy 105–106
Jewish Americans 42

Jews 42
Jobs, Steve 2, 61
The Joe Rogan Experience (September 2018) 75–80
Jones, Alex 76

Kandiyoti, Deniz 171
Kaphan, Shel 105
Kaplan, Joel 163n5
Kapor, Mitch 35
Karim, Jawed 163n1, 205
Karpf, David 109
Katz, Safra 3
Kavanaugh, Brett 163n5
Kay, Alan 107
Kelly, Annie 204
Kelly, Kevin 67
Khan, Lina 90–91
Kirkpatrick, David 182
Klaering, Laura 192
Kleiner Perkins 171
knowledge, privatisation of 198–202
Koch brothers 147
Kotler, Steven 67

labour practices, Musk, Elon 70
labour unions 194
leadership 64
leadership positions 170; women 41, 196
Lean In: Women, Work and the Will to Lead (Sandberg) 167, 169–171, 176, 177, 179
Leanin.org 178
leanness, Amazon 102–103
legal consent 38
legislative solutions 220
Lessin, Sam 121–122, 123
Levchin, Max 145, 157, 163n1
Levina, Marina 44
liberalism 130, 194, 195, 218; social democratic liberalism 194
Littler, Jo 11–12, 72–73, 178, 192
lobbying 15
Locke, John 29–30, 125
Long Now Foundation 111
Lowe, Lisa 41

Mackey, John 192
Malhotra, Neil 14, 192
managing the homestead, Sandberg, Sheryl 175–180
Mandell, Laura 173
Manne, Kate 176
mapping patriarchal network 8–11
Mark's Year of Travel 126–133
Marshall, P. David 72, 125–126

Martinez, Antonio Garcia 176
masculinity 59; geek masculinity 57–58, 63–66; hegemonic masculinity 58; Musk, Elon 80; paternal masculinity 117
Master, Blake 151
Mayer, Marissa 196
McCormack, Andrew 163n1
McEnery, Tony 22
McGirt, Ellen 197
McLuhan, Marshall 105
mediating the brand, Sandberg, Sheryl 180–181
Mejias, Ulises 4, 12, 31–32, 45, 96, 138–139
men: Black men 156; non-white men 156; versus women 203
Messerschmidt, J. 65
Microsoft 152
middle-class women, Facebook 183
Mies, Maria 216
migration status 41, 132–133
militarism 94–95
Mills, Charles 156
misogyny 161, 171, 176, 207; popular misogyny 204
Molyneux, Stefan 204
monopolies 152
Morozov, Eugene 44
motherhood, Sandberg, Sheryl 176–177
Mukherjee, Roopali 154
multiculturalism 153–154
Murray, Robin 118
Musk, Elon 2, 5, 11, 15, 27, 39, 40, 73, 145, 149; celebrity 59–63, 66–71; fatherhood 123; geek masculinity 63–66; households 31; ice bucket challenge 87; *The Joe Rogan Experience* (September 2018) 75–80; labour practices 70; relationship with Sandberg 170; relationships 10; rivalries 152; wealth 7
Musk, Justine 62

Nadella, Satya 41, 87
Nakamura, Lisa 30, 41–42, 154
National Conservatism 148, 162
National Labor Relations Act 194
neoliberal feminism 183
neoliberalism 149–150, 182, 195, 218; data 198–199
network of case studies 9
networks 146; pathway to tech patriarchs 217; *see also* patriarchal network
Neuralink 78
New Communalists 130

New Deal 194
New Left 106
Noble, Safiya Umoja 12, 38, 136, 157, 191
non-white men 156
Nosek, Luke 163n1
NVivo 12 software 223

Obama, Barack 158
O'Brien, Jeffrey 157
O'Brien, Walter 58
Ommanney, Charles 127
O'Neil, Cathy 44
O'Neill, Gerald 105, 110
O'Neill, Rachel 66
online misogyny 161
Option B: Facing Adversity, Building Resilience and Finding Joy (Sandberg) 167, 170, 179, 180
OptionB.org 178
Orgad, Shani 183
Ortner, Sherry B. 28, 29, 123
the other 117

Page, Benjamin 15
Page, Larry 8, 15, 39, 73, 74, 169, 209; celebrity and post-class politics 191–193; Google 189–191; ice bucket challenge 87–88; wealth 7; *see also* Google
PageRank 188
Palantir 145, 150–151
Palihapitiya, Chamath 172
Pao, Ellen 171
Parker, Sean 15, 31
Pateman, Carole 156
paternal American imperialism 189
paternal liberalism 190
paternal masculinity 117
paternalism 120, 126
paternalistic policies, Google 196
patriarchal architectures 30
patriarchal bargains 171
patriarchal households 220–221; Thiel, Peter 151–152; Zuckerberg, Mark 120
patriarchal network 5, 95; frontier 218; mapping 8–11; Sandberg, Sheryl 175–180
patriarchal system 28–29
patriarchy 28–33, 216–221; bargaining with 169–172; classic patriarchy 171
Pau, Ellen 41
PayPal 145
PayPal Mafia 145, *146*, 157, 163n1
Perry, Imani 17, 29, 30, 95

personhood 30, 36, 95, 139, 156, 194, 219; Thiel, Peter 158–162
Peterson, Jordan 76, 204
philanthrocapitalism 120, 179
philanthropy: celebrity and 87–90; Sandberg, Sheryl 178–179
Phillips, Whitney 36
Pichai, Sundar 41, 202
platform ecosystem 90
platform family technology 138
Plouffe, David 127
Poell, Thomas 90
political donations 1; lobbying 15
politics: celebrity and 125; post-class politics, Google 191–193; Thiel, Peter 158–159
popular feminism 184
popular misogyny 204
post-class politics, Google 191–193
postfeminist 36, 37, 120, 147, 154, 159, 192
postfeminist fatherhood 19, 120, 125
postfeminist paternalism 117
posttraumatic growth, Sandberg, Sheryl 181–184
pregnancy parking, Google 169–170
presence bleed 122
privatisation of knowledge, Google 198–202
privilege 42
privileged women 178
product launches, Musk, Elon 61–62
pronouns, concordance 172–175
protest 219–220
Puar, Jasbir 149, 150

Rabois, Keith 157, 163n1
race 30, 153; African-American 33, 135, 153, 157; Asian 41, 59; Asian-American 41, 57, 59; Black men 155–156; black 42; Facebook 136; racial hierarchies 40–42; social contracts 156; *Star Trek* 94–96; white 42
Rachmeler, Kim 101
Racial Contract 156
racial hierarchies 40–42
racial privilege 42
racialised patriarchal system 216
racism 153–154; Google 38, 197–198; tech industry 106; Year of Travel (Zuckerberg) 132
rape 160
Reagan, Ronald 125
Reddit 171
regulation 37–38

regulation of content 208
relationships 170
Republicans 149
resistance 219–220
responsibility to the world, Google 189–191
Rheingold, Howard 35, 37, 47–48n2
Ries, Eric 172
Riley, Talulah 60–62
rivalries 10–11, 152
Robber Barons 13–14, 39, 46
Roberts, Dorothy E. 38
Roberts, Sarah T. 208
Rockefeller, John D. 14, 220
Roddenberry, Gene 93
Rogan, Joe 71, 75–80
Roiphe, Katie 160
Rojek, Chris 88
Rollins, Jimmy 87
Romety, Ginni 3
Rosenberg, Jonathan 93, 200
Rottenberg, Catherine 178, 182–183
Rubin, Dave 149
Runciman, David 3, 13
Russell, John 137

Sacks, David 153, 155, 160, 161, 163n1
Salter, Anastasia 58, 63, 64
Salvation 63
sameness of products 152
Sandberg, Sheryl 3, 5, 6, 8, 31, 39, 73, 167–169, 196, 205; bargaining with patriarchy 169–172; concordance 172; feminism 175–176; frontier spirit 179–180; gendered genres 173; *Lean In: Women, Work and the Will to Lead* 169–171, 176, 177; managing the homestead 175–180; mediating the brand 180–181; motherhood 176–177; *Option B: Facing Adversity, Building Resilience and Finding Joy* (Sandberg) 167, 170; philanthropy 178–179; posttraumatic growth 181–184; relationship with Zuckerberg 180–181; relationships 9–10; wealth 7; *see also* Facebook
Sanders, Bernie 1, 76
Sardar, Ziauddin 36–37, 161
ScanSnap software 226
Schmidt, Eric 15, 93, 200
Schwab, Klaus 172
Scorpion 56–59
Scovell, Nell 167
Section 230 of the Communications Decency Act (1996) 136, 190

settler colonialism 87; *Star Trek* 93–94; *see also* frontier
sexual assault 160–161
sexual harassment 160
sexual violence 160–161
Shah, Premal 163n1
Sharma, A. 61
Shatner, William 92
Sheryl Sandberg and David Goldberg Family Foundation 178
Siapera, Eugenia 161–162
Silicon Valley 63–64, 88
Simmons, Russel 157, 163n1
Simpsons 65
Skeggs, Bev 12, 118, 130, 139, 183
Sketch Engine software 223
smartphones 16
Snowden, Edward 45, 89
social contracts 156
social democratic liberalism 194
The Social Dilemma (2020) 219
social justice 207
social media 64
space 10, 12, 14, 18, 34–35, 45–46, 73, 77; Bezos, Jeff 99, 110–111; Blue Origin 110; colonisation 34, 66–67, 105; cyberspace 36–37, 151, 158–159; deregulated space 92; domestic spaces 123; ideological space 128; public space 178, 184, 200, 207; reusable rockets 69; rockets 98, 104, 11, 170; ships 98; *Star Trek* 93–96; Thiel, Peter 151–152
SpaceX 10, 16, 40, 63, 68-69, 74
Spielberg, Steven 98
Standard Oil 13–14
The Standard Review 153
Stanford University 94
Star Trek 46, 65, 92–96, 110
Star Wars 155
Startup: Education 179
the state, Bezos, Jeff 90–92
Stewart, Patrick 92
Stone, Brad 73, 85–86, 91, 99
Stoppelman, Jeremy 157, 163n1
storytelling 169
Strauss, Neil 60, 66–67, 70
Street, John 72
Stross, Randall 124
Summers, Christina Hoff 160
Summers, Larry 178
Sunkara, Bhaskar 77
SuperSoul Conversations 167–168
surveillance capitalism 3
Swisher, Kara 87, 205

Takei, George 92–93
Taplin, Jonathan 15, 147
tax avoidance 91–92
taxes, Amazon 91–92
tech CEOs, celebrity 74
tech culture 105–106
tech industry, racism 106
tech patriarchs, pathway to 217
Tech-lash 3
technochauvinism 44
technological solutionism 44
Terman, Frederik 94
Terra Nullius 96, 107
Tesla 16, 61–62, 68, 74–76
textual gender 173
Thiel, Peter 2, 8, 11, 67, 68, 92, 144–148, 163n1; contrarian thinker 148–151; cyberspace frontiersman 151–153; *The Diversity Myth* (Thiel) 153–160; personhood 158–162; politics 158–159; relationships 10; rivalries 152; *Star Trek* 93; *Zero to One: Notes on Startups, or How to Build the Future* 151–152
traditional American family meals 133–135
Trump, Donald 1, 3, 117, 127–128, 133, 147, 150, 159
Trump, Ivanka 3
Trump Tech Summit 2016 1–3
Turner, Fred (media scholar) 36, 106–108
Turner, Frederik Jackson (historian) 96, 103, 104
Typhoid Mary (Mary Mallon) 182
Tyson, Neil deGrasse 67

unions 192, 194
Unity Biotechnology 11
universities 199–202

Vaidhyanathan, Siva 136, 181, 199, 201
Van Dijck, José 43, 90, 198
Vance, Ashlee 60–61
Vandermeyden, A. J. 205
vending machines 47

Wachter-Boettcher, Sara 157
The Washington Post 67
wealth 6–8
WEC (*Whole Earth Catalog*) 105, 108
Weinstein, Eric 77

Welch, Chris 137
Western 34; frontier 40, 46, 94, 96, 103, 111, 151; philosophy 155; texts 154
Wheeler, Mark 72
White, Richard 40, 46, 103–104
white supremacy 198
whiteness 42, 171
whites 42
Whole Earth Catalog (WEC) 105, 108
Why Him? 27–28, 33
Wilson, Julie 194
Winfrey, Oprah 167–169
Wise, Amanda 129
Wojcicki, Anne 191
Wojcicki, Susan 188, 196, 205–208
women: leadership positions 41, 170, 196; versus men 203; middle-class women, Facebook 183; privileged women 178; sexual violence 160–162; in tech industry 205–208
Wong, Julia Carrie 90
workforces: diversity, Google 196–198; racial hierarchies 40–42

Year of Travel, Zuckerberg, Mark 117, 126–133; family meals, 133–135
Yelp 157
Yiannopoulos, Milo 144, 147, 204
YouTube 205–208
Yuill, Simon 12, 118, 130, 139, 183

Zero to One: Notes on Startups, or How to Build the Future (Thiel) 151–152
Zuboff, Shoshana 3, 12, 39, 45–46, 92, 98, 182, 191, 195
Zuckerberg, Mark 3, 13, 15, 31, 39, 60, 65, 116–118, 191; AI 137–139; Axel Springer Award 98; Facebook corporate household 118–120; 'Grill Talk' 120–123; from hacker to paternal stateman 123–126; ice bucket challenge 87–88; relationship with Sandberg 180–181; relationships 9–11; traditional American family meals 133–135; wealth 7; Year of Travel 117, 126–135; *see also* Facebook
Zuckerberg-Facebook assemblage 117–119; hospitality 120–123